This Lake Alive!

An Interdisciplinary Handbook
for Teaching and Learning
about the Lake Champlain Basin

This Lake Alive!

An Interdisciplinary Handbook
for Teaching and Learning
about the Lake Champlain Basin

Written and Edited by Amy B. Demarest

With illustrations by Bonnie Acker and Holly Brough
Photographs by Lou Borie

Published by Shelburne Farms, Shelburne, Vermont

Printed with funding from the U.S. Environmental Protection Agency
through the Lake Champlain Basin Program (grant #001840-01-0).

Work for this book was supported in part by a grant from the Christa McAuliffe Foundation.

The Stewardship Institute of
SHELBURNE FARMS

Shelburne, Vermont 05482

Phone: 802-985-8686   *Fax:* 802-985-8123

Author and Editor: Amy Demarest, *Illustrators:* Bonnie Acker, Holly Brough, *Book Designer:* Elizabeth Nelson,
Editorial and Production Staff: Judy Elson, Holly Brough, *Copy Editors:* Suzi Wizowaty, Jennifer Ingersall

Editorial Board: Jeanne Brink, Colleen Carter, Mary Dupont, Judy Elson, Elise Guyette, Sue Hardin, Carol Livingston,
Karen Murdock, Tim Titus, Jill Vickers

Printed in Burlington, Vermont in the United States of America by Queen City Printers, Inc.
Printed on recycled paper.

*Bonnie Acker's cover illustration is a cut-paper collage created from both Japanese paper hand-dyed with watercolors,
and handmade paper from Langdell Paperworks in Topsham, Vermont. The inside illustrations were cut from
black paper originally used to protect new offset printing plates enroute to printing houses.*

Table of Contents

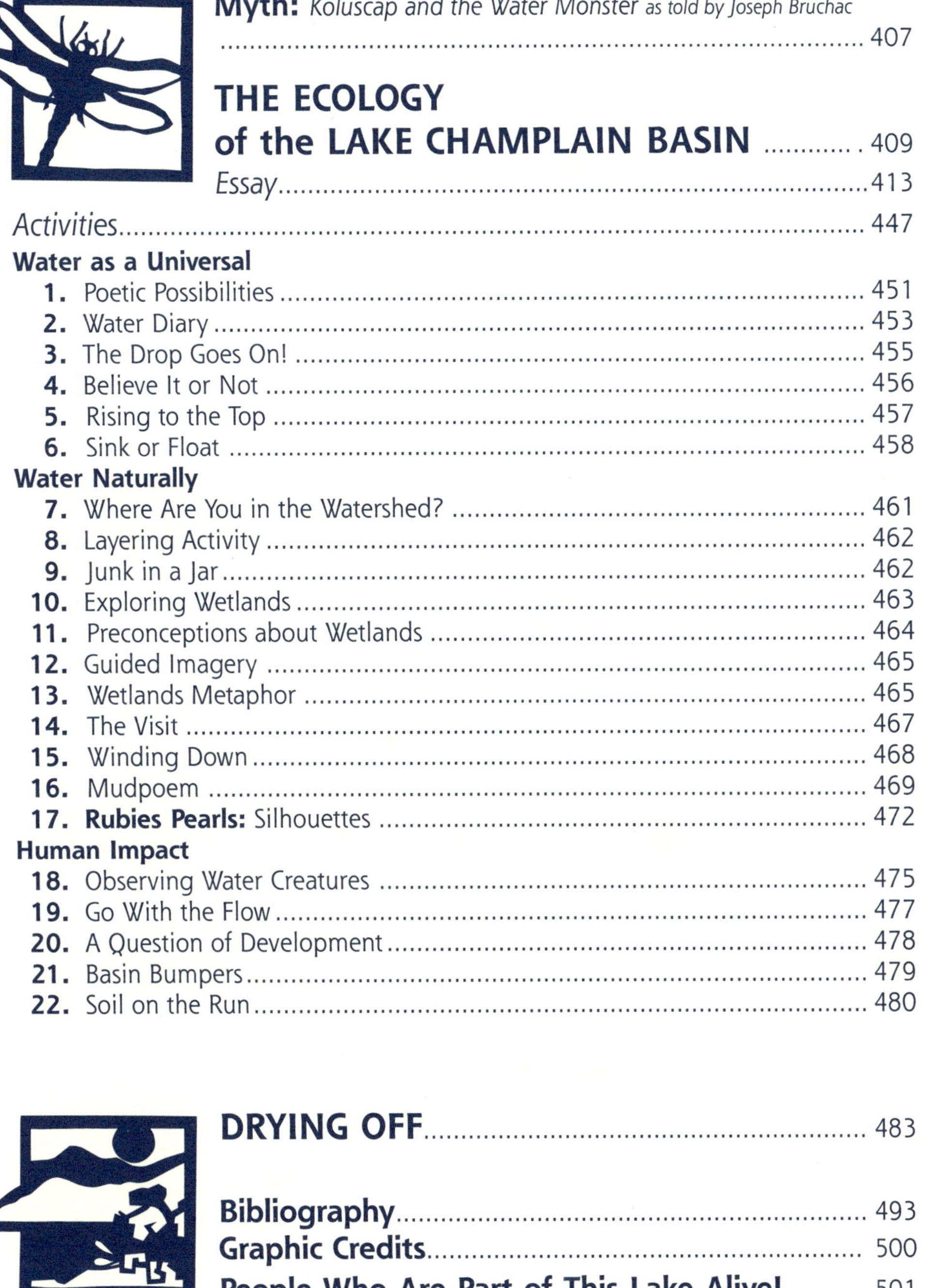

Foreword

I can honestly say that teaching and learning about Lake Champlain has been the single most exciting experience of my professional life.

In the summer of 1986, Barrett Smith, a teammate at Milton Jr. High and I took a writing course at the University of Vermont (UVM). We were asked to design an interdisciplinary unit to teach that fall; I still remember kicking around for a topic. One of us started talking about the lake and I remember a little something about an underwater vessel had trickled into what I now call my "pre-lake consciousness." Our first talks were about ice-fishing and tall tales, Abenaki legends and birch bark canoes. What we ended up designing that summer is still the framework for much of what I teach ten years later.

For me, learning about the lake quickly grew into an obsession and anyone who came to visit that summer was dragged on the ferry, to Ausable Chasm, or to the Shelburne Museum. I began to think about creating some sort of resource for teachers—so as I learned I gathered materials.

Carol Livingston, a seventh- and eighth-grade teacher at Camel's Hump Middle School, caught the "bug" when I presented a workshop at Chris Stevenson's Middle Grades Institute in 1987 and we have been lake collaborators ever since. We took a course on board the *Homer W. Dixon*, a double-masted schooner that is no longer sailing on the lake. Our "professors" on the boat were Mary Woodruff, Merritt Carpenter, Monty Fischer and Art Cohn. Summer jaunts and explorations fueled our curricula, which we have taught separately but collaborated on often. For this project she has been coach, friend, advisor and colleague.

Many people have taught different aspects of the lake study. Maureen Saunders, a Chapter One aide in 1987, team taught a class with me that researched jobs on the S.S. *Ticonderoga.* Our class performed skits on the boat and reenacted the crew's duties. This was one of my first experiences with a learning integrated field trip, an element that is now a significant part of this curriculum. When I moved to a fifth-grade classroom at School Street School, Bill Ladabouche and I teamed; he contributed many activities, including the creation of "All the News That's Fit to Float."

*author on board the **Homer W. Dixon***

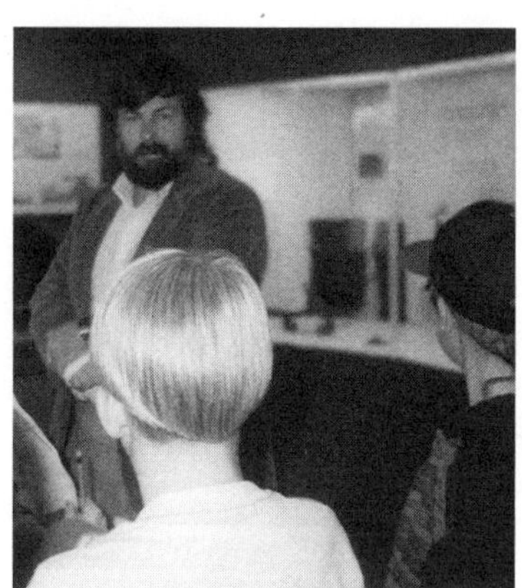

Tim Titus

I have had the privilege of working with two superb professionals in the Museum world, Garet Livermore at the Shelburne Museum, and Tim Titus, formerly at the Crown Point Historic Site. Garet and I coined the P.O.P. philosophy (see *Field Trips*). Tim has been a constant source of support, information and kindness. He has also served on the Editorial Board.

When I started teaching science to fifth graders, I took a course with Tom Hudspeth, professor of environmental education at UVM. The most important lesson I learned from him, while knee-deep in a wetland myself, was that the best way to teach about wetlands is to muck about in them as much as possible. I have tried to do that with my fifth graders.

Chris Stevenson and Judy Carr, two middle-level educators, have inspired the creation and growth of interdisciplinary studies all over this region. Each one, in his and her own way, gave me the strength and encouragement to create curricula that meant something to kids who grow up in the Champlain Valley.

In 1993, I began a working draft of a handbook on Lake Champlain. The one model I had in mind was the National Wildlife Federation's NatureScope series that I had used so often as a humanities teacher learning to teach the sciences. They were useful because they gave the teacher information as well as clearly designed activities. Although the book grew in scope and magnitude, that has remained the purpose of this work. I have tried to design each chapter for the teacher who might not be trained in a particular discipline.

I attended the Lake Champlain Leadership Institute as participant and instructor in the summers of 1993, 1994 and 1995. These exciting exchanges between leading experts in the basin and teachers from New York, Vermont and Quebec fueled my dedication to this project.

In 1994, I received a fellowship from the Christa McAuliffe Foundation to work full-time on this book. It was a wonderful time of research, writing and intellectual exchange so critical to my profession and so seldom available. Much of the writing of the book was completed during this time.

In many ways this book became a "conversation" between the significant people knowledgeable about certain areas and other teachers and educators who knew what was important for kids to learn. So many people participated in so many ways to this conversation.

Anyone who teaches Lake Champlain studies must pause every now and then and ask herself where we'd be without the tireless and extraordinary work of Art Cohn, diver, historian, and director of the Lake Champlain Maritime Museum. Art wrote the *Nautical Archeology* chapter for this book and contributed an essay, "The History of Lake Champlain," which served as the basis for the history essay I wrote for this book.

Art Cohn, Jeff Howe and Kris Kenlan wrote chapters; for these I served as editor. Judy Elson and I constructed the *Ecology* and *Living Treasures* chapters together with input from advisors. For some chapters, such as *History,* I began with someone else's work and built a much larger piece. Other chapters I wrote. Credits appear in the introduction to each chapter.

The Editorial Board read two versions of THIS LAKE ALIVE! in working draft form. Their comments and suggestions were invaluable. Members of the Editorial Board were Jeanne Brink, Colleen Carter, Mary Dupont, Judy Elson, Elise Guyette, Sue Hardin, Carol Livingston, Karen Murdock, Tim Titus and Jill Vickers.

In addition, many people with different areas of expertise read parts of this book. Many thanks to Michael Bouman, Sue Boyer, Barry Doolan, Laura Eaton, Laurie Eddy, Tom Hudspeth, Don Jarrett, Madeleine Little, Fred Magdoff, David Rider, Bill Romond, Mark Scott, Nick Staats and Pat Straughan.

Finally, many people contributed short articles, interviews or activities to this book. They are: Nancy Bazilchuk, Lou Borie, Joseph Bruchac, Colleen Carter, Lori Fisher, Elise Guyette, Sue Hardin, Dale Henry, Mark LaBar, Fred Magdoff, Karen Murdock, Deb Parrella, Joan Robinson, Nick Staats, Ruby Thibault, Mary Watzin and Don Wickman.

Suzi Wizowaty worked as copy editor for this book midway before she became full-time program director at Vermont Council on the Humanities. Her sparkling intelligence and ability to understand the true purpose of THIS LAKE ALIVE! meant so much to the integrity of this project.

I have been fortunate to have the partnership of Shelburne Farms and the many good people who work there. Judy Elson served as production manager, writer, advisor and source of much information and goodwill. Elizabeth Nelson, with her incredible sense of design, orchestrated the melding

Art Cohn

Student Contributors

Anthony Allard
Todd Archambault
Austin Barber
Cara Basiliere
Paul Berry
Amanda Boone
Colin Brady
Stephanie Bushey
Miranda Bushey
Debbie Clark
Tai Dinnan
Kyle Green
Sarah Hamilton
Robbie Hamilton
Mandy Labrie
Valerie Lamphere
Jamie Lewandowski
Becky Martell
Stuart McKenna
Jodi McQuillen
Jason Pariseau
Scott Payea
Samantha Price
Colleen Robie
Nora Sumner-Kopf
Kevin Stevenson
Chris Sweeney
Jonathan Turner
Mike Villemaire
Bachir Yahi

of a complex text, artistic illustrations, diagrams, photos and graphics and miraculously made it all beautiful. Holly Brough, *aka the fairy godmother of our story*, came to this project at the very end but saved us all. She has an eagle eye as well as sound judgment and spent countless hours bringing order to these pages. Holly also contributed the scientific illustrations for this book.

Lou Borie provided the majority of non-historical photographs that appear in these pages. His photographs and sensitivity to the text reflect his lifelong commitment to preserving the natural treasures of this region.

We have all delighted in working with Bonnie Acker, whose illustrations brought a new energy that sailed us to the finish line. We had all waited so long for the time to "bring in Bonnie" that when the day finally came it was better than Christmas. I feel honored to have her work appear on these pages.

Mary Dupont, my teammate at School Street School, served on the Editorial Board and survived teaching with me while I was finishing this book. Her dedication to kids and to her profession serves as a daily inspiration to me.

My husband, Fred Magdoff, read countless drafts of this manuscript, spent hours cajoling the Macintosh, wrote a short article on soils and always listened. Without his incredible store of patience, friendship, encouragement and support, I couldn't have imagined the completion of this project.

Last, and most importantly, I wish to thank the students of Milton, Vermont, with whom I have had the pleasure of studying their wonderful lake.

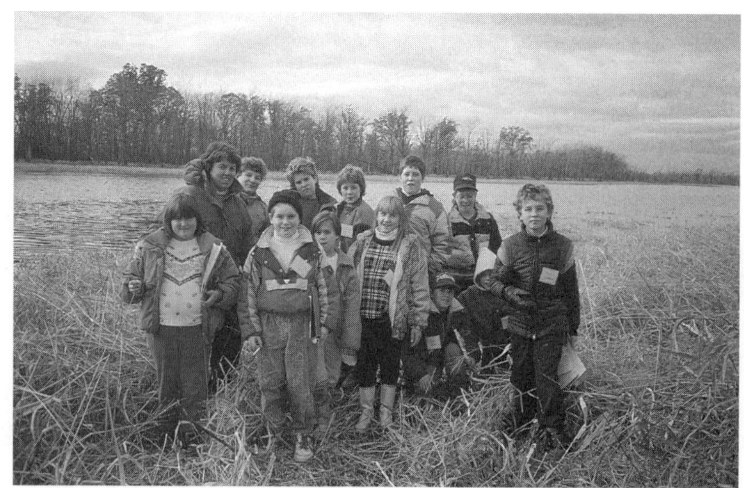

How to Use This Book

Everything in this book is submitted to you with the understanding that it will evolve and be embellished—and that's the point! We're all so good at what we do and every part of this book will undergo a multitude of permutations when you start to tailor it to fit you and your classroom. A resource as rich and varied as the Lake Champlain Basin means that your program will change as you engage your students in real, meaningful learning; because the lake IS alive!

This is not a curriculum; it is an opportunity to create curriculum. One reader likened THIS LAKE ALIVE! to a kitchen cupboard, not a recipe book. Many things will determine what pieces you use. You could choose to teach Lake Champlain solely as a math and science study with only a dollop of the humanities. It could be approached only as a course in geography or as "straight history." The possibilities are endless.

The chapters of this book are designed to help you create an interdisciplinary study of the Lake Champlain Basin. *Geology, Geography, History, Nautical Archeology, Living Treasures* and *Ecology* contain informational essays written for the teacher and student. These essays provide information that we deemed necessary to explore specific disciplines and they may be copied for classroom use. We struggled with the need to provide the teacher with necessary information and still maintain a reading level suited for students. We feel that with guidance, students can use these essays in the classroom. Chapters also contain short highlights of important topics in a format that will let you mix pieces from different chapters.

Activities are presented with the middle level learner in mind but can be adjusted to any age—including adults. They are designed to let you choose from a variety of learning modes. Because space became an issue as THIS LAKE ALIVE! grew in size (and they say there isn't such a thing as a Lake Champlain monster), we designed a "mini" handout. A "mini" gives suggestions for a handout, but since teachers often revise handouts to suit their needs, we didn't give our version a complete page. When we thought it important, we did present the ideas on a full page.

When I thought it was helpful to do so, I gave a very detailed description of how to proceed. For example, in the "Getting Started" section of *Getting Wet*, I even wrote down what to say! This was done to impart flavor rather than specifications. Usually, it reflects a tried-and-true practice that I have used because it continues to fit my students. Other suggestions for activities are explained very briefly in the column as "Other Ideas."

The *History* and *Ecology* chapters are the two anchors of this book. They are larger because they seem to serve as foundations for all the other pieces. In each chapter we provided key resources for the teacher. The bibliography in the back of the book contains complete information on these key resources and on other books and organizations mentioned in THIS LAKE ALIVE! Keep in mind that this listing is not comprehensive but what we thought would be most helpful.

Ruby Thibault, the art teacher at School Street School, designed activities for you to use in your classroom. Although many of us are reluctant to undertake art projects in the classroom, the art activities in this book, titled "Rubies Pearls," are designed for you to easily add a colorful dimension to your study.

Joan Robinson, the education director at the Flynn Theatre, reviewed and wrote drama activities for THIS LAKE ALIVE! Joan teaches creative drama at St. Michaels College and designed "Jo's Shows" to help students creatively interpret the many dimensions of the Lake Champlain Basin.

One problem that I don't think ever got fully resolved is the "Vermont-o-centrism" of this work. I live on that side of the lake, as do many of the consultants for THIS LAKE ALIVE! Although we are thinking more and more as a basin of people who share this land and water, many of our learning patterns and institutions are still tied to one state. My apologies to my neighbors in New York and Quebec for any omissions this caused.

If you have already been learning about the Lake Champlain Basin with children, I hope this book will fuel further work. If you have not been, you are about to start on a glorious adventure. Studying this land and water where we live is a truly wonderful experience—so open the cupboard and begin! Have a wonderful time!

You will see this graphic next to Jo's Shows.

Why Teach Kids About Lake Champlain

As expressed in the letter from Robbie, stewardship is probably the single most important inspiration for teaching about Lake Champlain. What happened to me, in a large way over ten years, happens to each child who studies the lake, who learns about its past, who contemplates its future. As they learn to love the lake, they want to protect it. That, really, is what this book is all about.

What are the hooks that will make a child growing up in New York, in Quebec or Vermont feel connected to this lake? There are many. Making a connection between a child and his or her past, between a child and this incredible natural resource, is the fire that fuels our work.

But a sound interdisciplinary study is also about other things. It is about what Chris Stevenson refers to as "rigor." It is learning the geography of your region—what a drainage basin is and what are its implications. It's about capitalizing proper nouns such as Crown Point, Benedict Arnold and Ojihozo. It's about learning to distinguish historical periods and discern what a person's life may have been like in the 1500s, canoeing up Otter Creek to fish and hunt for the winter's food, compared to the life of a person living in the 1800s in the busy seaport of Burlington and who perhaps worked on a steamboat. It's about learning to think clearly and critically and being able to express yourself orally and in writing, whether about applying lampricide in Lake Champlain's tributaries or drafting legislation on future marina development on the lake. It is about all these things, and, of course, more—but that's why I needed to write this book!

Dear Mr. Illick,

I am very interested in the history and future of Lake Champlain.

I love to fish and go swimming in the lake.

I wish Governor Dean and the State Senate could change the way Vermonters look at the lake. They should decrease the pollution, even though it isn't as much as California.

I love the lake. If people loved it as much as I do, the lake wouldn't have all the pollution.

Robbie Hamilton, Grade 5
School Street School, Milton, Vermont

Letter written to Mr. Rowland Illick, retired professor of geography, after a guest presentation of the Lake Champlain Committee's slide show, "The Ecology of Lake Champlain."

The Lake Champlain Basin

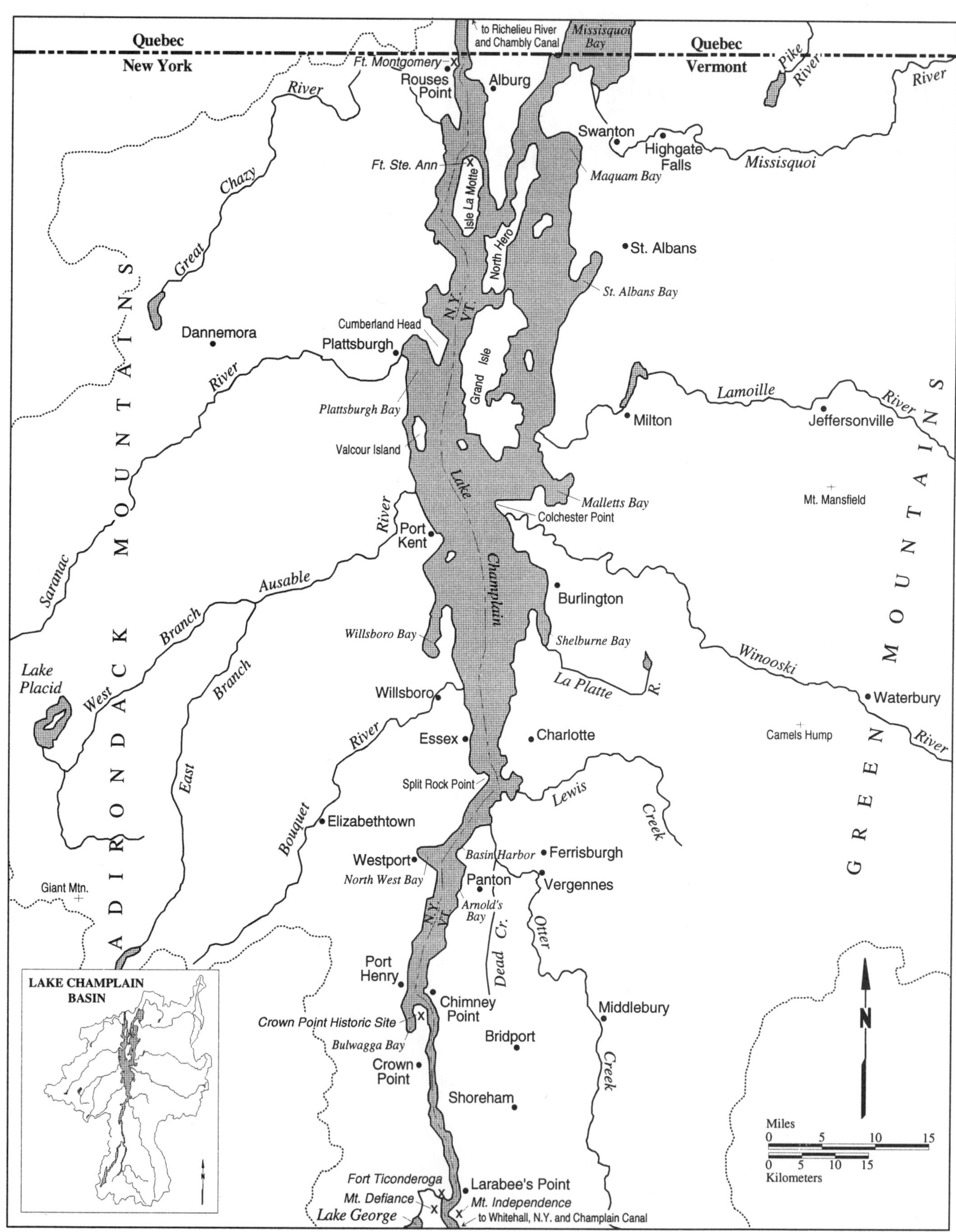

Getting Wet

Getting Wet

MAKING CONNECTIONS

This book is about connections. When building a strong interdisciplinary study, connections between community, school and home are critical. These connections are what will fuel your study and insure a meaningful learning experience for your students.

BUILDING CONNECTIONS *to your* COMMUNITY

As with any local study, it is important to tap into what your students already know about Lake Champlain. Many, having lived near its shore most of their lives, will surprise you with a wealth of knowledge and associations. They will tell you how beautiful the lake is and where they took their favorite boat ride and how much fun it was. Letting your students express this enthusiasm and giving it a place in the classroom will give your study a charge that no finely tuned lesson plan can match.

The first year we started our Lake Champlain study, we were swamped with stories about old camps on the lake, fishing tales and Champ sightings. There is a whole generation of grandparents out there whose favorite teenage memories are from the S.S. *Ticonderoga*'s last voyages on the lake, when dances were held routinely on its decks.

Because the collection of these stories involves family members and neighbors, a local study will link your classwork to your neighborhood in many exciting ways. You can invite people in to tell stories, send kids out for formal interviews, and find ways for kids to share their findings with their community.

There are so many good reasons to connect kids to the people and things that are nearby including:
- making connections to the real world,
- recording soon-to-be-forgotten skills and stories,
- broadening your scope of support and understanding of what is
  happening in the classroom,
- practicing students' skills of interviewing and learning from people.

There are many ways for students to study their "neighborhood" and see how it is connected to the Lake Champlain Basin, whether you are asking them questions based on the social sciences or on ecology.

One way is to ask your students to uncover the connections that people in their town have to Lake Champlain. This is an interview conducted by a Milton seventh grader, Todd Archambault.

"The person I interviewed was Alta White at 3:00 to 4:30 p.m. on Oct. 12, 1986. The interview was held in her Colchester, Vt., home.

She had a lot of stories to tell, she knows a great deal about the lake, like how they used to cut ice off the lake.

They cut the ice off the lake originally with hand saws. The saw was used in the same way we cut wood. They took the ice out of the water and put it on the horse drawn wagon with ice tongs. They pulled it to the ice house to save for the summer. Later they used a power saw to cut the ice and a conveyer to get it from the water to the truck.

Alta's father built and used a ferry. He built the ferry by lantern light for two winters in his shop. In 1910 his 36 foot long and 9 foot wide boat the **Frances Anne** *was put in the water.*

The boat was used mainly as a ferry but with the use of a scow he hauled bricks, sand and gravel. The sand he hauled was used to help fill in Sunderland Hollow.

When her father was young he worked on the sailboat that brought the bricks that were used in the Catholic Church in St. Albans.

I felt the hardest part was asking the questions because my father and Miss White would get off the topic like they talked about the type of engine that was in the boat.

The most interesting part was actually after the interview when she let us see the scrapbook she was keeping."

BUILDING CONNECTIONS *to your* STUDENTS

One of the most useful techniques I'm sure many teachers are familiar with is a student journal. Although students are free to write anything they wish in what I call "thinkbooks," they are content-based, not personal, journals. Specific topics are given, usually designed to evoke a response to an activity or class discussion, or to give them an opportunity to plan. With fifth graders, less reflective than seventh graders, I use it more often for writing "five good facts" or a "list of ideas" vs. "what do you think..." or "explain why."

At key points, I ask students to write a "Dear Ms. D." entry. It might be at a time when I sense some frustration, or after a class discussion where I think I have cleared up an issue about a project or activity and I need to hear from each student before proceeding. Sometimes it is used to just "tell me how things are going." For me, this connection is very important, especially when the pace picks up in the frenzy of an interdisciplinary study and I run the risk of losing touch.

Most thinkbook entries are written silently in class. Students always have the option of finishing an entry on their own time. If the entry is more of a specific task, such as "use four 'fort words' in good Crown Point sentences," it might be given as homework.

I check thinkbooks daily for completion, but only collect them once a week to read and respond to entries. (See *Assessment*, p. 332.)

Thinkbook Entries
- Write all the things you know about Lake Champlain.
- Write all the things you'd like to learn.
- Write a description about a place on the lake that you have been to.
- Write a song, poem or fishing ditty.
- Write about how we learn about people in the past. (Following discussion of primary and secondary sources.)
- Write about a time in history that's most interesting to you. (After our trip to the Maritime Museum.)
- Write about how the Abenakis depend on Lake Champlain to live.
- Write me a letter titled: "Dear Ms. D."

Dear Sam,

I wish you were here so you could see all the things that we got now you would be surprised. We got speedboats, ferries, and cars. We have houses and light houses. The lake is a lot dirtier than when you were alive. It must have been hard to paddle that canoe of yours down the lake. We have gunboats and army tanks now. We got a lot of different guns like rifles instead of a musket. People don't travel by boat much now that we got cars and trucks.

Jonathan Turner, Grade 5
School Street School, Milton, Vermont

This is a letter that a student wrote to Samuel de Champlain, explaining to him the things that have changed since Champlain's trip down the lake in 1609.

- Use five really good "fort" words in five great sentences about Crown Point.
- Write about your idea for your research project.
- Imagine a wetland. What do you think of?
- What is your idea for the story "Trip Around the Lake?"
- Write a letter to Samuel de Champlain titled: "Dear Sam." (See *It's About Time*, p. 190.)
- What are you going to teach the class during your research presentation?
- Describe the "touch lake" experience. (See *Field Trips*, p. 281.)
- Comment on your classmates' research presentations. What did you learn?
- Write a letter at the end of your unit titled: "So Long, Sam" or "See Ya Later, Lake."
- Write about a problem that Lake Champlain has. Explain a good solution. (After Lake Champlain Committee's slide show "Ecology of Lake Champlain.")

BUILDING CONNECTIONS *to your* FAMILIES

A key ingredient in a successful long-term interdisciplinary study is a strong connection between home and school. Send home a lot of information. This is critical if your study involves additional costs and schedule changes, but there are other reasons as well. As the unit evolves, your parents become part of it, thanking you for the opportunity to learn about the Lake Champlain Basin.

Throughout this book, there will be suggestions on how to send specific information home. Here are some general suggestions for successful parent involvement.

Be sure parents know early of:
• any additional costs for field trips and guest speakers (I usually include this information in a summer letter),
• any schedule changes that alter the regular school day,
• any special needs such as big boots for mud walks or help with an interview,
• the need for chaperones,
• the scope of the unit,
• any major research projects.

Cassie Steeves stands with her mother next to the Native American clay pot that Mrs. Sandra Steeves found while diving in Lake Champlain. The pot is on permanent loan to the Maritime Museum.

Taking It Home
This graphic appears throughout the book with a suggestion on how to build connections between the work you do in the classroom and the families of your students.

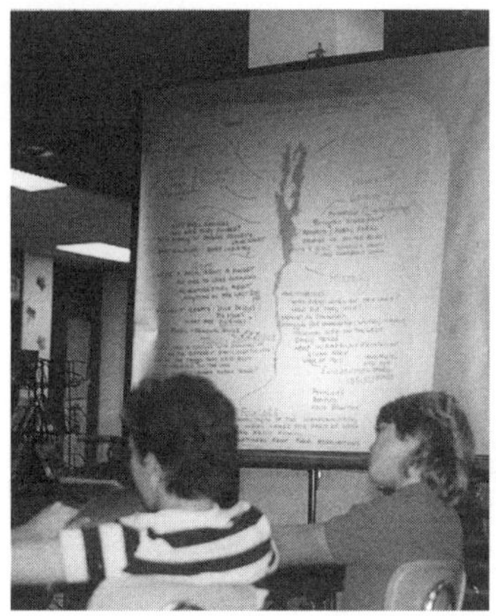

When undertaking a large unit of study, clarify student expectations in a handout sent home early in the unit. For example:

Each student will complete the following:
1. Geography map of Lake Champlain
2. Historical map of Native American peoples on Lake Champlain
3. Fact sheet of Lake Champlain
4. Creative writing: Trip Around Lake Champlain
    (historically and geographically correct)
5. Artistic contribution to timeline of person, place, artifact or event
6. Science paper on Lake Champlain animal or ecology issue
7. Contribution to lake glossary
8. Tests and quizzes

Each student will maintain the following:
1. Organization of notes in student notebook
2. "Thinkbook" journal entries in response to learning activities
3. Daily homework assignments

During your study, there are a lot of different ways to communicate the content of what you are doing.

• Have students write a letter home about an event that has just happened or is about to happen. Get the letter signed and returned.

• Have students ask their parents what they know about a particular topic such as the value of wetlands or the preservation of wrecks in freshwater. Students delight in learning more than the "general public" and if parents are asked in a friendly manner, they often will communicate the views of "J.Q. Public," so students can share their knowledge. Do this as an informal inquiry (see "Preconceptions About Wetlands" in *Ecology*, p. 464) or as a formal interview (see *Research and Inquiry*).

• Encourage parents to be involved in fact-finding. Parents who have had some involvement through boating, fishing, or even diving are great resources for your classroom. Welcome this information! Newspapers are also good sources of information for family fact-finding.

• Send home a family reading assignment that you think will be of interest to parents or older siblings. Allow a few days for completion and ask homework or response sheet to be signed by the adult or adults who participated.

Lake Champlain

	Mon.	Tues.	Wed.	Thu.	Fri.

Demarest 1994

GETTING STARTED

FREEWRITE

Here's a great way to begin studying Lake Champlain with your students.

"Let's start by thinking of everything you know about Lake Champlain. Think of all the things you might have done there, places that you've seen, boat trips, swimming....Maybe you've been on the ferry. Maybe you know some facts about the geography of the lake or its history or some things about people who live or work on the lake. Or maybe you know about an animal that you think lives there. Write down anything at all. Remember that there are no right and wrong answers in a freewrite, just the challenge of getting the ideas in your brain on paper. Please write quietly for three minutes."

On the blackboard or on a large piece of paper, cluster all the ideas that students wrote down. More ideas will come as you record.

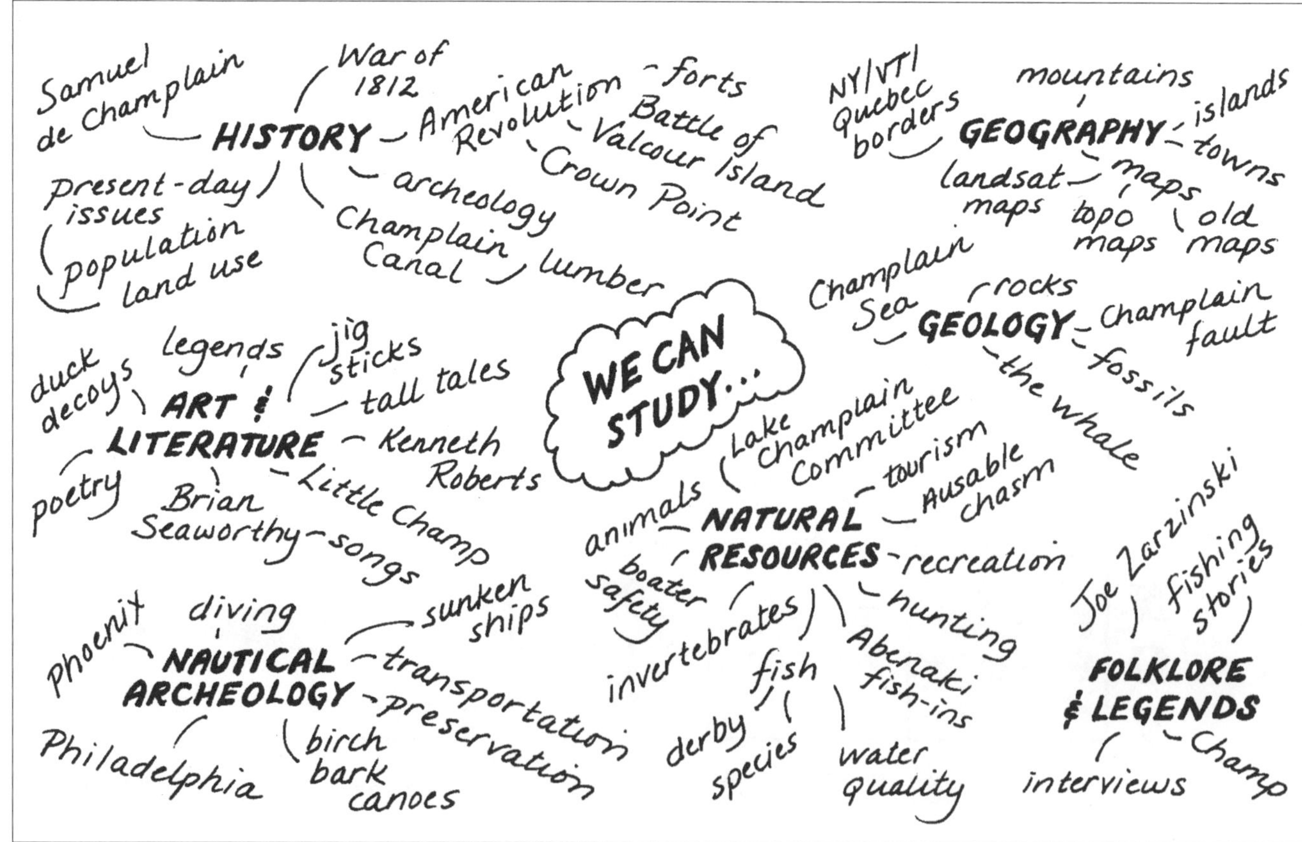

THE WORLD'S QUICKEST BULLETIN BOARD IDEA

Record (in bright markers) all the freewrite ideas on a piece of paper large enough to cover your whole bulletin board. Acknowledge with students how much information they already know. A room full of experts!

In the weeks ahead, have students add illustrations, photographs, data and additional narrative to the cluster.

Next, ask students to think of all the questions they might have, things they may not know about Lake Champlain:

> *"You have shown us all the things that you know about Lake Champlain. Now, like good scientists, we should think about some of the things we don't know and how we could find out more. Perhaps you have a special interest in history and want to know more about underwater wrecks or you are an engineer interested in bridges, or an ecologist interested in wetlands, or you have a concern about cleaner beaches. Maybe you want to know how many islands there are or how deep the lake is. Start writing and write quietly for three minutes. Don't stop! There are a million great questions to think of."*

After they have had time to write, ask them to share the questions. If students in the room know the answers, add them to the cluster, or add questions. If there are topics for which you have activities planned, take the opportunity to tell them about upcoming events.

Another thing that will be apparent, and vary according to the age of your students, is how concrete most of their questions are. When I went from teaching seventh grade to teaching fifth grade, this was most striking and led me to include much more fact-finding into our study. I couldn't believe a ten-year-old's insatiable appetite for FACTS. This will lead you into the next day's fact-finding activity, but should be maintained as a constant throughout the unit (see "Ten Excellent Facts," p. 16).

Invariably at this time, questions and topics will arise that you have had no plans to incorporate into your lake study. At times this can be very exciting and interesting—it can also drive you crazy! It's hard trying to match a student's interest with an unknown source. If you have decided to turn your students loose on a local resource, be prepared to do some digging around for sources.

One student writes:
"I would like to know more about your history...I already know that you are fun to play in."

- *How deep is it?*
- *How wide is it?*
- *How many islands are in it?*
- *How many fish live in it? (This is a fun one!)*
- *What is the longest tributary?*
- *Is Champ real?*
- *How many wrecks are at the bottom of the lake? Who found them?*
- *How many ferry crossings are there?*

• Develop a database on the computer to store facts as they accumulate.

• Assign students to be classroom experts on certain topics.

• Assign a news team to follow important lake issues in the news.

• Use math class to process Lake Champlain data. Lots of possibilities with area, distance and volume. Ferry crossings provide lots of possibilities for computation and time problem solving (see **Math**).

• Have a student or group of students write a "kick-off" news story about your study for the school or town newspaper.

• Make a big banner for outside your door announcing what your class is studying.

How you deal with this depends a lot on how you run your classroom. (See *Research and Inquiry.*) However you decide, I encourage you to use local sources and see if you might find a way for that student to pursue her interest. There will be many questions that emerge in local studies that you don't know the answers to and that is part of the fun. When I think of all the things that I didn't know about Lake Champlain when I started, it's sort of scary, but I also know that learning with my students, my first year, was one of the most exciting experiences of my professional life.

ASSIGNMENT

In your thinkbook, describe what you like best about the lake. It could be something that you know a lot about or something that you don't know much about.

OR

Write down five facts about Lake Champlain.

After your upbeat "kick-off," it's a good idea to share the nitty-gritty details of your upcoming unit. I usually hand them a list of expected classwork, a calendar (see p. 9), and a letter home.

"This week is incredible. A terrific tension has disappeared as the unit unfolds. Four months of work, dreaming and scheming. All that time I had been making it happen (arranging, scheduling, grants, memo, copying…). Now the unit is happening to me. Kids are writing songs, bringing in treasures, stories, planning research. There is an incredible amount of knowledge in this town about the lake. Art Cohn came and told us about the Champlain Canal and in class yesterday a kid explained to us how locks worked. He'd been through on his family's boat. I didn't even know there was a canal!"

ABD Teaching Journal

Activity: **Get the Picture**

• If you have the time and the resources, a slide show at the beginning of your study is helpful, especially if you can get shots of different parts of the lake that your students might not have seen. I have taken many slides over the years and often show them at the beginning of a unit. Shots include different parts of the lake as well as field trip sites. You can also make slides of pictures in books, but that is a complicated venture. Better yet, find a camera buff in your community who might have slides or pictures to share. Check with your local historical society.

• The Lake Champlain Committee and the Lake Champlain Basin Program both have excellent slide shows and are willing to come to classrooms. State offices that manage specific natural areas also have people who will come and visit.

Assemble a good collection of books related to Lake Champlain. Choose ones with pictures. It's okay to have duplicates for this activity, so borrow as many as you can. If you are short on books, tourist information is good, as is information on boating and fishing. Have the students sit in pairs and small groups. Explain that as we get older, adults encourage us to stop looking at the pictures in the books and only pay attention to the words! Say that today we are only going to look at pictures!

Take about a half hour to look at the pictures and encourage students to share what they have observed. Ask for students to share orally what they have observed or complete the "Source Search." (See *Research and Inquiry,* p. 308.)

It's great to have students start off with some concrete images of what they are going to be studying. We may refer to steamboats and assume that everyone knows what they look like, when that isn't the case at all!

Activity: **Treasure Hunt**

Assemble a large collection of brochures and maps. I usually make a two-pocket folder for each student that includes some of the following:

- Vermont Road Map
- Lake Champlain Basin Program fact sheets
- tourist brochures on important sites, including the places you are going!
- ferry schedule
- Vermont Guide to Fishing
- any related newsletters or publications

Make a set of trivia and fact questions like those on the next page. Assemble the students into groups of three or four and give each group its own set of questions. Questions for each group are the same.

Students work in their group to find the answers to questions and write answers on the back of cards. When they think they have all the answers, check to make sure they are right. They are the "winners." Enlist help from all students until each group is done.

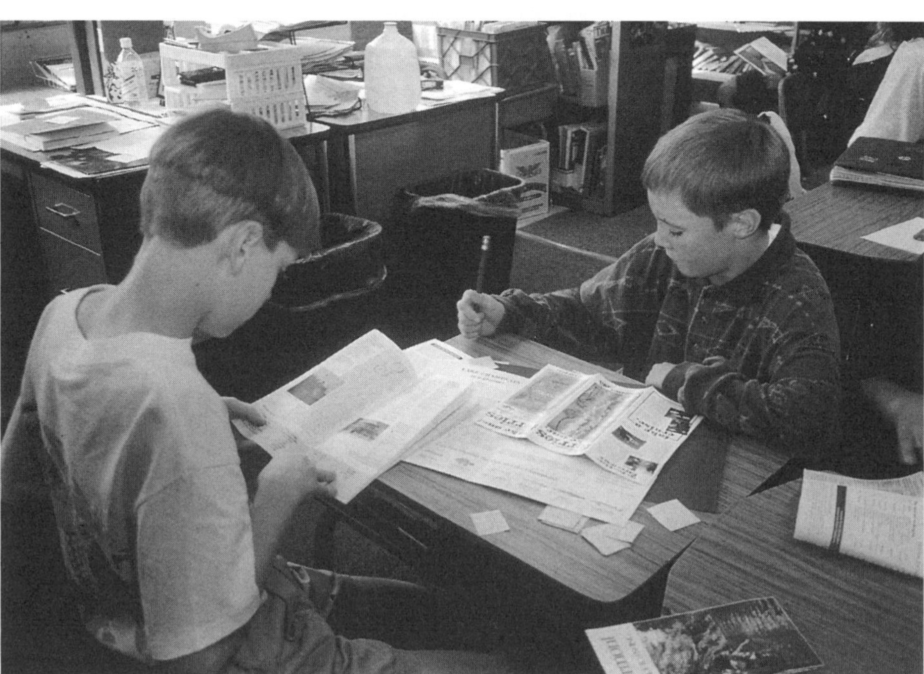

What is the telephone number for the Lake Champlain Ferries?	When was the zebra mussel first found in Lake Champlain?	How many square miles (area) is the lake?	What is the sum of the digits in the phone number of the "Friends of Fort Ticonderoga"?
What is the eastern border of Lake Champlain?	What town does the Charlotte ferry dock at in New York?	How many miles long is Lake Champlain?	How many years ago did glaciers move across this region?
What is the name of a tour boat that you can take to Fort Ticonderoga?	How many species of fish are in the lake?	What are the hours of the Lake Champlain Maritime Museum?	What state is the western border of Lake Champlain?
How many square miles is the Lake Champlain Basin?	What is the name of the river in Canada that "ends" Lake Champlain?	What is the cost of the Grand Isle ferry for a car and a driver round trip?	Is the Crown Point Historic Site open on Sundays?
When was the "Battle of Valcour Island"?	How many islands are in Lake Champlain?	Where is the original gunboat, the *Philadelphia*?	Where is the Ausable Chasm?
What is Fort Carillon called now?	How deep is the lake at its deepest point?	What time is the last tour of the Ethan Allen Homestead?	How wide is Lake Champlain at its widest point?

Activity: **Ten Excellent Facts**

During the first week, start fact-finding. Give the class a chunk of time to look through some of the sources related to Lake Champlain. Materials could be books, newspaper articles, maps and brochures. Ask kids to write what they think are ten excellent facts. Ask each student to compare his or her facts with a partner and come up with one list of important facts.

CLASS DISCUSSION *of* SIGNIFICANT FACTS

Discuss what makes a good fact, or what I call a "facty fact," rather than just a piece of information.

Example: The cost of a one-way ferry crossing from Grand Isle to Plattsburgh is a true piece of information; is it one of the ten most important facts about Lake Champlain that you want to include on the class list? Choosing these facts and rephrasing them is valuable class discussion as students become more confident experts on Lake Champlain.

Compile a list of ten "really good" facts. These can be copied over and posted in the classroom.

Facts About Lake Champlain

by Scott Payea, Grade 5, School Street School, Milton, Vermont

1. Lake Champlain is the sixth largest freshwater lake in the United States.
2. Lake Champlain is 400 feet deep at its deepest part.
3. The lake is 112 miles long.
4. Lake Champlain's widest part is 11 miles wide.
5. Ferry boats have been on the lake for 200 years.
6. Samuel de Champlain was the first white man to see the lake.
7. Lake Champlain used to be part of the Atlantic Ocean.
8. Thousands of years ago huge glaciers covered Vermont.
9. There are 80 species of fish in Lake Champlain.
10. There were many wars fought in the Champlain Valley.

Other Ideas

• *Continue this activity by asking two pairs of students to come up with one list.*

• *There are many facts in the column notes of this book. They can be copied onto small cards and used as sources or information for students to explain.*

Activity: **Mystery Box**

Assemble a box or a basket of artifacts or symbols relating to the lake.

Possibilities include:
• a plastic beluga whale
• a toy railroad car
• a piece of wood or lumber
• a sedimentary rock, or any kind!
• a French/English dictionary
• a beach hat, swimming goggles or bicycle helmet
• a piece of birch bark
• a bird's feather
• a dollar bill
• a box of laundry detergent
• a soda can
• a toy soldier or cannon
• a plastic cow
• an aquatic plant
• a Canadian dollar
• a fish hook
• a flipper
• a map, chart or tourist brochure
• any plastic animal found in the basin
• a zebra mussel (or picture)

Near the beginning of your study, after your students have some familiarity with the events and issues related to the lake, examine the "Mystery Box."

Ask each student to take an item and think of a way that this item is related to the lake. It could be a connection to an idea or an event, or something that might be true, but you're not sure! The relationships that students uncover will amaze you, as there are no "right answers." You may or may not choose to add information to the students' comments, depending upon your use of this activity. In other words, it can be used to teach, or it can be used to trigger the creative juices!

Main Lake

Ojihozo Creation Myth

as told by Joseph Bruchac

Kina. Listen. Long ago, when Tabaldak, the Owner, had finished making things, some of the dust of creation was still on the Owner's hands. So Tabaldak began to brush that dust away. It sprinkled down upon the earth. Where it fell upon the earth, the earth began to move about. It began to shape itself. It shaped itself a torso. It shaped itself a head. It shaped itself shoulders, arms and hands; it shaped itself hips. Then that earth which shaped itself sat up.

Awani gia? said Tabaldak. Who are you?

Ojihozo nia, said that earth which shaped itself. I am Ojihozo. I am the One Gathering Himself Together.

You are very wonderful, said Tabaldak.

Nda, said Ojihozo. No. You are the one who is wonderful. You are the one who sprinkled me.

Then Ojihozo looked around. All around was the beauty of the newly created earth. And Ojihozo became eager to get up and see it. But, like a small child eager to walk before he can, Ojihozo did not notice that he was not yet ready to walk. He had not yet shaped legs and feet. He was still connected to the earth.

So Ojihozo tried to stand. He pushed very hard to one side and he did not move. He pushed harder and harder, so hard that the earth was pushed up into mountains. Those mountains today are called the Green Mountains. But still he could not stand. Then Ojihozo pushed very hard to the other side. He pushed so hard that the earth rose up into mountains on that side, too. Today those mountains are called the Adirondacks. But still he could not stand.

Now Ojihozo reached out his long arms. He reached all the way to the mountaintops to either side of him. Then he pulled, trying to pull himself up. His fingers gouged down the channels of the rivers. Otter Creek, the Winooski, the Lamoille and all the other rivers were formed then. But still he could not stand.

Then Ojihozo saw that Tabaldak was looking at him. Tabaldak looked at him with that look of patience a parent shows when a child does something wrong but that parent is determined to let the child learn through his own mistake. Ojihozo looked at himself then. He saw that he was still connected to the earth. He did not have legs or feet yet.

Then Ojihozo reached down. He shaped legs and feet for himself. Then he stood. And when he stood, he left behind him a great hole in the earth. The waters flowed in and made that hole into a big lake. It is called Bitawbagok, The Waters In Between, by the Dawnland People, though on the maps it is called Lake Champlain. If you look at a map, you can see the shape there of a sitting person, his legs toward the north. That is the shape of Ojihozo.

Then Ojihozo walked around. He walked around for a long time seeing many things. But when he was done, he returned to the beautiful lake and the beautiful mountains he had made. This was where he wished to stay. He sat down upon a small island and changed himself into stone. He sits there to this day, watching over the mountains and the lake.

So the story goes.

Mt. Mansfield

The Geologic History of the Lake Champlain Basin

Our State Fossil

by Tai Dinnan, Grade 4, Charlotte Central School, Charlotte, Vermont

The bones of the Charlotte whale were found while digging the Rutland and Burlington Railroad in 1849. Workers thought they belonged to a horse or cow so they kept on digging until a curious local farmer, John G. Thorp, questioned their find. He thought the bones were unusual and called Zadock Thompson at the University of Vermont. Zadock brought the bones to UVM to examine and identify them.

Unfortunately, the bones were dipped in "animal glue" to preserve them from desiccation, which made it impossible to prove the exact age of the skeleton. We do know that "Charlotte" lived during the time span of the Champlain Sea, 10,000 to 12,500 years ago. Today the skeleton of "Charlotte" is on display in the Perkins Museum of Geology at UVM where visitors are welcome to see her. The Charlotte Historical Society has placed a historic marker near the site where the bones were found. You can go and see it at the railroad crossing on Thompson's Point Road.

A few years ago, Jeff Howe from the Perkins Museum decided the bones should be the state fossil. He asked for help from the Charlotte Historical Society and students from Charlotte Central School to bring this idea to the state government. Charlotte representative Hazel Prindle introduced a bill to declare "Charlotte" the official State Fossil. C.C.S. students then traveled to the state capital, Montpelier, to meet with a special committee and Governor Howard Dean. The state legislature later passed the bill and Governor Dean signed it into law at a ceremony at the Charlotte Central School on June 7, 1993!

The Charlotte whale was a White whale. Other names for it are Beluga, White porpoise, and Sea Canary. It was a toothed whale and is recognized by its grayish white color. It lived about 10,000 to 12,500 years ago. It is not known exactly what its habitat was, but now Belugas live in the colder Arctic Ocean, the North Atlantic, and the North Pacific. They prefer shallow waters and rivers. These whales eat fish including char, sand lance, capelin, pollack, cod, and salmon, plus shrimp and octopus. Belugas are 3 to 5 meters long and weigh about 1.5 tons while the calves measure about 1.5 meters at birth. The Beluga has up to 11 teeth in each side of its upper and lower jaw (at least 32 total) and lacks a dorsal fin which makes it easy to identify. Along with their camouflage, Belugas have the ability to turn their heads from side to side. They also are able to look over and under their shoulders to protect themselves from predators such as polar bears and killer whales.

Scientists do not know exactly how Charlotte died. They think it either died out at sea or it died of hunger in shallow water. It was buried over time and was undiscovered for thousands of years.

Introduction

The Geologic History of the Lake Champlain Basin was written by Jeff Howe for this publication. Jeff Howe oversaw the renovation of the Perkins Geology Museum at the University of Vermont (UVM) and served as the director/curator of the museum from 1992 to 1994. Much of the research that Jeff did—that is used in this essay—was funded by a grant given by the Lintilhac Foundation to the Perkins Museum. These funds and the creative work of Jeff Howe are responsible for the fine resource the museum is today. Jeff Howe is currently the Director of Museum Programs at the Delaware Museum of Natural History in Wilmington, Delaware.

Barry Doolan, Chairman of the Geology Department at UVM, reviewed this chapter and provided help with the graphics.

The Geologic History of Lake Champlain

1.3 billion years ago	**Ancient Adirondacks** This mountain range was formed.
450 million years ago	**Iapetus Ocean** This ocean was a shallow tropical sea. Its shells and organic debris were cemented in limestone.
440–350 million years ago	**Green Mountains** This mountain range was formed.
5 million years ago	**Ice Age** Glaciers carved the soft sedimentary rock in the Champlain Valley.
21,000 years ago	**Glaciers** Glaciers started melting northward toward New England.
14,000–15,000 years ago	**Lake Vermont** A large, deep lake was formed as the glaciers melted then blocked the outflow of water.
13,000 years ago	**Champlain Sea** The sea replaced Lake Vermont when ocean water from the north flooded the basin. The sea supported varied marine life, like the Charlotte whale!
11,000 years ago	**Lake Champlain** The lake was formed when the area was cut off by glacial rebound, sea water was flushed out.

The Geologic History
of the Lake Champlain Basin

THE EVOLUTION
OF THE LAKE CHAMPLAIN BASIN

Lakes of all shapes and sizes are situated all over the world in different environments. Some lakes are small and round and sit high in the mountains. Other lakes are huge and cover vast areas of land. Lake Champlain is long and narrow and is surrounded by mountain ranges on both sides. How did that come to be? To understand how the Lake Champlain Basin was formed, we need to go back a billion years...

Long ago, North America was covered by huge sheets of glacial ice. The Ice Age was a time when massive glaciers formed in the north and slowly moved southward. They eventually reached the area of the Ohio River, Cape Cod and New York City. The glaciers that covered the Champlain Basin covered land that was one billion years old. But these glaciers are only a recent part of a long geologic history of the Champlain Basin. To understand how the basin came to be it is necessary to return to a time when the land we now know as Vermont and New York did not exist.

A billion years ago the earth was much different than it is now. There were no plants or animals on the land. The only life on the planet included a wide variety of microscopic plants, bacteria and a few primitive animal forms. As simple as these life-forms were, they had been evolving for over two billion years. Photosynthesis by microscopic plants over those years gradually changed our atmosphere from one that contained noxious gases, such as methane and sulfur dioxide, to one that was rich in oxygen. It was this oxygen-rich atmosphere that allowed other more complex life-forms to evolve.

The Ice Age is also called the Pleistocene Era, which lasted from 2.5 million to 10,000 years ago.

The age of the earth is approximately 4.6 billion years.

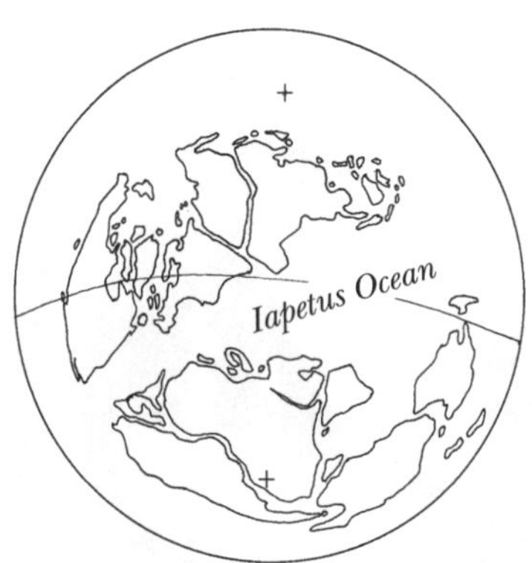

the world 400 million years ago

THE ADIRONDACK MOUNTAINS

The Champlain Basin as we know it did not exist a billion years ago. However, mountain-building events had formed a huge range of mountains that were as large as the Himalayas are today. These were the original Adirondack Mountains. Geologists know that the Adirondacks were once over 20,000 feet tall because the rocks that are now exposed could only have been formed at the base of a pile of rocks that deep. Erosion over the last one billion years has removed the overlying rock.

In many places in the Adirondacks, metamorphic rocks, formed from enormous heat and pressure, yielded fine specimens of minerals such as garnet, anorthosite and diopside. Because of these rocks, the Adirondacks are very popular with rock enthusiasts today, in addition to being a favorite vacation spot for skiers, hikers and nature lovers. For over 500 million years, the Adirondacks eroded in silence, finally being reduced to a range of low hills, lower than the Adirondack Mountains we see today.

THE IAPETUS OCEAN

About 600 million years ago, another catastrophic event caused the surface of the earth to rupture, or "rift," in the approximate area that is now the Champlain Valley. As the rift grew in width and the opposite sides slowly moved apart, the space in between was filled by sea water, forming a warm, shallow ocean.

The ocean that formed in this area was called the Iapetus Ocean. It was full of rapidly evolving life, including trilobites, cephalopods, bryozoans and gastropods and primitive corals. On Isle La Motte, an island in northern Lake Champlain, the remains of a rich reef from the Iapetus Ocean can still be seen. The reef shows many fossils. Although once at the bottom of a warm ocean, the fossils on Isle La Motte are now in the middle of a farmer's cow pasture. Many locations around Lake Champlain yield fossils of things that once lived in the Iapetus Ocean.

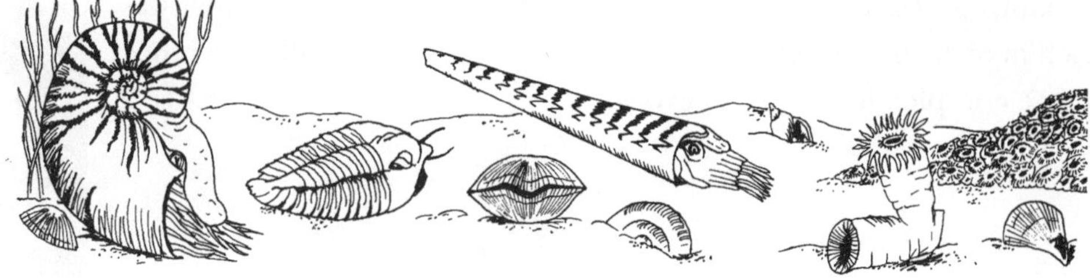

THE GREEN MOUNTAINS

Because the surface of the earth is constantly in motion, the Iapetus Ocean slowly began to narrow, eventually closing completely. In the final stages of closure, the land masses on opposite sides of the ocean collided. This happened slowly over millions of years and it caused the ground to crumple, fracture and fold. This movement formed another huge mountain range, the Appalachian Mountains, which were not quite as high as the original Adirondacks, but still magnificent in size. The Green Mountains, which now cover the state of Vermont, were formed as part of this Appalachian range. They were formed some 450 million years ago and have also eroded to just a fraction of what they once were.

Much of the rock color in the Green Mountains is due to the metamorphic mineral chlorite. Biologists might say the Green Mountains got their name from the color of the trees. Geologists on the other hand, could say the mountains got their name from the color of the rocks. What do you think?

THE CHAMPLAIN THRUST

It took a tremendous force to create the Green Mountains. An outstanding example of this power is the Champlain Thrust, which runs along the northeastern shore of Lake Champlain from St. Albans to south of Burlington. As the Green Mountains were forming, enormous forces deep in the earth caused a huge slice of rock to break free and be forced upwards above rocks that were much younger in age. This "thrust fault" can be seen most spectacularly at Lone Rock Point near Burlington. Lone Rock Point is famous and geologists and geology students from all over the world come to observe and study this fault formed by compression.

Champlain Thrust at Lone Rock Point

THE GREAT HIATUS

From the formation of the Green Mountains 400 million years ago until the "recent" glaciation, there is very little record of events here in the Champlain Basin. This gap in the story is called the Great Hiatus.

Although no clear record marks this time period, ample evidence in other parts of New England suggest that a great deal was happening in this region. The age of dinosaurs and the formation of the modern Atlantic Ocean both happened during this time. The entire Champlain Basin was highly mountainous and undergoing extensive erosion. Sediments from this erosion were carried away and deposited in other places, far from the Champlain Valley. This erosion removed much of the "old" surface, leaving low rounded hills. Dinosaurs may have roamed over what is now Mt. Mansfield and Whiteface Mountain, but the fossil traces, if there were any, have eroded away over time.

THE BRANDON LIGNITE

The only known window into the Great Hiatus is the Brandon Lignite, a tiny deposit of iron-rich clay and lignite (a crude form of coal) found near Forestdale, Vermont. In the Brandon Lignite, scientists have discovered the remains of plant seeds and fruits about 25 million years old. These indicate that, at that time, this area was much warmer, perhaps like the climate in South Carolina. Geologists are not certain how the Brandon Lignite escaped being destroyed by erosion and glaciation. They have suggested that a small piece of the area was pressed into the soft clay below it and protected.

PLATE TECTONICS

Although the idea of plate tectonics has been developed in only the last 30 years, it is regarded as one of the most significant ideas in science, equal in importance to the discoveries of Galileo and Madam Curie. Rather than a discovery made by one scientist, it was developed by geologists working together worldwide. Plate tectonic theory is still being developed and continues to be modified as new evidence becomes available. This is the way that science operates: by continually redefining what we think to be true as new discoveries are made.

As early as the 1500s, when the first reliable maps of the earth were drawn, geographers noted that the coastlines of Africa and South America fit together almost perfectly like two pieces of a giant puzzle. There was no good explanation at the time for how entire continents might move apart such a great distance.

In the 1960s, scientists began to gather evidence from the bottom of the ocean that suggested that the crust of the earth is composed of large "plates" that move about slowly on molten rock. Along boundaries where these plates collide, their edges crumple, forming mountain ranges and volcanoes. When the edges of the continental plates pull apart, they form depressions that fill with sea water. These depressions can grow over time into large oceans. When plates slide alongside of each other (as they do in California), they cause frequent (and often destructive) earthquakes.

THE PLEISTOCENE—THE AGE OF GLACIERS

The earth has had many Ice Ages throughout its history, but the most recent, and the one that most affected the Champlain Basin, began about 2.5 million years ago. This period, from the formation of glaciers until their final disappearance about 10,000 years ago, is known as the "Pleistocene."

Glaciers form when the climate of the earth becomes such that more snow falls in a given winter than can melt the following summer. If these conditions exist for hundreds to thousands of years, snow piles up to enormous depths. When the weight of the overlying snow becomes great enough, the glacier begins to move outwards at its base, very similar to the way a pile of applesauce spreads at the bottom as more spoonfuls are added to the top.

This buildup of snow is what occurred in the northern latitudes of the earth during the Pleistocene Age. A center of snowfall in northern Canada produced a glacier that slowly migrated southward into New England. A lobe of this glacier penetrated between the Adirondacks and the Green Mountains, filling the valley and finally covering all of the mountains as well! At one time the thickness of the glacier in the Champlain Valley was over a mile high!!

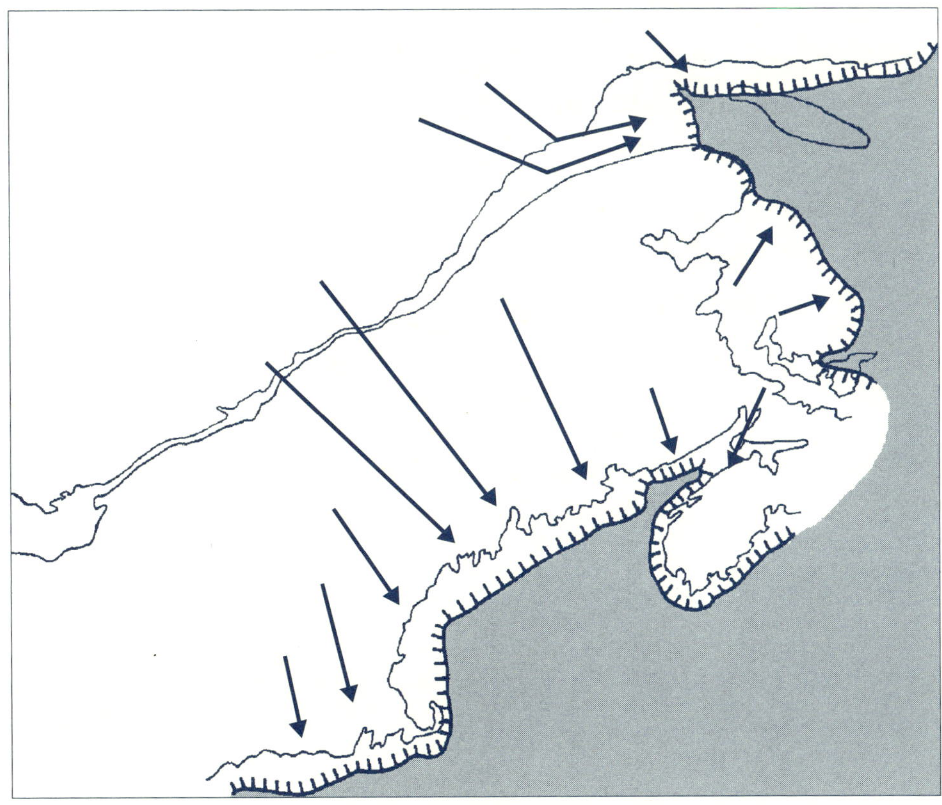

18,000 years ago, glaciers covered most of New England.

Lake Vermont

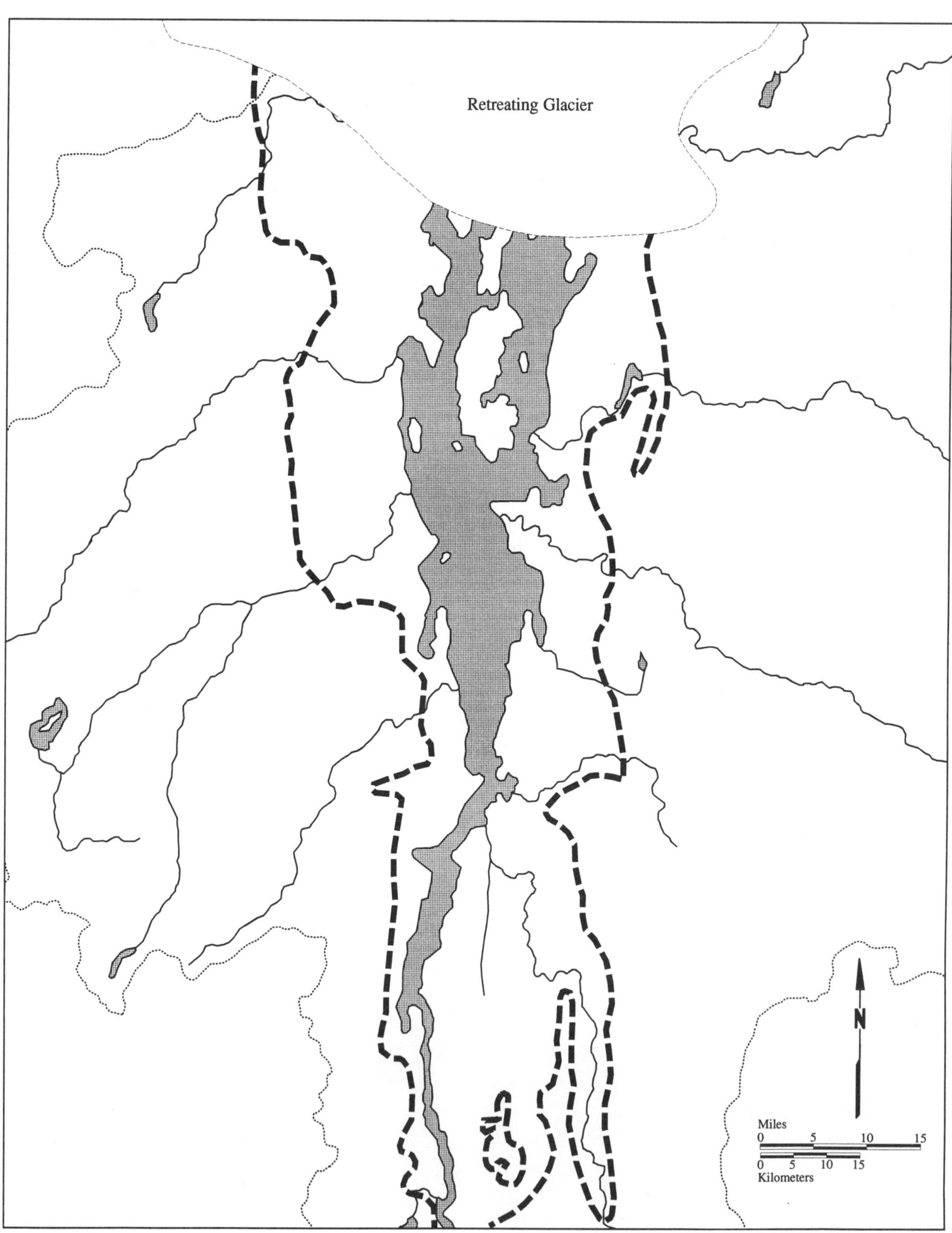

Credit: *Northern Cartographic. Used with permission.*

LAKE VERMONT

About 20,000 years ago, the climate of the earth changed again and the glaciers began to melt. As they retreated northward, enormous quantities of meltwater thick with sand and silt poured off the glaciers and flooded the land at their bases. As the ice melted through the Champlain Basin, meltwater was blocked to the north by the glacier and to the south by huge dams of rock, mud and jammed ice. A deep freshwater lake was formed, much deeper than present-day Lake Champlain, and it covered many hundreds of square miles in Vermont and New York (Canada was still covered by ice). This lake had many stages but is generally referred to as Lake Vermont.

THE CHAMPLAIN SEA

As the glacial ice continued to melt northward, it brought changes to this region. By about 13,000 years ago, the ice lobe had melted back to northern New York and Vermont, exposing land that had been covered by glacial ice for many thousands of years. The ice that had prevented Lake Vermont from draining melted and the lake level dropped many hundreds of feet. The general warming of the climate caused glaciers to retreat worldwide, causing the level of the oceans to rise from the increased meltwater. Thousands of feet of ice had covered the Champlain Valley. The weight of all this ice had depressed the land below the level of the sea for many years. This lowland was quickly flooded by the rising sea. Freshwater Lake Vermont was replaced by an extension of the ocean known as the Champlain Sea. It was no longer a freshwater lake but very much like a large inland bay, connected to the ocean by the valley that today contains the St. Lawrence River. The discovery of the skeletons of over a dozen white (or Beluga) whales from this time period, as well as the remains of other ocean fossils such as seals, salmon, herring and mussel shells, are evidence that this area was once part of the ocean. These fossils have been found in portions of New York, Vermont, Ontario and Quebec, all areas once covered by the Champlain Sea.

On land, the valleys were clogged with sediment runoff from the melting ice. Sand and gravel ridges remained to mark former sites of the ice. Plants that could grow in the cold and Ice-Age mammals, such as the woolly mammoth and caribou, followed the retreat of the glaciers. From the south and west came the first humans, following the herds of grazing animals into new and productive lands. Archeologists call these people Paleo people.

The extent of the Champlain Sea

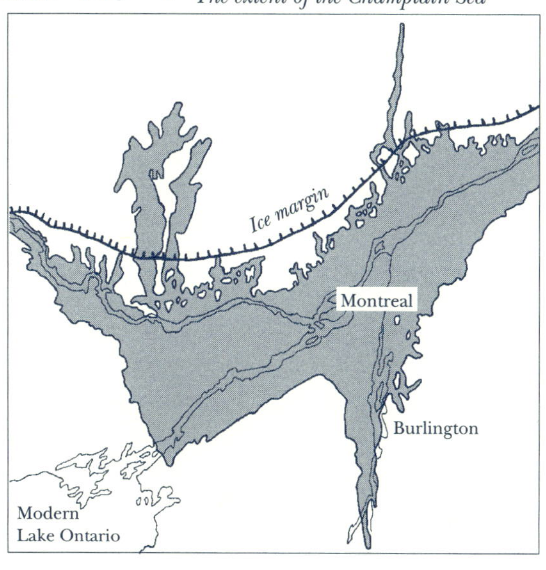

The Champlain Sea

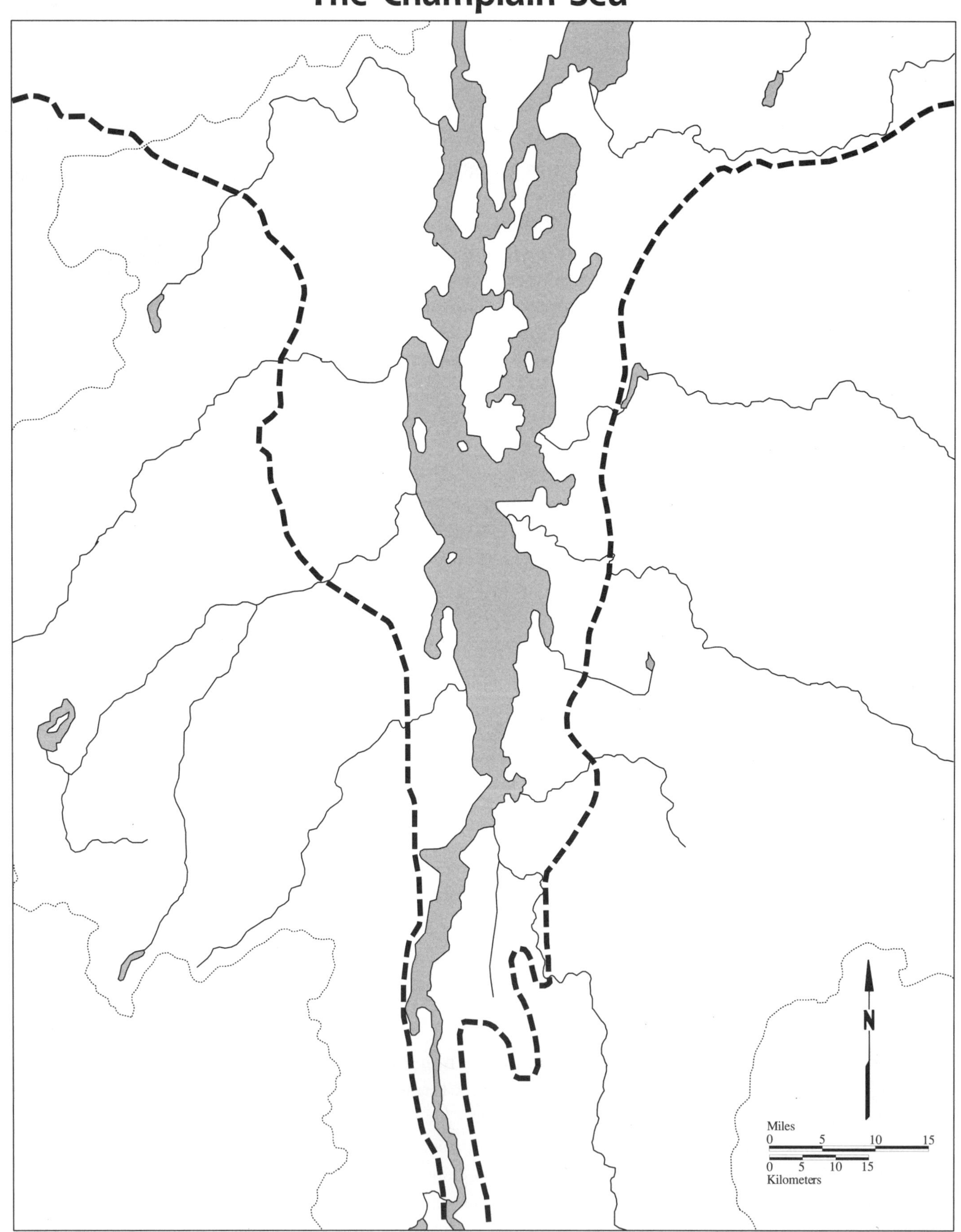

Credit: *Northern Cartographic. Used with permission.*

LAKE CHAMPLAIN

As the Champlain Valley continued to rebound from the weight of the glacial ice, the surface of the Champlain Sea rose until it attained an elevation greater than that of sea level. When this occurred, the salty water of the Champlain Sea began to flow slowly northward to the valley of the St. Lawrence and back to the ocean. As the rivers surrounding the basin continued to flush it with freshwater, the Champlain Sea slowly gave way to the freshwater lake that we know today as Lake Champlain. Lake Champlain has existed in its approximate present form for at least 9,000 years.

THE FOSSIL HISTORY OF THE LAKE CHAMPLAIN BASIN

The different kinds of fossils found in the Champlain Basin offer many interesting clues to plant and animal life in the past. A fossil is seldom composed of the original bone, teeth or plant fiber of the organism, but instead is composed of rock material that has slowly, over many, many years, replaced it. If the remains of an animal or plant are deposited quickly in soft mud or sand, they are protected from rapid decay in the atmosphere. Over time, the original material is replaced by dissolved minerals in the ground, eventually producing an exact copy, called a fossil. Sometimes a print of a plant or animal is left behind and is slowly filled in with more sand or mud. When the filled print hardens, it becomes a "cast" and looks just like the original shell, leaf, footprint or animal skeleton. Casts are also fossils.

THE EARLIEST FOSSILS

The oldest fossils that have been found in the Champlain Basin are those of creatures that lived in the warm, shallow Iapetus Ocean that covered this area over 450 million years ago. At this time, the land was barren and windswept, with no animals (or even plants!) living on it. All life on the earth at this time was confined to the oceans.

The fossil remains of trilobites, cephalopods, gastropods, bryozoans and graptolites are often found in the black shales and limestones along the shores and islands of Lake Champlain. In rocks that were deposited in areas that were beaches in the ancient sea, evidence of ripple marks, animal tracks and worm burrow holes can still be seen, similar to those seen on modern beaches.

PLEISTOCENE FOSSILS

In 1848, the tusk and two teeth from a woolly mammoth were discovered near Mt. Holly, in south-central Vermont. Mastodons and woolly mammoths lived in cold and rugged tundra environments and followed the retreating glaciers northward. The remains of numerous mammoths found in both New York and Vermont suggest that these animals once lived in the region surrounding Lake Vermont. The remains of caribou, hare, fox and deer have also been found. There is also evidence to indicate that the Paleo people who followed the large animals also inhabited this region shortly after the glaciers retreated.

The Charlotte Whale

In August of 1849, railroad workers were laying the tracks of Vermont's first railroad near Charlotte. As they worked they came upon the bones of a strange animal buried in over ten feet of sticky blue clay. Thinking the bones to be those of an old cow or horse they continued to dig until a local farmer, who knew very well what cow and horse bones looked like, asked them to stop.

They notified Professor Zadock Thompson of the University of Vermont. Professor Thompson came to the scene to observe the strange bones and to carefully collect as many pieces as he could find. Thompson was a self-taught naturalist with few books and was operating in what was at that time a northern wilderness, far from the museums and colleges of Boston and New York City. Despite these hardships, he was able to reconstruct the skeleton, and after consulting with scientists in Boston and Paris, declared the bones to be those of a white (or Beluga) whale! This caused quite a sensation. How do you get the bones of an ocean-going whale buried beneath ten feet of clay in a field in Charlotte, Vermont, which is hundreds of miles from the nearest ocean?

Since that time, over 15 other whale fossils have been found in New York, Ontario and Quebec. We now know that the whales swam in the Champlain Sea and were buried in the sediments when they died— most likely of natural causes. At the time of Zadock Thompson, however, this idea was very new and controversial. Pictures of the "Champlain whale" appeared in geology textbooks as early as the 1860s. In 1993, a bill declaring the Charlotte whale the "Official State Fossil" of Vermont was signed into law by Governor Howard Dean.

Since the Charlotte whale is "only" about 10,500 years old, and its bones have not yet been mineralized, some people question whether or not it is really a fossil. Others argue that because the Charlotte whale represents the preserved remains of an ancient life-form that is no longer present in the area, it can rightfully be classified as a fossil. Do you agree?

CURRENT RESEARCH *on the* LAKE CHAMPLAIN BASIN

Today, much of the paleontological research in the Champlain Basin involves tiny microscopic fossils that can only be viewed with a microscope. These fossils, foraminiferans (or "forams" as many scientists call them), represent the shells of one-celled animals very similar to the amoeba. Scientists that study them are called micropaleontologists.

To study these tiny fossils, researchers drop weighted coring tubes from boats in Lake Champlain to collect samples of the sediments on the lake bottom. Back in the lab, scientists carefully remove the core samples, weigh them and label them, and then remove the sections that they want to study. The muds and clays of the sample are dried and sifted to remove the mineral and clay grains, leaving the forams. By carefully noting the types of forams they find, the composition of their shells and how deep they were found, micropaleontologists can reconstruct the changes that have taken place in the lake and the climate over time.

Geologists continue to study the rocks, minerals, fossils, folds and faults in the area to enrich our understanding of the area's past history. There is much work yet to be done, because there is so much story yet to be told and so many questions that remain. Perhaps you will make the next great discovery!

The Geologic History
of the
Lake Champlain Basin
Activities

These activities provide possibilities for the "non-geology teacher" to explore rocks with kids. Many geology activity books provide similar and more extensive ideas for activities.

Jeff Howe reviewed the following activities and offered these comments for teachers to consider:

To attempt to understand the enormity of geologic time, have your students count silently to themselves, as fast as they can, for exactly one minute. When they have finished, go around the room and see how far each student counted. Obtain a class average. On a calculator (or by hand) have one student multiply how far the class counted in one minute by 60 minutes and then 24 hours and then 365 days to determine how far you could count in one year. Continue with the math to determine how long it would take the class, counting as fast as they could, taking no time to sleep or eat, to count all of the 4.6 billion years in the Earth's history. The answer is around 30 years!

On a topographic map of New England, connect all of those areas in the Champlain and St. Lawrence lowlands that are the same approximate elevation as the base of Mt. Philo. Although glacial rebound was uneven throughout the region, this exercise will provide a rough approximation of the shoreline of the Champlain Sea. Compare your map to a map of the Champlain Sea. Note that Burlington and Montreal would be underwater.

Ask students to imagine conditions that would prevent fossils from being preserved in this area for many millions of years at a time. HINT: Either no organisms were present, no preserving conditions were present, or the evidence was removed by erosion.

There is no "right answer" to this question but the suggested scenarios appear valid to geologists. Fossils are not preserved because of the lack of preserving conditions and ongoing erosion. Pose the question to students and solicit other possible scenarios.

QUESTIONS

- What are some of the important events and changes that have led to the formation of the Champlain Basin?
- What caused these changes to take place?
- What methods do geologists use to discover how the earth changed so many years ago?
- What do fossils tell us about the Champlain Basin? Why are some fossils older than others?
- What is a glacier? How does it form? Why are there no glaciers in the Champlain Valley today?

KEY RESOURCES

- The Nature of Vermont *by Charles W. Johnson*
- NatureScope: "Geology: The Active Earth"—*National Wildlife Federation*
- Written in Stone *by Chet Raymo and Maureen Raymo*
- The Roadside Geology of Vermont and New Hampshire
  by Bradford Van Diver
- The Roadside Geology of New York *by Bradford Van Diver*
- "Paleontology of the Champlain Basin"—*available from office of the Vermont State Geologist*
- Natural History of Vermont *by Zadock Thompson*
- The Big Beast Book: Dinosaurs and How They Got That Way *by Jerry Booth*
- The Perkins Museum of Geology at the University of Vermont—*field trip*
- Button Bay State Park—*field trip*
- Mt. Philo State Park—*field trip*

Word Bank

Adirondack Mountains
amoeba
bryozoan
cast
cephalopod
Champlain Sea
Charlotte whale
chlorite
erosion
foraminiferan or "foram"
fossil
garnet
gastropod
glacial rebound
glacier
graptolite
Green Mountains
hiatus
Iapetus Ocean
Ice Age
igneous rock
lobe
Lake Vermont
mammoth
metamorphic rock
methane
microfossil
oxygen
photosynthesis
plate tectonics
Pleistocene
rift
sedimentary rock
sulfur dioxide
thrust fault
trilobite
tundra

Activity: **The Rock Connection**

TEACHER NOTES *and* INFO

The next three activities are designed to let students informally explore rocks. They will learn some basic vocabulary, guess (hypothesize) how the rocks were formed and what they are made of, and record various observations. The activities can be done as a series of explorations or as single activities. It is helpful, however, to start with "Rock Talk" as an introduction to basic geological concepts and terms. It can then be used as a reference for the other activities. There is some overlap in the purpose and outcomes of the activities.

Tell students (give them two weeks' notice) that they will have to find and bring in a rock. They must find it (not buy it), and it must be local. Tell them it will, if they choose, be broken.

A lot of science starts to happen as students start to bring their rocks into class and share observations and knowledge. I just recently integrated geology into my study of Lake Champlain. It was not a subject of which I had any previous knowledge and I didn't feel very confident. Having the students bring in their rocks was a great comfort. The rocks generated a lot of scientific discussion, excitement and sharing of information; this was a lot better than depending on the teacher for information—and much more beneficial!

These activities focus on the student as scientist: observing, recording, asking questions and hypthesizing answers before all the information is known. Later activities give more attention to exploring and understanding basic geological facts and concepts.

It is helpful to have a class set of magnifying glasses when students are observing their rocks. Students can set up stations with their rock samples.

Activity: **Rock Talk**

Using an overhead projector, review with the class the information on the handout "Rock Talk" (see next page). Students will begin with a blank worksheet like the one below (with only vocabulary words in bold). Have them fill in the blanks with terminology they understand as you work through the questions and discuss the answers. Students can refer to their completed worksheets as they examine and think about their own rocks.

All the Talk about Rocks

What's a Rock?

Minerals ____

Crystals ____

Rocks ____

How are Rocks Formed?

Igneous ____

Sedimentary ____

Metamorphic ____

How are Rocks Identified?

Luster ____

Hardness ____

Cleavage ____

Streak ____

Rock Talk

What are Rocks? How Do They Differ From Minerals?

Minerals - Nonliving compounds of elements that are only found in nature. They are the building blocks of rocks. They can form crystals.

Crystals - Solid substances with atoms arranged in an orderly pattern, which usually form flat surfaces. There are seven crystal "systems" based on shape.

Rocks - Solid mixtures of one or more minerals. They make up the inorganic portion of earth.

How are Rocks Formed?

Igneous - Formed when magma or molten rock from deep inside the earth cools. Sometimes forced by pressure (volcanoes).

Sedimentary - Formed near earth's surface by wind, water and weather. Erosion moves sand or soil over earth. When they settle together, they form layers.

Metamorphic - Formed when extreme heat, pressure and major shifting of the earth causes changes in igneous or sedimentary rocks. They look folded or squeezed.

How are Rocks Identified?

Luster - How does light react with its surface? Is the rock glossy? metallic? dull? pearly? shiny? chalky? greasy? Can you make up a name that describes it better?

Hardness - Scratch it and see! Can you scratch it with your fingernail? with a penny? with a nail? Can you scratch a piece of glass with it? Do your rocks scratch each other? Which one is the hardest? Which is the softest?

Cleavage - (ALWAYS WEAR SAFETY GLASSES WHEN BREAKING ROCKS!!!) How does it split? Does it break along flat planes or does it break irregularly? Are you sure? (Look carefully.)

Streak - Rub your rock on a streak plate provided by your teacher. What color is the powder? Is it the same color as the rock? Why?

Activity: **Classifying Rocks**

Other Ideas

• *Students can learn to identify their rocks blindfolded: pass the rocks around in a circle and ask students to hold on to the one that they think is their own.*

• *Have a rock swap with other schools.*

• *As a "pre" activity, students can sort a large collection of rocks according to different attributes. This is different than testing attributes and can be done informally to start observing rocks closely.*

There are many different ways to classify rocks. In this activity, have students put all their rocks into one collection. Then they can proceed to classify the entire collection into different categories. Some possible categories are suggested below. You may also want to do this activity in small groups or arrange work stations.

1. Classify all rocks by color. Record your findings by making a colored rock chart.

2. Classify all rocks by texture such as: rough, shiny, smooth, cracked. Think up more categories and compare your results.

3. Classify all rocks by weight. Verify your findings by using a scale.

4. Think up ways to classify your rocks in different ways. Compare your results. Surprise us!

Activity: **Rock Mystery**

Ask students to write in their thinkbooks about how they think their rocks came to be. They will not necessarily come up with the right answer, but educated speculation or forming a hypothesis is an important part of science.

Ideally, see if you can arrange a visit from a local rock hound or a visit to a geologist or a geology museum. Have students bring their rocks and test their hypotheses.

To encourage them to further examine and evaluate their rocks, have students complete a worksheet like the one below.

"I don't have any clue about how my rock was formed but I'll take a guess. Maybe my rock was formed from extreme heat or pressure. Maybe my rock is metamorphic."

Miranda Bushey
Grade 5, Milton

My Rock

1. Draw your rock here:

2. Using words, describe your rock. Include sentences about its size, weight, color, shape and hardness. Pretend you are describing your rock to a person who cannot see or feel.

3. What is the single most prominent characteristic of your rock? (Shape, color, size, etc?)

4. How do you think your rock was formed?

Activity: **Characteristics of Rocks and Minerals**

You will need:
- hammer or tool to break rocks
- sock or covering to prevent shattering
- magnet
- 5-10X magnifying glass
- rock and mineral guidebook
- streak plate or unglazed porcelain penny
- steel scissors or a file
- rock collection with samples of:

  igneous-volcanic rock
  (basalt, obsidian, tuff and pumice)

  igneous-plutonic rock
  (granite and gabbro)

  sedimentary rock
  (sandstone, limestone, shale conglomerate, and coal)

  metamorphic rock
  (slate, quartzite, schist, marble)

  This rock collection should also include semi-precious samples such as pyrite, hematite, agate, calcite, copper, silver, turquoise, a selection of crystals *(quartz, amethyst, fluorite, calcite, etc.),* and at least one geode.

TEACHER NOTES *and* INFO

Attributes of rocks can be tested with a rock kit that you borrow, buy or assemble yourself. If you go to a rock store, let the staff know you are collecting for educational purposes. Maybe they will give you a discount. A real rock collection works best for testing, but you can also use the rocks that students brought in. You may not get many different kinds of rocks, though. The "tests" that you will be running are the same that geologists use to classify rocks. They also conduct many other tests.

STUDENT ACTIVITY

If you have enough materials, arrange cooperative groups. Each group will need a sampling of rocks, testing tools and a chart of attributes (see "How Would You Describe It?"). Depending on the age group of your students, you may want to set up a supervised station for the rock breaking. It's always great to have a parent volunteer for this type of lesson. If you don't have enough materials, set up stations with a collection of rocks and tools. In this case, each student (or pair of students) would have a copy of the chart.

Review with students how to test for the different attributes. Pick a rock and demonstrate (without naming the rock aloud). **Example:** quartz

COLOR - *Quartz is usually colorless or white, but it may be pink, smoky gray, yellow, or purple if it contains impurities.*
STREAK - *Quartz should leave a white streak.*
LUSTER - *Quartz has a glassy luster because it shines a little like glass.*
HARDNESS - *The steel probably can't scratch the quartz, so it is considered a hard mineral.*
NAME - See if students can name the rock. Use mineral guides at this point.

This activity can be adjusted to have students individually test the attributes of their rocks and then work in cooperative groups to identify their rocks.

STUDENT HANDOUT - "How Would You Describe It?"

How Would You Describe It?

Attribute	Rock 1	Rock 2	Rock 3	Rock 4
COLOR - Observe and record the color of the rock.				
STREAK - What color does your mineral leave when streaked or scratched across a streak plate or un-glazed porcelain? *Note: Sometimes it will be hard to distinguish the streak of hard minerals.*				
LUSTER - How does your mineral reflect light?				
HARDNESS - If you can scratch a mineral with your fingernail, it is **very soft**. If you can scratch it with a penny but not your finger-nail, it's **soft**. If you can scratch it with steel scissors or a steel file, it's **medium**. If the scissors or the file won't make a scratch, it is **hard**.				
NAME - Can you name the rock? (Use mineral guides.)				

Activity: **Walk the Big Walk**

• Use the information in this article about the events since the disappearance of the glaciers and have students design another walking timeline (with another scale of their creation). Include human habitation and the presence of woolly mammoths!

• Although the number of "steps" in this activity is convenient, Jeff Howe suggests that students divide whatever distance is at their disposal (parking lot, soccer field, hallway) by the requisite number of years. This allows them to construct their own path, using good math skills along the way.

Credit: *Activity adapted by Lisa Borre of the Lake Champlain Basin Program and Charlotte Mehrtens of the UVM Geology Department from the BIG BEAST BOOK by Jerry Booth. Used with permission.*

TEACHER NOTES *and* INFO

This activity shows geologic time relevant to the creation of Lake Champlain. Since this is a very hard thing to grasp, "walking the years" as a series of steps helps. The steps give a scale that the students can relate to. You need a large space such as a parking lot or a playing field to do this in.

Make big signs with the following information:
1. Earth formed 4,600,000,000 years ago.
2. Adirondack Mountains formed 1,100,000,000–1,400,000,000 years ago.
3. Iapetus Ocean opens 600,000,000 years ago.
4. Green Mountains formed 450,000,000 years ago.
5. Atlantic Ocean opens 200,000,000 years ago.
6. Glaciers advanced over North America 100,000 years ago.
7. Champlain Sea formed 12,000 years ago.
8. Lake Champlain formed 8,000 years ago.

Explain that one step equals 50 million years. Pick a starting point and have a student hold a sign and "move back in time." The spacing of students on this large timeline gives them a reference point to talk about geologic time.

1. Earth formed = 90 steps.
2. Adirondack Mountains formed = 25 steps.
3. Iapetus Ocean opens = 12 steps.
4. Green Mountains formed = 9 steps.
5. Atlantic Ocean opens = 4 steps.
6. Glaciers advanced over North America = sideways step.
7. Champlain Sea = balance on big toe.
8. Lake Champlain = balance on little toe.

Rubies Pearls

Activity: **Fossil Print**

YOU WILL NEED:
- petroleum jelly
- plaster of paris
- plastic margarine containers and covers
- spoons for mixing
- chosen object with which to print fossil
- straws cut in one-inch lengths (optional)

STUDENT ACTIVITY

Beforehand, students need to choose an object with which to make their fossil print. It could be a shell, piece of coral, bone or the hard part of a plant.

1. Lightly grease the inside of the plastic cover with petroleum jelly.
2. Lightly grease the object that will be used to make a print.
3. Mix plaster of paris in the plastic container. (Mixing directions are on the package.)
4. When ready, pour into the covers quickly.
5. Set the object in the plaster.
6. Put pre-cut straw pieces in the plaster which, when removed, will make a hole. When dry, place a string though the hole to hang.

One hour later, or the next day:
1. Pull up the object.
2. Pull up the straw.
3. Pull off the plastic cover.

Activity: **Geology You Can Eat**

TEACHER NOTES *and* INFO

The language of this activity is directed toward young learners. I found it so enticing that instead of changing the format to match the rest of this text, I left it as is. If you are going to do the activity, it makes sense that the "cooks" have a copy of the directions.

STUDENT ACTIVITY

To get a good look at what happens to rock strata, it is a good idea to make your own. You could do it with sand, silt, and seashells, but then you'd have to wait around for thousands of years before you could see the results.

A much quicker way is to use flavored gelatin. It's easy to make, it's a lot less messy, and when you're done looking it over and experimenting with it, you can eat what's left for dessert!

First, mix up a batch of limestone, more commonly known as lime gelatin. We'll say that this stratum formed when the area was under the ocean. To create the limestone, put the gelatin in a measuring cup, add boiling water, and stir. Add a little less water than called for in the directions on the box. Let your limestone cool in the mixing cup for about 15 minutes; then pour it into the pan. Place the pan so it is level in the refrigerator and leave it until the gelatin is completely set.

Next, make a stratum of sandstone, the kind that forms from sand deposited by a river. Fossils are often found in this kind of stratum, so we'll need some fossils, too. In this case, the sandstone will be raspberry gelatin and the fossils will be pieces of banana.

Cut the banana into small chunks. Mix the gelatin in the measuring cup as you did before and let it cool for about 12 minutes. Mix in the banana. Pour this mixture into the pan on top of the "limestone." Make sure the limestone is completely firm, so the two layers don't mix together. Place the pan back in the refrigerator until it is cold and firm.

Our next stratum will be a thin layer of coal formed when the area was part of a huge swamp. In this case, crushed graham crackers will be our coal. So crumble up five or six graham crackers and sprinkle them on top of the sandstone.

Next, mix up half a box of the lemon gelatin. This will be another layer of sandstone. Pour it on top of the graham crackers and return your growing formation to the refrigerator for more cooling.

For our final layer we need a siltstone. Make the rest of the lemon gelatin and let it cool in the measuring cup. Then stir in about 1/2 cup of whipped cream or topping. Pour this mixture evenly over the top of your formation. Put the whole thing back into the refrigerator.

One thing you'll notice is that the banana fossils are hidden away under a number of other layers. How will they ever be found? Fortunately, things don't stay put in nature. Rock strata may not be as soft as gelatin, but they do stretch and bend and even break, just like gelatin layers, when they are subjected to the heat and pressure generated by the earth.

There are a number of different ways that the fossils can work their way to the top of the pile. Cut a 4" x 4" square of the formation, and you'll see how this might happen.

Uplifting - There are tremendous pressures building up inside the earth. These pressures form mountain ranges, and at the same time they twist flat strata of rock into all sorts of bizarre shapes. Slide a knife under the center of your gelatin square and lift. The strata will bend so far and finally break. Once the pieces are standing on end, you'll see something interesting—one edge of the sandstone with the fossils is now on the surface.

Overthrust - There's another way that strata can get mixed up. Cut another square of gelatin. Gently and evenly push in from opposite sides of the square so that the center rises up and one half flops over on the other half. When this happens in the earth, geologists call it an overthrust.

Faulting - The surface of the earth is full of big cracks called faults. Sometimes the land on one side of the fault will be uplifted, or raised, above the land on the other side. This is another way that fossils can work their way to the surface.

Once your formation has set, take a look through the side of the dish. You've created in an afternoon a series of strata that would take millions of years to form in nature.

Where are the oldest gelatin strata? Right. On the bottom. And the youngest? On top.

If a couple of miniature paleontologists happened to wander across this area right now, they'd probably discover some great banana fossils!

Notice that the older strata are no longer under younger ones. In fact, half of the youngest stratum is on the very bottom. Geologists must study rock strata very carefully to determine their relative ages.

You can demonstrate the effects of faulting with another square of gelatin. Slice the square into two parts with a spatula. Then use the spatula to lift up one half. If it is raised high enough, the layer containing your fossil bananas will be exposed.

Erosion - Fortunately for paleontologists, sedimentary rocks are constantly being worn away from above by rain and wind, so fossils are constantly being uncovered. We can show this with a cupful of warm water and another square of stratified gelatin.

Place the gelatin on a paper towel on a plate. Tilt the plate over a sink or bowl that will catch the water, and slowly pour a stream of warm water on one edge of your square. Gradually, the top layers will melt away, exposing the fossil (banana) layer.

The wind also erodes sediments. To show this, take a blow dryer, turn it to warm, and aim it at a square of gelatin. In a few minutes the top layers will begin to dissolve. Soon banana fossils will be uncovered.

Notice how small pieces of banana flow out with the melting gelatin. This happens with real fossils too. When paleontologists find a few small bone fragments lying on the ground (which they call float), they often find the rest of the fossil by looking in the rocks directly above it.

Marker Beds - Coal beds like the one formed by your graham crackers are very important to paleontologists because they can be seen very easily. A gelatin geologist looking at your formation, for example, could always be sure that wherever she spotted graham crackers she would also be likely to find bananas in the next layer. Real fossil hunters often use the dark black coal beds as "markers" because they are easy to spot among all the light gray and brown layers. By knowing where the fossil-rich strata are in relation to the coal, they can zero in on the areas where they are most likely to find fossils.

Of course, in nature the rocks don't melt. They're just slowly broken down and carried away.

Credit: *Activity reprinted with permission from the BIG BEAST BOOK: DINOSAURS AND HOW THEY GOT THAT WAY by Jerry Booth.*

The Geography of the Lake Champlain Basin

Champ's Trip

by Valerie Lamphere, Grade 7, Milton Jr. High School, Milton, Vermont

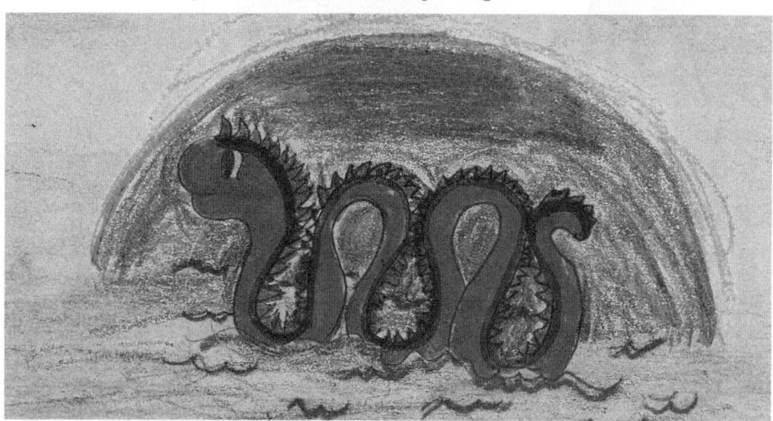

Hi! This is Champ, the Champlain Monster. I've been here for quite a while. You don't look so pretty after that. Now, this is my story of how I got to Snake Den Harbor, which is close to Bullwaga Bay, where I am often sighted.

It all started one night in the prehistoric age. I was going to bed for a cool nap when, suddenly I woke up. BAM! It's the Twentieth Century. The rock I was on turned out to be an island, now called Valcour. It's a nice spot but not sheltered enough for me. So I figured I'd ask for directions. I met a snapping turtle named Varco.

He said the best place to hide was at Snake Den Harbor near the narrows of the Lake. So I set out heading south.

I stopped to surface near Colchester Point, there I caught my first sight of Humans. They were shrieking and their yelling was deafening to me. I dove down again. I passed a ferry and on the bottom of the ferry, I saw some writing. It said:

**STATE OF VERMONT FERRY
ON LAKE CHAMPLAIN**

So that's where I was! Lake Champlain! Soon I hit Four Brother's Islands. I spent the night there. I was halfway to my destination! I had traveled 14 miles.

My next stop was Bullwaga Bay. Late that night, a ship tried to capture me! That was it! I was gone! I advanced a few miles to reach the straits. I was home at last at Snake Den Harbor.

And that's my story of how I got to Snake Den Harbor!

The Geography of the Lake Champlain Basin

When you study geography, you learn about the land and the stories it has to tell. Lake Champlain and the land around it have affected what humans have done in this area for thousands of years. The lake provided food for the people who lived here. Until only recently, it was a main transportation route for the people of this region. For the Woodland people, the lake was a political barrier between two groups, the Iroquois and the Western Abenaki. When the Europeans moved into the region, they depended on the lake as a main highway, the way people had done in the past and would continue to do for three hundred more years. The lake has been the stage for numerous battles, trade and commerce. Tourist brochures now refer to the lake as the "west coast" of New England. Some people still depend on the lake for their food and many people use the lake for pleasure and recreation.

You may be lucky to live very close to the lake or have had the opportunity to visit there. If you have, you probably have some pictures in your head of what the lake looks like on a sunny, sparkly day—or a wild and wavy day. You may have a clear image of what the Adirondacks or the Green Mountains look like as they rise from either side of the lake. Maybe you can visualize the path of a tributary as it meanders towards the lake. As you learn more about the geography of Lake Champlain and the land around it, try to remember some of the pictures you have in your mind.

The Adirondacks in New York and the Green Mountains in Vermont are the high boundaries of the Lake Champlain Basin. The mountains help define an area of 8,234 square miles that covers land in New York, Vermont and Quebec. All the rain that falls within this special area drains into Lake Champlain. Small streams and creeks and large tributaries carry this water into Lake Champlain.

The lake itself covers 415 square miles and is 120 miles long. It is a narrow lake, only 12 miles wide at its widest part. One writer compared it to a "silver dagger" that struck through the mountains. How long does it take to travel the length of the lake in a motorboat? How long does it take in a canoe?

Although you'll probably find plenty of people who think differently, many think that the Main Lake is the most beautiful part of Lake Champlain. Sunsets over the Adirondacks are a main attraction for Vermonters. Do New Yorkers rise early to watch the sun rise over the Green Mountains?

Land in the basin is 56% Vermont, 37% New York, 7% Quebec.

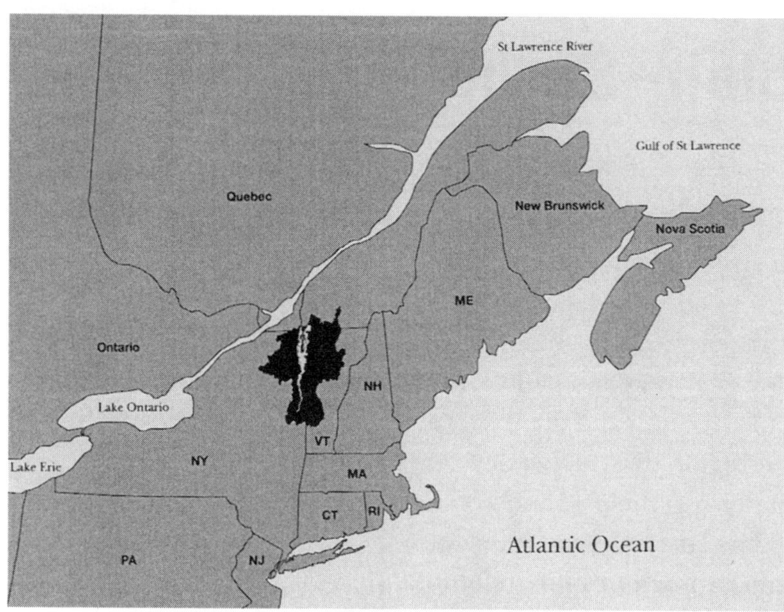

Lake Champlain has 587 miles of shoreline. It begins in Whitehall, New York, and flows northward toward Canada. Near Ash Island, it empties into the Richelieu River, which drains into the St. Lawrence River. It is sometimes called the "sixth Great Lake." It is called this because of its kinship to the five Great Lakes, not because of its relative size.

Lake Champlain is surrounded on the west by the Adirondacks and on the east by the Green Mountains. The land ranges from the highest peaks of the Adirondacks to the lowlands of the Champlain Valley. Average temperatures around the basin vary according to elevation, especially during the spring, summer and fall. Temperatures are usually colder in the mountains and warmer in the lower elevations. The Champlain Valley tends to have the longest growing season in the area. That's why it's easier to grow melons near the lake.

Sometimes the same storm will bring snow to the mountains and rain to the lake and surrounding lowlands. Most of the weather patterns come to Lake Champlain from the west, crossing the Adirondacks on the way. As the air hits the Adirondacks, it is forced higher and thus becomes cooler. Cooler air can hold less moisture than warmer air, so it drops more rain or snow in the higher elevations. When the air travels down the east side of the mountains toward the lake, it gets warmer and there is less precipitation because the warm air holds onto the moisture. The storm also has "lost" some of its moisture while crossing the mountains. When the air rises up again over the Green Mountains, precipitation will increase again .

Tributaries that drain into Lake Champlain provide 91% of the lake's water. Major tributaries include the Missisquoi River, Lamoille River, Winooski River, LaPlatte River and Otter Creek in Vermont; and La Chute River, Lake George, Bouquet River, Ausable River, Saranac River and the Great Chazy River in New York. The remaining 9% of the lake's water comes from precipitation and condensation that falls directly into the lake. About 600,000 people live in the Champlain Basin and at least 150,000 use Lake Champlain as their source for drinking water.

The temperature of still air decreases about 3.5°F for every 1,000 feet in elevation. The average temperature on Mt. Mansfield is about 14°F cooler than that in Burlington, some 4,000 feet below.

When there is less precipitation after storms cross a mountain range, it is called a "rain shadow."

The volume of Lake Champlain has been calculated as 909 billion cubic feet of water, which equals 6.8 trillion gallons of water.

A 1990 census recorded 607,788 people living in the basin.

LAKE CHAMPLAIN ECOSYSTEM

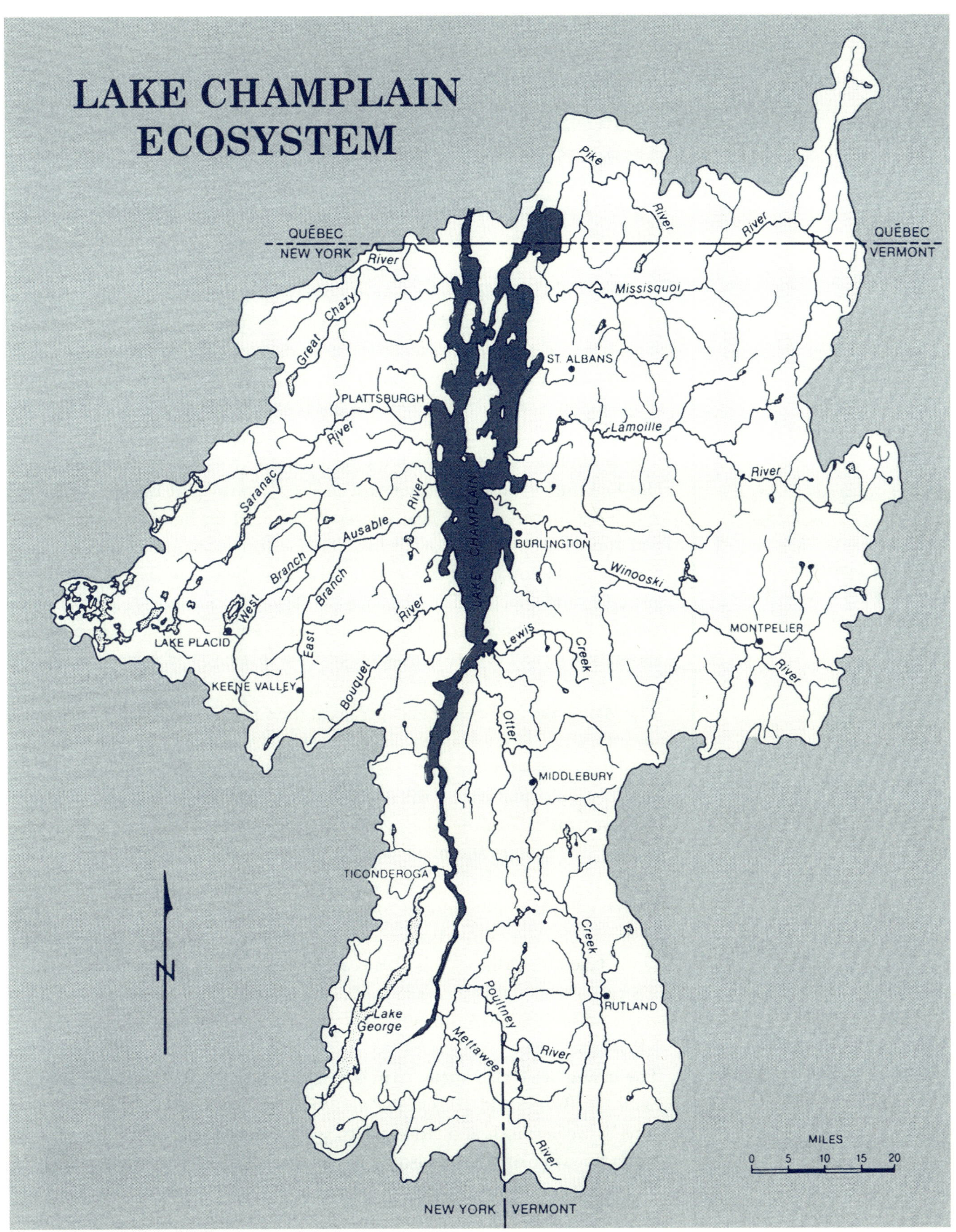

REGIONS *of the* LAKE

The lake is divided into five sections that are determined by geographic boundaries and characteristics. These five sections act like different lakes and are considered as such when scientists consider pollution problems and planners look at land-use issues. They are five different "living regions."

For example, although the average depth of all of Lake Champlain is 64 feet, if you calculated the average depth of each region, it would vary drastically. The Main Lake is over 400 feet deep at its deepest part, whereas most of the South Lake never is deeper than 40 feet. Imagine all the ways that lake depth alone would change the qualities of the different regions.

The South Lake is the long narrow part of the lake that starts at the mouth of the Poultney River and runs north to the Crown Point Bridge. It is very much like a river and is a favorite nesting ground for herons. Eurasian milfoil and water chestnut love it too, because the water in the South Lake is warm and shallow. It looks very different from the rest of the lake. It is very primitive and unspoiled and has marshy vegetation on the edges. Not many people live on the shores of the South Lake, but it was very important as a navigation route because it linked Lake Champlain to harbors further south.

The Main Lake, or Broad Lake, begins at the Crown Point Bridge and opens into the wide open expanse of lake. West of Grand Isle County in Vermont, the lake narrows again and becomes the Richelieu River that flows into Canada. The Main Lake is the deepest, widest and largest section of the lake and contains 81% of the lake's total volume of water. This part of the lake is popular for boaters and many people live on the shores of the Main Lake.

Mallett's Bay is southeast of Grand Isle and is separated from the Main Lake by an abandoned railroad causeway. Mallett's Bay is the most restricted part of the lake. In addition, this area is a very popular summer recreation area. There is a real "traffic problem" in the summertime with sailors, speed boaters, wind surfers and kayakers making their way out to the Main Lake.

The Inland Sea or Northeast Arm is east of Grand Isle. This section starts at Sand Bar Bridge and ends at the mouth of Missisquoi Bay. "The Gut" that runs between South and North Hero is considered part of the Inland Sea. Water flows in from the Missisquoi Bay and north from Mallett's Bay, keeping the Inland Sea relatively healthy. This is a very quiet section of the lake and is a favorite place to catch yellow perch, northern pike and Atlantic salmon.

In 1823, the Champlain Canal was built. This canal linked the lake to the Hudson River and made Lake Champlain one of the most significant trade highways in the world.

A 1993 boat study showed an 86% increase in the number of boats in high use in Mallett's Bay since 1980.

Most of the Missisquoi Bay is in Canada. It begins at the delta of the Missisquoi River and extends into Quebec. The bay is cut off from the lake's northward flow and is shallow and warm. Like the South Lake, the bay has problems with aquatic plants.

Regions of Lake Champlain

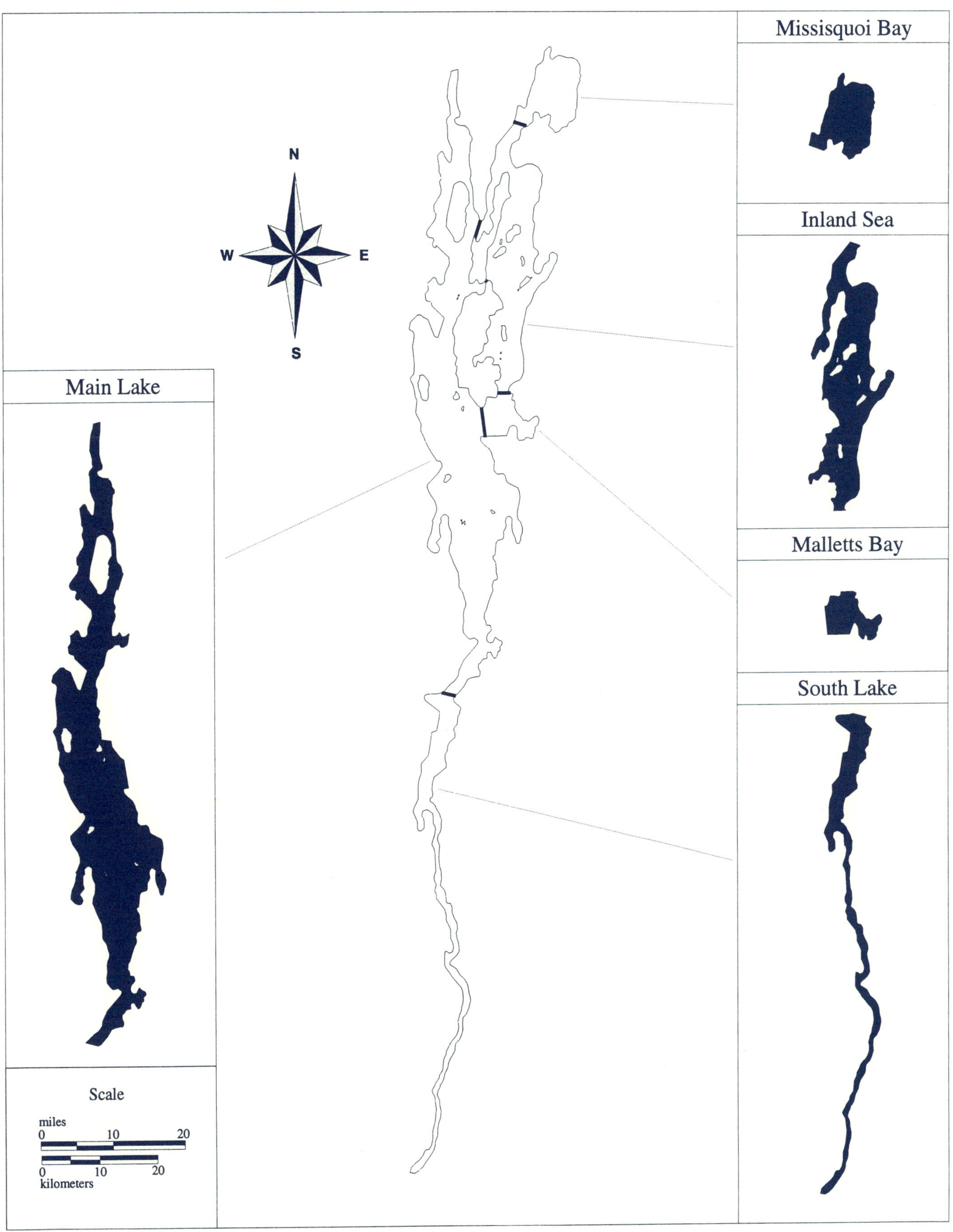

Islands of Lake Champlain

About seventy-five islands dot the surface of Lake Champlain. They lend variety to the scenery, pique the explorer's imagination, and afford the photographer a chance to record nature as it cycles through the seasons. When a sudden storm blows up, sailors find refuge in the lee of an island. The Lake Champlain islands are a haven for those who wish to escape the turmoils of the world, a living textbook for the student and scientist, and a home to thousands of migrating waterfowl, shorebirds and songbirds.

Islands are fragile and it sometimes is not clear how to protect them. While many Lake Champlain islands are well suited to public use, others are strictly private. Some islands support populations of birds that must not be disturbed while they are nesting.

Popsquash was the original nesting site of the common tern. The tern was driven out by the ring-billed gull, but naturalists have worked to protect nesting areas and reestablish the tern population. Young Island has a large colony of black-crowned night herons. Boaters are often warned to stay off certain islands during critical nesting times.

The name of an island often tells some of its story. Almost a third of the islands carry the name of a former or current owner. Savage Island was named for James Savage, a surveyor who worked on this property in 1789. Metcalf Island, which is located near the mouth of the Missisquoi River, was inhabited by a fur trader named Metcalf, who carried on his business in the 1760s. Ball, Young, Knight, Johnson, and Sawyer are all thought to be named after former owners. Many other islands are named by those who knew and loved them. People who fished, bird-watched or farmed probably named Shad, Fish Bladder, Gull, Hen and Garden Islands. Some islands have received their names from their vegetation or geological features such as Cedar, Juniper, Birch, Mud, Rock, Cave and Marble. Other names are descriptive such as Sunset or Lazy Lady.

Sometimes the names of islands change. A famous island, Ojihozo, is of great importance to the Native Americans. It is named after the creator who turned himself into a rock in the middle of Lake Champlain so he could forever enjoy this beautiful spot. Newcomers renamed it Rock Dunder, but many people still call it Ojihozo, its original name. Four Brothers Island shows up on an old map as Four Sisters Island.

The future of these islands is unclear. Will they remain wild and untouched? Will they be subdivided for camps and summer homes? Will the wildlife found nowhere else in Vermont or northeastern New York still be welcomed "home" each nesting season? Growing population pressures, rising land prices and increasing property taxes affect the status of these scenic islands. Change is coming, but how it occurs and what it looks like will be influenced by important decisions made by citizens like you.

Credit: *Adapted with permission from "A Portrait of the Lake Champlain Islands," by the Lake Champlain Islands Trust.*

The different bays and open water, the tributaries and the wetlands, the shapes of the lake and the land around it tell the different stories of Lake Champlain. One place may have been the bluff where a hunter made camp, or a bay where a smuggler could hide from the patrol boat. It may have been that gentle slope to the water on which a settler wished to plant fruit trees or a rock on which a child liked to sit and fish. The places of the lake tell the stories.

Just as people have chosen different parts of the lake for different reasons, so too the fish, birds and other creatures have found the places that are best suited to them. Warm-water fish such as pickerel and bass seek the shallow water of a wetland to lay their eggs, while cold-water fish, such as trout and salmon, prefer the clear, cold bottom of the Main Lake. The islands of Lake Champlain provide favored "hotels" to migrating birds. Herons congregate in rookeries in the Missisquoi Wildlife Refuge where a single tree may house five or six nests. We know that Champ prefers the deep water near Snake Den Harbor where he can hide in peace and quiet!

Carleton's Prize (pictured below) was named after the British general who chased Benedict Arnold down the lake from Valcour Island. Chasing the American fleet in the early morning mist of October 12, 1776, Carleton saw what he thought was a ship and gave the order to fire. When the fog lifted, the "vessel" was an island.

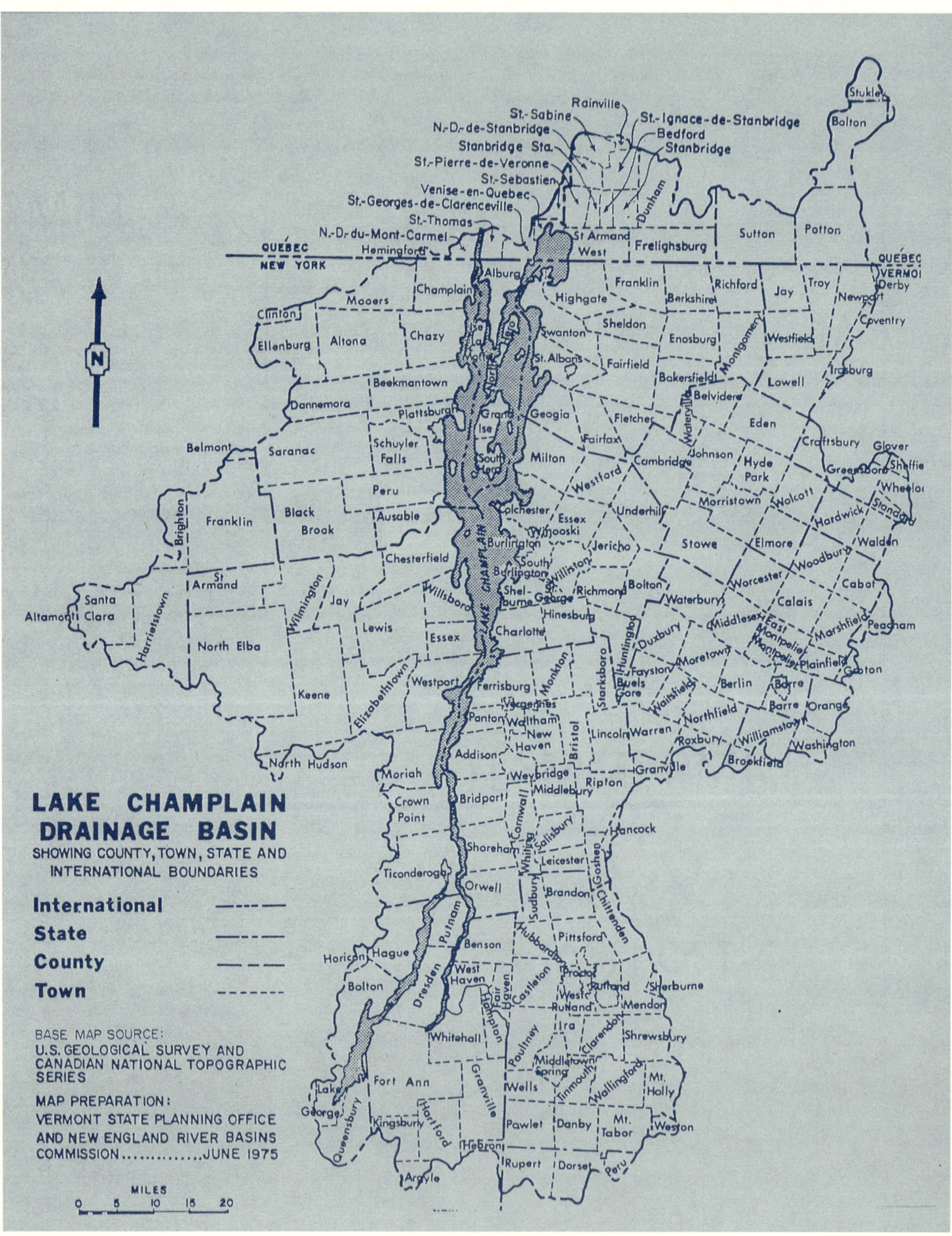

LAKE CHAMPLAIN
DRAINAGE BASIN
SHOWING COUNTY, TOWN, STATE AND
INTERNATIONAL BOUNDARIES

International
State
County
Town

BASE MAP SOURCE:
U.S. GEOLOGICAL SURVEY AND
CANADIAN NATIONAL TOPOGRAPHIC
SERIES

MAP PREPARATION:
VERMONT STATE PLANNING OFFICE
AND NEW ENGLAND RIVER BASINS
COMMISSION.............JUNE 1975

MILES
0 5 10 15 20

N

Stukley
Bolton
Rainville
St.-Sabine
N.-D.-de-Stanbridge
St.-Ignace-de-Stanbridge
Stanbridge Sta.
Bedford
Stanbridge
St.-Pierre-de-Veronne
St.-Sebastien
Venise-en-Quebec
St.-Georges-de-Clarenceville
St.-Thomas
N.-D.-du-Mont-Carmel
Hemingford
Dunham
Sutton
Potton
St Armand
West
Frelighsburg
QUEBEC
NEW YORK
QUEBEC
VERMONT
Derby
Alburg
Champlain
Franklin
Highgate
Berkshire
Richford
Jay
Troy
Newport
Mooers
Clinton
Sheldon
Coventry
Swanton
Enosburg
Montgomery
Westfield
Ellenburg
Altona
Chazy
Fairfield
Irasburg
Beekmantown
Bakersfield
Lowell
Dannemora
Waterville
Belvidere
Plattsburgh
Grand
Isle
Geogia
Fletcher
Eden
Craftsbury
Glover
Sheffie
Belmont
Saranac
Schuyler
Falls
South
Hero
Milton
Fairfax
Johnson
Hyde
Park
Greensboro
Wheelo
Franklin
Black
Brook
Peru
Ausable
Colchester
Essex
Cambridge
Westford
Morristown
Wolcott
Hardwick
Standar
Brighton
Winooski
Underhill
Walden
Burlington
Jericho
Stowe
Elmore
Woodbury
Cabot
Chesterfield
South
Burlington
Williston
Richmond
Bolton
Worcester
Calais
St
Armand
Wilmington
Jay
Shel-
burne
St.
George
Waterbury
Middlesex
East
Montpelier
Marshfield
Peacham
Santa
Altamont Clara
Harrietstown
Lewis
Willsboro
Hinesburg
Huntington
Duxbury
Moretown
Montpelier
Plainfield
Goton
North Elba
Essex
Charlotte
Starksboro
Fayston
Buels
Gore
Berlin
Barre
Keene
Elizabethtown
Westport
Ferrisburg
Monkton
Waitsfield
Barre
Orange
Vergennes
Lincoln
Warren
Northfield
Williamstown
Washington
North Hudson
Panton
Waltham
New
Haven
Roxbury
Brookfield
Addison
Weybridge
Ripton
Granville
Moriah
Middlebury
Crown
Point
Bridport
Cornwall
Salisbury
Hancock
Shoreham
Whiting
Leicester
Ticonderoga
Orwell
Brandon
Chittenden
Sudbury
Pittsford
Putnam
Benson
Hubbardton
Horicon
Hague
Proctor
Dresden
West
Haven
Castleton
Rutland
Sherburne
Bolton
Poultney
Rutland
Mendon
Whitehall
Hampton
Ira
Clarendon
Shrewsbury
Middletown
Spring
Tinmouth
Wallingford
Mt.
Holly
Lake
George
Fort Ann
Wells
Queensbury
Kingsbury
Hartford
Granville
Pawlet
Danby
Mt.
Tabor
Weston
Hebron
Peru
Argyle
Rupert
Dorset
LAKE CHAMPLAIN
LAKE GEORGE

The Geography
of the
Lake Champlain Basin
Activities

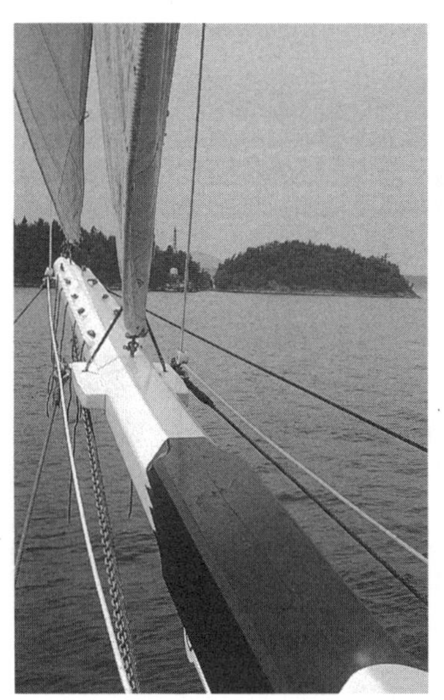

The activities in this chapter represent a sampling of different geography activities that you can use when you are integrating geography into an interdisciplinary study. These activities were developed in consultation with David Rider, geography teacher at Bellows Free Academy, St. Albans, and former co-coordinator of the Vermont Geographic Alliance. He offers this perspective on geography instruction:

> *In the past decade, instruction in geography from grades K–12 has been organized around five themes of geography. These content organizers set the stage for eighteen standards within the National Geography Standards. The five themes are present throughout the Standards. The five themes and the standards were developed by the Geographic Education National Implementation Project (GENIP). GENIP is a consortium of four geographic organizations: the Association of American Geographers, the American Geographical Society, the National Council for Geography Educators and the National Geographic Society.*

THE FIVE THEMES *of* GEOGRAPHY

1. Location *(Absolute and Relative)*

Where in the world is it? What is it near? How is it connected to other places?

2. Place *(Physical and Human Characteristics)*

What physical and human characteristics make this place unique? (See chapters: *Geology, History, Ecology* and *Living Treasures.*)

3. Human-Environment Interaction *(Relationships Within Places)*

People interact with and change their environments. How has the environment been altered? Why was it altered? What are the consequences of these changes? (See chapters: *Ecology, History* and *Living Treasures.*)

4. Movement *(Mobility of People, Goods and Ideas)*

Travel, communication and migration are examples of how people connect with each other. How does your family/community/state/nation depend on other areas? How has the movement of people influenced the demographics of your area? (See chapters: *History* and *Nautical Archeology.*)

5. Regions *(How They Form and Change)*

Areas on the Earth can be defined by certain unifying characteristics, either human or physical. What human or physical regions can you identify within your own state? (See chapters: *Geology, History, Ecology.*)

QUESTIONS

- How does the geography of Lake Champlain affect how people live in the basin?
- How are parts of the lake different from each other?
- How are fish and wildlife affected by the lake's geography?

KEY RESOURCES

- Vermont Land and Resources *by Harold Meeks*
- Vermont Geographic Alliance
- The Nature of Vermont *by Charles W. Johnson*
- A Portrait of the Lake Champlain Islands *published by the Lake Champlain Islands Trust (out of print)*
- "Lake Champlain North, N.Y.-VT" and "Lake Champlain South, N.Y.-VT"— *U.S. Geological Survey (USGS) topographic maps*
- "Lake Champlain Atlas of Navigational Charts"—*R.W. Vogel*
- "Raised Relief Map of Champlain Valley: Lake Champlain" and "Raised Relief Map of Lower Champlain Valley: Glens Falls"—*Hubbard*
- "Lake Champlain Region: Road Map and Guide"—*Northern Cartographic*

Native American Place Names

azeskoimenahan (muddy island) - Isle La Motte

bitawbagok (waters in between) - Lake Champlain

bitawbagwizibok (between-lake river) - Richelieu River

gitsimenahan (big island) - Grand Isle

madegwasewapskak (at rabbit rock) - Mt. Philo

masipskwebik (flint water) - Missisquoi Bay

moziozaganek (moose shoulder) - Camel's Hump

mozôdebiwajok (moosehead mountain) - Mt. Mansfield

onegigwizibok (otter river) - Otter Creek

senapskaizibok (stone rock river) - Ausable River

senipôganitegok (stone pipe river) - La Platte

winozkitegok (onion river) - Winooski

wintegok (marrow river) - Lamoille River

zalônaktegok (sumach cone river) - Saranac River

Jeanne Brink provided the Abenaki place names.

Activity: **Making a Map of Lake Champlain**

TEACHER NOTES *and* INFO

Students need a solid grounding in the geography of Lake Champlain. Even if your study is mostly historical or scientific, it is helpful for students to be familiar with present-day locations and distances.

STUDENT ACTIVITY

Each student will make a map of Lake Champlain. Because the location of the borders and islands are sometimes confusing on a blank map, the most important first step is coloring in the blue of the lake correctly! Before we do any labeling, I put up an overhead with the lake's outline and the water colored in correctly and ask students to carefully color the surface of the lake. I then proceed through the labeling process in layers, so that what is on the overhead is exactly what they are working on.

1. Show transparency of blank map on overhead.
2. Overlay with overhead (A) that has just blue lake filled in. Ask students to draw in lake, being careful of bays and islands.
3. Proceed with next overlay. Students proceed through each step with you:

    (B) Borders—Vermont, New York, Quebec

    (C) Tributaries—label major tributaries

    (D) Major towns and cities—label major towns and cities

At this point, I hand out the complete basin map along with other maps so students can add more information to their own maps. Encourage them to choose information from many different maps. Discuss other things to include:

- historical sites and points of interest
- hometown (and student's house!)
- sites of field trips and tourist attractions
- major roads
- fishing accesses
- sites of shipwrecks

STUDENT HANDOUTS - Blank basin map and complete map ("The Lake Champlain Basin," p. viii)

You will need:
- copies of blank map of the basin (see p. 69)
- copies of complete map, "The Lake Champlain Basin" (see p.viii)
- blue-colored pencils
- prepared overheads
- additional maps for student reference

• *Use a state road map or a map of Lake Champlain to calculate distances from your town to the lake, routes to field trip and historic sites and the time of these trips. Use scale bar to estimate the length of boat trips on the lake. Students can also design their own questions about locations and distances.*

• *Use an overhead to project the outline of the lake on the wall. Have students paint or draw and label as a class project. A large map could include a variety of themes. Underwater wrecks, state parks, historic and tourist sites are some of the possibilities.*

• *Have students design a "Jeopardy Game." You or a group of students design categories of answers and questions and students say whether something is true or false. This can be done with or without a map for reference.*

• *Use a variety of sources (map of Native American places; maps with more details of harbors, bays, island names; nautical charts; map of historical sites) and discuss how, and reasons why, places got their names. Be a toponymist!*

• *Before you start making maps, discuss the outline of Lake Champlain and its implication. If you were living in the 1500s, where might you want to make your village? Why? If you were building a fort in the 1600s, where might you put it? Why? This is a good opener to start students thinking about the interaction between people and geography, e.g. shipbuilding, farming, mills.*

* *Write 5* **true** *statements about Lake Champlain geography.*
* *Write 5* **false** *statements about Lake Champlain geography.*

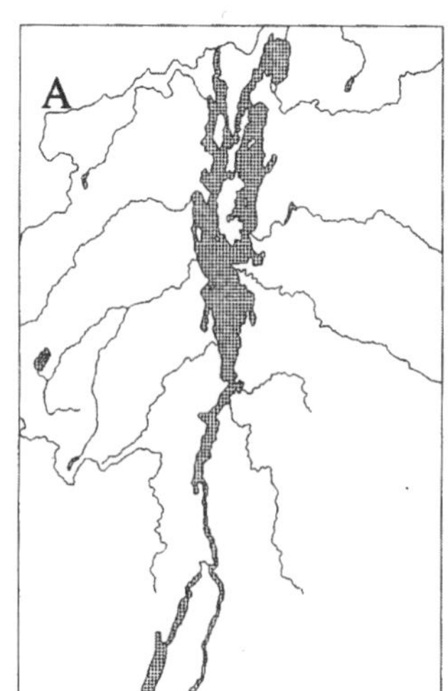

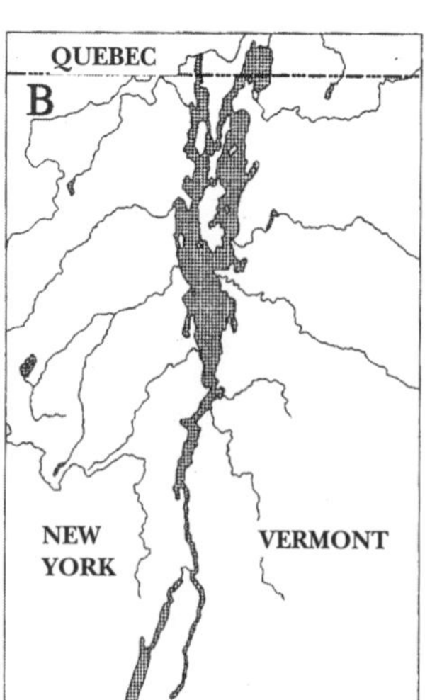

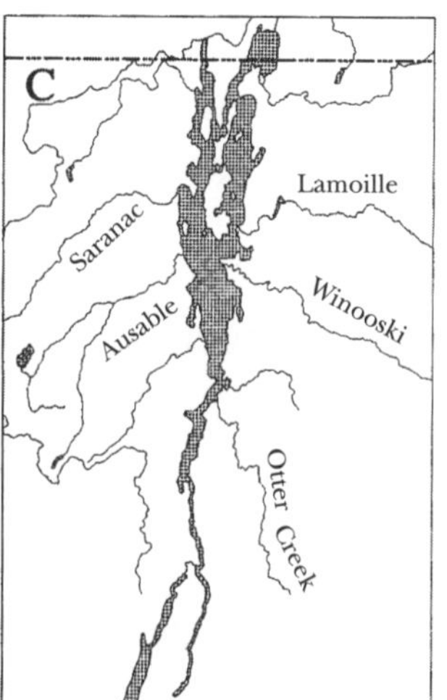

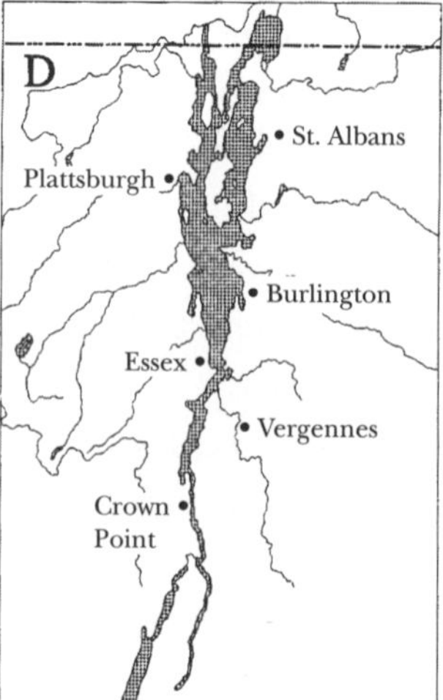

The Lake Champlain Basin

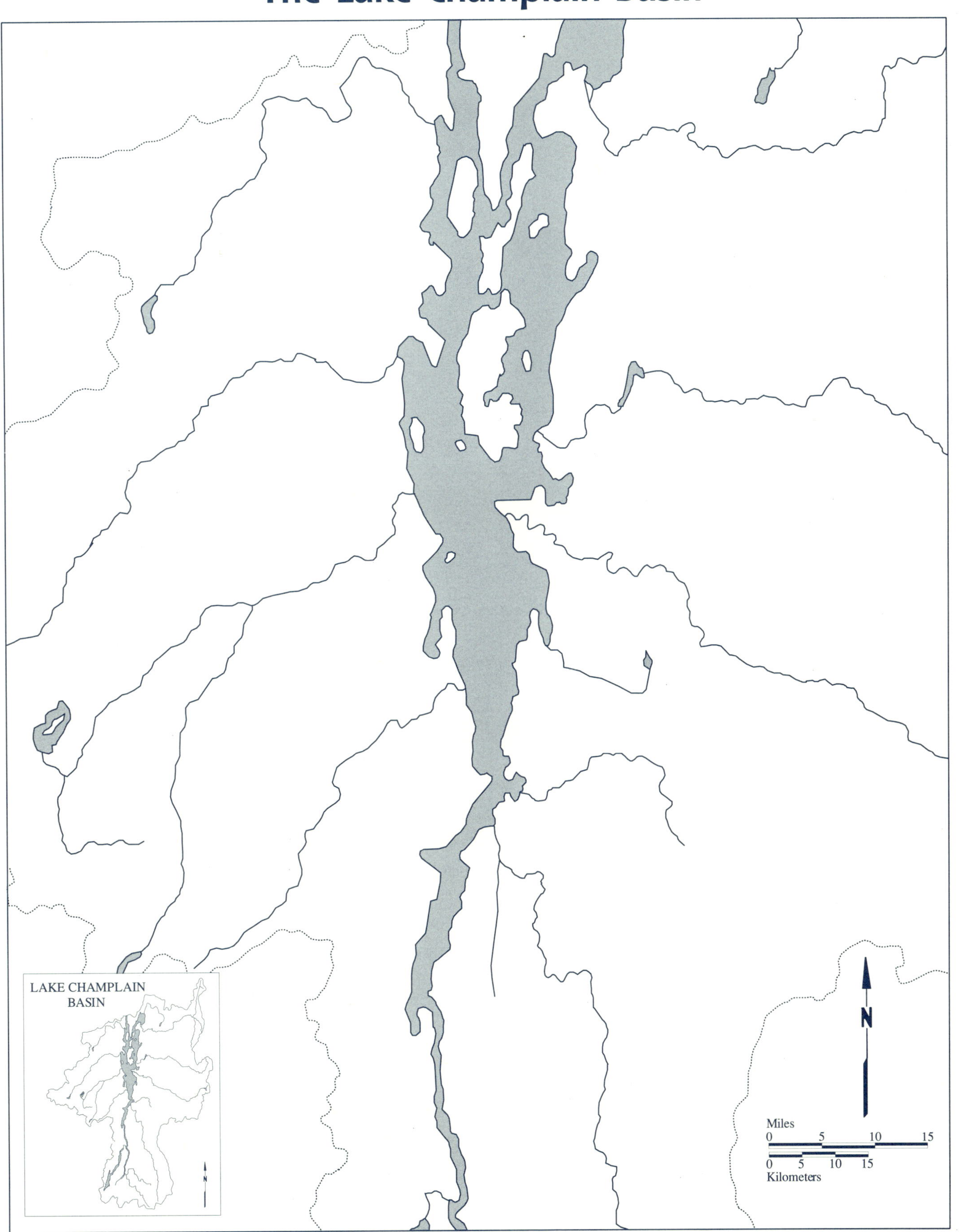

Credit: *Northern Cartographic. Used with permission.*

Activity: **Regions of the Lake**

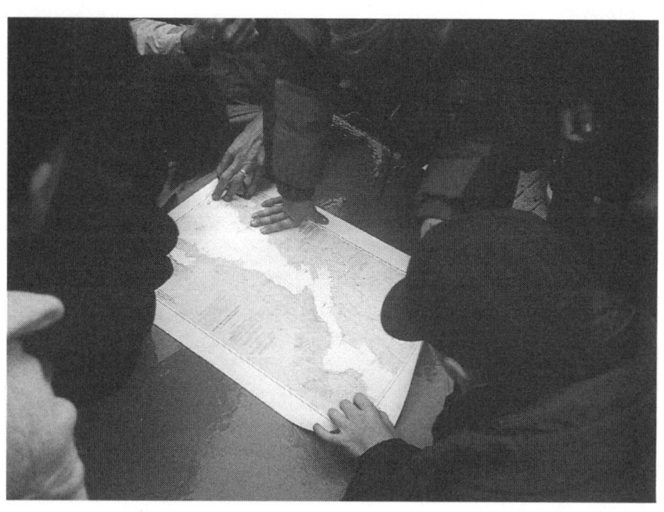

TEACHER NOTES *and* INFO

Make a set of "puzzle pieces" of the five different lake regions for each group. Use the outline of map pieces from the map, "Regions of Lake Champlain," (see p. 59), ideally enlarged and mounted on cardboard.

This activity requires that students have a mental image of the region they are working on. By students self-selecting, you may have all areas of the lake covered. This activity may be difficult if you live far from the lake or have few resources.

Using the previous essay, "The Geography of Lake Champlain," maps, brochures and pictures, ask students to elaborate on the attributes of each region. Some photos are provided on the next few pages.

Taking It Home

Ask students to ask parents and neighbors about these regions. These could be formal oral interviews or just treasure hunts to collect information. Pictures, stories, impressions, facts all count as treasures!

STUDENT ACTIVITY

In small groups, students use materials to identify characteristics of each region. They will use the handout to gather information.

Make a worksheet with questions such as:
• What is the shape of your region?
• What are the characteristics of this region?
• Describe in your own words what makes this region different from other parts of the lake.
• What plants and animals live in this region?
• What kind of things might have happened here 500 years ago? 200 years ago?
• What kind of pollution/water-quality problems might this region have?

When all the groups have completed gathering information, ask them to complete one of the following (or discuss as a class or in small groups which task they would like to do).

• Design a "habitat for sale" ad to attract a particular animal that you think would want to come live in your region.
• Design a "land for sale" ad to attract a person who you think would like to purchase land in your region.
• Make a case (speech, poster, song) for why your region should be protected from development and maintained as a natural preserve.
• Make a case (speech, poster, song) for why your region should be the site of a 300-slip marina.
• Design a skit that tells the important information about your region.

A. Inland Sea

A. Inland Sea
B. Inland Sea
C. Missisquoi River Delta and Bay
D. Missisquoi Wildlife Refuge
E. South Lake
F. Harvesting milfoil in South Lake
G. Mallett's Bay
H. Mallett's Bay
I. Burlington on Main Lake
J. Main Lake

B. Inland Sea

E. South Lake

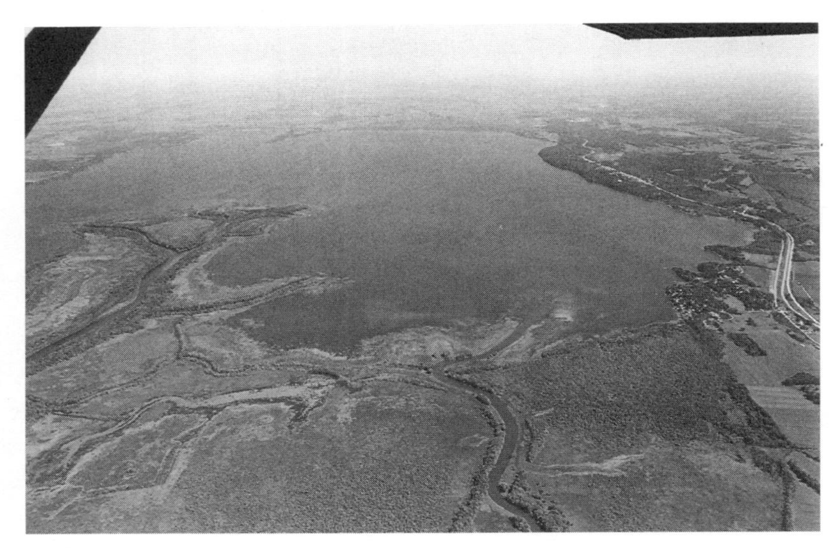

C. Missisquoi River Delta and Bay

F. Harvesting milfoil in South Lake

D. Missisquoi Wildlife Refuge

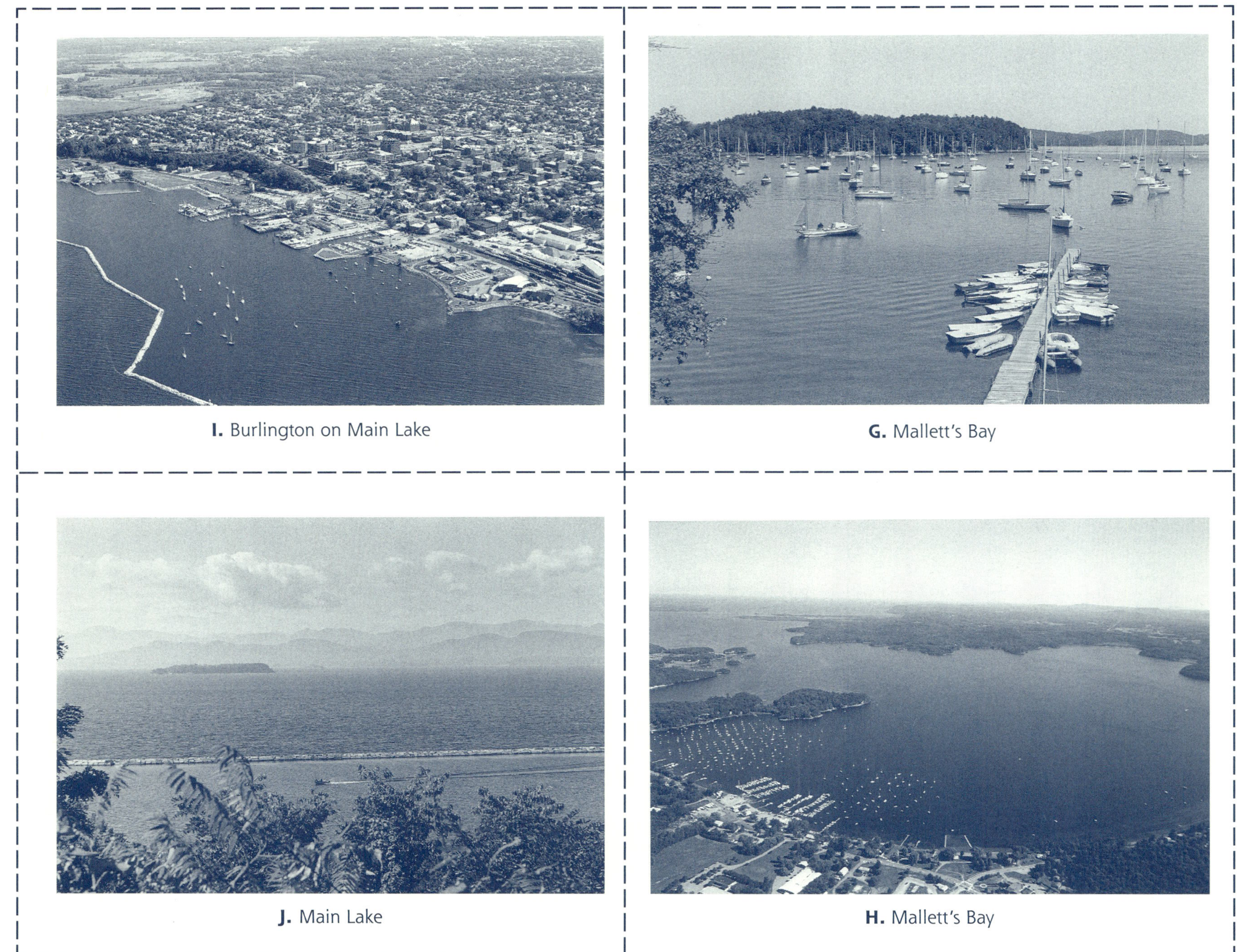

I. Burlington on Main Lake
G. Mallett's Bay
J. Main Lake
H. Mallett's Bay

Activity: **Reading a Map**

TEACHER NOTES *and* INFO

Below is a sampling of questions using the Vermont Department of Tourism's Official State Highway Map. It is possible to use a variety of maps to help kids discover geography facts. You can design more questions based on the map you are using.

Reading a Map

Look at the map scale and make a scale ruler. 1 inch = _______ miles

1. Estimate the distance from Milton (Civil War Monument) to Shelburne. __________ miles

2. If a school bus averages 50 mph, how long would this trip take? _________________

3. Find the route from Milton to Basin Harbor via Vergennes. Estimate the distance. ________ miles.

4. How long should it take the school bus? _____________________

5. Estimate the length of the lake from Benson Landing to Cantic, Quebec. ________ miles.

6. Find the widest part of the lake. Estimate the distance. _______ miles.

7. Find the distances between these communities on the lake:

Burlington—Port Kent	_______ miles	Burlington—Plattsburgh	_______ miles
Burlington—Shelburne Bay	_______ miles	Burlington—Port Henry	_______ miles
Plattsburgh—Shelburne Bay	_______ miles	Plattsburgh—Basin Harbor	_______ miles

Using the map, choose locations that will make these sentences true. Write in your answers.

8. How far must you travel if you went by boat from _____________ to _____________
    to _________________? _______ miles

9. It's about the same distance to travel by boat from _____________ to _________________ as it
    is to travel from _________________ to _________________.

Activity: **Comparing Lakes**

TEACHER NOTES *and* **INFO**

It is often incorrectly written that Lake Champlain is the sixth largest lake in North America. It's a common misconception that probably comes from it being called the sixth Great Lake. (Misconceptions are good things to share with students. You can even say that the author of this book always thought this was true!) In fact, Lake Champlain is the sixth largest freshwater lake in the continental United States. This activity compares the surface area, length, depth and elevation of Lake Champlain to other lakes in North America.

STUDENT ACTIVITY

Ask students to speculate how large Lake Champlain is. How could they explain its size to someone who has not seen it? How does it compare to other lakes? Discuss depth and volume as ways to compare bodies of water. Which is the best measure to use? Why?

Complete a bar graph that compares Lake Champlain to the fifteen lakes, using the table of information on the following page.

Have a discussion about how the size of Lake Champlain has affected what human beings have done on the lake. Has the depth affected human activity? Has the volume? Would our history be different if the shape of the lake was different? Do the shape and size affect what kind of ecological problems there are? Do they affect what animals live here?

Compare the volume of Lake Champlain to other things in the world that students might be able to imagine.

Example: Compare the volume of Lake Champlain to how many gallons of water New York City uses in a day. If we plugged the Richelieu River and attached a hose that ran all the way to New York City, how many days could we supply New York City with water?

Other Ideas

Ask students to design a project that:
• compares the size of the fifteen lakes in some other way than a bar graph
• compares the depths of the lakes using a bar graph
• compares the volumes of the lakes using a bar graph.

A nonscientific estimate calculates that New York City uses 1.4 billion gallons of water a day (for resident and business use). Lake Champlain has an estimated volume of 6,800 billion gallons of water (or 6.8 trillion). Based on these numbers, Lake Champlain could supply New York City with water for 4,857 days—or 13 years and 112 days!

FIFTEEN LARGEST LAKES IN NORTH AMERICA

Lake	Area (sq. mi)	Length (miles)	Depth (feet)	Elevation (feet)
Superior	31,700	350	1,330	600
Huron	23,000	206	750	579
Michigan	22,300	307	923	579
Great Bear	12,096	192	1,463	512
Great Slave	11,031	298	2,015	513
Erie	9,910	241	210	570
Winnipeg	9,417	266	60	713
Ontario	7,550	193	802	245
Nicaragua	3,100	102	230	102
Athabasca	3,064	208	407	700
Reindeer	2,568	143	720	1,106
Nettiling	2,140	67	N/A	95
Winnipegosis	2,075	141	38	830
Nipigon	1,872	72	540	1,050
Manitoba	1,799	140	12	813
Champlain	435	120	400	96

Credit: *1996 INFORMATION PLEASE ALMANAC.*

Note: *The level of Lake Champlain has actually been rising. The lake level given here is the mean lake level over the last 100 years. The maximum range between high and low averages in a year is 9.4 feet.*

The History of the Lake Champlain Basin

The Magical Furs

by Anthony Allard, Grade 5, School Street School, Milton, Vermont

May 11, 1778. Edward Peters woke up excited. He had to help his father set traps so they could sell the fur in Skenesborough, New York. They had big traps for things like bears and catamounts. They had small traps for rabbits and medium-sized traps for foxes and wolves. In all, there were 26 traps they had to set.

Every day after school Edward went to his job as a blacksmith and a tanner. Edward did little jobs like making nails, starting and putting coal on the fire, fitting boots, making and selling other leather items, getting water and wetting the leather. When Edward had free time he would work on a knife and a leather backpack. He made 50 cents a week and by the time fall came he had 12 dollars.

Finally the day came when Edward had to leave. They packed food, water and clothes. They put everything in their canoe and paddled down the river (Otter Creek) and out onto Lake Champlain. By midday, the sky clouded, the wind blew and they both knew a storm was coming. The waves got bigger and suddenly a huge wave flipped their canoe over. In the water Edward saw the furs sinking to the bottom. Quickly he swam after them and brought the furs back to the surface. Edward and his father swam back to shore and walked 10 miles to Skenesborough. It was dusk when Edward and his father arrived. Exhausted, they got a room at an inn. The next morning Edward's father went to sell the furs and Edward went walking around town. On his walk he met an old Indian and traded for a necklace. The necklace had four bear claws on it and in between each bear claw was a red bead. Edward also traded furs of a fox, wolf, catamount, and a cougar. Then the Indian said, "Furs magical. You become animal."

Edward put on the necklace and put the furs in his leather backpack. Then he went back to his father. His father had sold all their furs and made a lot of money. While Edward packed, his father went and bought a dress for Edward's mother, tools to make a new canoe, and the rest he put in the bank.

They walked six miles to the lake where they found a man to take them home on his schooner. On the schooner Edward wondered if what the Indian said was true. When nobody was looking he wished he was a fox and suddenly he was a fox. He changed himself back to a person and started whittling. He carved things—his favorite animals and two Indians. During the night the schooner ran aground. Quickly everyone grabbed their things and rushed to the lifeboats. They rowed to shore and spent the rest of the night there.

When Edward and his father got home they started working on a new canoe with the tools they just bought. Edward thought a moment. He liked being an animal better than being a person. So he asked his father if he could leave home. Edward's father said yes. Edward went to the edge of the woods, changed into a wolf and ran deep into the woods.

Introduction

In the study of history and geography, it is important to see how human beings use natural resources, and how patterns of use change over time. The essay is written in sections that give an overview of the separate historical periods outlined in Art Cohn's original essay. Each section attempts to describe how human beings interacted with the lake, what tools and transportation they used, and how these things affected their lifestyles.

The first section describes how Native Americans first used this region. It is mostly about the Woodland people, the people who were here when the Europeans penetrated this region. It does not explain, to the same degree, 12,000 years of human habitation that preceded the Woodland era. There is a great deal of material about Paleo-Archaic habitation of the Champlain Valley. For most teachers, this material falls under the discipline of archeology, which is not a subject that is treated fully in this book.

As is the case with all of this book, but painfully so in this section, there is simply too much material to include and I have had to make some choices based on my point of view. I hope the sources cited will enable you to make your own choices about the additional material that you share with students.

Canoes have been used for centuries in this region. This is a Penobscot canoe.

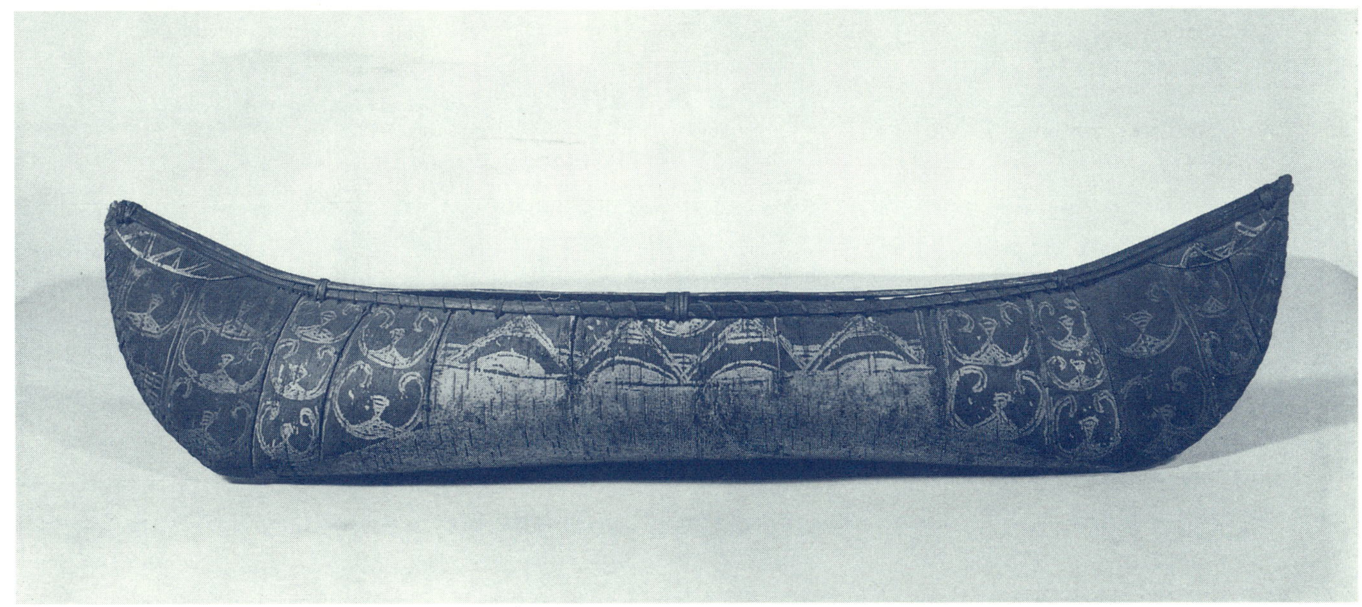

The History
of the Lake Champlain Basin

NATIVE AMERICANS

People have lived in this region for 12,000 years.

THE PALEOLITHIC PERIOD   10,000 B.C.–7,000 B.C.

About 12,000 years ago, a two-mile-high glacier blanketed the rocky mountains of what is now Vermont and New York. The ice had moved down very, very slowly from the north when the earth's climate cooled. The earth then began to warm and the glacier slowly receded. As the glacier melted, it revealed smaller rounded mountains that had been ground down by its great weight.

At first there were no people living in the frozen environment, but the climate warmed, and plants, then animals and then the first people came to this region. The area was covered by a great saltwater sea that had flowed in from the Atlantic Ocean. The Champlain Sea was surrounded by a tundra-like environment, where great herds of caribou roamed. Moose-elk, mastodons, woodland musk-ox and mammoths also found good grazing on the open plains.

Skilled hunters tracked the movements of these animals and the men, women and children used the meat for food, and the skin and bones of these animals for shelter and clothing. They wasted nothing. The gigantic mammoth bones were stood on end and tied together to frame a small shelter. Animal skins were laced together with sinews to keep out the wind, rain and snow. Some families made their homes in caves.

The men hunted with fluted spear points. The women used stone and bone tools to prepare the food. In addition to the land animals that the men hunted, people ate salt water animals such as walrus and clams.

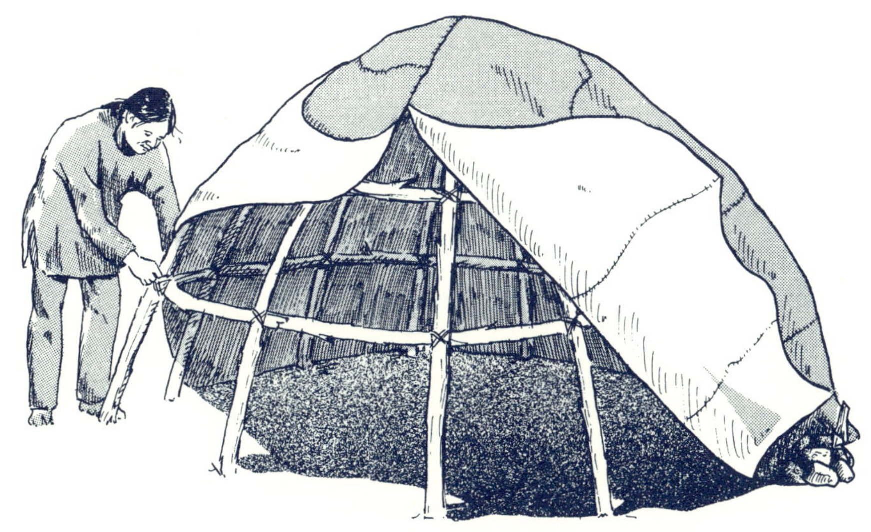

THE ARCHAIC PERIOD   7,000 B.C.–1,000 B.C.

As the glaciers retreated to the north, a great weight was lifted and the land gradually rose. The Champlain Sea was cut off from the ocean and gradually became fresh water. The climate grew warmer. Forests grew where none had grown before, causing the great herds to migrate north. New, smaller animals began to inhabit this region.

The people had to adapt to these changes. The walrus would not have disappeared in a single season, but the hunters would have known from the stories passed down that the hunting was different "in the old days."

The people living in the Champlain Valley invented new methods for hunting smaller animals such as squirrel and deer. They made new hooks and spears for fishing the freshwater creatures in the lake. People used the new and abundant building materials of bark and wood for their homes and utensils. They continued to use stones and bones for tools and jewelry.

The atlatl was a tool developed during the Archaic Period to increase the power of a hunter's throw.

THE WOODLAND PERIOD   1,000 B.C.–1600 A.D.

> *The Woodland People are the ancestors of people living in this region today and the cultural ancestors of all who live in the Champlain Valley. Archeologists have found significant sites that tell about these peoples' daily lives. We know more about the Woodland People because their descendants live here today and have, through a strong tradition of oral history, kept alive many of the beliefs and practices of ancient times. European newcomers also recorded observations of Woodland People, but not as extensively as elsewhere in New England, and these observations were clouded by a prejudice about Native people.*

The people classified by anthropologists as Woodland were the sole inhabitants of this region from 1,000 B.C. to 1600 A.D., when the Europeans arrived. During this time, language groups and tribes that we know today developed into distinct identities. Tribes are sub-units of a larger classification called a language group. Several tribes may speak different languages that have something in common. They may understand each other's language. This is the case with people who speak Italian, French and Spanish; these languages sound very different, yet all began as Latin many centuries ago. They are part of the romance language group.

People who lived on the eastern shore of Lake Champlain, the People of the Dawnland, were Western Abenaki. The Western Abenaki peoples inhabited most of what is now Vermont and New Hampshire as well as parts of southern Quebec and northern Massachusetts. The various tribes that made up the Western Abenaki peoples, such as the Missisquoi, Sokokis and Cowasucks, shared similar cultures and belonged to the same language group. The Abenaki did not organize as large formal tribes with one leader. They made decisions in small family groups. There were no written laws that controlled what people should or should not do. Customs and lessons were handed down through oral tradition and held society together.

Lake Champlain, or Lake Bitawbagok, the "waters in between" as it was then called, was the western edge of Ndakinna, the land of the Abenaki. They believed the lake was the center of their universe. It was in the lake that the transformer Ojihozo chose to rest after making the world, because it seemed to him to be the most beautiful place of all.

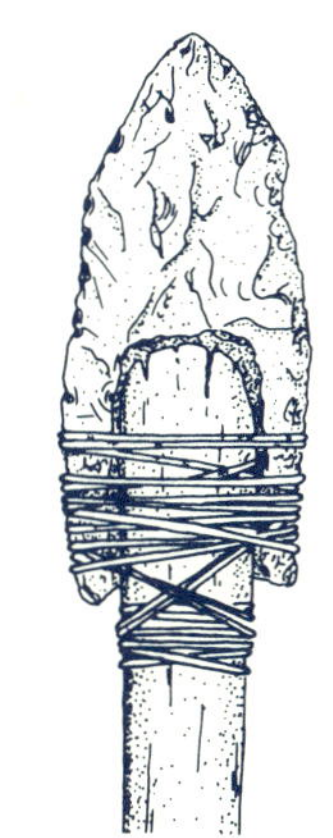

fluted point spearhead

"Indians" is not a correct term for the ancestors of our region. It was first used when European explorers thought they had landed in India. They didn't know about the continent of North America.

The Abenaki name for the lake was Lake Bitawbagok, which meant the "waters in between." The Iroquois name was "Caniadari Guarunte" or "the door to the country."

Abenaki of this region call themselves "the people" and believe that their ancestors have always inhabited this land. They call this land "Ndakinna" or "our land."

The Abenaki belong to the Eastern Algonquian language group.

The Iroquois lived on the western shore of Lake Champlain. The tribe that lived closest to the lake was the Mohawk. The Mohawk were part of the Iroquoian language group that lived toward the west of the Great Lakes and north into what is now Canada. Iroquois lived to the south and southwest of Lake Champlain, but they hunted in the Adirondacks and traveled in small hunting groups up the lake for fish and game.

At the time of European contact, five Iroquois tribes organized themselves into a confederacy called the Iroquois Nation or Confederacy. One author explains the confederacy in these words:

> *"The Five Nations dug a great hole, and in it they buried all the weapons of war. Above these they planted a Tree of Peace with long leaves. In its top they set an eagle to watch in all directions and give warning of the approach of any enemy that might try to cut down the Tree.*
>
> *The Tree of Peace grew and grew, and all the Five Nations seated themselves beneath its pleasant shade. When they saw there was plenty of room, they invited other nations to join them under the spreading branches."*

The Abenaki and the Iroquois used the lake as a source of food and transportation. They traveled in bark or dugout canoes. More often than not they shared the plentiful resources the lake offered. At times there was fierce conflict, but there was also cultural and social exchange. Archeologists have found evidence that some Iroquois lived on the eastern shore of the lake—Abenaki territory—and believe these excavated sites were refugee camps or temporary hunting camps. Also, Abenaki hunted and fished on the western shore, which was Iroquois territory.

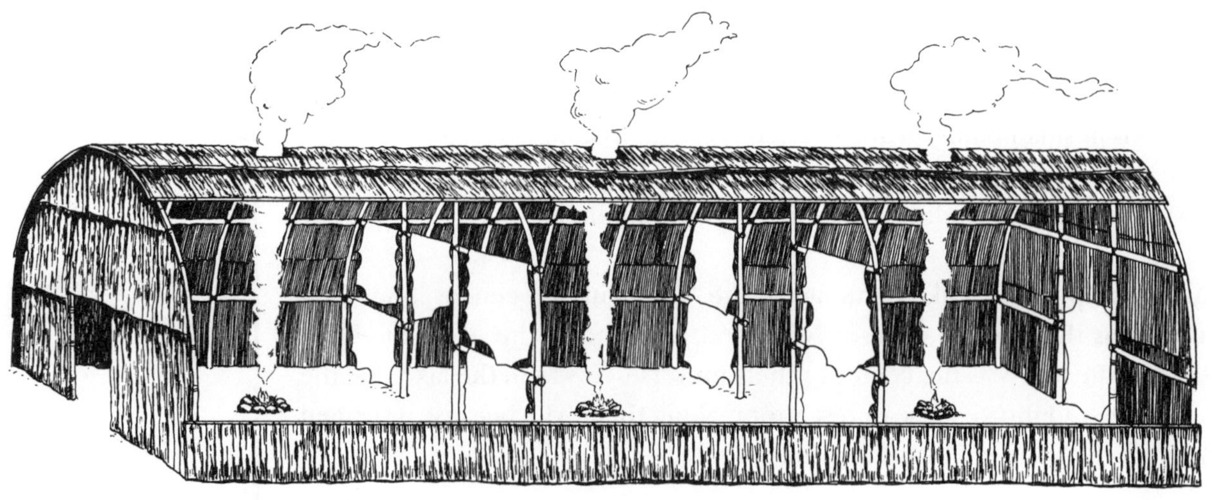

Territories during the Woodland times were clearly defined but not owned in the same way people own land today. A family group would belong to a certain section of land and be responsible for taking care of it. Another group could not hunt there unless it had permission.

Each hunting territory was around a tributary or stream of a larger river, such as the Missisquoi. The rivers were the main means of transportation. When a river was not frozen, people used it for travel to all sections of their territory. When the river was frozen, they would either walk on it with snowshoes or use trails that went alongside it. Smaller trails ran off at right angles from the main trail and divided a territory into quarters. The family only hunted and trapped one quarter at a time, giving the other three portions time to replenish the supply of game.

The hunting was done by the men. In the late winter, they hunted deer and moose. They wore snowshoes so they could travel faster than the moose that got stuck in the deep snow. Woodland people developed the bow and arrow to hunt smaller game. In the spring, the men caught fish and captured birds with nets. Villages were often located near the rapids of a river where fish were plentiful.

In the winter, the women were busy with household chores such as cooking and making clothing and utensils from hides and fur, bark and spruce root. They would decorate some of these things with porcupine quills, moose hair and paint. Woodland women were the first in this region to make pottery containers. This made a big difference in how food was stored and transported and made work much easier, just as the invention of the icebox made things easier for our great grandmothers. In the spring, the women gathered maple syrup and wild greens. In the summer, they grew the crops and gathered wild plants and berries. In the fall, they gathered nuts and were busy preserving crops. Villages often moved nearer to the lake in the summer and closer to the shelter and food supply of the mountains in the winter.

The Iroquois did more farming than the Abenaki. The women of both groups were in charge of the planting and the harvesting. Iroquois women were heads of a clan; tribes were divided into clans. Women did not become chiefs but they chose which men were chiefs.

An arrow, or "mini-spear," was a much more efficient tool for killing a rabbit than a spear. It allowed a hunter to kill small game quickly and quietly. The development or invention of the bow and arrow was a major technological breakthrough for Woodland society.

The Iroquois believe that corn, beans and squash are sacred life-giving foods and call them "The Three Sisters." They believe that The Three Sisters were the first gifts from the Sky Woman who came to "Turtle Island" or Earth.

The Iroquois and the Abenaki people developed trading networks with tribes as far away as the Great Lakes. One day, in the sixteenth century, they encountered new goods coming from a tribe in the north. The goods included brass, wool and iron. The new tribe was called the "French."

The time when Native Americans were the only caretakers of this land was about to come to an end. Along with the new goods, the French brought European diseases that destroyed large numbers of native people. Europeans had built up immunities against these diseases, whereas people living on this continent had not. They had no way to fight the plague, smallpox, measles and typhoid fever that raged through the villages. In some areas these diseases killed 90% of the population. In addition, the system of land stewardship that Native Americans had practiced for thousands of years left them vulnerable to European intrusion.

EUROPEANS COME to the CHAMPLAIN VALLEY

Colin Calloway, in his book DAWNLAND ENCOUNTERS, writes about an ancient prophecy:

In the sixteenth and seventeenth centuries, the superpowers of Europe laid claim to North and South America. The British and Dutch settled along the Eastern seaboard and the Spanish sought control of lands further to the south. The French settled north of Lake Champlain.

The French had settled first in Quebec and made friends with the Algonquin. The Algonquin helped the French build their significant, profitable fur trade by sharing important information about survival in their land. When the Iroquois people became competitors in this fur trade and raided some French trading posts, the French declared them enemies. This made the French alliance with the Algonquin stronger and together they vowed to fight the Iroquois.

One of the French explorers to travel to this region was Samuel de Champlain. Samuel de Champlain was born in 1580 in a French seacoast town. At an early age he decided he would become a mariner. He participated in a number of expeditions from Europe to North America. Champlain proved to be a great navigator, map maker and journalist. He had heard about "a large lake with beautiful islands and a great deal of beautiful country surrounding it" and was anxious to see this new place. He had also promised the French government that he would help fight Iroquois enemies, as well as record

The Algonquin, sometimes spelled Algonkins, were also a part of the larger Algonquian language group. The spelling often causes confusion.

The Battle

Aparty of French and Algonquin explorers entered the lake on July 4, 1609. In his journal, Champlain described what he saw:

"The next day we entered the lake, which is of great extent....I saw four fine islands....There were also many rivers falling into the lake, bordered by many fine trees of the same kinds as those we have in France....Continuing our course over this lake on the western side, I noticed some very high mountains, on the top of which there was snow."

They made their way peacefully down the lake until they met what they believed to be an Iroquoian war party at the southern part of the lake. Champlain described the battle in his journal.

"We both began to utter loud cries, all getting their arms in readiness. We withdrew out on the water and the Iroquois went on shore, where they drew up all their canoes close to each other....When they were armed and in array, they despatched two canoes...to inquire if they wished to fight. [They] replied that they wanted nothing else....

As there was not much light...it would be necessary to wait for daylight...as soon as the sun rose, they would offer us battle....The entire night was spent in dancing and singing on both sides, with endless insults and other talk...."

The next morning:

"Our men began to call me with loud cries, and...to give me a passageway; they opened in two parts and put me at their head, where I marched some twenty paces in advance of the rest until I was within about 30 paces from the enemy, who at once noticed me, and, halting, gazed at me, as I did also at them. When I saw them making a move to fire at us, I rested my musket against my cheek and aimed directly at one of the chiefs. With the same shot, two fell to the ground, and one of their men was so wounded that he died some time after."

Champlain fired more shots at the Iroquois and *"arrows flew on both sides."* The Iroquois, who must have been terrified by their first experience of gunfire, retreated into the woods. Champlain pursued them, *"killing more of them."* Champlain described the victory and concluded, *"And, having made good cheer, danced and sung, we returned three hours afterwards with the prisoners."*

information about the region. The battle between Champlain and the Iroquois was very important because it changed forever the traditional method of resolving conflict on the lake. People had fought in groups, facing off until one side conceded defeat. When the Europeans brought firearms, the native people developed new tactics of sneak attacks and ambush—tactics they used alongside their European allies.

Historians believe that the reason the Iroquois were so bitter toward the French is that four Iroquois chiefs were killed in that battle. It is possible that the Iroquois group was on a diplomatic mission. The Iroquois, not knowing about the power of guns, could not have anticipated the casualties. The loss of leadership was a huge blow to the Iroquois nation.

After the battle between Champlain and the Iroquois, many native people chose sides; these loyalties would last for 150 years. The native people, who had lived for centuries with a system of land stewardship that Europeans did not understand, were in a dangerous situation. Many friendships had been made with the new settlers; Native Americans had offered important advice on surviving in the new land. Some stayed and fought along with their new neighbors. Often, they headed to the hills where things seemed safer, leaving behind land that was already cleared and appeared unoccupied because it was not marked by fences and stone walls. Some native people moved north to what is now Canada. Many stayed and tried unsuccessfully to maintain their claim to their land. Native people would continue to make different choices and they would not successfully organize to try to claim their land until the twentieth century. In the meantime, business interests, supported by a widely accepted feeling of racial superiority, led the Europeans to assume that the land was theirs to claim.

EUROPEANS STRIVE
to CONTROL the CHAMPLAIN VALLEY

For the next 150 years, Europeans moved into the Champlain Valley. The British, who had claimed much of southern New England, moved northward. The French, still interested in the fur trade, moved south and west from their bases in New France, in the area we know today as Quebec. Both groups sent armies to defend the land they claimed.

England and France, longtime enemies in Europe, brought their fight to the New World. They learned quickly that the lake and its tributaries made an exceptional highway for moving armies. In summer, canoes and "bateaux" could move invading forces and in winter, the ice provided a surface for armies on snowshoes. Both countries knew that if they could control the lake, they would control the whole region. With assistance from Native American allies, they fought a series of smaller conflicts over land.

Across the lake from Crown Point at the southern end, the English erected a small fort at Chimney Point. This fort, built in 1690, was only occupied for a short time. In 1730, the French built upon this same land. The wooden fort on Pointe à la Chevelure (Chimney Point) was fully manned with 30 men in 1732. The construction of this fort violated the Treaty of Utrecht.

The Treaty of Utrecht was signed by the French and the British in 1713 at the end of the Queen Anne's War. The treaty said that Split Rock, near present day Essex, New York, was the boundary; the French must stay north of that point. Crown Point was 20 miles south of Split Rock. This boundary was an age-old boundary between Iroquois and Abenaki people.

In 1734, the French began to build a stronger fort across the lake at Crown Point. This fort, called Fort St. Frederic, became a French stronghold in the valley and became a base of operations against the British in the south.

The French government wanted to make life attractive to new settlers so it built a windmill where soldiers and settlers could grind grain and make bread. The windmill was also armed with six swivel cannon called "pierriers."

Peter Kalm, a visitor to the fort in 1749, wrote that for dinner *"...they ate clear soup, wheat bread and various kinds of relishes, then a dish of cooked meat, sometimes fried after being cooked; occasionally beef or mutton, squabs or fowl...often the third course was green peas or fried fish..."*

Until the 1740s, the main form of transportation was water travel via bark canoes and bateaux. Canoes were excellent for quick travel and raiding parties. The bateaux were used to haul cargo or a larger number of troops. In 1742, at Fort St. Frederic, the French built the first true sailing vessel to travel the lake. The *Vigilant* was a small schooner.

THE FRENCH *and* INDIAN WARS *or* SEVEN YEARS' WAR

As things heated up between the French and the British, the French doubted Fort St. Frederic would stand up under British attack. In 1755, they started to build a new fort, Fort Carillon, further south and near Lake George. The British were intent on capturing these French forts. From Albany, they launched the "Crown Point Expeditions" (1755–1759) to attack the French strongholds at the southern part of the lake.

In 1758, the British assembled the largest of these expeditions. In July, 15,000 men rowed across Lake George toward Lake Champlain. It was an armada, "the largest army ever assembled in North America." They traveled in 900 bateaux, 135 whaleboats, rafts that carried artillery and three small radeaux.

Only 3,600 French troops waited at Fort Carillon, under the leadership of General Marquis de Montcalm. The British were led by General James Abercrombie and his second in command, a young British nobleman named

The British Army had "Regulars" who were paid soldiers or "Redcoats." "Provincials" were colonists fighting for the British Army. Most Iroquois fought with the British. The Abenaki fought with the French. The British Army paid soldiers from other European countries to fight in the colonies.

a Black Watch captain

George Viscount Howe. Howe was not a typical British officer. He fought alongside the troops, did his own laundry, carried his own bedroll and was very popular with the troops. He made a lot of adjustments to military life "in the wild." He had his men cut their hair and discard their wigs, cut off the tails of their redcoats and throw away any useless clothing.

Lord Howe was killed the day before the planned assault on Carillon in a scouting mission. This hurt the morale of the army and the expedition floundered another day. Without this delay, and the misjudgment of General James Abercrombie, historians feel that the British would have won. Rather than using artillery to assault the fort from a distance, however, Abercrombie sent his troops to attack a log and earth palisade that was on a high ridge near Carillon. The French had quickly constructed it while waiting for Abercrombie to attack. The French, though small in numbers, were able to mow down the British troops from the heights of Carillon.

Fighting under the British were many Scottish soldiers who wore Black Watch plaid quilts. They were led by the music of bagpipes. One account tells of a wounded bagpiper who leaned against a tree and continued to play a mournful song until he died. Of the estimated 1,900 killed or wounded, 1,000 were Scottish Highlanders. The British troops retreated to Lake George. It was a miserable defeat.

The French were lucky to have survived the attack in 1758, but in 1759, the British returned. This time, General Jeffrey Amherst was in command. The British attacked both French forts. The French withstood the attack for a few days, but soon retreated to their ships. Rather than leave their forts to be used by the British, they blew them up before escaping.

The French had lost on land, but their very small fleet of ships remained on the lake that summer. In October, Amherst, with two recently built ships, cornered the French vessels on the western shore of the lake. The French sank their own ships and retreated overland to Canada. They knew the British had beaten them off the lake.

In 1760, the British captured the French fort at Isle aux Noix and met additional troops in Montreal to finally beat the French into surrender. This last victory signaled the end of 150 years of French rule in North America and, specifically, the end of French control of Lake Champlain.

The story of the Forty-second Scottish regiment inspired Robert Louis Stevenson to write a famous poem called "Ticonderoga." The poem tells the legend of a man who would meet a ghost at a place called Ticonderoga. The soldier went into battle not knowing the old name for Carillon was Ticonderoga; it was indeed where he died.

MORE PEOPLE MOVE *to the* CHAMPLAIN VALLEY

From 1760 to 1775, new settlers moved into the Champlain Valley. Many were former British soldiers who had fought in the valley and had liked it. There were rivers to power mills, ore to make iron and timber to sell to European shipbuilders.

People who moved into the valley at this time are often referred to as "white" or "British." Not all of the new inhabitants were white, however, as some families brought African-American slaves. There were also a few free blacks, most notably Lucy Terry Prince and her family, who moved here in 1764. There were also a multitude of people moving into the area from other countries such as Scotland and Ireland, like Philip Skene, an Irishman who served in the British Army. In addition, the French, who had settled in New France, did not all disappear when the British took control. And, of course, many Abenaki and Iroquois, many of whom had fought in the French and Indian Wars, remained in the region.

The Royal Proclamation of 1763, which established British boundaries after the Seven Years' War, included a clause that said land could not be purchased from Native Americans except by proper authorities and in open council. This should have guaranteed protection to Abenaki lands, but it did not. Feeling the threat of British settlement, Native Americans negotiated leases for long-term control and formally appealed to British authorities to honor these agreements.

The land in Vermont became known as the "Grants" because land was granted to the newcomers by the governors of New York and New Hampshire.

Ignoring Native American land claims, the governors of New Hampshire and New York granted land to the new settlers. People, many from Connecticut and New York, began to move onto the land. Among them, the Allen brothers—Ethan and Ira—from Connecticut traveled the territory to find the best lands to purchase.

One of the famous families that came to the Champlain Valley during this time was the Story family, who moved from Connecticut to Salisbury, Vermont. One author describes Ann Story as "a great woman who could cut off a two-foot log as quick as any man in the settlement." Her husband was killed while cutting down a tree, but Ann decided to settle in the Grants with her children and make the most of it. She survived raiding parties and harsh winters and acted as a spy during the American Revolution.

An Irishman named William Gilliland, who had served in the British Army, purchased land on the New York side. The story of his trip from "civilized" Albany to the shores of Lake Champlain tells what it was like to travel in those days.

Gilliland had quite a bit of money and assembled a group of workers to settle his new land. The group that gathered in Albany included a minister, two millwrights, a carpenter, a clerk, five weavers, a housekeeper and an indentured servant. They were joined by two drovers who led twenty oxen, one bull and some calves. On May 18, 1764, they loaded eighty barrels of supplies onto four boats and set sail. Along the way they picked up two farmers, a wagon maker and a blacksmith. They reached Ticonderoga Landing on June 1 and spent two days portaging boats and goods overland to Lake Champlain. The drover was left behind with the cattle while the rest of the crew made their way north to the mouth of the Bouquet River. They made a decision about where to build a sawmill and returned to the mouth of the river, threw out a fishing seine and hauled in 60 large fish. The group was in good spirits. Two weeks later, they started construction on a settlement that would become Willsboro. This was the first village of its kind to be built between Crown Point and Canada.

Settlers like Gilliland, although not as wealthy, continued to move onto land issued to them by the governor of New York or New Hampshire. This created quite a problem when a title was sold to two different people for the same land! Conflicts over Native American land claims were not settled. It was more complicated when the people who were selling the land didn't really own it. Conflict arose between the people holding New Hampshire grants and people holding deeds from New York. Local militia groups were formed to defend land claims.

One local militia group was called the Green Mountain Boys. They lived in the Grants, land that is now Vermont. They were commanded by Ethan Allen and defended their land claims against the "Yorkers." When the tensions between Great Britain and the American colonies exploded into armed conflict, Ethan Allen, the Green Mountain Boys and the people of the Champlain Valley found themselves right in the thick of things.

On the eve of the American Revolution, the Iroquois Confederacy, which had maintained political unity for two hundred years, could not reach agreement on which side to fight. They agreed to "cover the council fire" and let each group choose its own alliances. Because of this decision, it was difficult for the Iroquois to reorganize after the Revolution. In addition, without the alliance of the British, which had strengthened their position for many years, they were more vulnerable to the U.S. Government's control. In 1779, General Washington authorized an invasion of Iroquois villages and after the war, President Washington oversaw the policies that seized Native land and moved the Iroquois to reservations.

The Abenakis were in the same dilemma. Some chose sides and fought in the Revolution, but many remained neutral and withdrew from their villages to safer places. Lands claimed by Europeans were never formally relinquished by the Abenaki.

The displacement of Native peoples and their fight to reclaim land and restore their way of life is a long, sad story that will not be told in these pages, but it is a story you should learn more about.

THE AMERICAN REVOLUTION COMES to the CHAMPLAIN VALLEY

Three weeks after the Battles of Concord and Lexington in April 1775, the American Revolution began in the Champlain Valley. Ethan Allen and the Green Mountain Boys, with Benedict Arnold from Connecticut, took the British fortress of Ticonderoga on May 11, 1775. Soon after, Seth Warner and another group of Green Mountain Boys captured Crown Point. Arnold and Allen established "headquarters of the Army" at Crown Point.

Crown Point, the head Quarters of the Army

At Crown Point, they captured 111 pieces of artillery: 105 cannon, 2 howitzers and 4 mortars.

The taking of Fort Ticonderoga was the first American action against the British in the Revolution. There was hardly any fighting, but it boosted the colonists' morale. The capture of Fort Ticonderoga and Crown Point gave the rebels a large amount of artillery. The cannons became famous because soldiers hauled them overland to Boston, where they were used to fight off the British.

The American rebels also captured the two large vessels on the lake, one a schooner called *Katherine*, which the rebels renamed the *Liberty*. Benedict Arnold and his crew took this schooner and surprised the British garrison at St. Johns. There he captured the other large vessel on the lake, known as the "King's Sloop," and renamed it the *Enterprise*. These two vessels captured in May of 1775 have been called the first vessels in the American navy.

Benedict Arnold, a commissioned officer in the colonial army, was just beginning an extraordinary military career. His actions would have a huge influence on events in this region, although history focuses on his later career, when he turned traitor and sided with the British.

Arnold and the Green Mountain Boys were sure that the lake would be very important in the fight against the British. They tried to persuade the Congress, located in Philadelphia, to use Lake Champlain for an invasion of Canada. A decision was made to attack Quebec City from two sides. Congress sent one army, under the command of Benedict Arnold, through the Maine and the Canadian wilderness. Richard Montgomery and his army went north on Lake Champlain. Montgomery's army captured St. Johns, Chambly and Montreal. Arnold's force emerged from the wilderness having suffered hunger, cold and sickness during their march. The two armies joined in front of the strong walls of Quebec in late fall. The weather was turning cold and the troops enlistments were about to run out. Arnold and Montgomery made a plan to attack the fortress on New Year's Eve, even though the odds were against them.

It was a nighttime attack, covered by a blinding snowstorm. Montgomery and many of his officers were killed. Arnold was wounded; the attack failed. For the rest of the winter, the army suffered greatly from a lack of supplies. They became sick with smallpox and dysentery.

Imagine the morale of the soldiers stationed hundreds of miles from home fighting for an army that couldn't always send supplies to keep them warm and fed. The young country found the task of supplying the American Army a difficult and often impossible one. When troops were stationed in Canada, 120 barrels of pork and flour were shipped from Albany every day in a dozen bateaux. In transport, the seal on the barrels could crack and the brine that preserved the meat would spill. Often the meat that arrived was spoiled. In addition, it was hard to send enough cannon and ammunition over the great distances between the army stations.

the Liberty

In the spring, a British army arrived at Quebec and the Americans were forced into a hasty retreat. Hundreds of sick men died as the Americans withdrew to Fort Ticonderoga and Mount Independence. Dr. Lewis Beebe described this scene at Fort Ticonderoga:

> *"Last evening we had one of the most severe showers of rain; it continued almost the whole of the night with unremitted violence; many of their tents were ankle deep in water. Many of the sickly their whole lengths in the water, with one blanket only to cover them. One man having the smallpox bad, and unable to help himself, drowned when a current of water came through his tent.…We buried two more yesterday and two more today.…"*

In the Champlain Valley, the war in 1776 was about who could control Lake Champlain. Both sides started a race to see who could build the most ships. The Americans brought in carpenters from the coast and set up operations in Skenesboro. A now-healed Benedict Arnold was made commodore of the fleet. The British established a shipyard at St. Johns. Both sides built impressive fleets. The two fleets met at Valcour Island in the fall of 1776.

The battle ended when Arnold's fleet fled south and retreated to Fort Ticonderoga. American forces frantically strengthened their defensive positions at Ticonderoga and Mount Independence. They called in the militia and waited for a British attack. Instead, the British, concerned about the coming winter and the fifteen thousand American troops prepared to meet them, decided to return to Canada. Historians feel that this decision gave the Americans

Skenesboro, named after Philip Skene, an Irish soldier, is now Whitehall, New York.

*The British faced a special challenge in getting some of their ships to Lake Champlain. Some that were built on the St. Lawrence were disassembled and hauled over the rapids at Chambly and reassembled. One named the **Inflexible** was taken apart in 30, 6-ton sections, and hauled overland. It was reassembled at St. Johns in 38 days. On October 11, the two squadrons met at Valcour Island.*

The Battle of Valcour Island

In late September, 1776, Benedict Arnold sailed north to meet the British. The plan was to find a secure place to wait for the British. He chose the channel behind Valcour Island and wrote to his commanding officer: *"[It] is a good harbor...where we shall have the advantage of attacking the enemy in the open Lake."* The large British gunboats could not turn quickly and Arnold hoped this would give him an advantage.

Arnold was worried about the lack of training of his soldiers and he wanted more cannon. Supplies were slow to arrive. The soldiers waiting on board could see the snow that had already fallen on the Adirondacks. Scouts sent to St. Johns sent back reports that underestimated the firepower of the warships. The American fleet waited almost three weeks at Valcour Island.

The scouts for the British Army had not located Arnold's fleet. When the British fleet finally sailed down the lake on October 11, it sailed right by Valcour Island. The British had to reposition their boats when they finally saw the American fleet.

The Battle of Valcour Island lasted over three days. On the first day, the Americans fought the larger British fleet for five hours and lost the schooner *Royal Savage*, the gunboat *Philadelphia* and over 60 men.

The *Royal Savage*, the only ship that matched the British ships in size and firepower, was lost early in the day. The British destroyed its mast and rigging and captured 20 Americans before they could escape. Aside from the massive firepower of the British gunboats, a group of British soldiers and Native Americans, presumably Iroquois, were firing on the Americans from the shore. The gunboat, the *Philadelphia*, was sunk later in the afternoon. By the end of the day, the Americans were clearly beaten.

Arnold realized he was over-matched and would have to retreat. Then, he designed a bold plan. Under the cover of night, Arnold was able to row his remaining vessels, single file, past the British blockade set up at the south end of the island. Soldiers wrapped rags around their oars to quiet them as they sneaked by the British fleet.

The next morning, the British were mortified to find that the Americans had escaped. General Carlton, commander of the British fleet, was "in a rage." The British immediately gave chase. The fleeing American squadron was caught on October 13, below Split Rock. From there, they fought a $2\frac{1}{2}$-hour running battle down the lake.

Arnold, on board the galley *Congress*, realized his battered vessels could not keep fighting. He directed his five rear-most vessels into Ferris's Bay and destroyed them on purpose, so the British could not capture them. Arnold then escaped overland to the American lines at Ticonderoga with his men. The British now controlled Lake Champlain.

an advantage; they would not have to fight the British until the following spring. This is why the Battle of Valcour Island is called an American victory.

During the winter of 1776–77, the Americans reduced their troops stationed at forts on Lake Champlain. Chief Engineer Jeduthan Baldwin began work on a great floating bridge to connect Fort Ticonderoga, also called Fort Ti, and Mount Independence. The "Great Bridge" was an engineering marvel of its time. Footings for the bridge were built on the ice. They were basically huge boxes, like log cabins without roofs. They were filled with stones and lowered through the ice to act as anchors for a floating log road.

top view of wooden crib structure of Great Bridge

The next spring, in June of 1777, an army of 8,000 British and Hessian (German) soldiers advanced up the lake toward Ticonderoga. This army was under the command of General John Burgoyne. There were only 2,000 men defending Fort Ticonderoga and Mount Independence.

On July 5, 1777, threatened by this large British force, the Americans abandoned their lake fortifications and began an organized retreat.

Some of Burgoyne's forces chased them to Hubbardton, where the only battle fought on Vermont soil delayed the British. The colonists defeated the British at the Battle of Bennington. However, the British continued the chase into the Hudson Valley where American forces were massing to stop them. The ultimate showdown came near Saratoga. Horatio Gates commanded the American force and Benedict Arnold was one of his generals. In a major battle, the British were defeated and forced to surrender. This was the turning point of the Revolution: the French then joined the American cause and things began to go better for the Americans.

The next year saw the front of the war shift south. In the Champlain Valley, small British raiding parties, with Iroquois allies serving as soldiers and scouts, continued to harass residents. Some, like Peter Ferris and his son Squire, were captured and taken back to Canada as prisoners. Most valley residents were ultimately forced to abandon their homes and withdraw to safer territories. Only a few, like the Story family, stayed where they were and weathered the storm.

PEACE *and* SETTLEMENT

After the final American victory in 1783, people returned to their homes and new settlers moved in. With poor or nonexistent roads, the major thoroughfares were still the lake and the rivers. Soon ferries, log rafts, sloops and schooners joined the canoes and bateaux on the lake.

The Champlain Valley was beginning its commercial climb. As new settlements emerged, new means were developed to transport people around the lake. Burlington on the Vermont side and Whitehall and Essex in New York were centers for the new commerce. Workers in these towns built most of the trading sloops that appeared on the lake.

With all the new business and trading, the best and only trade route to outside markets was north to Canada. Livestock, grain, lumber, potash and iron were shipped north in return for salt, manufactured goods and other goods not available in the valley.

Logs that were shipped to Canada were lashed together to make huge rafts. Sails were crudely fastened to propel the rafts northward. Crews made tents and lean-tos and lived on the rafts.

The War of 1812

In the early 1800s, France and Britain were still enemies. England wanted to stop the U.S. trade with France, much of which was concentrated in the Champlain Valley. English ships on the Atlantic stopped and seized American ships and kidnapped American sailors. The new nation, led by Thomas Jefferson, was angry about being told what to do by the British and declared it illegal to trade with Britain. The conflict between the British and the Americans was bad news for the many people in this area who made their living selling and transporting goods to Canada. The U.S. Government sent custom officials and army troops on gunboats to patrol the lake, but smugglers still ignored the law. During the time that the embargo was in effect, trade to Canada actually increased.

After years of mounting tension, President James Madison, who succeeded Jefferson in the White House, declared war on Great Britain on June 18, 1812. The U.S. Navy saw that Lake Champlain, so near to Canadian waters, would once again be an important waterway to control. It sent Lt. Thomas MacDonough to build a navy to fight the British.

The first year, MacDonough kept control of the lake. But the British were building ships on the Richelieu River at Isle aux Noix. After a series of British raids into the lake in 1813, the naval race was on.

MacDonough had chosen Vergennes as the site for his naval shipyard. The Otter River had powerful waterfalls and was an excellent place to build ships. There was an abundance of timber and Vergennes had established businesses such as a blast furnace, iron foundry, forges, wire factory and grist and sawmills. Crews began work. The first ship was completed 40 days after the first tree was cut down. These were the largest sailing vessels ever to appear on Lake Champlain.

The shipbuilding race that followed was similar to the one that took place during the American Revolution. When the British learned of the American progress, they began construction of a 39-gun frigate. This would be the largest warship ever built on Lake Champlain. In a frantic response, MacDonough oversaw construction of the 20-gun brig, the *Eagle*, in 19 days.

In September, 1814, MacDonough sailed north to meet the British. He stationed his fleet in Plattsburgh Bay. American land troops stationed themselves on the south side of the Saranac River. The British army advanced to the northern banks of the Saranac and waited for the British navy to appear and dispose of the American fleet before advancing further. The British warships arrived, anchored facing the Americans, and the two sides opened fire. There was an intense and bloody engagement, now known as the Battle of Plattsburgh. The Americans won. This brought an end to the naval contest for the lake and also helped bring the wider war to a successful conclusion a few months later. The lake was again at peace.

THE COMMERCIAL ERA

TRADE *and* COMMERCE

After the War of 1812, a new commercial era followed for Lake Champlain. The lake was busier than ever before, with many new ships that could go faster and carry more goods. The Champlain Valley was able to provide America with many things it needed to build a new nation. People made their living harvesting many of the natural resources of the area and transporting them to other parts of the country. Ships carried cargoes of lumber, pulpwood, iron ore, marble, granite and coal.

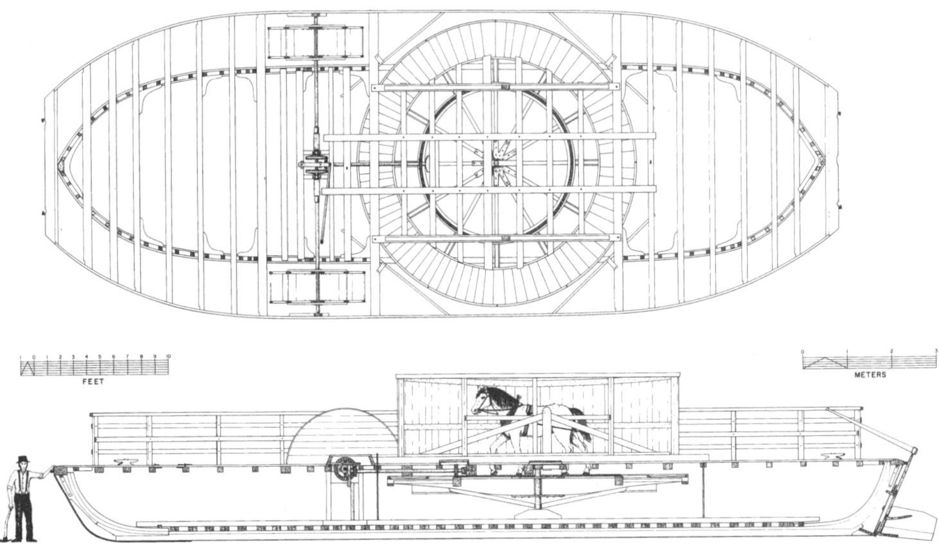

One of the most interesting boats on the lake during this time was a ferry boat powered by horses! The two horses, facing opposite directions, walked on a wheel that was geared to paddle wheels that drove the boat. There was another design, a variation on this theme, where three horses on each side walked on treadmills that drove the gears.

In an effort to cut the cost of transportation, the federal government decided to build a canal that would link Lake Champlain and the Hudson River. The Champlain Canal was completed in 1823. Goods could now be carried all the way to New York City, a major seaport. They could also be shipped to the Midwest through the Erie Canal and the New York State canal system.

The Chambly Canal was completed in 1843 and linked the lake to the St. Lawrence Seaway. Lake Champlain, now linked to the ocean at both ends, was a major trade corridor, a main highway like today's interstate.

CANAL BOATS

There were two kinds of canal boats. The most common, called a standard canal boat, was pulled by mules or horses. When it reached the open lake, either it was towed or its cargo was transported by steamboat to its final destination. The sailing canal boat was equipped with a sail and a centerboard and worked the same as a standard canal boat in the canal. When it reached the lake, crew members lowered the centerboard to provide stability, raised the sail and set forth on the open lake to make their delivery.

Some canal boats carried passengers and were outfitted with cabins for sleeping. They were very crowded. Charles Dickens, a famous author who traveled on Lake Champlain, said the rows of bunks were like bookshelves and the passengers were like volumes; once they were in place they couldn't move! Many of the passengers in the 1830s and 1840s were immigrants going west.

Working canal boats were mobile homes for whole families who lived on them year-round. Boats were often handed down to the next generation and children grew up learning only the life of a canaller.

As a child, Martha Robbins lived on a canal boat with her family. During the years 1897 to 1907 she traveled up and down Lake Champlain from New York City to Canada. She has written:

> *"The cargo from the North might be lumber, hay, or spruce pulpwood from Three Rivers [Canada] cut in two-foot lengths and you had real spruce gum to chew! If the cargo was pulpwood, you might drop off from the tow at Ticonderoga but usually Fort Edward."*

In 1868, there were 600 recorded registrations of water vessels of all kinds: steamers, canal boats, schooners, sloops and tugs. The estimated total weight of these boats was 40,000 tons.

In 1848, over 4,000 immigrants, mostly Irish, traveled on Lake Champlain on their way west.

"...at that age my one big ambition was to ride one of the mules while towing."

Martha Robbins

Even though it may sound exciting, life on a canal boat had its problems. There were accidents and sickness. There was no room to run and play. A child couldn't go to school on a regular basis. That may seem like fun, but after a while, children probably missed seeing their friends each day! Young children were often tied to the towing post or deck to prevent them from falling overboard.

Canal boats didn't last that long and often leaked. Rather than spend hours pumping out water, canallers used their imagination to fix the leaks. One such device was called the "medicine spoon." They used a long handle to push a container to the place under the boat where they thought the leak was. The container, either a box, or open potato sack, was filled with dried horse manure or sawdust. As the water seeped in, the dry material plugged up the hole. It seems pollution wasn't one of their main concerns.

*The **Vermont** was the first steamboat to begin commercial service on any of the world's lakes. Soon the **Congress**, like many other steamboats of the time, had regular routes up and down Lake Champlain.*

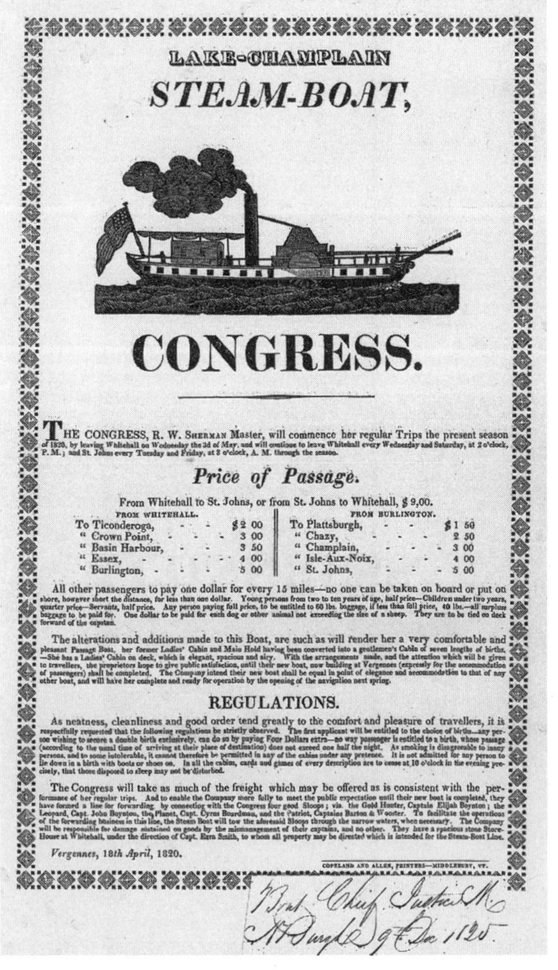

LAKE-CHAMPLAIN
STEAM-BOAT,

CONGRESS.

THE CONGRESS, R. W. Sherman Master, will commence her regular Trips the present season of 1820, by leaving Whitehall on Wednesday the 3d of May, and will continue to leave Whitehall every Wednesday and Saturday, at 2 o'clock, P. M.; and St. Johns every Tuesday and Friday, at 8 o'clock, A. M. through the season.

Price of Passage.

From Whitehall to St. Johns, or from St. Johns to Whitehall, $ 9,00.

FROM WHITEHALL.		FROM BURLINGTON.	
To Ticonderoga,	$2 00	To Plattsburgh,	$1 50
" Crown Point,	3 00	" Chazy,	2 50
" Basin Harbour,	3 50	" Champlain,	3 00
" Essex,	4 00	" Isle-Aux-Noix,	4 00
" Burlington,	5 00	" St. Johns,	5 00

All other passengers to pay one dollar for every 15 miles—no one can be taken on board or put on shore, however short the distance, for less than one dollar. Young persons from two to ten years of age, half price—Children under two years, quarter price—Servants, half price. Any person paying full price, to be entitled to 60 lbs. baggage, if less than full price, 40 lbs.—all surplus baggage to be paid for. One dollar to be paid for each dog or other animal not exceeding the size of a sheep. They are to be tied on deck forward of the capstan.

The alterations and additions made to this Boat, are such as will render her a very comfortable and pleasant Passage Boat, her former Ladies' Cabin and Main Hold having been converted into a gentlemen's Cabin of seven lengths of births. —She has a Ladies' Cabin on deck, which is elegant, spacious and airy. With the arrangements made, and the attention which will be given to travellers, the proprietors hope to give public satisfaction, until their new boat, now building at Vergennes (expressly for the accommodation of passengers) shall be completed. The Company intend their new boat shall be equal in point of elegance and accommodation to that of any other boat, and will have her complete and ready for operation by the opening of the navigation next spring.

REGULATIONS.

As neatness, cleanliness and good order tend greatly to the comfort and pleasure of travellers, it is respectfully requested that the following regulations be strictly observed. The first applicant will be entitled to the choice of births—any person wishing to secure a double birth exclusively, can do so by paying Four Dollars extra—no way passenger is entitled to a birth, whose passage (according to the usual time of arriving at their place of destination) does not exceed one half the night. As smoking is disagreeable to many persons, and to some intolerable, it cannot therefore be permitted in any of the cabins under any pretence. It is not admitted for any person to lie down in a birth with boots or shoes on. In all the cabins, cards and games of every description are to cease at 10 o'clock in the evening precisely, that those disposed to sleep may not be disturbed.

The Congress will take as much of the freight which may be offered as is consistent with the performance of her regular trips. And to enable the Company more fully to meet the public expectation until their new boat is completed, they have formed a line for forwarding by connecting with the Congress four good Sloops; viz. the Gold Hunter, Captain Elijah Boynton; the Leopard, Capt. John Boynton, the Planet, Capt. Cyrus Boardman, and the Patriot, Captains Barton & Wooster. To facilitate the operations of the forwarding business in this line, the Steam Boat will tow the aforesaid Sloops through the narrow waters, when necessary. The Company will be responsible for damage sustained on goods by the mismanagement of their captains, and no other. They have a spacious stone Store-House at Whitehall, under the direction of Capt. Ezra Smith, to whom all property may be directed which is intended for the Steam-Boat Line.

Vergennes, 18th April, 1820.

COPELAND AND ALLEN, PRINTERS—MIDDLEBURY, VT.

STEAM TRAVEL

At the same time as more and more people became involved in canalling, a few people were busy developing a new form of technology. For years, inventors had been experimenting with ways to apply steam power to watercraft. In 1807, Robert Fulton finally produced a vessel that successfully navigated the Hudson River. Two years later, the steamboat *Vermont* was launched on Lake Champlain. The steamboat was built at the foot of King Street in Burlington by a crew working for James and John Winan. Nothing like the *Vermont* had ever appeared on Lake Champlain. It had a regular route from one end of the lake at Whitehall all the way north to St. Johns, Quebec.

People who had been making money shipping goods on sailboats were not very happy about this new technology. Other people thought steamboats were dangerous and would never think of riding on one. Still, there were others who were anxious to be part of the change, either as passengers, builders or owners. There was a big competition to be the biggest steamboat company on Lake Champlain. Companies tried to undercut each other's prices and build larger, faster and fancier boats. Shipbuilding companies sprang up along Champlain's shores. Boats carrying passengers or freight steamed up and down the lake making stops from Whitehall to Canada.

One traveler, Basil Hall, commented in 1827:

> *"The machinery was unusually noisy, the boat weak and tremulous, and we stopped, backed, and went again at no fewer than eleven different places, at each of which there was such a racket that it was impossible to get any rest. If a passenger did manage to doze off…he was sure to be awakened by the engineer's bell or the sharp voice of the pilot calling out, or he might be jerked out of his berth by a sound thump against the dock."*

Nine years later, in 1836, Charles Dickens had a much more pleasant trip:

> *"There is one American boat which I praise very highly, but no more than it deserves….The steamboat, which is called the **Burlington**, is a perfectly exquisite achievement of neatness, elegance, and order. The rooms…are choicely furnished and adorned with prints, pictures and musical instruments; every nook and corner of the vessel is a perfect curiosity of graceful comfort and beautiful contrivance."*

*The interiors of these nineteenth century steamboats, such as the **Vermont II** pictured here, were very elegant.*

A small company that ran a ferry service from Vergennes was owned by Louis and Philemon Daniels. Philemon, who ran the company after her husband died, was the first woman in the world to carry a pilot's and a master's license for a steamboat. She worked in taffeta skirts, wore lots of jewelry and had a strong "boiler room voice," that she used to shout out commands to her crew.

Steamboat travel was not without its share of accidents. In July of 1875, passengers on the steamer *Champlain* were suddenly awakened. Pilot Eldredge was at the ship's wheel when the steamer, traveling at a fast speed, ran right into high rocky land near Westport, New York. Second pilot Rockwell rushed on deck to see what had happened. Eldredge calmly asked him, "Can you account for my being on the mountain?" Rockwell answered, "Yes, Mr. Eldredge, you were asleep."

Another famous disaster was the burning of the *Phoenix*. On September 5, 1819, in the middle of the night, a fire broke out in the pantry of the steamer *Phoenix*. All but six people aboard escaped to safety. The burning ship sank off the Colchester Reef and has since been discovered by divers.

*The burning of the **Phoenix** was one of the most famous and mysterious accidents on the lake. Although a candle in the pantry was the probable cuplrit, there was speculation at the time whether owners of commercial sailing vessels were to blame.*

In 1906, the side-wheeler S.S. *Ticonderoga* was completed by the Champlain Transportation Company, the oldest steam company in the world. The Ti, as it was called, was the last steamship built for Lake Champlain travel. The 200-foot ship was very grand. It had a large dining room, elegantly carpeted halls filled with plush chairs, a barbershop, purser's office, promenade deck, and many cozy compartments.

In 1826, the first lighthouse was built on Juniper Island.

With the number of boats on the lake higher than ever before, improvements were made to improve travel and safety. The Burlington breakwater and the Colchester Reef Lighthouse are two familiar examples of this type of public improvement, paid for by the federal government. During these years, the lake was an extremely busy place. Many different kinds of boats did different jobs. Iron ore, marble and lumber were transported over the lake. People built large houses on prospering waterfront communities, notably in Burlington, Vermont, and Essex, New York.

The sailors and workers on the lake didn't know that another big change was on the horizon, the coming of the railroads. Reaching Burlington in 1849 and extending its lines throughout the area, the railroad first helped and then destroyed lake commerce. In the beginning, it was fashionable for travelers from New York City to first take a train and then a steamship to a fancy hotel on the lake, like the Hotel Champlain at Point Bluff, New York, south of Plattsburgh. But things changed.

Railroads could operate year-round and were more dependable than the winds on Lake Champlain. The commercial fleet steadily declined until, at the turn of the century, there were only a handful of sailing vessels and remnants of the canal-boat fleet being towed on long rafts by steam-tow boats. Early in the new century the steamboats started to feel the increasing pressure from the railroads and from yet a new source of competition—the automobile. Lake Champlain had entered the twentieth century.

In 1870, the Delaware and Hudson Railroad bought the Lake Champlain Steamboat Company and ran the schedule so tourists could use trains and steamboats to reach their destinations.

Hotel Champlain at Point Bluff, New York

MODERN TIMES

TOURISM BECOMES *the* MAIN INDUSTRY

The lake scene was changing. In the late nineteenth century, recreational boating became popular. Hotels around the lake advertised the great fishing and the history of the Champlain Valley in order to attract visitors. People built permanent year-round camps on the lake shores, replacing tent-camps that had been used only in summer.

Commercial harbors were not the active centers that they had been. Boats that had been critical in the commercial development of this whole region were abandoned. Today, the fuel barges, the last holdovers from the days of commercial canal use, are almost totally gone.

Today, Lake Champlain is a place to have fun. Pleasure craft such as sailboats and motorboats are the main form of "transportation." Jet skis and windsurfers compete for space on the open water. Tourism is the main industry. It brings millions of dollars to the region when people come to fish, boat or stay near the lake's shores.

A common way to discard of a vessel was simply to let it sink; this was much cheaper than trying to remove it from the lake.

In 1995, one fuel barge still operated once a week on Lake Champlain, bringing fuel from New York City to Plattsburgh.

PEOPLE WORK *to* PRESERVE *the* PAST

At the beginning of the twentieth century, many important relics of the past lay in ruins around the Champlain Valley. In 1909, the Pell family began efforts to restore Fort Ticonderoga. It is now a fully restored fortification. Crown Point, neglected since the American Revolution, had been used as a cow pasture; residents took its stones and bricks to build barns and houses. In 1910, the state of New York took possession of the site and began preservation efforts. In 1955, the S.S. *Ticonderoga*, no longer in use on the lake, was hauled overland to the Shelburne Museum in a major engineering feat.

*the **Ticonderoga**'s overland journey to the Shelburne Museum*

In 1935, L.F. Hagglund found and raised the *Philadelphia*, Benedict Arnold's gunboat that had sunk at the Battle of Valcour Island. The original *Philadelphia* is at the Smithsonian Museum in Washington, D.C. In 1989, an ambitious crew at the Lake Champlain Maritime Museum built a life-size replica at the museum to educate the public about the past. *Philadelphia II* was launched in the summer of 1991.

More wrecks are still being found and the State of Vermont has established five wrecks as underwater preserves. Anyone who wants to continue to learn about the history of Lake Champlain may want to consider taking a scuba-diving course!

Homer St. Francis, elected leader of the Abenaki nation in 1979

NATIVE AMERICANS PROCLAIM *their* HERITAGE

Native Americans who hid their identities for many years now proclaim their heritage with pride. They now demand that their indigenous rights to fish and hunt along Lake Champlain be restored. They claim sovereign or independent status, and feel that therefore they should not be governed by state laws that restrict hunting and fishing to certain seasons and quotas.

In 1979, Abenakis held an unlicensed "fish-in" along the banks of the Missisquoi River to dramatize what they felt was their right to free fishing and hunting. The right to hunt and fish means more than securing a source of food; it is symbolic of a much larger issue. If the Abenaki can practice these time-held traditions, then they can also preserve a pride in their heritage. No government should deny this important link to the past.

"The fish-in was done with pride. There was tremendous pride, cohesion and joy."

Nakki Goranin

On May 5, 1995, at an Abenaki powwow, a huge crowd gathered. Dorous Churchill, coordinator of the youth dance troupe that led the grand entry said, *"When I see this happening and a youth group going out there and performing with honor and dignity, you can see there is a future for our people....I didn't think I'd see an event like this in this area in my lifetime."*

POLLUTION BECOMES *a* CONCERN

Pollution became a big concern in the twentieth century. People began to realize that we needed to change some practices. In 1905, a U.S. Geologic Survey team issued a "Report on the Pollution of Lake Champlain," which outlined some major industrial and municipal problems.

Because the lake's waters are shared by Vermont, New York and Quebec, organizing to clean up the lake has always been a difficult task. An early leader in helping to clean up Lake Champlain was

the Lake Champlain Committee formed in 1963. Working on both sides of the lake, it is a citizen's action group dedicated to involving people in water monitoring and bringing political pressure on policy makers. They worked to create the New York-Vermont-Quebec Cooperative Agreement that led to the establishment of the Lake Champlain-Adirondack Biosphere Reserve in 1989.

In 1990, the federal Lake Champlain Designation Act called for the development of a pollution prevention, control and restoration plan for Lake Champlain. The Plan was developed under the auspices of the Lake Champlain Basin Program, a collaborative effort involving federal, state and local organizations from New York, Vermont and Quebec. OPPORTUNITIES FOR ACTION: AN EVOLVING PLAN FOR THE FUTURE OF THE LAKE CHAMPLAIN BASIN was released in October, 1996. Over $18 million dollars have been devoted to demonstration projects and research, monitoring, planning and outreach efforts related to the Plan.

It is the feeling of these action groups and many citizens that a comprehensive plan must involve all people living in the basin. Beach closings in 1987 were one of the many sirens to the public that something was wrong with the waters of Lake Champlain. At the present time there are many dollars being spent and much discussion about the future of Lake Champlain. One thing is certain, the future of Lake Champlain lies in the hands of young people who live, work and play in the basin.

THE LAKE CHAMPLAIN MONSTER

One of the more popular characters of the twentieth century is Champ, Lake Champlain's own monster. Although believers claim he has been around for centuries, he has received a lot of publicity in the twentieth century. In 1947, Professor Leon Dean described a sighting by three fishermen:

> *"The lake was calm, the water sparkling and clear, the trio unsuspecting, when a tremendous splash attracted their attention. Out of the depths, as they looked, reared a huge dark form which moved swiftly off to the northwest. Its body was composed of three segments separated by about five feet of water, and its overall length was estimated at about twenty-five feet. In the distance it surfaced again."*

In 1982, the Vermont Legislature issued a law to protect Champ. There was some disappointment when new sonar technology failed to uncover Champ's hiding place. In the summer of 1993, a crew of scientists from Japan filmed a television show on the monster.

the Crown Point Bridge

Pretend a visitor from the past has paid you a visit and you are flying together over the lake in an airplane. Think of all the ways the view surprises your guest. The shoreline is dotted here and there with marinas and condominiums. Land that was pasture is filled with houses, and you see large highways crossing the landscape. As you think of all the ways that the lake scene has changed, consider all the ways that these changes affect our lake.

Look around you. Is everyone talking about how to clean up Lake Champlain? Do you feel that we are all working together to preserve this precious resource? Unless you are involved in something very unique, probably not. But there are many questions concerning the preservation of Lake Champlain that will fall in your hands.

There are many questions for you to think about as the lake enters the twentieth century. What is important to you about Lake Champlain? In order to solve the problems of the future, you will need to figure out what these problems are and how to solve them. Part of this process is knowing the history of Lake Champlain. Lessons from the past mark the paths we have taken and signal a course for the future. The rest is up to you!

The History
of the
Lake Champlain Basin

Activities

T he activities in the following section are designed to correspond to the main historical periods in the preceding essay. Activities represent a balance of reading and interpretation, primary sources, hands-on activities and geography. I avoided lists of comprehensive questions and vocabulary exercises with the idea that teachers will design their own methods to process the information with their class. These decisions will be based on the amount of background knowledge your students have and their reading level. Obviously, a clear understanding of the information and vocabulary is critical.

Each section contains a list of useful words. I considered including a glossary of terms, but this seemed not as useful as giving you a more flexible "word bank" to use as you wish. See *Language Arts* for some possibilities.

Each section also contains "key resources," works that I consider indispensable if you are studying that historical period with students. There's a danger in doing this, of course, because there will always be a source that someone else feels is more important. But teachers' time is precious and I've been told this would be helpful. In addition to the sources cited in each section, the following two books are indispensable when studying the lake's history:

- Sails and Steam in the Mountains *by Russell Bellico*
- Lake Champlain: Key to Liberty *by Ralph Nading Hill.*

Native Americans

QUESTIONS

- How was the lake important to early people?
- What tools/practices did they use to survive near the lake?
- How did those tools/practices change over time?
- How was the lake part of their world view ?
- What animal and plant life sustained human life?
- What was the attitude people had toward the natural resources?
- What things did a child have to learn in order to survive?

KEY RESOURCES

- The Original Vermonters: Native Inhabitants, Past and Present *by William Haviland and Marjory Power*
- Vermont: A Cultural Patchwork *by Elise Guyette*
- The Original People: Native Americans in the Champlain Valley *booklet from an exhibition at Clinton Community Historical Museum*
- The Abenaki *by Colin G. Calloway*
- The Iroquois *by Barbara Graymont*
- The Wind Eagle *edited by Joseph Bruchac*
- New York State Museum in Albany, New York—*field trip and educational resources*

Word Bank

Abenaki
Algonquin
Archaic
arrow
atlatl
bark canoe
Bitawbagok
bolla
bow
caribou
Champlain Sea
deer
dugout canoe
elk
firestone
fur
hammerstone
hides
Iroquois
legend
longhouse
mastodon
moose
Ndakinna
Ojihozo
Paleo
pemmican
scraper
spear
wampum
wigwam
Woodland

Native Americans

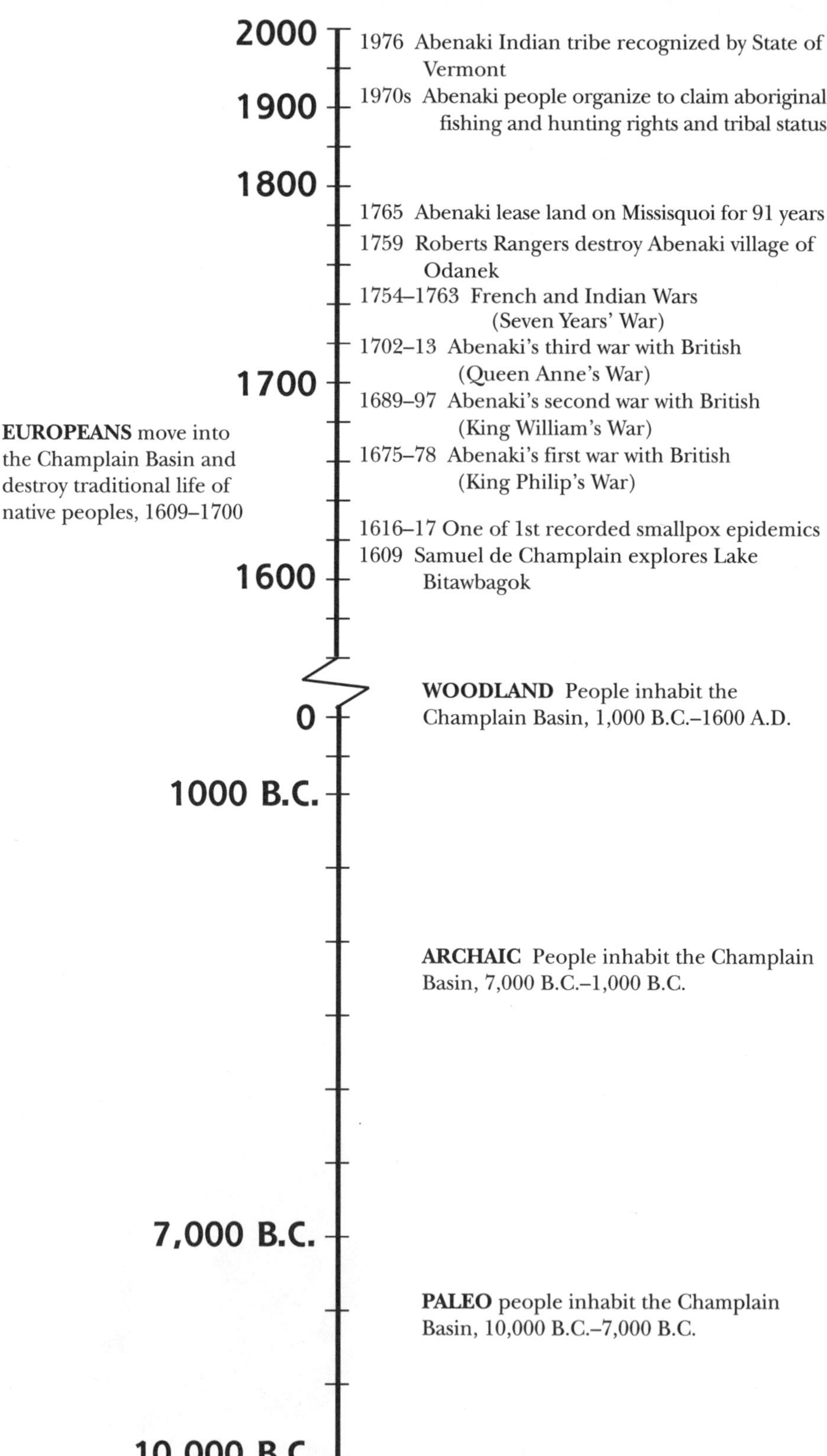

Activity: **"The Hunt"**

arrowhead

TEACHER NOTES *and* INFO
Read the story "The Hunt" by Elise Guyette. Design a handout with the questions shown below.

STUDENT ACTIVITY
After you have read the story, discuss and have students fill out the activity sheet.

STUDENT HANDOUT - "The Hunt"

Name: _______________________________

The Hunt

1. What jobs do people have?

2. What tools do they use?

3. What weapons did they use?

4. Explain how the hunters trap and kill the mastodon.

Beginning of Hunt •————————————————————————————————————• *Dead Mastodon*

5. Explain what they do after the kill.

The Hunt

by Elise Guyette

Imagine a young toolmaker thrilled by the prospect of a mastodon hunt. Caribou was the preferred animal of the Paleohunters, probably because it was so abundant and easier and safer to kill than some of the larger mammals, but a mastodon would provide an immense amount of hide, meat and fat to last through the winter. Preparations for a mastodon hunt would generate a great deal of excitement.

Pere searches near the family home for just the right flint to make a new spear. When he finds some suitable pieces, he returns home to begin carefully chipping out the basic shape with his hammerstone. With his bone hammer he splinters off smaller chips to make a sharp point. All the while he dreams of being the first to wound the mastodon—a great honor.

One of the young women who will accompany the hunters is excitedly packing her cutting and scraping tools into a moose-hide pouch. This is her first hunt. Lai has never seen a mastodon before and the thought of the huge creature thrills her. She gathers her empty baskets and pouches for carrying the butchered animal back home. She must also help the other women prepare their traveling food: dried meat mixed with fat and dried fruit.

Finally the day comes when the group leaves on the hunting trip. Traveling by foot to the mastodon migration route takes several days. When they are near the route, scouts are sent out to watch for the prey. When the scouts spot mastodon, they alert the hunters.

The men decide to dig a trap and cover it with saplings. Excitedly, they cut the small trees and prepare the hole. They also make torches out of wood and dry grass to be used in frightening the animal toward the trap. When preparations are complete, the men practice their spear throws and stretch their muscles like athletes getting ready for a competition. Their lives depend on their physical readiness for the job ahead.

Finally the hunters creep quietly toward the grazing mastodons. The men hide in the tall grass and wait. Soon a young female mastodon strays from the herd. It is what the leader, Shon, has been waiting for. He gives the signal. Pere and Shon use a hot coal to light their torches. Quickly they run behind the mastodon and put the flickering flame to the prairie grass.

Huge mastodons are not afraid of anything—except fire. The moment the herd senses danger they gather together for protection. Soon the smoke turns the peaceful animals into a mass of stampeding behemoths.

The female mastodon turns toward the herd, but it is too late. A wall of fire burns and crackles between them. With a frightened screech, she charges in the opposite direction. The men are waiting. They run toward her, shouting and waving their torches, to veer her toward the trap. The frightened mastodon could easily turn on them and crush them. The hunters run as fast as they can, frantically hoping she won't. She charges blindly in the direction of the trap.

Some men have stayed behind at the sapling-covered hole. They see the bellowing behemoth speeding in their direction. They light their torches and send a prayer that the beast will crash into the trap and not into them. They race toward the frightened animal waving their torches, turning her toward the pit. In her panic, she plows right into the trap, trumpeting in pain.

Pere and Shon race breathlessly toward the mastodon. Pere arrives first. While some men throw rocks at the beast to divert her attention, Pere thrusts his spear into her throat. Others are on her immediately with spears and knives. With a final cry of pain, the great beast slumps lifelessly against the walls of the trap.

The men dance ecstatically around the mastodon, celebrating their great victory. Pere jumps on the animal's back, ablaze with excitement that he was the first to wound the animal. He will be honored when they return home. The men offer thanks to the mastodon for giving its life so the people can eat. Soon the exhausted men retreat to rest. They call the women to do their job.

Lai and the others move toward the pit. She cannot believe that such a magnificent animal exists. She stares in amazement at the animal that the men have just killed. Holding the bear claw hanging from her neck, she sends a prayer of thanks that no one was hurt during the hunt. Now it is time to work.

First the women build fires around the area to keep scavengers away. They spend hours skinning the mastodon and then dividing the carcass into smaller portions. While some women cut the meat into smaller strips and hang them out to dry, Lai helps to scrape the hide on one side. When finished she rolls up the hide for easy transport back to camp. The downy undercoat and tough outer hair will be removed later at home.

The next task is to melt the enormous amount of fat taken from the beast. Later the women pour the fat into cleaned intestines and other pouches they brought from home. Finally when the meat is dry, which could take days, the women pack for the long trip home. It is also their job to carry everything back. The family will eat well this winter.

Activity:
The Lesson of the Legend

TEACHER NOTES *and* INFO

This is an activity that explores legends as a primary source. You might want to read some other legends and just enjoy them together and have discussions about the values that cultures hold and how a culture expresses these values. Read aloud the Iroquois legend "The Earth on Turtle's Back."

STUDENT ACTIVITY

After reading the legend, discuss with your students the following questions.
• What is a creation myth?
• What might you guess about the Iroquois people from reading this story?
• What are the things that they thought were important?
• What are the things that you think they cared about?
• What is being said about water and water creatures?

Make a response sheet to use with discussion/work groups. Students can complete it as they listen to this or another legend. This process helps students to identify the basic elements common to most legends.

ENTERTAINMENT	CREATION
What is entertaining about this legend?	What or who is being created?
VALUES/LESSONS What lesson is being taught? What values are evident in this legend?	**POWER** What or who is the source of power in this legend?

STUDENT HANDOUT - "The Earth on Turtle's Back"

The Earth on Turtle's Back

as told by Joseph Bruchac

Before this Earth existed, there was only water.

It stretched as far as one could see, and in that water there were birds and animals swimming around. Far above, in the clouds, there was a Skyland. In that Skyland there was a great and beautiful tree. It had four white roots, which stretched to each of the sacred directions, and from its branches all kinds of fruits and flowers grew.

There was an ancient chief in the Skyland. His young wife was expecting a child, and one night she dreamed that she saw the Great Tree uprooted. The next morning she told her husband the story. He nodded as she finished telling her dream. "My wife," he said, "I am sad that you had this dream. It is clearly a dream of great power and, as is our way, when one has such a powerful dream we must do all that we can to make it true. The Great Tree must be uprooted."

Then the ancient chief called the young men together and told them that they must pull up the tree. But the roots of the tree were so deep, so strong, that they could not budge it. At last the ancient chief himself came to the tree. He wrapped his arms around it, bent his knees and strained. With one great effort, he uprooted the tree and placed it on its side. Where the tree's roots had gone deep into the Skyland there was now a big hole. The wife of the chief came close and leaned over to look down, grasping the tip of one of the Great Tree's branches to steady her. It seemed as if she saw something down there, far below, glittering like water. She leaned out further to look and, as she leaned, she lost her balance and fell into the hole. Her hand slipped off the tip of the branch, leaving her with only a handful of seeds as she fell, down, down, down, down.

Far below, in the waters, some of the birds and animals looked up.

"Someone is falling toward us from the sky," said one of the birds.

"We must do something to help her," said another. Then two Swans flew up. They caught the Woman From The Sky between their wide wings. Slowly, they began to bring her down toward the water, where the birds and animals were watching.

"She is not like us," said one of the animals. "Look, she doesn't have webbed feet. I don't think she can live in the water."

"What shall we do, then?" said another of the water animals.

"I know," said one of the water birds. "I have heard that there is Earth far below the waters. If we dive down and bring up Earth, then she will have a place to stand."

So the birds and animals decided that someone would have to bring up Earth. One by one they tried.

The Duck dove down first, some say. He swam down and down, far beneath the surface, but could not reach the bottom and floated back up. Then the Beaver tried. He went even deeper, so deep that it was all dark, but he could not reach the bottom, either. The Loon tried, swimming with his strong wings. He was gone a long, long time, but he, too, failed to bring up Earth. Soon it seemed that all had tried and all had failed. Then a small voice spoke. "I will bring up Earth or die trying."

They looked to see who it was. It was the tiny Muskrat. She dove down and swam and swam. She was not as strong or as swift as the others, but she was determined.

She went so deep that it was all dark, and still she swam deeper. She went so deep that her lungs felt ready to burst, but she swam deeper still. At last, just as she was becoming unconscious, she reached out one small paw and grasped at the bottom, barely touching it before she floated up, almost dead.

When the other animals saw her break the surface they thought she had failed. Then they saw her right paw was held tightly shut.

"She has the Earth," they said. "Now where can we put it?"

"Place it on my back," said a deep voice. It was the Great Turtle, who had come up from the depths.

They brought the Muskrat over to the Great Turtle and placed her paw against his back. To this day there are marks on the back of the Turtle's shell, which were made by Muskrat's paw. The tiny bit of Earth fell on the back of the Turtle. Almost immediately, it began to grow larger and larger and larger until it became the whole world.

Then the two Swans brought the Sky Woman down. She stepped onto the new Earth and opened her hand, letting the seeds fall onto the bare soil. From those seeds the trees and the grass sprang up. Life on Earth had begun.

Activity: **Trust and Trade**

TEACHER NOTES *and* **INFO**

This activity explores the traditional use of wampum in Iroquois culture.

Wampum was used by the Iroquois to commemorate an important event or mark an occasion or understanding. It was used as the historical record of the Iroquois people. Most often, it was a string or belt woven together with beads made from bones or shells. The pattern of shells would tell the story of the event or understanding.

When some group wanted to invite another group for an important meeting, they would send a string of wampum. It would give the word of both parties that they would live by the agreement. By giving wampum, the giver was making a promise that he was speaking the truth. One writer compares it to the way people swear on the Bible today.

Paul Wineman from the Albany State Museum said the person would "pick the belt up and the words came back out." In Iroquois culture, there was a person designated to be the "keeper of the wampum." The keeper would memorize the story of the belt. This person knew what the symbols meant and could "read" the story to the people.

The steel tools of the Europeans meant that wampum could be made more quickly, and it was used more often, sometimes to seal treaties between Europeans and Native Americans. Europeans, in their dealings with the Native people, used wampum as a kind of currency. But Europeans misunderstood the true meaning of wampum. It was never regarded as money by the Native Americans.

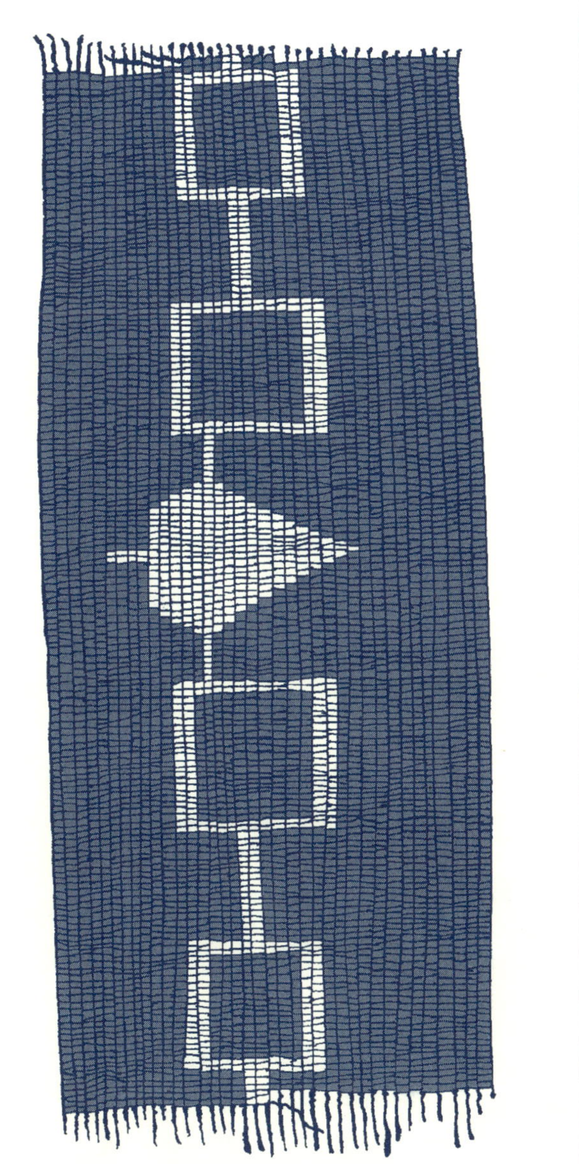

This is an artist's rendition of an Iroquois wampum, the Hiawatha Belt, which symbolizes the formation of the League. The center pine tree represents the League; the joined rectangles symbolize the several nations.

STUDENT ACTIVITY

Summarize the use of wampum and the traditions surrounding it and discuss the European misunderstanding of wampum.

Discuss the following questions:
- How are agreements developed between **nations** today?
- How are these agreements sealed?
- How are these agreements broken?

- How are agreements developed between **individuals** today?
- How are these agreements sealed?
- How are these agreements broken?

- In friendships, how do you know that you can trust someone?
- When is it important to keep your word?

As a class or individually, design a symbol or code that communicates that you will keep your word. Decorate as a shield or emblem or stamp.

Note: Students are not being asked to imitate wampum, which is a sacred tradition to the Iroquois. The purpose of this activity is to understand the concept of trust and to design something that represents that trust to others.

European Settlement
1609-1775

QUESTIONS

- What kind of folks made their way through the "wilds" to settle here?
- What was life like for them?
- Why did people come to live in this region?
- What kinds of tools and skills did they need for survival?
- What things did they learn from Native Americans to survive?
- How did whites change life on the lake?
- How did European settlement affect Native Americans?

KEY RESOURCES

- Otter Creek: The Indian Road *by James E. Petersen*
- Dawnland Encounters: Indians and Europeans in Northern New England *by Colin G. Calloway*
- Crown Point Historic Site—*field trip and educational resources*
- The Fall of Quebec and the French and Indian War *by George Ochoa*
- The French Occupation of the Champlain Valley from 1609 to 1759 *by Guy O. Coolidge*
- Peter Kalm's Travels into North America *by Peter Kalm*
- Western Abenaki, 1600–1800 *by Colin G. Calloway*
- Voyages of Samuel de Champlain, 1604–1618 *journals edited by W.L. Grant*
- Life in Acadia *by Rosemary Neering and Stan Garrod*

European Settlement 1609-1775

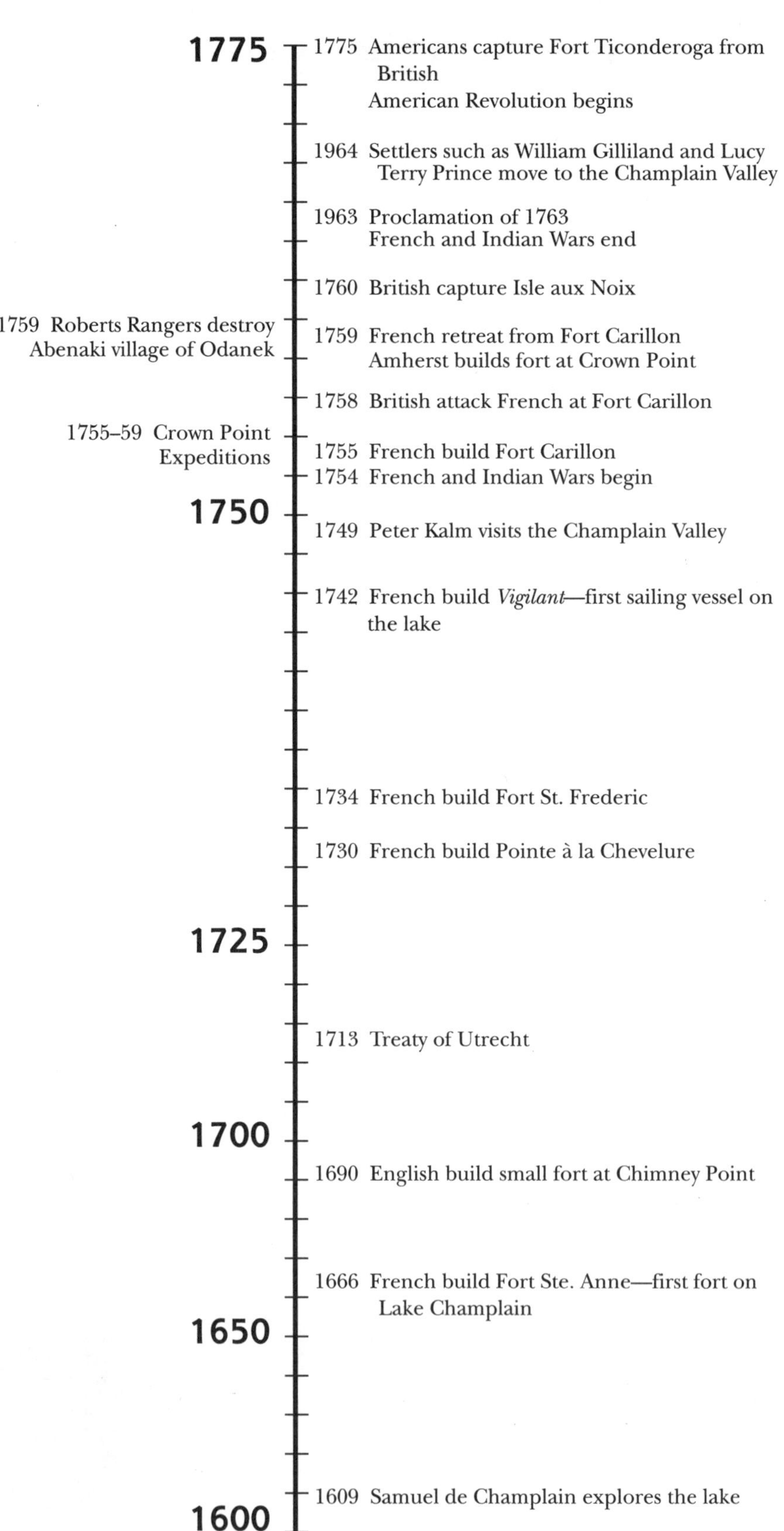

Activity: **Powder Horns**

TEACHER NOTES *and* INFO

If you had a musket, you needed a powder horn to carry gunpowder. The horns of bulls, cows and oxen were readily available—tough, lightweight, and sparkproof. They were unaffected by heat or cold, waterproof and, because of their shape, would float if dropped in water.

To make a powder horn, the owner would:
• boil it in water to soften it,
• clean out the inside,
• cut off parts of both ends,
• bore a hole in the closed end,
• boil it again,
• scrape one or two raised rings to hold the strap,
• scrape all of horn until smooth,
• make a wood plug for the base of the horn,
• seal the plug with beeswax,
• make a small wooden stopper for the small end,
• use a knife and a needle to decorate the horn.

Powder horns were engraved in two basic ways: with a map or with the owner's name and a location. Map horns can show the owner's home area or someplace the owner traveled. Name/location horns have the owner's name and pictures about the place where it was made, e.g. an outline of a fort, a deer or a fishing scene. Powder horns were never mass produced, so each one was different. The powder horn thus tells clues about its owner. Encourage students to include drawings that mean something to them personally.

STUDENT ACTIVITY

Share the information about how powder horns were made. Discuss the different things they could draw on their powder horns. Students might want to jot down some ideas first. Give each student the handout, "Paper Powder Horn Outline," when they are ready to make a final draft.

STUDENT HANDOUT - "Paper Powder Horn Outline"

Powder horns were collected by the army and filled with gunpowder, then returned to their owners. Soldiers had to mark their horns to identify them as theirs. It became stylish to make designs on powder horns.

Note: *Tim Titus notes that the engraving of powder horns is not scrimshaw. Scrimshaw appeared after the Revolution and was confined to nautical topics.*

Using a real horn is not advisable!

Credit: *Activity adapted with permission from "Crown Point and Its Powder Horns in the 1700s" by Tim Titus.*

Paper Powder Horn Outline

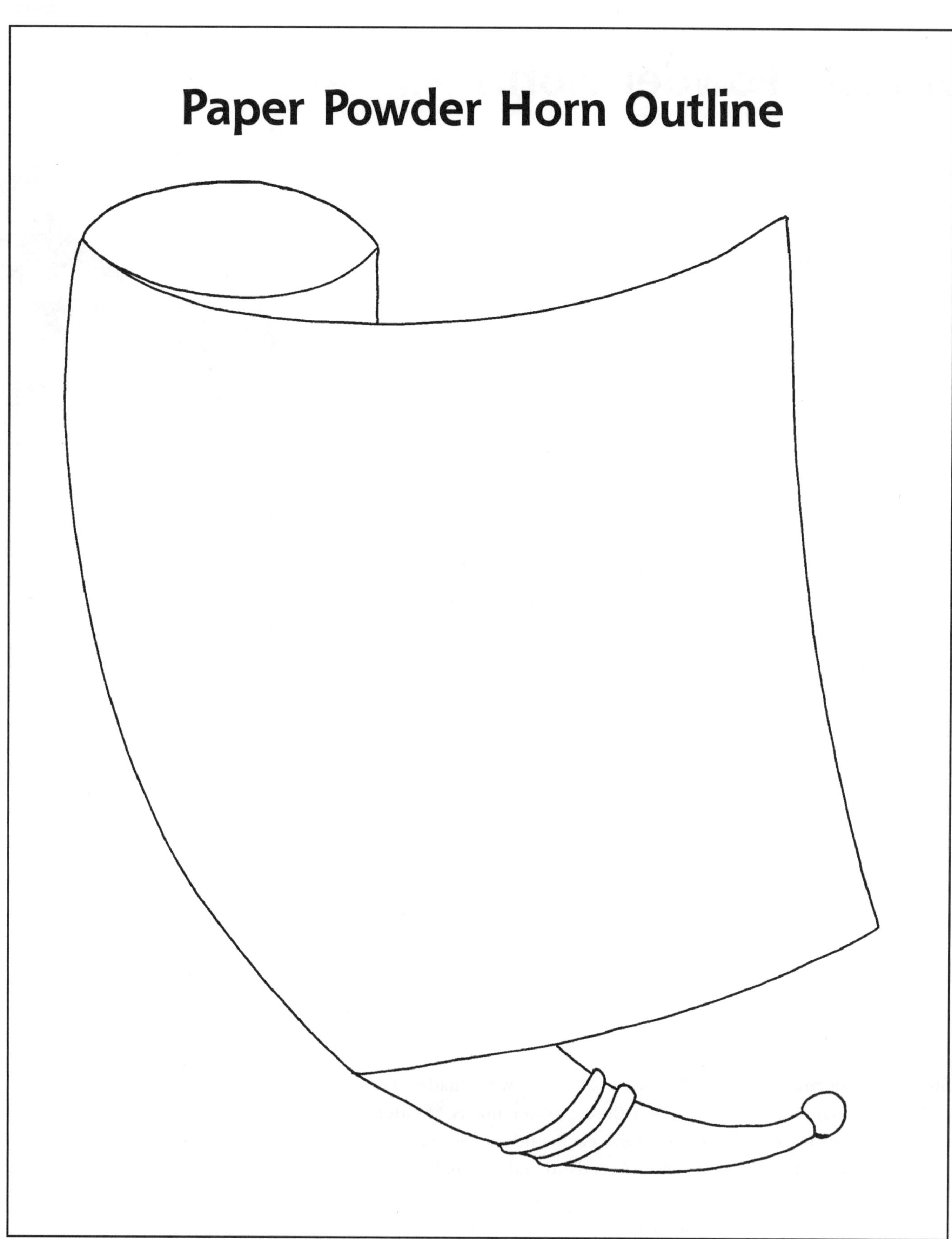

Activity: Expressing Your Point of View

arrowhead

TEACHER NOTES *and* INFO

"Since the Beginning of Time" is the speech that an Abenaki delivered to the Governor of Quebec at the north end of Lake Champlain, September 8, 1766. There was a meeting to settle boundaries between Quebec and New York and Native Americans were there to settle their disputes. The speech and the book it comes from, DAWNLAND ENCOUNTERS, are a fascinating and poignant telling of the efforts of the Abenaki people to hold claim to their land in the face of European intrusion.

STUDENT ACTIVITY

Share with the class the speech, "Since the Beginning of Time." Discuss with the class the point of view expressed in the speech. What concessions had the Native Americans already granted? How had things changed? What did the speaker want? It is important that students note that 150 years after contact with the Europeans, Native Americans spoke in a voice that demanded respect and an explanation for the unauthorized use of their land.

Contrast this to the point of view of the Europeans. Discuss all the things that Europeans had done on the assumption that the land was theirs to claim. It might be helpful to make separate listings on newsprint of events and attitudes of both sides. Note that all Native Americans didn't feel one way and all Europeans another way. History is never that simple. Although the two world views were different and this meeting illustrates a significant conflict in American history, the issue should not be oversimplified.

Divide the class into two groups (Native Americans and Europeans) and give each side one of the lists of events and attitudes.

First, ask the students to decide who they are in the group.
Possibilities if Native American: chief, chief's family, chief's council of advisors.
Possibilities if European: French Governor, Council of Advisors, mill builders, members of navy.

Ask students to imagine a parcel of land that they are familar with. The enactment could start with a portrayal of how Native Americans had used this land for hundreds of years. Then ask them to enact the scene when the first agreement was made.

Suggest that the scene begin with the French scouting out the land, deciding it is well-suited to their needs and approaching Native Americans with a proposal. The scene would conclude with an agreement drawn between French and Native Americans. After the improvisation, ask students what parts could be more historically accurate. Then replay with suggestions. Next, tell them that 18 years have passed and the Europeans have come to rebuild and expand the mill. The Native Americans catch wind of their plans and call a meeting. Impassioned speeches from both sides follow.

If a conclusion is reached, end with that and hold a class discussion on what students think about the solution. If the group cannot reach a conclusion, bring the scene to a close and discuss why both sides were unable to find a solution.

STUDENT HANDOUT - "Since the Beginning of Time"

Since the Beginning of Time

B rother

We the Misiskoui Indians of the St. Francis or Abenaki Tribe have inhabited that part of Lake Champlain known by the name of Misiskoui [since a] time unknown to any of us here present, without being molested or any one's claiming right to it, to our knowledge, except about eighteen years ago, the French Governor Mr. Vaudreuil and Intendant came there, and viewed a spot convenient for a saw-mill to facilitate the building of vessels and bateaux at St. Johns, as well as for the use of the navy at Quebec; and on the occasion convened our people to ask this approbation, when they consented and marked out a spot large enough for that purpose, as well as for the cutting of the saw timbers, about half a league square, with the condition to have what boards they wanted for their use gratis. But at the commencement of last war, said mill was deserted, and the iron work buried; after which we expected every thing of the kind would subside. But soon after peace was made, some English people came there to rebuild the mill, and now claim three leagues in breadth and six in depth, which takes in our village and plantations by far. We therefore request of you, brother, to enquire into this affair, that we obtain justice as it is of great concern to us.

Activity: **Sequencing a Story**

TEACHER NOTES *and* **INFO**

Read the story of Hocquart with your class. It is helpful for students to have a copy of the story as you read.

STUDENT ACTIVITY

After you read the story, talk about what it was like for children to settle in New France in the 1700s. What jobs did they have to do? What tools did they use? What skills did they use? What did they know that children today would not know?

Hand out the sequencing sheet. In pairs, have students rearrange the events in the story according to the order in which they actually happened. When they get the order checked against the answer sheet, they can fasten the events on construction paper with glue.

STUDENT HANDOUTS - "Hocquart" and "Cut and Arrange"

Other Ideas
• *Use the events as captions and, individually or as a group, draw the scenes of the story.*

Note: *Monsieur LaFleur built the homes at Hocquart **before** Marcel took the journey down Lake Champlain and Marcel traveled on the Richelieu River **before** he got to the main lake.*

Artwork by Chris Sweeney, Grade 5, School Street School, Milton, Vermont

Cut and Arrange in Correct Sequence
Check with teacher before you glue!

A. Pierre laughs at the bear.

B. Marcel and Pierre carry buckets of water to their pumpkin patch.

C. Maman screams "Mon Dieu."

D. Monsieur LaFleur and others build homes and name settlement Hocquart.

E. A bear sticks its head in the LaFleur cabin.

F. Marcel rides in Lake Champlain with his family to a new home.

G. Marcel and Pierre clean up damage caused by the bear.

H. Maman, Marcel and Pierre scramble up into the loft.

I. The bear burns itself on the hot samp.

J. Marcel and Pierre smell the maple syrup cooking.

K. The bear and cubs leave the cabin.

L. The LaFleur family paddles the canoe down the Richelieu River.

M. Marcel wonders whether the animals have the same feelings as people. END

N. Marcel unpacks supplies: horn cups, wooden plates and blankets.

O. The LaFleur family arrives by canoe at Hocquart.

P. The bear enters the cabin with two cubs.

Q. The bear shows its angry, pained expression to the boys in the loft.

Answers: D, L, F, O, N, B, J, E, P, C, H, I, A, Q, K, G, M

Hocquart

by Elise Guyette

Marcel was so excited he couldn't even talk. He sat in the middle of the dugout canoe that was gliding along Lake Champlain and stared at the thick forests on either side. His brother, Pierre, sat near him, while Maman and Papa paddled the canoe. After days of paddling first down the Richelieu River and then the lake, nights of camping in the woods and eating meals filled with wood ashes, they were finally near their new home.

Marcel's papa (Monsieur LaFleur) and some other men had come to this part of New France from Montreal a year ago to build their homes. They had picked a place near the stockade in case they needed help against the English or their Indian allies. The seigneur who owned the land had given them cornmeal and tools to help them get started. They built several cabins and a small church and called their settlement Hocquart.

"I can't wait to see everything," Marcel said. It was hard for him to contain his excitement after being forced to sit still for so long. After what seemed like forever, the LaFleurs' canoe angled toward the shore.

 "This must be it!" Pierre cried. The thrill in his voice matched Marcel's mood. As soon as the canoe beached on the crescent-shaped shore, he and Pierre ran up the steep bank. In a small clearing stood a small cabin. Behind the cabin was a forest of huge trees. It was so dark that Marcel could not see beyond the first few trees.

As he helped unload the canoe, Marcel wondered where the Indians lived. They had taught Papa how to grow beans, corn and pumpkins. Papa had said that many Indians had visited him during the winter he lived here alone. Papa said they were friendly and he enjoyed their company.

Finally, Marcel got a glimpse of the inside of the cabin. There was no door—just an old blanket covering the opening. Inside was one room with a loft up above. The big fireplace would easily keep the cabin warm in the winter. A large table stood in the middle of the room with wooden benches on both sides. A rope bed stood at the right. Underneath was a trundle bed, which would be pulled out at night for the boys. Marcel helped unpack horn cups, wooden plates and blankets. Once settled, his family would begin planting crops, gathering berries and roots, and drying meat for winter.

One evening, Marcel and Pierre were carrying buckets of water to their pumpkin patch when they smelled a kettle of samp (porridge) cooking. Marcel was tired of eating samp and fish all the time. He longed for a cup of milk, but no farm animals could survive in the grass-less forest. He hoped Papa would come back from hunting with a rabbit. Rabbit stew would be delicious. As they started back to the cabin, they smelled a new aroma.

"Smell that," Marcel said, inhaling.

"Mmmm, smells like maple sugar. Maman must be sick of the plain old mush, too," Pierre answered.

They went inside and saw their maman setting the boiling samp aside to cool. At that moment, they heard a strange noise outside. Their senses had already become attuned to the everyday sounds and smells of the forest in which they lived. But this sound and smell were different. Their bodies automatically went on alert.

In the next instant, the blanket covering the doorway moved aside and a bear stuck her head in.

"Mon Dieu!" Maman cried. The boys opened their mouths in silent cries of alarm, not knowing what to do. "Quickly, up in the loft," said Maman, pushing the boys toward the ladder. All three scrambled up, and maman pulled up the ladder after her. From above, they watched the bear enter with two cubs and go straight for the samp.

"She smelled the sugar too," whispered Marcel. The bear picked up the kettle and drank some of the scalding samp. She immediately let out a roar and threw down the kettle. Her paws went into her mouth as if she were trying to get the samp out.

Pierre started laughing. When the bear heard him, she angrily tried to reach them in the loft. Pierre instantly quieted and they all shrank back as far as they could. Marcel felt the blood drain from his head as he looked into the pained and angry eyes of the bear. He prayed to God to send the bear back into the forest.

After a few minutes of watching the bear flail at the loft and toss the tables and benches around, Marcel's muscles were so tense they were almost paralyzed. Finally, the bear gave one last roar and left the cabin, her cubs trailing behind.

Silence filled the cabin. Marcel's muscles began to relax, and he became aware of his heart pumping furiously and blood surging to his head. Never had he been so scared. After a few minutes, they were all breathing easier, and Maman hugged the boys to her. "Thank God we're safe," she whispered.

"You're so dumb to laugh at the bear," Marcel said to Pierre when he found his voice again.

"How was I supposed to know the bear would get mad?" protested Pierre.

"This is no time to argue," said Maman, setting down the ladder, "We've got to clean this place up."
They climbed down to start the chore, still shaky from the encounter. Marcel couldn't get the look in the bear's eyes out of his mind. He thought that animals must have the same feelings that people do.

Credit: *VERMONT: A CULTURAL PATCHWORK by Elise Guyette.*
Based on a true occurrence in Vermont. Used with permission.

American Revolution
1775-1783

QUESTIONS

- How important was the Champlain Valley in the American Revolution? Why?
- What was it like for soldiers who fought?
- What was it like for the people living in the basin who were not fighting in the war?

KEY RESOURCES

- Rabble in Arms *by Kenneth Roberts (abridged version available from the Lake Champlain Maritime Museum)*
- The Gunboat Philadelphia and the Defense of Lake Champlain in 1776 *by Philip K. Lundeberg*
- Lake Champlain Maritime Museum—*field trip and educational resources*

Word Bank

Ann Story
Benedict Arnold
brig
caisson
cannon
Chambly
Crown Point
Ethan Allen
Ferris Bay (Arnold's Bay)
fort
Fort Ticonderoga
frigate
galley
garrison
Gen. Horatio Gates
Gen. Guy Carleton
Gen. Philip Schuyler
Gen. Richard Montgomery
"The Green Mountain Boys"
gunboat
hard tack
hotshot
Ira Allen
militia
Mt. Defiance
Mount Independence
Onion River
Peter Ferris
Philadelphia
Philip Skene
radeau
rigging
rowboat
scow
scurvy
Skenesborough (Whitehall)
smallpox
St. Johns, Quebec
Valcour Island
William Gilliland

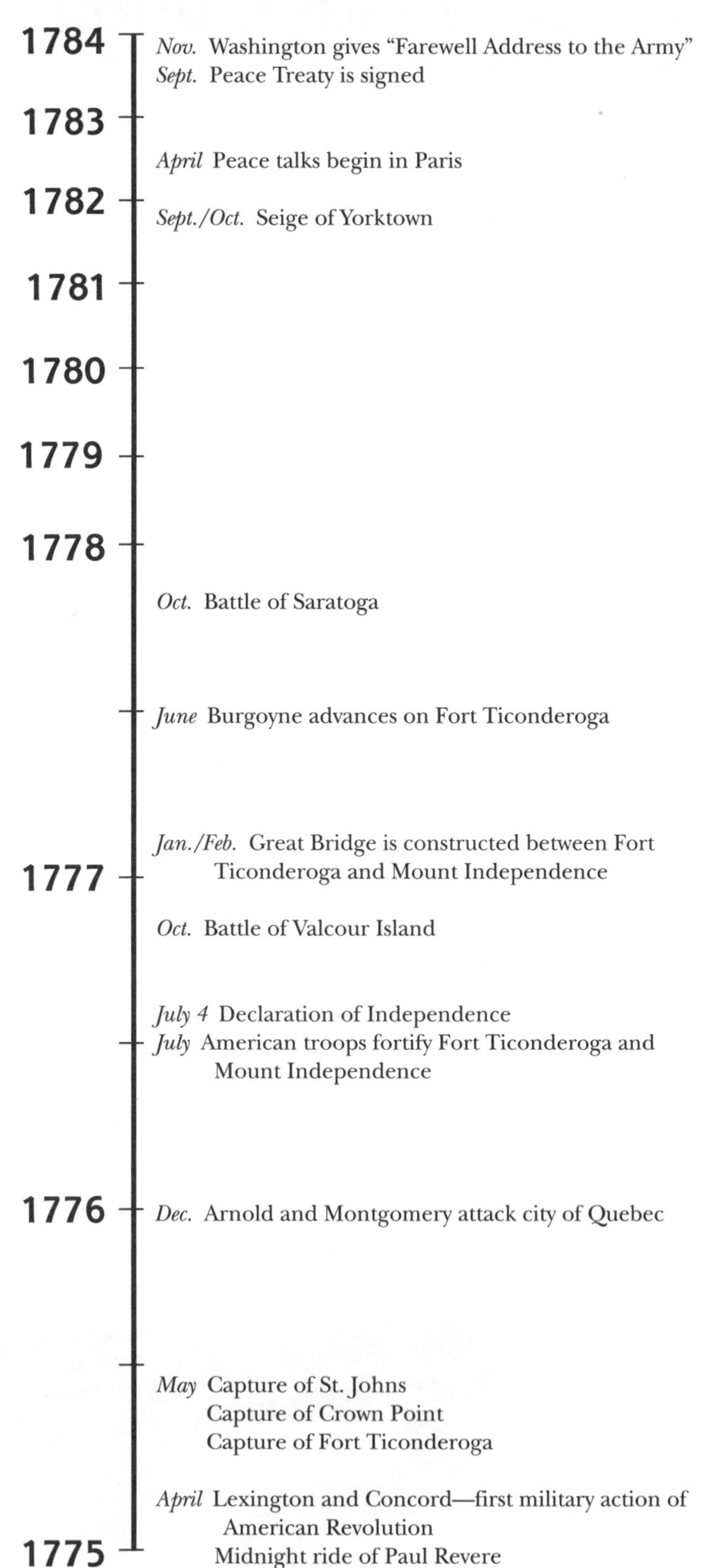

Activity: **Mount Independence**

TEACHER NOTES *and* INFO

Mount Independence was a very important encampment during the American Revolution. Over the years, there has been much interest in the site, spurred by citizens' groups, archeological research and most recently, Don Wickman's master's thesis: "Built with Spirit, Deserted in Darkness. The American Occupation of Mount Independence, 1776–1777." In the summer of 1996, the state of Vermont opened a new visitor's center and the site is much more accessible to the public. It is a wonderful place to visit with students and is relatively untouched—with barely a trace of the frenzied activity during the winter of 1776. The students are forced to imagine what took place and as my teammate Mary Dupont said, "the site is a living memorial to the spirits of the soldiers who lived there. The air was almost heavy with their presence." Before we visited the site, we did this activity. It is a helpful way to learn about soldiers' lives with or without a visit to Mount Independence.

Don Wickman

STUDENT ACTIVITY

Read the article with the students. Most of Wickman's research was based on journals written by people who were there. He provided this summary article and the quotes for THIS LAKE ALIVE! Discuss how historians find out information about the past. Although primary sources give specific information that can be verified, often journals provide material that the historian has to use to make an educated guess as to what the human experience was.

Assign small groups. Give each group three or four quotes to interpret from the collection of quotes in this activity. Students should work together to interpret the quotes and then determine what they can feel certain took place and what they can infer. After the interpretation is complete, ask each group to present their understanding of one quote that they liked best. Although we just asked the groups to tell us about the quotes, there are many possibilities for creative interpretation.

Note: Spelling in "Quotes from Mount Independence" is from journals as read by Don Wickman.

STUDENT HANDOUTS - "The Story of Mount Independence," "Quotes from Mount Independence" and "Mount Independence Research"

The Story of Mount Independence

by Donald Wickman

In July 1776, the demoralized and disease-ravaged American Northern Army straggled into Ticonderoga. It was their final stop on the retreat from the failed invasion of Canada. The American generals chose Ticonderoga because of its strategic location. The fort guarded the portage from Lake George and commanded the narrow channel of Lake Champlain. However, the old, crumbling fort had a weakness: the strongest walls faced in the wrong direction; they were not designed to face a threat from the north.

The Americans looked for a new site. Across the lake was a high plateau surrounded on three sides by water. It was called East Point. It jutted northwards into the lake and provided a lookout over Ticonderoga. Three brigades moved from Ticonderoga to begin carving encampments out of the "howling wilderness."

At this time, six thousand men were at the forts. Most of the men were infantry with several companies of artillery. After the first three months of work, the appearance of East Point had changed drastically. At the northern point an extensive water battery guarded the channel. Protecting the rear of that battery, men constructed a horseshoe-shaped fortification which stood higher than Ticonderoga. A log-and-stone breastwork protected the one-and-a-half mile land perimeter. On the point's highest elevation, work had begun on a wooden picket fort set in the configuration of an eight-pointed star. It would shelter eight barrack buildings. All this construction was accomplished by a disease-ridden garrison in a summer when it rained one third of the time. The feet of thousands of men churned up the heavy clay soil.

East Point was named Mount Independence when Congress adopted the Declaration of Independence on July 4, 1776. Other places in the area were also named after the patriotic values of the times: Mt. Defiance, Liberty Hill, and Mt. Hope.

The encampments on Mount Independence were like orderly small cities. Camps were laid out in formal arrangements, with the housing consisting of tents and wooden and brush huts. Some of the senior officers had framed houses. Men were assigned daily tasks about camp involving guard duty, participating in work or fatigue parties, plus regimental drill. Each day men were issued standard rations for their meals: fresh or salted meats and an allowance of flour. There was a serious shortage of vegetables in the diet. Added treats could be purchased through the sutlers, the men who gave out provisions from the army.

Between the bland diet, poor food handling practices, fetid living conditions, the rains and subsequent stagnating puddles of water, Mount Independence served as an incubator of disease. Though the first outbreaks of illness began in August, they came to a deadly head in September. Smallpox had been purged, but replacement germs surged through the ranks, striking enlisted man and officer alike. Malaria, typhoid, typhus and dysentery incapacitated many. So intense grew the wave of disease that the total of sick men at Mount Independence and Ticonderoga ballooned from 1,878 on the twenty-fourth of August to over 4,000 thirty days later.

The number of healthy soldiers was barely enough to man the extensive lines. Only American control of Lake Champlain prevented a British advance from Canada. By mid-October the scourge of disease had subsided. Frosts had eliminated the malaria-bearing mosquitoes, the most debilitated soldiers were discharged and the supply and quality of food improved. By the time the British were able to advance on Mount Independence and Ticonderoga in late October, they discovered a numerically superior American army lodged behind intimidating earthworks fortified with artillery. Being both outnumbered and threatened with the onset of colder weather, British General Guy Carleton made the fateful decision to withdraw. The attack against the Champlain Valley forts would have to be postponed until the following spring. The 1776 campaign in the north closed with the British navy masters of the lake, but with the path towards Albany still barricaded by the American fortifications at Mount Independence and Ticonderoga.

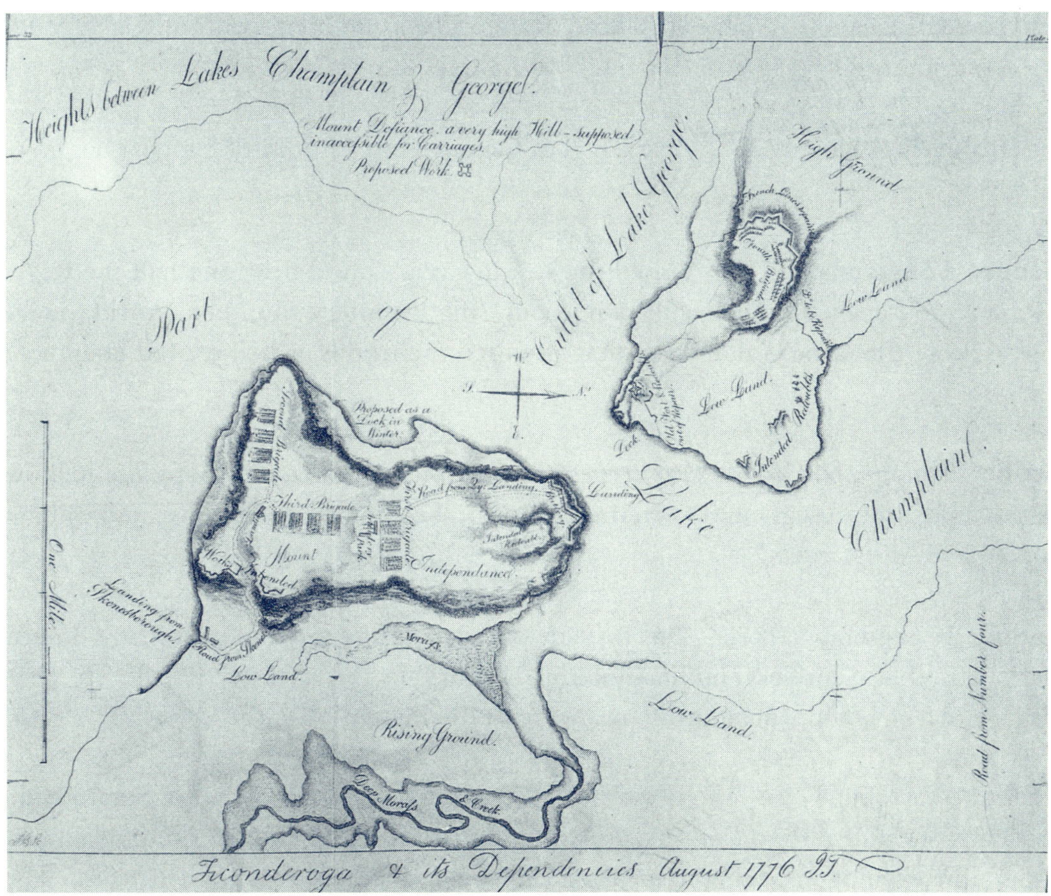

Quotes from Mount Independence

Anthony Wayne: 23 August 1776 - "[Ticonderoga region] appears to be the last part of the world that God made & I have some ground to believe it was finished in the dark—that it was never In-tended that man shou'd live in it is clear—for the people who attempted to make any stay—have for the most part perished by pestilence or the sword.

"I believe it to be the Ancient Golgatha or place of Skulls—they are so plenty here that our people for want of Other Vessels drink out of them whilst the soldiers make tent pins of the shin and thigh bones of Ambercrumbies men—"

Benjamin Beal: 18 July 1776 - "Lt. Thayer is gone a fishing this afternoon & I hope he will get many fish We have nothing but Pork & beans"

Benjamin Beal: 24 July 1776 - "We have had no fresh meat this 40 days"

Timothy Tuttle: 30 July 1776 - "we had a Potpy & a Large wheat suit Pudding, I Believe Nigh a Pecke, it had to be Almost all Day & when it was Done I could not Eat But Little it was so Homespun"

Samuel Kennedy: 10 August 1776 - "The army, both officers and men, continue sickly of Putrid, Nervous, Bilious intermitting & remitting fevers with fluxes &c. &c."

Timothy Tuttle: 11 August 1776 - "a man Dy'd in Camp was sick But Little time he has gone the way of that all Living Must go"

Lewis Beebe: 1 September 1776 - "Visited the sick in camp, found near one half the Regt. unfit for duty, and many whose situation was truly dangerous. the dysentery, Jaundice, Putrid, intermitting & Bilious fevers, were the prinicipal diseases that attended the troops, which proved fatal in a variety of instances."

Lewis Beebe: 5 September 1776 - "Our army, especially the Continental Troops, are half unfit for Duty: the small pox, the fatiegue has worn them out, and brot many to the grave, and will many more unless immediately discharged."

Lewis Beebe: 19 September 1776 - "Our Brigade paraded at ten in the morning, was entertained with a lifeless, tasteless, Senseless and inanimating discourse by the revd. Mr. Porter. However as he had the badge of a chaplain, I shall say no more about the matter."

Lewis Beebe: 2 October 1776 - "In the afternoon was visited by Mr. Brick, Capt. Stanton, and Lieut. Claghorn: had a Sociable dish of Conversation, after we had drank together and took leave of each other. I spent the evening in writing to my friends."

Benjamin Beal: 3 August 1776 - "pleasant....We had a piece of rost Beef a good pudding for dinner"

Benjamin Beal: 4 September 1776 - "our regiment sick with fever and ague"

Benjamin Beal: 29 September 1776 - "sunday stormy...We spent our day in reading and talking of our folks that were dresssed up and going to meeting"

Ammi Robbins: 8 September 1776 - "Our regiment in a most miserable condition, I could wish they were all dismissed. Visited this day tent by tent and could not pass one single tent among the soldiers wherein there were not one or more sick...."

Ammi Robbins: 10 September 1776 - "The groans of the distressed in the camp are real affecting... Not fifty men really fit for duty"

Ammi Robbins: 29 September 1776 - "Was rosed last night by a violent shower—the roof leaked and it poured in upon our bed."

Persifor Frazer: 21 September 1776 - "I have a very severe spell of the flux and bilious fever. It had reduced me very low and weak. I thank God I am in as good spirits as ever tho very much reduced in flesh.

"2 or 3 of the Yankee colonels have died lately—more of them are sick; indeed the most of them look like specters."

Samuel Wigglesworth: 27 September 1776 - "Nearly half this regiment is entirely incapable of any service, some dying almost every day.

"...It would make a heart of stone melt to hear the moans and see the distress of the sick and dying."

Jonathan Burton: 2 October 1776 - "I took my walk out of camp for my health as at other times when off duty."

Ammi Robbins: 22 September 1776 - "Attended divine service on the parade ground—a convenient place built up for me, the whole brigade under arms attended, and great number of other officers and spectators. I preached from Daniel v, 23, with great freedom and plainness. A very attentive audience; was hoarse and some exhausted after I got through. The officers and soldiers observed the Sabbath in such a manner that it seemed more like a Sabbath-day than any I have seen in the army. Met at evening, at which I proposed to amend and reform the singing which had a good effect. Prayed, sang, and dismissed."

Mount Independence Research

Group Members: _____________________

____

____

____

FACT	GUESS
Interpret the quote and write what you **know**, or are quite certain to be true.	Interpret the quote and write what you **think** might be true about what the soldiers thought, believed or had to deal with.

Activity:
Hero: Benedict Arnold

Benedict Arnold

TEACHER NOTES *and* INFO

Benedict Arnold is a controversial figure in American history. Most textbooks only refer to him as a traitor and disregard his illustrious career on Lake Champlain.

STUDENT ACTIVITY

Read the short biography with your students. After you have finished, have a discussion with your class.

- What events helped Benedict Arnold be a hero?
- Do you think he was a hero?
- What events led to his "fall from grace?"
- Explain why you think this happened.
- What parts were Arnold's doings and what parts were events or government?
- Discuss Arnold's place in history. What do you think it should be?
- Who are our heroes today?
- Do we have any fallen heroes?

Write a thinkbook entry about:
- Benedict Arnold's place in history.
- What makes a hero.
- Nominate someone you know/respect as "Hero of the Year."

STUDENT HANDOUT - "Benedict Arnold"

Note: *If you want to read more about this interesting character, try THE MAN IN THE MIRROR by Clare Brandt or BENEDICT ARNOLD: PATRIOT OR TRAITOR by Willard Sterne Randall.*

Benedict Arnold

Benedict Arnold was born in the colony of Connecticut in 1741. At age 14, he ran away from home to join the British troops fighting in the French and Indian War. He served in the Lake Champlain area. When the glory of a soldier's life faded, he deserted the army and returned home. He became a merchant and joined the Connecticut militia.

At the beginning of the Revolutionary War, Arnold was sent to Vermont to lead the attack on Ft. Ticonderoga with Ethan Allen. The two men argued about who was in charge. More credit went to Allen although Arnold had an official command. After the capture of the fort, Arnold set up headquarters at Crown Point and planned to attack Canada. On a schooner he renamed the *Liberty,* Arnold sailed to St. Johns and captured a second vessel, which he renamed the *Enterprise.*

Throughout Arnold's military career, he had a great deal of problems getting along with people. He always wanted to be in charge and he made enemies easily. Some military men doubted his reliability.

Because of these conflicts, Arnold was relieved of his command at Crown Point soon after his return from St. Johns. He still wanted to serve in the Army and went to see General Washington who put him in charge of an expedition through the Maine wilderness. The plan was for Montgomery to come up Lake Champlain to meet Arnold and capture the city of Quebec. Arnold's expedition was wrought with difficulties. Bateaux had been hastily built of green wood and didn't withstand the journey, men had to portage through ice-cold waters. Many of the supplies were damaged and one of Arnold's junior officers turned back with some of the provisions. Still, Arnold proved himself as a leader. His men, bedraggled and sick, were still willing to follow him into battle against the British in Quebec.

Arnold and his troops had to wait almost a month for Montgomery and were weakened by the cold; their morale was low. By the time the attack took place in a blinding snowstorm, it was doomed to fail. Montgomery was killed and Arnold badly wounded. Arnold led a lengthy retreat to Crown Point.

Once healed he oversaw the construction of a fleet of boats to meet a British invasion. In October, the little navy engaged a British fleet at the battle of Valcour Island. Arnold outwitted the British in a nighttime retreat and escaped down the lake. He was the hero of the day.

In 1777, Arnold was overlooked by the Continental Congress for a promotion. Arnold resigned from the Army. On the personal request of Washington, he returned and fought with great distinction against the British at Saratoga. There he was wounded, but not recognized for his brave deeds.

In 1780, after receiving the command of the American post at West Point, he made arrangements to surrender it to the British in exchange for a high rank in their army and a large sum of money. The plan was discovered before it went into action and Arnold fled to the safety of the British army. The following year he went to London and lived the rest of his life in England.

The War of 1812

QUESTIONS

- What events caused the War of 1812?
- What was the importance of the commerce established on Lake Champlain?
- Who was involved in smuggling and why?
- How were the issues and events similar to those of the American Revolution?

KEY RESOURCES

- The Eagle: An American Brig on Lake Champlain during the War of 1812 *by Kevin Crisman*
- The War of 1812 in the Champlain Valley *by Allan S. Everest*

War of 1812

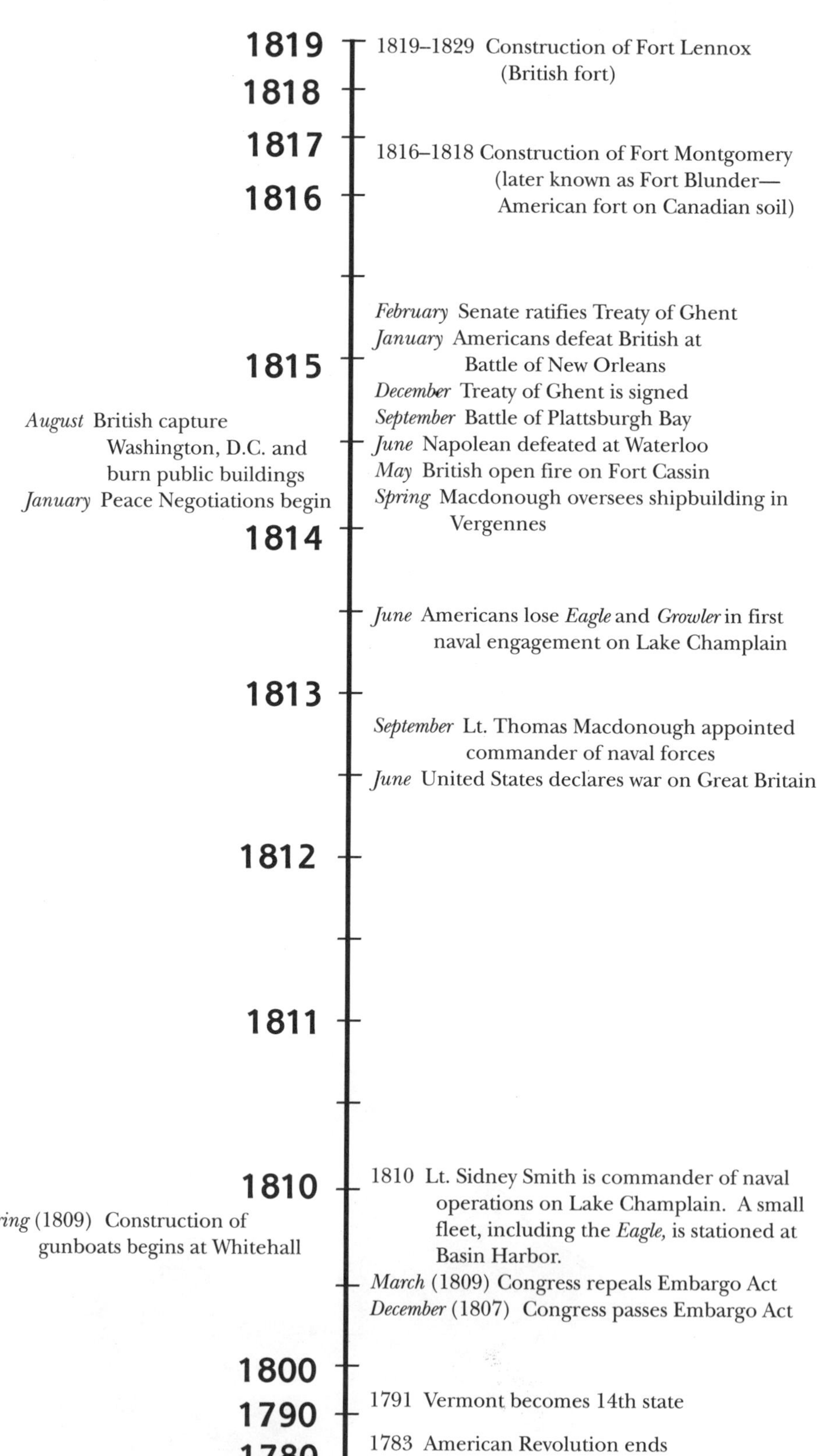

1819
1818
1817
1816
1815
1814
1813
1812
1811
1810
1800
1790
1780

1819–1829 Construction of Fort Lennox
(British fort)

1816–1818 Construction of Fort Montgomery
(later known as Fort Blunder—
American fort on Canadian soil)

February Senate ratifies Treaty of Ghent
January Americans defeat British at
Battle of New Orleans
December Treaty of Ghent is signed
September Battle of Plattsburgh Bay
June Napolean defeated at Waterloo
May British open fire on Fort Cassin
Spring Macdonough oversees shipbuilding in
Vergennes

August British capture
Washington, D.C. and
burn public buildings
January Peace Negotiations begin

June Americans lose *Eagle* and *Growler* in first
naval engagement on Lake Champlain

September Lt. Thomas Macdonough appointed
commander of naval forces
June United States declares war on Great Britain

1810 Lt. Sidney Smith is commander of naval
operations on Lake Champlain. A small
fleet, including the *Eagle*, is stationed at
Basin Harbor.
March (1809) Congress repeals Embargo Act
December (1807) Congress passes Embargo Act

Spring (1809) Construction of
gunboats begins at Whitehall

1791 Vermont becomes 14th state
1783 American Revolution ends

Activity: **Comparing Wars**

TEACHER NOTES *and* **INFO**

Historians often say that the War of 1812 was just a continuation of unresolved issues from the American Revolution.

STUDENT ACTIVITY

Discuss the above idea with your students.

• What were some general issues that were the same? (*Issues of independence, "not wanting to be pushed around," tariff and taxation.*)

• How old was the United States of America in 1812? (*It was an adolescent! There's food for a good discussion here about adolescence and independence. The United States, only 34 years old, hadn't "proved itself" to its "parent," Great Britain. The issues of seizure of ships and impressment must have been strongly felt by those who had recently fought in the Revolution.*)

• What do we know about the two presidents at the time? (*Both were signers of the Declaration of Independence, intellectual leaders of the American Revolution, ardent patriots and committed to the economic autonomy of U.S. business interests.*)

• What are some similarities between what happened on Lake Champlain in 1812 and in 1776? What issues can we recognize as similar? What events are similar? (*A furious shipbuilding race took place between both sides. America was once again fighting against a powerful British army. MacDonough, like Arnold, picked his site in a bay in order to face the British. The American victory on the lake led to the final victory of the war elsewhere.*)

Close your discussion with a writing activity in the thinkbook. Two possible assignments could be:

• compare 1776 and 1812

• compose a letter from Thomas Jefferson about why we should fight Britain. Title the letter, "It's Time We Grew Up."

Activity: **The Black Snake**

TEACHER NOTES *and* INFO

This is a story about an event known as "The Black Snake Affair." It shows that Vermonters were of different minds about their loyalty to the United States. Read "The Black Snake Affair" with your students.

STUDENT ACTIVITY

Discuss some of the questions raised by the essay.

• Vermont was 17 years old in 1808. How might this have affected people's loyalty?

• What is meant by a "faraway government?" Are there any issues today involving state's rights?

• How did people express loyalty and patriotism in the 1800s? How do people express these today?

• What do you think about the judicial system as portrayed in the essay and what do you think about capital punishment in this setting?

STUDENT HANDOUT - "The Black Snake Affair"

Other Ideas
• Simulate a courtroom where students have to argue for or against the innocence of Cyrus Dean.

The Black Snake Affair

Around noon on August 4, 1808, a party of soldiers rowed from Lake Champlain into the mouth of the Winooski River. Their eyes scanned the shoreline. These 12 men were members of the state militia. They were led by Daniel Farrington of Brandon. The soldiers were looking for the *Black Snake,* a 40-foot, single-masted boat, known up and down the lake for smuggling potash to Canada. It was called the *Black Snake* because its hull was painted with black tar. (Some say this kept it from being spotted at night.) Its captain, Truman Mudgett of Highgate, was equally famous.

A year before, President Thomas Jefferson had passed the Embargo Act. It made trade with England and Canada against the law. People were angry. Their business was cut off and the potash trade forbidden. They saw no reason to let the faraway United States Government tell them what to do. "If we can't trade lawfully," they said, "we'll turn to smuggling." So, by boat and by pack horse, they carried potash to Canada and exchanged it for cash or store goods. From Canada the potash went to England.

Many Vermonters thought that smugglers were heroes. They turned a blind eye to the smugglers' lawbreaking. Others felt that the United States Government and the president should be obeyed. They said that the smugglers were traitors for selling to England.

The United States Government sent customs agents and militia to patrol the border. This is why Lieutenant Farrington and his men were on patrol that day. Just ahead of them by the shore, they spotted the *Black Snake.* She was unguarded. They took her in tow. Suddenly, Truman Mudgett and his crew appeared and demanded the *Black Snake* back. When Lieutenant Farrington refused, they opened fire and killed a soldier. Farrington and his men landed and charged the smugglers. In the fight, another soldier and a Burlington farmer who was working nearby were killed. Most of the smugglers were captured there or as they fled to Canada.

The trial of these men stirred up anger between those who supported the United States president and the embargo, and those who did not. So many Vermonters agreed with smuggling that it was hard to pick a fair jury for the trial. Ethan Allen, Jr., son of the famous hero, was dismissed from jury duty after saying the prisoners were not guilty of any crime and should be set free.

Finally, at the trial run by Chief Justice Royall Tyler, most of the smugglers were convicted. One of them, Cyrus Dean, was charged with the murder of the soldiers and sentenced to hang. His execution in Burlington in 1809 was attended by 10,000 spectators. Truman Mudgett was released, but others in his band were imprisoned, given 50 lashes, or pilloried.

Credit: *Adapted with permission from article in "Green Mountaineer," publication of the Vermont Historical Society.*

Activity: **Political Cartoons**

TEACHER NOTES *and* INFO

Discuss political cartoons with your students. You might want to bring in some current cartoons to share with the class, such as the one to the left from the *Burlington Free Press.*

STUDENT ACTIVITY

Copy and distribute the cartoon below. It is a rendition of a political cartoon about the Embargo of 1807. In this cartoon, a snapping turtle that represents the Embargo is biting the pants of a man loading a barrel on a ship. The cartoonist shows that the embargo, a law that forbids trade with another country, hurts business. Discuss the cartoon and ask students to design their own cartoon, either individually or in groups.

Commercial Period

1814-1890

QUESTIONS

- How did transportation change on the lake during the Commercial Period?
- How did jobs and commerce change?
- How did different people feel about the changes on the lake?

KEY RESOURCES

- Life in the Colchester Reef Lighthouse *by Gordon P. Manning*
- Two Centuries of Ferry Boating *by Ralph Nading Hill*
- Shelburne Museum—*field trip and educational resources*
- Skenesborough Museum—*field trip and educational resources*

Word Bank

B. Langdon
beacon
Burlington
canal boat
canal sloop
canaller
Chambly Canal
Champlain Canal
Colchester Reef
commerce
Delaware and Hudson
    Railroad
donkey
draft
Essex
ferry
General Greene
horse ferry
Hudson River
James and John Winan
Lake Champlain Steamboat
    Company
lighthouse
log raft
lumber
paddlewheel
Philemon Daniels
Phoenix
Robert Fulton
sailing canal boat
seaport
shipwright
smuggling
St. Albans
standard canal boat
steamship
Whitehall

Commercial Period 1814-1890

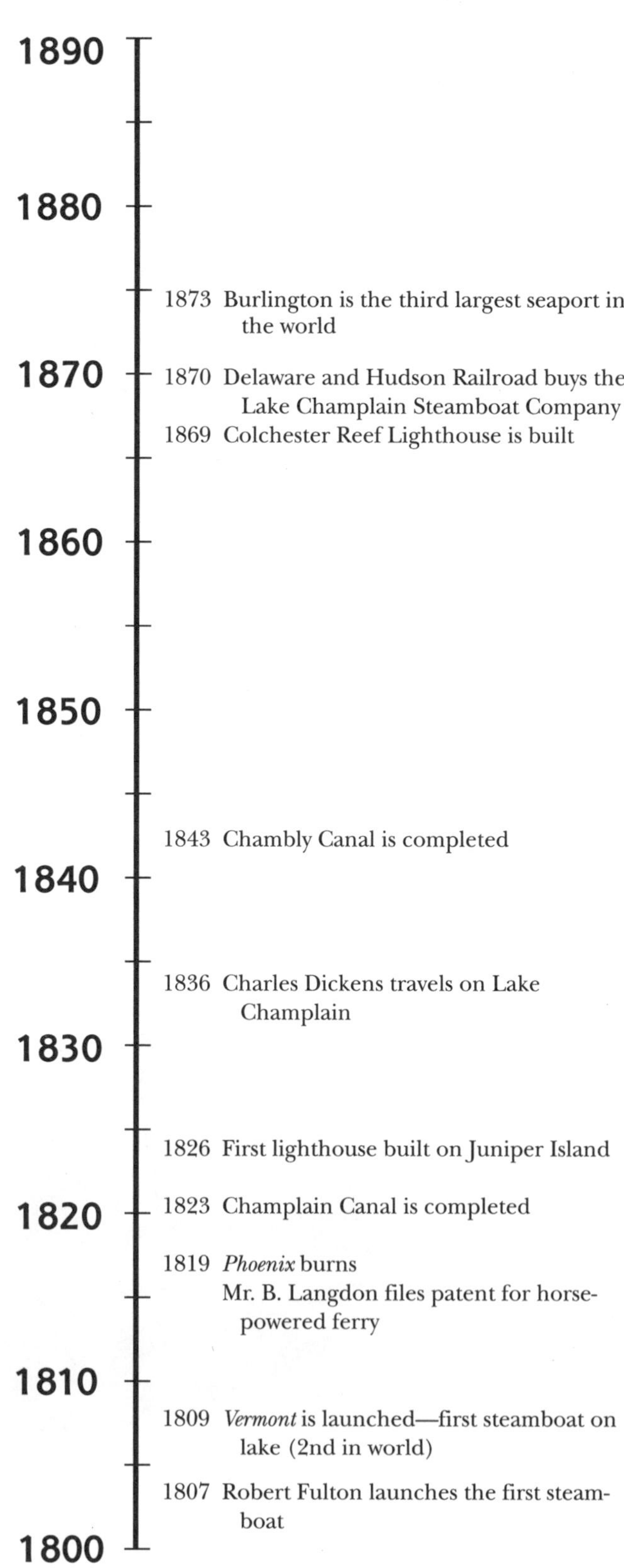

Activity:
The Burning of the Phoenix

TEACHER NOTES *and* INFO

The burning of the *Phoenix* is a great story and easily lends itself to dramatization. The process could be extensive or limited. Decide how long you will spend on the dramatization. Sometimes a group of students comes along that is just right for an extensive drama activity. The number of skills that are employed during a drama production—language arts, problem solving, group cooperation and organization—are endless.

STUDENT ACTIVITY

This is a complicated story to dramatize. Joan suggests two possibilities that can be done as a prelude to a full play production or as separate activities.

1. Interviews

In a TV newscast format, ask for volunteers to be interviewed. Tell the students that you're looking for these characters to talk with: Jahaziel Sherman, Richard W. Sherman, Colonel Thomas, John Howard, D.D. Howard, Mr. Hall, McVein, Sion Howard, the thief, passengers, onlookers during the confrontation with the thief, and crew members. If no one volunteers, take one of the roles and encourage the children to ask you questions. Once you've set an example, others will no doubt volunteer. It is important to focus on the questions that don't require memory of the facts, but rather interpretation of the facts. For example, ask passengers: *What were your first thoughts when you learned there was a fire? What did you lose in the fire? How cold was the water? What kinds of travel plans do you have in the future?*

2. Scenes

Divide the students into pairs and have them decide who is A and who is B. Tell them that A will be John Howard and B will be a sleeping passenger. Ask each pair to decide where the bar is and where the cabin is and to locate themselves in those settings. Then begin narrating the pantomime for them to act out:

> *"Passenger, you are sleeping soundly in your cabin. John, you're going to the bar to check on your money. You go around the bar. You open the cash box*

and start counting your bills. Suddenly, you smell something burning. You open a door to the hall and see a fire. Immediately, you grab the bills and stuff them in your coat pocket. You rush to the cabin to knock on the door loudly. Passenger, you sit up, startled. You go to the door and open it. John explains the problem. Passenger, you go to change from your night cloths and then realize there's no time. You grab a couple of personal items and run with John to the deck. Both of you pull down the life boat and gently, carefully, put it in the water. As John holds the rope to the boat, the passenger jumps in. John jumps in afterwards. Both of you row together quickly away from the burning ship, coughing as the smoke catches you. You get far enough away to feel safe. You look back at the burning ship." FREEZE.

Other scenes can be narrated in this way; e.g. captain and passenger looking for things that can float and jumping with them overboard; thief and Sion Howard. If time and interest allows, you can build a full enactment from these scenes, adding dialogue and a larger cast.

Here are some ideas if you decide to make a play of the burning of the *Phoenix*:
• List the characters in the plot. Remember, angry sailboat captains and members of the public who thought steamships were dangerous can also be characters.
• Discuss the different scenes. You might decide to only include the main scenes in the story or to design sub-plots about some of the passengers, or about people who were not on the boat.
• Decide how roles will be assigned and what other jobs are necessary for your production. Will you be writing scripts? Designing sets?

The burning of the *Phoenix* is an unsolved mystery. What clues are there in the story that point to arson? What clues could be added to the story? Do you want to solve the mystery or leave it unsolved?

STUDENT HANDOUT - "The Phoenix: Part One"

The Phoenix: Part One

The *Phoenix* operated for four seasons on regularly scheduled runs between Whitehall, New York, and St. Johns, Quebec. The fare for the entire length of the lake was $10. A minimum fee of $1 was required no matter how short the passage. Servants traveled for half fare. Animals not exceeding the size of a sheep were permitted, but they had to be tied forward of the capstan.

Passengers were expected to be on their best behavior, as shown by the company's rules and regulations: *"As the steamboat has been fitted in elegant style, order is necessary to keep it so; gentlemen will, therefore, please to observe cleanliness, and a reasonable attention not to injure the furniture; for this purpose, no one must sit on a table, underneath penalty of a half dollar for each time, and every breakage of tables, chairs, sofas or windows, tearing curtains or injury of any kind will be visited with the severest penalty of the law."*

While the company thrived, it was not without its share of troubles. Engines were constantly breaking down, sometimes sinking a boat, and fires were always a threat.

On the night of September 4, 1819, the *Phoenix* left Burlington harbor with a total passenger list and crew of 46 people. The boat's regular captain, Jahaziel Sherman was ill with a fever and confined to his home in Vergennes. His 21-year-old son, Richard W. Sherman, was in command.

"We left Burlington at 11 p.m. with everything in apparent good order about the vessel, a regular watch being kept at night," recalled Captain Sherman. *"I remained on deck until we passed the reef of Colchester...passengers, I think had all retired. Having been up all the night previous, I told my pilot to call me at Crab Island...and then went below to my stateroom, lay down and fell asleep, the wind blowing fresh from the northeast."*

During the night, as the boat steamed into a northerly wind in the broadest part of the lake, John Howard, a special messenger from the Bank of Burlington, went to check $8,500 in Montreal bills that he was taking to Canada to exchange. The money had been put behind the bar for safekeeping with his son, D.D. Howard, who was a steward and barkeeper on the *Phoenix.* While checking the money, John Howard discovered the boat was on fire.

He *"at once aroused all the passengers in the gentlemen's cabin, and from thence rushing to the ladies' cabin awakened all there, all got on deck as fast as possible—most of them in their night clothes."*

As people frantically made their way to the deck, one passenger remembered, *"A vivid light illuminated every object beyond the splendor of a noonday sun. I fancied it was the torch of death to point me and my fellow travelers to the tomb."*

About 20 people boarded the first lifeboat, including D.D. Howard with his father's money, a Colonel Thomas, who took charge of the boat, and all the women passengers. The second lifeboat could have carried all the rest on board, but was cut loose before it was filled to capacity. As it pulled away from the burning vessel, one passenger remembered, *"The cries for assistance from those who could not swim were pitiable."* At least one of the passengers, a Mr. Hall from Middlebury, proposed they go back for the people left behind. But the plea was silenced by the engineer of the steamer, a man named McVein, who threatened *"to knock the first man overboard with an oar who should rise to make the first attempt"* at turning back.

Still on board the *Phoenix*, the young captain and John Howard assisted the remaining 11 people into the water on anything they could find that would float. Planks, tables and chairs were all thrown overboard.

Upon landing on Providence Island, Colonel Thomas and D.D. Howard each took charge of a lifeboat and returned to the burning *Phoenix* in the hope of finding survivors. Five of the eleven people who had been left behind were rescued. The captain, the last to leave the boat, clung to a table leaf for two hours before he was picked up. *"I at once ordered my men to put about and go back to the wreck,"* he later recalled, *"in the hopes of saving others."* They rowed around the wreck several times, but saw no signs of life.

Before returning to the burning *Phoenix*, D.D. Howard had left the money his father gave him with some of the passengers for safekeeping. When he returned to Providence Island, he discovered someone had stolen the money.

Another son of John Howard's, Sion, was sent to pursue the thief. He caught up with the man at Bell's Ferry. When confronted, the thief refused to hand over the money and threatened to kill anyone who attempted to take it. After receiving no assistance from the onlookers, Sion *"armed himself with a club and advanced resolutely and demanded the money."* The thief relented and was immediately arrested.

The most common theory about the cause of the fire is that a candle was accidentally left burning in the galley by a crew member. However, some people wonder whether the company was hiding something. A mechanical malfunction would have made the company look much worse. The candle theory was much more calming to those who had doubts about the safety of steamboats.

There was no way of proving, however, that a candle caused the fire. In fact, some circumstantial evidence points to arson. Many sailing merchants were angry about having lost business to the new steamship companies: could someone intentionally have set fire to the *Phoenix*?

The charred remains of the *Phoenix* drifted several miles to come to rest off Colchester Point. No one knows for sure how long she stayed grounded.

In all likelihood, the wreck was trapped by ice and was dragged clear of the reef when the ice melted in the spring of 1820. Off the reef, the *Phoenix* quietly slipped beneath the surface to rest on the sloping bottom some 15 fathoms below. She remained there, undetected and preserved for more than 150 years.

Credit: *Adapted with permission from the "Phoenix Project," a publication of the Champlain Maritime Society and the Vermont Division for Historic Preservation. The Champlain Maritime Society is no longer in existence.*

Activity: **The Ticonderoga**

TEACHER NOTES *and* INFO

The S.S. *Ticonderoga* is currently undergoing a restoration that began in 1993 and is expected to be completed in 1997. Although the ship was actually built in the twentieth century, it is the "sole survivor of an era" when steamboats were the main form of transportation on the lake and it is significant because it is the last ship of its kind left in the world.

STUDENT ACTIVITY

Read aloud the following article: "The Ticonderoga."
Have students complete the following worksheet: "Facts about the Ticonderoga."

STUDENT HANDOUTS - "The Ticonderoga" and "Facts about the Ticonderoga"

The Ticonderoga

H i, I'm the *Ticonderoga*, but people call me the Ti for short. I was built in Shelburne Bay, Vermont, in 1906 by the Champlain Transportation Company. I'm a pretty big and heavy steamship. I'm about 220 feet long and I weigh over 892 tons. That's a lot considering I only draw eight to nine feet when under way, and six feet when standing still.

When I was built in 1906 I cost $170,000, but if you tried to make a replica of me now, it would cost over $2.7 million. During the time I served I was the pride of the lake. My speed was 23 miles per hour.

At full throttle I burn two tons of coal an hour. I was capable of carrying over 24 tons of coal in storage. I have a small crew of 28, compared to my passenger capacity of 1,200 people. My crew consists of a captain, a chief engineer, a first assistant engineer, four firemen, a purser, a stewardess, a freight clerk, a bartender, two hall and recess boys, a cook, three waiters, a scullion and a mess boy.

I was the last of the vertical-beam, side-wheeler steamships that provided passenger and cargo service on rivers and lakes in the United States. When I was in service I took a lot of people for rides. For instance, in the summer of 1953, I carried over fifty thousand passengers around the lake. Now that I'm at the Shelburne Museum, I usually come close to doubling that amount when people come to see me. When visitors come they always have memories of traveling on me.

Along with carrying passengers, I was, at one time, a ferry for cars. I could carry 20 to 30 cars just like the diesel ferries. I didn't really like having to carry cars because they were heavy. I carried a variety of animals as cargo—horses, cows, sheep and goats. Each fall I would go up to Isle La Motte to pick up apples. In one season I was able to take seventeen thousand barrels of apples back to Burlington.

On September 23, 1913, I was called upon to do an unusual task—transport an elephant named Minnie from Burlington to Plattsburgh. She was the star of a show touring the region. Transporting an elephant on a steamboat was exciting enough, but there was a problem. When standing up straight, Minnie was taller than the deck where she was staying! However, Minnie was an intelligent animal and obeyed her keeper's instructions. For the whole voyage she never even tried to stand up. When we got to Plattsburgh, she was overjoyed to be able to stand up straight. The cost of transporting her was the same as that for two horses. We didn't have a rate for elephants!

In my whole history, I was only seriously damaged once. It was on August 17, 1919. I had left Burlington for Plattsburgh filled with passengers. I was rounding the north side of Isle La Motte when suddenly I was grounded on Point au Fer Reef. The water poured through the large gash in my hull. The crew tried to back me off but they were unsuccessful. Then the engineers, fearing that my boilers would explode, quickly doused my fires. All three hundred passengers were taken off to safety in lifeboats. They patched my side and a tugboat towed me to the shipyard. The *Chateaugay* replaced me for the rest of the season.

The greatest honor I had was when I carried President Taft from Plattsburgh to Burlington. As I left the port, twelve hundred Plattsburgh infantrymen and thirty-five horses marched for the president up and down on the barge I was pulling.

After 47 years of service, I started to cost more than I was making, so people decided to bring me to the Shelburne Museum, where I am now. It took 65 days, 20 hours and 28 minutes of hard work to get me here. They had to build a railroad from the lake to the Shelburne Museum, a distance of about two miles. They hauled my 892 tons over the railroad.

Credit: *Adapted with permission from an anonymous manuscript from the Shelburne Museum.*

Facts about the Ticonderoga

Hi! I'm the Ticonderoga. Call me _______ for short. I was built in _____________ Bay,
_1_   _2_
Vermont, in _______. I am about _______ feet long and I weigh over _______ tons. I draw
_3_   _4_   _5_
_______ to _______ feet under way, _______ feet standing still.
_6_   _7_   _8_

When I was built in 1906, I cost $_______. Today, I would cost $_______ to build. My
_9_   _10_
speed was _______ miles per hour. At full throttle, I burn _______ tons of coal an hour. I could
_11_   _12_
carry _______ tons of coal in storage. My crew is _______ people, but I can carry _______
_13_   _14_   _15_
passengers. I was the last vertical-beam _____________ steamship to provide passenger and
_16_
cargo service on any river or lake in the United States. In the summer of 1953, I carried

_______ people around the lake. At the Shelburne Museum, where I am now, _______ people
_17_   _18_
[*figure the number*] visit me. I also was a car ferry and could carry _______ to _______ cars. I also
_19_   _20_
carried animals—_________, _________, _________ and _________.
_21_   _22_   _23_   _24_

At Isle La Motte, I picked up _________ and once carried _________ barrels. In 1913,
_25_   _26_
I carried an elephant named _____________. I had an accident on _______ 17, 1919, near
_27_   _28_
Isle La Motte. My most honored guest was President _____________. _______ infantry men
_29_   _30_
and _______ horses came with him. My move to the museum took _______ days, _______ hours
_31_   _32_   _33_
and _______ minutes. I traveled on a _______ -mile railroad.
_34_   _35_

Answers: **1**. Ti, **2**. Shelburne, **3**. 1906, **4**. 220, **5**. 892, **6**. 8, **7**. 9, **8**. 6, **9**. 170,000, **10**. 2.7 million, **11**. 23, **12**. 2, **13**. 24, **14**. 28, **15**. 1,200, **16**. side-wheeler, **17**. 50,000, **18**. 100,000, **19**. 20, **20**. 30, **21**. horses, **22**. cows, **23**. sheep, **24**. goats, **25**. apples, **26**. 17,000, **27**. Minnie, **28**. August, **29**. Taft, **30**. 1,200, **31**. 35, **32**. 65, **33**. 20, **34**. 28, **35**. 2.

Activity: **Animals We Love**

TEACHER NOTES *and* INFO

Most of the educational material related to canals is related to the Erie Canal and the larger New York canal system. The Champlain Canal, and later the Chambly Canal, were linked to this network and one can assume that much of the culture that thrived on the canals was the same in our area. There is some material available, but I feel that Lake Champlain's canal culture is an untapped educational opportunity for those of you that want to go looking. The study of canals can include the technology of the locks as well as the culture of the people who worked and traveled on the canals.

STUDENT ACTIVITY

Discuss the importance of animals on the canal.

• What are the things that this canaller admires most about his horses? Why were these qualities important? What was the relationship between the canaller and the animals that pulled the boat?

Discuss the use of animals for work.

• How are animals used for work in New England? (*logging, sugaring, assisting people who are physically-impaired, herding*)

• In other parts of the United States? (*pulling sleds or plows, Seeing Eye, assisting people who are physically-impaired*)

• In the world? (*lots of possibilities*)

• Why else are animals important? (*love, companionship, entertainment*)

• What about animal research?

Invite students to:

• stand and make an impromptu tribute to an animal that they respect and or love,

• write a formal tribute to an animal they respect or love in the form of an essay, poem or song and then illustrate and exhibit it.

STUDENT HANDOUT - "Attend, All Ye Drivers"

Attend, All Ye Drivers

"Attend, All Ye Drivers," is a "bragging song" collected by Harold Thompson in the 1930s from Mrs. W.W. Hay of South Glens Falls, New York. Mrs. Hay learned it in the 1890s from her uncle, Walter Rozelle of Fort Edward, New York.

Attend all ye drivers, I sing of my team.
They're the fleetest and strongest that ever was seen.
There's none that will toil with such speed down the creek
Or start at the word of the driver so quick,
Derry down, down, down, Derry down.

There's Dandy, my leader, looks boldly ahead,
With his tail raised aloft, and majestic his tread.
He has a bright, shining coat of a beautiful bay,
His eyes sparkle bright as the sun at noon-day.

(verses continue on next page)

He's a roarer, no doubt, there's few can match him,
Once let him loose, and the devil may catch him.
At the call he is ready like a reindeer to jump,
Obedient, when ordered he stands like a stump.

The next in procession is Charlie, a buster,
General Pluck might feel proud on his back at a muster.
So graceful he moves in the midst of his team,
So strong, you would think he traveled by steam.

And lastly my Jimmie, my saddle-horse true,
It's hard to tell how much this horse cannot do.
He has the pride of an emperor, the wisdom of kings,
He moves o'er the ground like a bird on its wings.

The three altogether in motion outdo,
Any team of their age, the whole canal through.
Should any company try to go by us,
We'll show them our steam whenever they try us.

While Baker and Walbridge their packets run daily,
Proud Dandy and Jimmie and Charlie so gaily,
Will waft all the passengers through the canal,
In spite of all others, and in style, so they shall.

Credit: *THE CANALLER'S SONGBOOK by William Hullfish. Reprinted with permission.*

Activity:
Beacons of the Future

TEACHER NOTES *and* INFO

If you have a copy of LIFE IN THE COLCHESTER REEF LIGHTHOUSE by Gordon P. Manning, read aloud selections from the book to enhance students' understanding of daily life in a lighthouse.

Read together the essay "Life in the Lighthouse."

STUDENT ACTIVITY

• Ask students to list all the responsibilities of the keeper and his family. How did the lightkeeper's job become outdated? Discuss jobs that are outdated today. What kinds of changes occur that make jobs become outdated or unnecessary?

• Ask them to speculate what jobs will be outdated in 50 years. (Be prepared for them to include teachers!) What mechanisms and practices might replace these tasks? A good example might be the process of laying asphalt and repairing roads. Think of concrete tasks that will be replaced with specific new technology.

• Ask students in cooperative groups to choose a job that they think will become outdated. Describe how that job is done now, discuss why it will become outdated and determine how the same task will be done in the future. Have students present their work orally or on a poster board with two drawings side-by-side, under the headings "Now" and "Then."

STUDENT HANDOUT - "Life in the Lighthouse"

the Colchester Lighthouse

Life in the Lighthouse

Sailors on Lake Champlain had to be careful to avoid the reefs and shoals off Colchester Point. During the day it was easy enough to see the water breaking over the rocks and shallows of the reef. But at night and in the fog an error in navigation could send a vessel to the reef—a sure disaster for the boat and its crew. In response to growing commercial traffic on the lake in the 1850s, the U.S. Lighthouse Service built a lighthouse in 1869 on Colchester Reef. A Burlington engineer, Albert Dow, won the competition for its design.

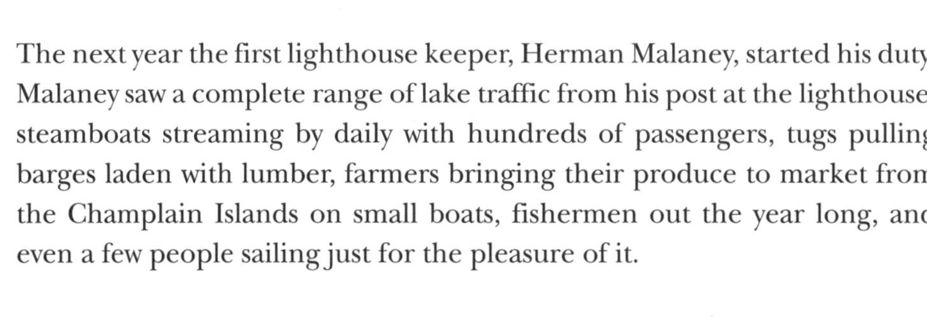

The next year the first lighthouse keeper, Herman Malaney, started his duty. Malaney saw a complete range of lake traffic from his post at the lighthouse: steamboats streaming by daily with hundreds of passengers, tugs pulling barges laden with lumber, farmers bringing their produce to market from the Champlain Islands on small boats, fishermen out the year long, and even a few people sailing just for the pleasure of it.

The keeper's job was a trying one. His duty lasted 24 hours a day until the winter cold turned the waters to ice. Constant vigilance was required to watch for any changing weather that reduced visibility on the lake. Each night the beacon shined from dusk until dawn. Its kerosene lamp demanded constant attention, as an improperly trimmed wick reduced the lamp's visibility to zero in a few minutes. When the keeper saw that fog had cut the visibility to less than three miles, he triggered a mechanism that rang the bell three times a minute. The keeper's family had little sleep on foggy nights!

Government ships supplied coal, kerosene and other essentials. To supplement the food supply, the keeper grew vegetables on a nearby island. For keepers with families, tending the garden was the children's responsibility. They rowed the half mile to the island daily.

Life in the lighthouse kept the whole family busy. Some children worked with their fathers performing maintenance duties. Others helped their mothers put food by to last the long winter. When ships struck the rocks, the entire family sprang into action. The wife and the eldest child kept the beacon going, while others stood by to help distressed sailors.

In 1933, the last keeper left the lighthouse when a modern automatic beacon replaced the light. The lighthouse stood empty for 19 years before it was moved to the Shelburne Museum in 1952.

Modern Times
1900-Present

QUESTIONS

- How has life changed on the lake since the early 1900s?
- What technology has caused those changes?
- How are citizens managing the natural and cultural resources of the Lake Champlain Basin?

KEY RESOURCES

- Lake Champlain Committee—*newsletter and educational resources*
- Lake Champlain Basin Program—*publications and educational resources*
- Lake Champlain Maritime Museum—*newsletter and educational resources*
- Lake Champlain Basin Science Center—*field trip and educational resources*
- Shelburne Farms—*field trip and educational resources*
- U.S. Fish and Wildlife Service–Lake Champlain Fish and Wildlife Resources Office—*publications and educational resources*
- Opportunities for Action—*Lake Champlain Basin Program*

Modern Times

Activity: **Who Owns History?**

TEACHER NOTES *and* INFO

People in the basin may be unique in the ways that they have worked at and had success with preserving the cultural resources of the Champlain Valley. This success is based on problem-solving, cooperation, allocation of funds and the hard work of many individuals. Many of these decisions are still being made and it is important to let students join the discussion.

STUDENT ACTIVITY

There are numerous ways to explore these issues with students. Here are a few suggestions.

• Discuss and interpret the quote from Ralph Nading Hill. Ask students to suggest ways that knowledge of the past can drive the quality of our future.

• Discuss with students the question of historic preservation. Immersing a boat in freshwater is the best way to preserve a boat's structure, but everyone can't dive to see wrecks and artifacts. Where should these historical relics be kept? Who should see them? Who should pay for the preservation of these wrecks, underwater and on land?

• Discuss with students questions regarding historic artifacts. Who owns the artifacts at the bottom of the lake? The Vermont Historic Preservation Act of 1975 and the New York Historic Preservation Act of 1980 (and related state laws) establish that artifacts/wrecks found underneath the lake belong to the states of Vermont and New York. A historical site is defined as a place where more than one object is related to another as opposed to isolated objects or artifacts. Divers can retain isolated objects if they report the finding; you cannot disturb a site. What should be done with artifacts that are found? Ask students what they would do if they found an important relic.

• Read the following article. Discuss with students the problems that need to be solved in finding and documenting a historic wreck.

STUDENT HANDOUT - "The Phoenix: Part Two"

"They [artifacts of lake's history] are the tangible survivors of an area whose stock-in-trade is history. Places without history, like moonscapes, can be beautiful, but without footprints to follow, are all but meaningless. A present without a past is unthinkable. If we had not fathomed where we were we could not reckon where we are. Nor have the least inkling where we are bound."

> *Ralph Nading Hill*
> LAKE CHAMPLAIN:
> KEY TO LIBERTY

*Ralph Nading Hill spent much of his life studying the history of the lake and was the driving force behind moving the **Ticonderoga** to the Shelburne Museum.*

The Phoenix: Part Two

In August of 1978, on the outer reef of Colchester Point, three divers plunged into a three hundred foot ravine. The divers, Don Mayland, a scuba instructor, and two students, Dick Hubbard and Don Mudgett, swam down the smooth slope. At 90 feet they stopped. The water was cold, about 48˚F, and the visibility was no more than 20 feet through the dim olive-green light.

The sensation of diving in deep water is often disorienting. The pressure, the darkness and the danger of "the bends" make many beginners nervous. As the divers swam across the shoals, Mudgett suddenly signaled that he was having trouble. Mayland swam over and tried to calm him down. Just over Mudgett's shoulder a black silhouette of a ship's bow loomed out against the vast darkness.

Mayland was mesmerized for a moment. But he quickly realized that he didn't have time to see whether the image before him was real or some figment of his imagination. Shaking himself loose from the vision, he signaled to start ascending.

When the divers reached the surface, Mayland burst out of the water shouting, "I've seen a wreck! There's a boat down there!" Hubbard yelled that he too had seen it. After Mudgett felt better, the three divers went down again.

They followed the slope of the ravine, but when they reached their depth, there was no sign of a ship. They searched the surrounding area. No ship. They could not stay at that depth any longer without risking decompression sickness.

Although they did not dive again that day, Mayland and Hubbard were intrigued enough to go back to the site. During the course of the summer, two other divers, Bill Oswald and Dick Sell, joined them. They dived twice without finding anything. Then on September 4, 1978, they spotted the boat.

Before the cold weather turned them away from the lake, they made two more visits to the wreck, trying to find something that might help them identify it. Sketches by Dick Sell suggested that it was a sailing vessel of some sort, but there were no artifacts of any significance that might give a clue to its identity.

Over the winter Mayland researched histories of the lake in an effort to identify the boat. As the 1979 diving season approached, he grew more restless to have the answer to the question that lay on the shoals off Colchester Point.

During the summer the four divers continued to dive on the boat. Meanwhile, Mayland learned that Vermont had a state archaeologist employed by the Division for Historic Preservation who might know about the ship.

"I entered the office, told her what we had found, and handed her a pottery chip from the boat," Mayland recalls. "She immediately told me I was in violation of state law."

State archaeologist Giovanna Neudorfer (now Peebles), was only half joking. She explained that under Vermont law anything of historic value found in the Vermont portion of the lake must be reported to the Division. It is the responsibility of the state to protect historic sites. She told Mayland that the year before, Art Cohn, another diving instructor on Lake Champlain, had applied for and received a permit to search for a steamboat called the *Phoenix* that had burned and sunk off Colchester Point in 1819.

Cohn had first learned of the *Phoenix* from Captain Merritt Carpenter, a local historian and captain for the Lake Champlain ferries. The *Phoenix* had been the second steamboat on the lake and part of the thriving Lake Champlain Steamboat Company's fleet before it burned. Cohn surmised that the remains of the boat must still be somewhere off Colchester Point.

It was early September by the time Cohn, Mayland, and the other divers met to discuss the wreck. In comparing notes they felt certain that the boat Mayland had found was the *Phoenix*. In August of 1979, Cohn, Mayland, Sell, and Hubbard dived again to make a positive identification of the wreck.

Both Mayland and Cohn agreed now that they had enough evidence to apply for a joint permit from the state to explore the boat. They also felt that they needed more than just a permit if the boat was to be properly documented. They wanted to organize an expedition. The question, however, was where in the world were they going to find the financial resources and personnel for such a venture?

A lot of discussion took place among interested individuals. The Lake Champlain Committee was involved and Monty Fischer, then chairman, along with Art Cohn, Merritt Carpenter and others orchestrated many lake awareness activities. They formed the Lake Champlain Maritime Society, which became the organization that spearheaded diving explorations until the formation of the Lake Champlain Maritime Museum in 1986. The Maritime Society's first project, funded by the Vermont Division for Historic Preservation, was the *Phoenix* Project.

Credit: *Adapted with permission from the "Phoenix Project," a publication of the Champlain Maritime Society and the Vermont Division for Historic Preservation.*

Activity:
Design a Tourist Brochure

TEACHER NOTES *and* INFO

Gather some brochures for students to review. Discuss the format. Most brochures are two-sided and folded in thirds. Discuss the different information that is packed into a brochure. Brochures often include maps, facts, chronologies, descriptions and illustrations.

Subjects can be favorite places, historical sites, wetlands, pollution sources (an informational tourist brochure!), or fishing spots. Topics can be general, e.g. "Fun Places to Go on Lake Champlain," or specific e.g. "The S.S. *Ticonderoga.*"

This activity is easier if students have received a packet of maps and brochures that they can refer to. (See "Treasure Hunt" in *Getting Wet,* p. 14.)

Other Ideas
• A less time-consuming but fun option is to design a tourist poster. This can include one illustration and a snappy caption!

STUDENT ACTIVITY

Ask students to design a tourist brochure about the Lake Champlain area. Decide what format you will use. Some students may be more comfortable with two sides and one fold. The brochure should include:

- text—that describes your topic in prose
    - illustration—at least one!
    - map—that shows where your topic is.

You can also include:
- all the possibilities that you discussed!

Activity:
To Ski or Not to Ski; That is the Question!

TEACHER NOTES *and* INFO

There are a number of timely issues concerning the use of Lake Champlain to explore with your students. Jet skis are very popular and students may already be involved in conflicts over their use. You could invite adults involved in this debate to visit your class before or after your class explores the issue with this activity.

STUDENT ACTIVITY

1. Divide the class into halves.

2. Tell one half that they are members of the Lake Champlain Sailing Club. They each own sailboats (of varying sizes) and have spent much of their free time sailing to different areas of the lake. They love the quiet sound of the wind blowing the sail. The other half are owners of jet skis. They are thrilled by the speed of the ride and the freedom to skim over the waves.

3. Begin a dialogue between them by saying:

   "I've brought your two groups together because I understand that you'd like to set some rules for the use of Lake Champlain and you are having problems coming to consensus. What are your concerns?"

4. Encourage them to debate their different points of views. Then ask them to switch roles so they can see both sides. Through your leadership, try to work towards consensus in the second round of debates.

Sources

Based on an essay: "The History of Lake Champlain" *by Art Cohn* and "A Short History of the Abenaki" *by Elise Guyette*

Additional sources for essay and activities:
From Steamships to Sidewheelers *by Kevin Crisman*
Sails and Steam in the Mountains *by Russell P. Bellico*
Lake Champlain: Key to Liberty *by Ralph Nading Hill*
The Original Vermonters *by William Haviland and Marjory Power*
Otter Creek *by James Peterson*
Vermont: A Cultural Patchwork *by Elise Guyette*
"The Original People: Native Americans in the Champlain Valley" booklet from an Exhibition at
    Clinton Community Historical Museum
"The Earth on Turtle's Back" from Native American Stories *told by Joseph Bruchac*
The Western Abenakis of Vermont: 1600-1800 *by Colin Calloway*
The Iroquois Trail *by M.R. Harrington*
People of the Longhouse *by Jillian and Robin Ridington*
The Wind Eagle *edited by Joseph Bruchac*
Dawnland Encounters: Indians and Europeans in Northern New England *by Colin Calloway*
Centuries of Ferry Boats *by Ralph Nading Hill*
Life in the Colchester Reef Lighthouse *by Gordon P. Manning*
The Eagle: An American Brig on Lake Champlain during the War of 1812 *by Kevin Crisman*
Resource material from Crown Point *by Tim Titus*
Resource material from Maritime Museum *by Laurie Eddy*
Resource material from Shelburne Museum *by Garet Livermore*
Samuel de Champlain biography *by Joe C.W. Armstrong*
Peter Kalm's Travels into North America *by Peter Kalm*
Journal of Dr. Lewis Beebe *by Lewis Beebe*
Interviews with Paul Wineman at Albany Museum, Jeanne Brink, Tim Titus and Elise Guyette
"The Phoenix Project" printed by The Champlain Maritime Society and Vermont Division for
    Historic Preservation
"The Black Snake Affair," *The Green Mountaineer*, Winter 1990/1991
"Attend, All Ye Drivers" from The Canaller's Songbook *by William Hullfish*
"I am the Ti," author unknown, from the Shelburne Museum archives
"Built with Spirit, Deserted in Darkness. The American Occupation of Mount Independence, 1776-
    1777." Master's Thesis *by Don Wickman*
"The Champlain Monster," *Vermont Life*, Summer 1970
"The Rise and Fall of William Gilliland," *Press-Republican* (Plattsburgh, New York) *by Lorraine Lilja*

It's About Time

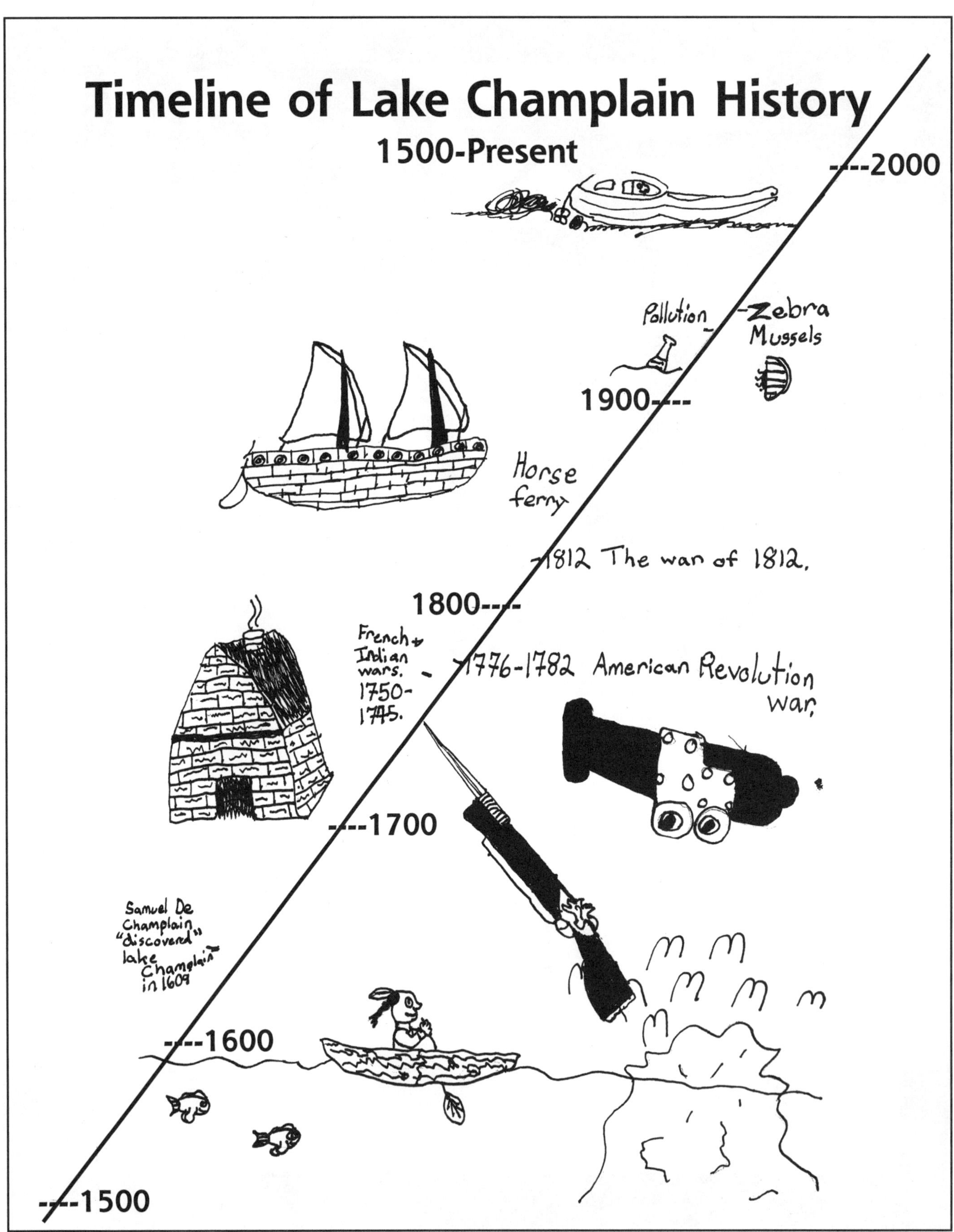

Artwork by Stuart McKenna, Grade 5, School Street School, Milton, Vermont.

Introduction

One of the hardest things to teach students is how the past is a dynamic, changing element in the human experience. Students tend to think of the present and the past as two separate, stagnant "chunks." The past contains everything from mastodons to horses-and-buggies, from black-and-white television to one-room schoolhouses. There is pre-Nintendo time and Nintendo time. Teaching kids about the complexity of the past and the progression of time within the past is an exciting challenge of the social sciences. Many history activities tend to accentuate the contrast between past and present without weaving the threads that connect us to the past or the different parts of the past to each other. Using a natural resource that's been around as long as the lake has is an exciting way to explore this complexity with young minds.

We also teach events in the past as if they were inextricably linked to one another in a predetermined chain of events. One of the more interesting things about studying the American Revolution is learning about the people who lived in these parts who remained loyal to the King of England. They didn't know that they were living in the future United States of America. When we study the development of technology, we seldom explore what people thought about these changes. When steam travel came to the lake, not everyone knew that it would become the dominant and relatively safe form of transportation. When an Abenaki man spoke in 1766 to the heads of white government, he spoke in a clear voice that outlined his people's claim to the land they had inhabited for thousands of years. He didn't know that the tides of history had changed and the influx of the white man would ignore his pleas. As we ponder the ecological issues that face Lake Champlain at the turn of the twentieth century, we don't know whether the solutions we are currently exploring will save our lake or not. We are living in the present and do not know what the future will bring. Every moment in the past has at one time been the present. Our task is to give children a chance to experience that past moment in all of its complexities, without our knowledge of the next event clouding the view.

I have outlined some activities designed to help kids understand how the lake, people and times changed. These activities span several time periods

and thus are different from the activities offered in the history section, which are designed for a specific time in history.

Also, some activities outlined in this chapter are discussed more fully in other chapters. For example, there are numerous writing activities in *Language Arts*; the ones here specifically relate to teaching about time.

Timelines

TEACHER NOTES *and* INFO

Timelines are an important activity to help students visually organize abstract historical information.

During your study, it is important to give as many visual representations as possible. Maybe because I'm a visual learner myself, I find these pictures critical to the understanding of history. For example, a trip to the Lake Champlain Maritime Museum, with its multitude of graphic displays, provides learners with "pictures" of the progression of history. If you can't get to the museum, provide as many visuals as possible with books, photos and bulletin boards. Notes on the Maritime Museum's slide show and lecture provide a basic chronology of dates that students will be using throughout the study. (See "Lake Champlain History," p. 196.)

It is helpful while making timelines to "talk the dates." Encourage students to make a true statement.

Examples:
• The first fort was built on Lake Champlain ___ years after Samuel de Champlain sailed down the lake.
• Vermont became a state ___ years after the American Revolution.
• People have lived in this region for ___ years.
• The *Phoenix* was discovered ___ years after it was sunk.

This also can be given as a formal homework assignment:
Write down five historical facts in your thinkbooks.

There are a number of different kinds of timelines. One timeline that is not in this section is a nautical archeology activity called, "As Time Floats By." This activity employs a particular theme and can be adapted to many other topics. (See "As Time Floats By" in *Nautical Archeology*, p. 217.)

A few examples of using timelines to explore the passage of time follow.

Activity: **Just Imagine!**
A Timeline of 12,000 Years

Make a timeline that shows human habitation over 12,000 years. The activity illustrates the contrast between the huge time of Native American habitation (12,000 years) and the 400 years of European settlement.

Get a section of flagging tape that is at least 45 feet long. The timeline will represent the time from 10,000 B.C. to the present day. Mark off segments of time in 100-year sections (i.e. 600–700 B.C.). Four inches = 100 years. Use a permanent marker. Mark the Paleo, Archaic and Woodland archeological periods. Mark Champlain's voyage in 1609.

Share the timeline with your students. Students can stand in a large circle and read sections of the tape and make observations as they discover what it shows. Discuss the huge changes that have happened in a very short period of time.

Activity: **Time Flies:**
Make an Illustrated Timeline

Review important dates in the lake's history by putting "Lake Champlain History" (see p. 196) on an overhead projector. Students have copies of the worksheet and I fill in on the overhead as we discuss important events. The class can usually provide information as you go. Each student writes down the correct information on his or her copy.

I then hand out blank timelines (see p. 195). We transfer some of the basic information onto the timeline; again, I use the overhead. Then I turn the class loose to add dates that they choose. After students fill in information they can illustrate the timelines with historically accurate graphics.

You can also add other dates such as your birthday or the year students were born or other important dates in history!

This idea of using flagging tape came from Barry Doolan, who made a geologic timeline to share with his students.

Note: The blank timeline provided in this book runs from 1500–present. You could design your own blank timeline using any length of time.

Activity:
Getting the Big Picture:
Large Illustrated Timeline on Bulletin Board

Use as reference the "Date Chart" of information on the following page. Fill it in with your students. Discuss all the different pictures that help tell the story of a particular time in history. You may want to just focus on a particular theme such as technology.

Arrange dates 1500–2000 on the bulletin board. Assign each student the task of choosing one artifact, scene, happening, ship (the possibilities are endless) to illustrate and post in its correct location on the timeline. Depending on space and time, student work can be small (use blank index cards) or larger (use oak tag). If they are all the same size, they can be mounted and placed in a book after you take down your bulletin board.

Have some pictures photocopied and ready for students unable to find or make up their own. Students can also make little fact cards to decorate the timeline. This is a great task for students who have completed their illustration!

Note: A wonderful book to read aloud and share with students is A RIVER RAN WILD by Lynne Cherry. The superb illustrations and story portray the passage of time on a river in Massachusetts; the story and details are similar to the tales our rivers tell.

Name: ___________________________________

Date Chart   Lake Champlain

Time	1500s	1600s & 1700s	1800s	Today
Lake & Land				
Transportation				
Tools				
Work				
Food				
Homes				
Important Events				

Activity: **Hands-On Learning**

TEACHER NOTES *and* INFO

Some museums have kits that contain artifacts that students can handle. An example of a great one is "12,000 Years of History" from the Discovery Museum in Essex Junction, Vermont. It has some wonderful artifacts, tools and projectile points from Native American cultures. The kit also has a great slide show. If you can't get a kit, it is sometimes possible to find a private collector who will lend you some materials.

Note: There is a procedure for handling ancient objects. The Shelburne Museum recommends wearing white gloves.

Although we tend to think of artifacts as old things, you could adapt this activity to any object.

Example: a "what's-it?" activity with "mystery" modern boat artifacts. If you use modern objects, omit Question 4.

STUDENT ACTIVITY

Share some artifacts with the class and practice observation skills by using questions from the worksheet. Arrange students in small groups. Each group will have one artifact.

After each group has had an opportunity to discuss its artifact and complete the worksheet, have each group share its findings with the class.

Identifying Your Artifact

Group: _________________
____
____
____

1. Observe your artifact.
Write three statements that describe your artifact.

____
____
____

2. Discuss how the artifact was made. What materials and tools were used? Write down how you think it was made.

____
____
____

3. Discuss how this artifact was used. Is there more than one possibility? Write down how you think it was used.

____
____
____

4. Discuss what you think is the modern counterpart to this artifact. How is this same task accomplished today? Compare and contrast the two artifacts. How are they different? How are they similar?

Activity: **A Stitch in Time**

TEACHER NOTES *and* **INFO**

This is an art project where students choose at least four dates, arrange the dates on a chosen quilt pattern, then draw scenes, artifacts or people that represent those dates.

STUDENT ACTIVITY

Give each student one square piece of paper (8" x 8" works fine). Explain the process of choosing a quilt pattern design that will divide their square into four sections. They will be choosing four dates to represent artistically on each section of their one square. You could choose to make squares on cloth and use permanent cloth markers or cloth paint.

Display squares on a wall as a quilt of all the students' squares. Ruby Thibault suggests making some creative stitching to hold the quilt pieces together. If your squares are paper, you can use marker after your squares are fastened on the wall to "sew" them together. If they are cloth, you might want to learn some folk-art stitching patterns to finish off your quilt (or use fabric markers).

STUDENT HANDOUT - "Lake Champlain Time Quilt"

Lake Champlain Time Quilt

Decide on your quilt pattern.

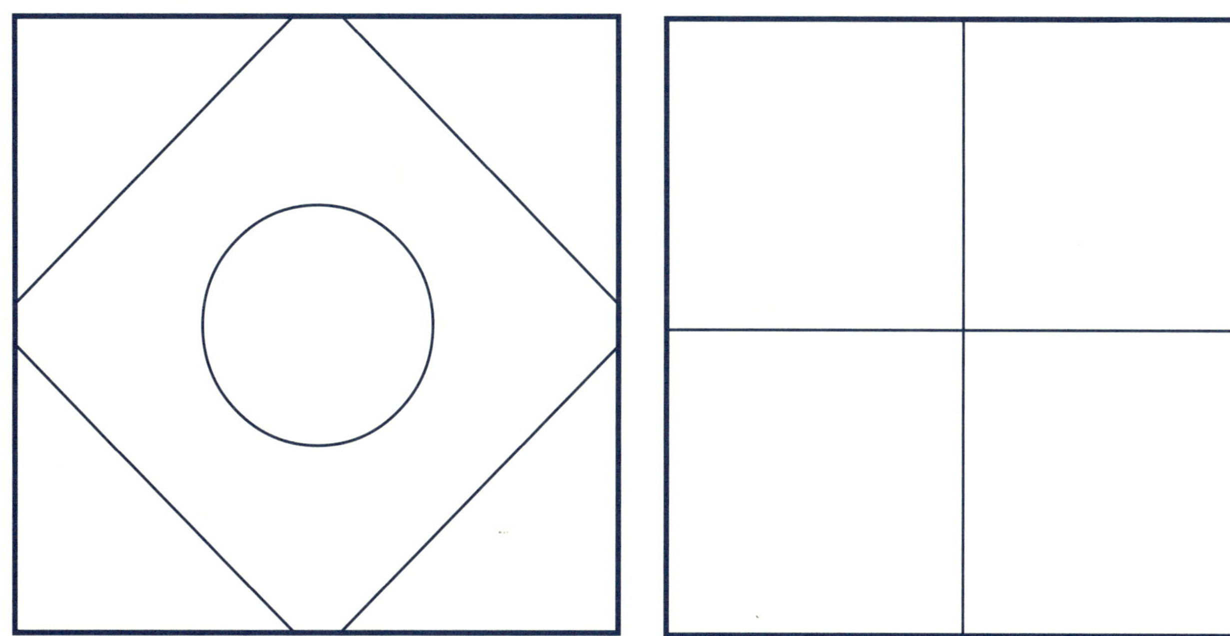

Your quilt square must be divided into 4 sections.

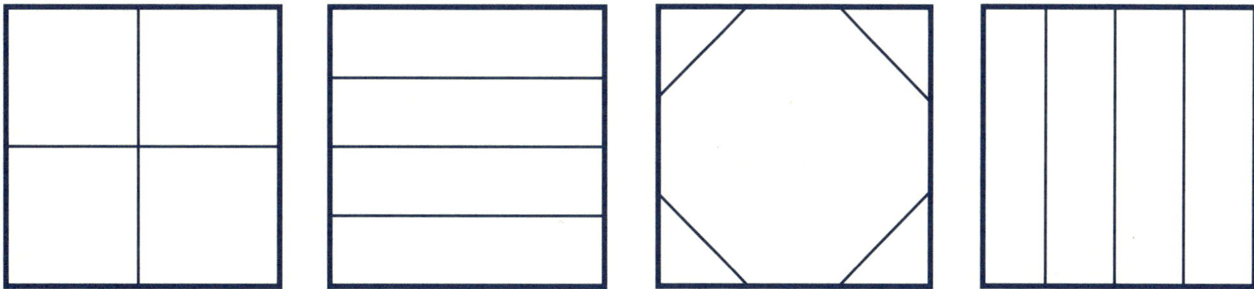

Each section will illustrate a different time period.

Label each section with a date.

Your quilt pattern could have more than four sections.
A fifth (or sixth) section could include a poem on your quilt square!

You might choose to put a border on your quilt!

Jo's Shows

Activity:
"Last Sailing of the Ti"

TEACHER NOTES *and* INFO

There are a number of drama opportunities in an interdisciplinary study. This technique is called "Freeze Frames." Students learn about one activity and have some time to practice their activity. At a certain point, the teacher calls "FREEZE" and the actors freeze in position. The scene is as if someone pushed the pause button on a VCR. After you practice a little you can let the actors "roll it" and continue the activity. The scene then becomes a play!

After you visit the Shelburne Museum and your students have experienced the nature of the jobs and happenings first hand, have them dramatize the last sailing of the Ti. Students in small groups will have time to learn more about their jobs and to plan the enactment. One highlight of this activity for me is that every year I find that two or three of my students' grandparents were at the dance on the last sailing.

The following areas are acted out:

1. boiler room   2. captain's deck   3. purser's office   4. kitchen

The performance can have a beginning, middle and end with a freeze at each point. Students need to decide on the beginning of their actions and the middle and the end.

Other Ideas
• You may want to think about doing a performance with all the actions happening simultaneously. A narrator could circulate and observe each action; other groups would continue silently and the scene that the narrator is speaking of could proceed with soundtrack.

The rest of the students could be given the following roles of characters:

• 3 girls from Burlington and their great-aunt. The girls want to be silly but the great-aunt holds a very careful guard on them.

• 2 older gentlemen who now are rather dignified and smoke cigars as they stroll on deck. They had worked as scullery mess boys in the summer of 1928 and reminisce.

• 2 shy boys who are very nervous about being at the dance and who spend most of the time watching the crew do their work.

• 2 girls from New York City who are very well-behaved but very incredulous at the view of Lake Champlain.

• 2–3 students may choose to be the character of a grandparent or someone who the students may have interviewed about the last sailing of the Ti.

Writing

TEACHER NOTES *and* **INFO**

There are endless ways to use writing to explore time on Lake Champlain. Here are some ideas!

STUDENT ACTIVITY: *My Favorite Time*

Write about a time on Lake Champlain. Include as many details (from field trips and class work) about life on the lake as you can. You might begin, "My favorite time in history is...."

STUDENT ACTIVITY: *Just One Place*

Write about one place on the lake. Imagine a spot that you know. Describe the way that place changed through time. Make a three-part drawing to accompany your essay that shows three different times in history.

STUDENT ACTIVITY: *Burlington Waterfront*

Discuss how life changed on the lake on one spot: the Burlington waterfront.

1. Imagine the land at the mouth of the Winooski River and what it must have meant to the Abenaki. Picture lots of trees, maybe a small settlement on the land that is now Battery Park, perhaps a small group arriving on canoe from the larger settlement near the mouth of the Winooski River.

2. Read aloud this description of Burlington harbor in 1790 (from LAKE CHAMPLAIN: KEY TO LIBERTY):

> *"In 1790, Horace Loomis, one of the city's early citizens, took up residence in a log house on what is now Pearl Street....At this time only four buildings perched at the edge of the woods on the lake. A few logs fastened to the bank served as the first dock, but most lake men anchored in deeper water, rolling their barrels of molasses overboard and floating them to shore."*

Note: You can use your local area. Contact the historical society for graphics that might help students envision the change over time.

The Abenaki name for the Winooski River is the "Winozkitegok" or the "onion land river."

3. Show this painting of Burlington harbor c.1830 (available as poster from Shelburne Museum).

4. Show a slide or postcard of the present-day waterfront (taken from the ferry) or use this aerial photo.

5. Discuss the actual details of how this place has changed over time and the implications of those changes (i.e. jobs, ecology, population, technology, etc.).

6. Discuss what the waterfront might be like in 2050.

STUDENT ACTIVITY: *So Long, Sam*

At the end of your Lake Champlain study, write a closing entry in your thinkbook as a letter to Samuel de Champlain, titled "So Long, Sam."

Brainstorm with kids what the lake looked like when Samuel de Champlain sailed down it in 1609. Discuss the changes that occurred after 1609. Have students write letters to Sam explaining some of the changes that they think are important.

Dear Sam,

Hi! I'm a student at Milton Jr. High. You probably haven't heard of a high school. A high school is a place where you learn, and they serve you really gross food with artificial ingredients.

A lot has changed since you were here in 1609, when you found Lake Champlain. Your nice clean lake that you knew is now a polluted lake. The once beautiful lakeside is now covered with houses and developments. I'd love to tell you more, but I really gotta go! Bye!

AGFA,

Debbie Clark, Grade 7, Milton

P.S. Write back if you have some spare time in the future.

STUDENT ACTIVITY: *Old News*

Create news stories from different time periods. After you have studied a certain time in the past, assign students the task of writing a "news story" from that time period.

Taking It Home

Interview someone
- 20 years old
- 40 years old
- 60 years old about one topic or one place on the lake.

Write up your interviews. Add three illustrations that show the different impressions these people had.

Activity:
Trip Around Lake Champlain

TEACHER NOTES *and* INFO

Every year this major writing activity seems to change. It began with a geography focus and students had to include references to geographical features and places on their "trip." Some years it has been stories about historical events with a lot of time spent on sorting out the nuances of each historical period. In the last few years, I have incorporated more sciences into my study. Now the "history" story is an option but students can also choose an adventure story that includes a scientific or nautical discovery or an adventure that "tells a science story." Whatever way you structure it, writing a major story about the lake gives students the chance to retell the stories they have learned—and that's what learning is all about!

STUDENT ACTIVITY

1. Brainstorm information as a pre-writing activity. Use a blank grid for each historical period to develop information with your students. I use the overhead projector and through class discussion, we fill in the information. Use as your reference the completed grids on p. 193. This can be done as a class or in cooperative groups. After the work is completed, make posters with the information. Display them in the room for reference during writing time.

2. Discuss the importance of historically accurate information. I use the example of a sailor working on a sloop in the 1700s. What's wrong if he stops for a snack and eats Doritos?

3. Use the worksheet "Trip Around the Lake" as a story starter.

4. Use your writing process to complete final product.

5. Give students time to make illustrations and exceptional covers for their stories.

STUDENT HANDOUT - "Trip Around the Lake"

Other Ideas

• *Some years there are students who want to explore the future of Lake Champlain! Use the grid to generate endless possibilities: hover craft, biosphere, underwater habitat, no zebra mussels!*

• *The grids can be made into a small booklet for students to use as a reference. Copy the grid page and cut into four sections so that each mini-page has a century's worth of story ideas!*

Trip Around the Lake

In order to write a great trip around the lake, you must make some choices about what's going to be in your story!

1. WHEN will your story take place? 1500s? 1600s? 1700s? 1800s? 1900s? Maybe you will write about the future? Explain below WHEN your story will happen.

2. WHERE will your story happen? What details can you include from all the things we have seen? Describe below WHERE your story will happen.

3. Now the most fun! WHAT will happen in your story? Will it be a fishing story, a revolutionary battle, a canoe trip, a ferry boat ride, a swim, an underwater diving expedition? What can you think of? Describe below WHAT will happen in your story.

Great! You are ready to begin. Have a great trip!

If My Story Happens in the 1500s

Transportation

dugout canoe
bark canoe
small raft
walking
snowshoes

Tools/Weapons

spear
bow and arrow
rock knife/tool
arrowhead
snares/traps

Food

corn/squash/beans
fish
game - venison/muskrat/rabbit
berries
nuts
roots (gathering)

Housing

huts
wigwam - made of wood, hide, bark
longhouse
cave
lean-tos

Things That Could Happen

play a game, dance
make a canoe
make tools
cook over a fire
tell/hear stories
- in a longhouse
- around a fire
build a shelter
hunt, fish, trap
see Champ
Abenaki meet Iroquois
c. 1609 - talk about "new tribe" of
Europeans

If My Story Happens in the 1600s-1700s

Transportation

dugout canoe
bark canoe
raft
bateau
sailing ship
schooner
sloop
wagon
horse
snowshoes

Tools/Weapons

spear
bow and arrow
arrowhead
musket/rifle
ax
adze
cannon
knife
tomahawk
swivel gun
grape shot
traps/snares

Food

corn/squash/beans
fish
game
berries/nuts/roots/(gathering)
flour
molasses

Housing

wigwam
longhouse
cabin
fort
hut
(shelter on boats)

Things That Could Happen

trap beaver
Abenaki and Iroquois
meet Europeans
Europeans meet
Abenaki and Iroquois
clear land
hunt
explore
build cabin
French and Indian War
American Revolution

If My Story Happens in the 1800s

Transportation

canoe
sailing ships
steamboat
canal boat
tug boat
barge
log raft
snowshoes

Tools/Weapons

rifles/musket
plow
cannon
ax
saw
traps

Food

grow your own food
fish
game
supplies at general store
trapping
garden
hunting

Housing

wigwam
longhouse
cabin
larger houses (2 - 3 stories)
brick houses

Things That Could Happen

work in engine room - steamboat
cut/transport lumber
steamboat races
War of 1812
visit Burlington
- *3rd largest seaport in the world*
work in lighthouse
travel on canal boat
make snowshoes, birchbark canoes,
ash splint and sweetgrass baskets

If My Story Happens in the 1900s

Transportation

canoe
sailboat
steamboat
railroad
ferry
motorboat
underwater diving
car
waterski
windsurf
jet ski
kayak

Tools/Weapons

rifle
tractor/plow
hammer
chain saw

Food

supermarkets
pizza
fish
game
Doritos
ice cream
gardens

Housing

brick
cement
large office buildings
wood houses

Things That Could Happen

fishing trips
boat ride
hunting
discover wreck
first/last ride of the Ti
ride *Spirit of Ethan Allen*
powwow
canoe trip
visit historical site
find ancient artifact
discover zebra mussel

If My Story Happens
in the __________

Transportation

Tools/Weapons

Food

Housing

Things That Could Happen

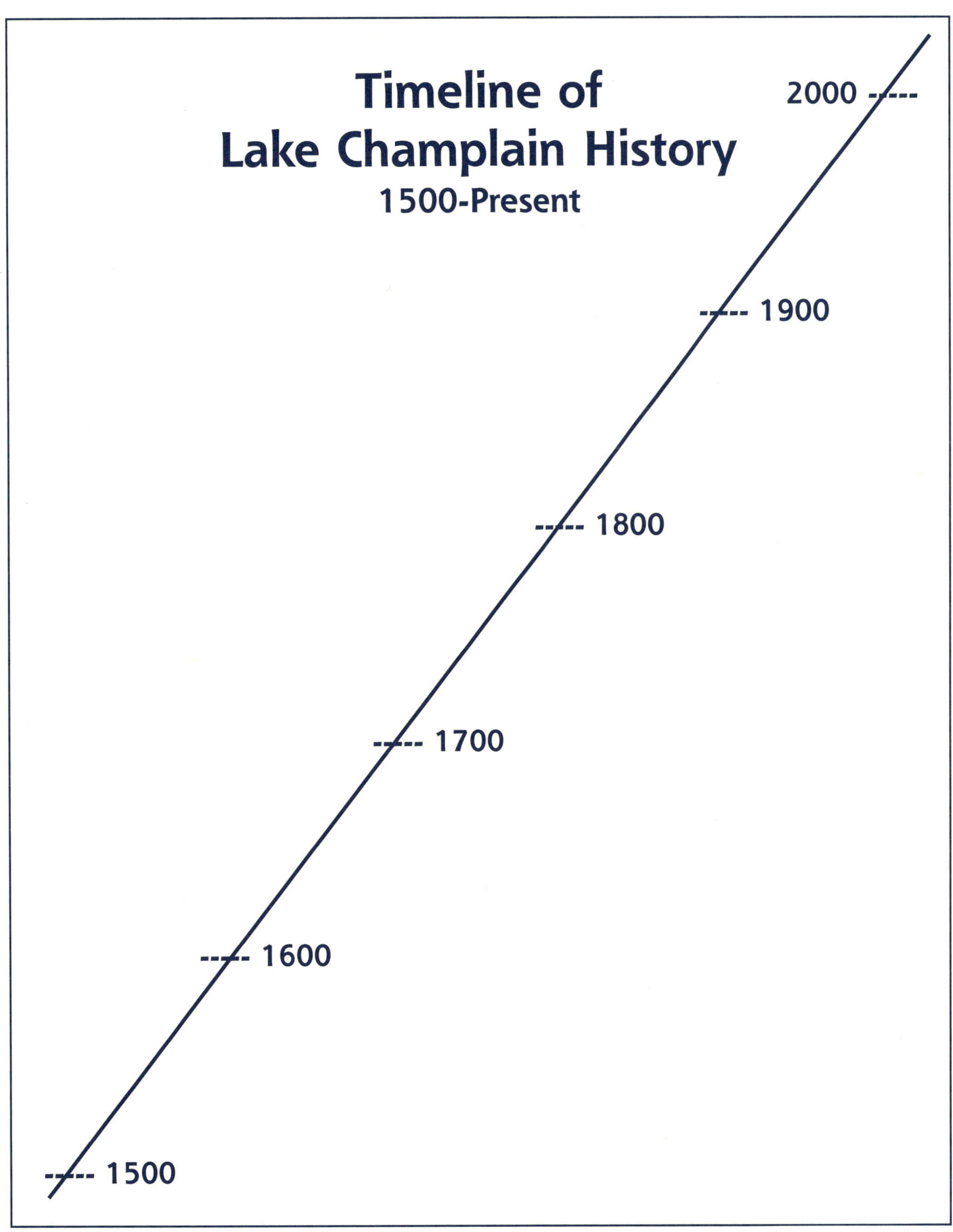

Timeline of
Lake Champlain History
1500-Present
2000
1900
1800
1700
1600
1500

Lake Champlain History

1. ______________________ were the "original navigators."

2. In 1609, ______________________ "discovered" Lake Champlain.

3. For many years after that, both ______________________ and ______________________ wanted control of the Champlain Valley.

4. They wanted the ______________________ to build ships.

5. They built many ______________________ on Lake Champlain to house their soldiers.

6. ______________________ and ______________________ fought the French and Indian War, 1759–1763.

7. After the War ended, many people wanted to move to the land that is now Vermont. It was claimed by the colonies of ______________________ and ______________________.

8. One group that was angry about this was called ______________________.

9. Before they settled this problem, the ______________________ began.

10. Two important leaders during this conflict were ______________________ and ______________________.

11. They captured ______________________.

12. The Battle of ______________________ was important when Arnold escaped from the British.

13. After the War, many people wanted to resettle the Champlain Valley. Because the roads were bad, Lake Champlain was the ______________________.

14. At first, people used ______________________ and ______________________ for transportation on the lake.

15. In the 1790s, they used ______________________ and ______________________.

16. In 1809, the first ______________________ was built on Lake Champlain (the world's second).

17. In 1812, the United States fought the ______________________ in the War of 1812.

18. In 1823, the ______________________ Canal was finished.

19. In the 1830s, people used ______________________ and ______________________.

20. In the 1870s, ______________________ was the third largest lumber port in the world!

Answers: 1. Native Americans, **2.** Samuel de Champlain, **3.** British and French, **4.** wood, **5.** forts, **6.** British (Iroquois) and French (Abenaki), **7.** New York and New Hampshire, **8.** Green Mountain Boys, **9.** American Revolution, **10.** Ethan Allen and Benedict Arnold, **11.** Fort Ticonderoga, **12.** Valcour Island, **13.** main highway, **14.** canoes and bateaux, **15.** sloops and schooners, **16.** steamboat, **17.** British, **18.** Champlain, **19.** steamboats and sailing canal boats, **20.** Burlington.

Nautical Archeology in the Lake Champlain Basin

What is Nautical Archeology?

Text by Sarah Hamilton. Artwork by Kyle Green
Grade 5, School Street School, Milton, Vermont

There are many different tools that you can use when studying nautical archeology.

Scuba divers use a vacuum-like tool to help them suck up the dirt and other small artifacts. Then they use a smurf pool to search through what they had sucked up.

Nautical archeology means underwater archeology, or the study of things that have happened in the past that are left underwater. Just like archeology you look for artifacts that will help you find out about our history. In this case, underwater history.

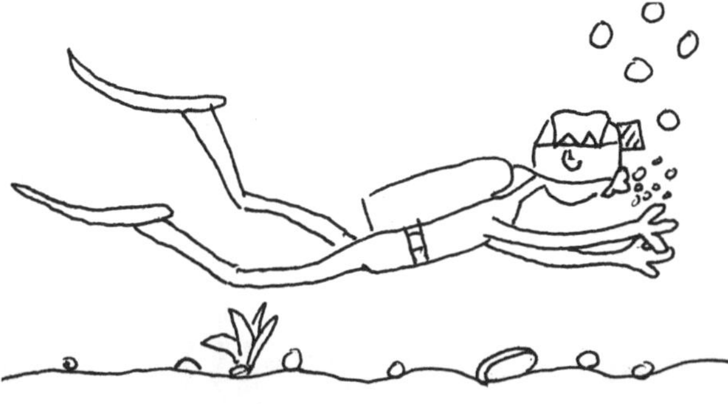

Most nautical archeology artifacts are found by scuba divers.

When you have found an artifact you have to tell the state or you will be breaking the law. You also have to handle the artifacts carefully.

Introduction

This essay was written by Art Cohn, whose vision and leadership has prompted much of the activity described in the chapter. I edited it and made changes to fit the language and intent of THIS LAKE ALIVE!

Ten years ago, few people knew that there were boats beneath the waters of Lake Champlain. Indeed, there are hundreds of them and they are probably one of the most significant collections in the world.

This essay outlines the importance of this collection and current efforts to preserve the underwater treasures. It is a timely piece of writing and both the threat of zebra mussels and the possibility of many more finds may change the tale told here.

Most importantly, the story of these ships provides tangible relics to help students unravel the past. Any teacher who has taken her students to the Lake Champlain Maritime Museum or had a diver visit the class can attest to the incredible interest and excitement that these boats create. Because of the work done by the outstanding staff at the museum, students can sit on board the life-size replica of the *Philadelphia II* and shout the commands of a captain in the American Revolution, simulate a dive on an underwater wreck (no talking), and see an incredible amount of boats and related nautical artifacts, photos and artwork that tell the tale of days gone by.

Dale Henry, one of the more well-known staff persons at the museum, is featured here in "Champ's Chat." I interviewed him on board the *Philadelphia II*.

Philadelphia II docked at the Lake Champlain Maritime Museum

Nautical Archeology
in the Lake Champlain Basin

People love shipwrecks. Maybe it's because we have heard so many stories about underwater treasures that the idea of shipwrecks stirs our imagination. Lake Champlain has an extraordinary collection of underwater wrecks, perhaps the largest in North America. But the treasure on these vessels is not gold or diamonds. The treasure is the clues and links to the past that these vessels provide.

Like many things, our sense of historical appreciation runs in cycles. In the 1960s and 1970s, people weren't thinking or talking much about Lake Champlain. Waterfronts were less active, ferry service was reduced and the lake's last steamboat was retired and moved to the Shelburne Museum. Most likely, there weren't many students who learned about the lake in school. A fourth grader from the town of Addison, Vermont, would have known that Arnold's Bay was a place with good fishing, not a place where an important naval battle was fought during the American Revolution.

In the 1980s and 1990s, many things happened to bring the lake into the public eye. You are living at a time when there is an incredible amount of discussion on all fronts about what should be done to save this precious resource. Scientists, geologists, historians, farmers, anglers, city planners and lots of ordinary citizens are involved in this dialogue.

One of the sparks that triggered this new awareness was the discovery of a vast collection of shipwrecks and other historic sites beneath the waters of the lake.

If you know your country's history, you know that many important chapters were written right here on Lake Champlain. This history can be studied by looking at the different kind of boats that were used throughout history.

The first boats that traveled for centuries on Lake Champlain were dugout and bark canoes. In recent history, there has been an incredible variety of ships. In the 1700s, people used bateaux, flat-bottomed vessels, primarily for transporting military supplies and soldiers. When the French, British and Americans staged war on the lake, they used naval vessels: sloops, gunboats,

row gallies, radeaux, gondolas and other ships of war.

These military vessels were displaced by early ferries, log rafts, lake sloops and schooners. Steamboats were a main mode of travel during the nineteenth century. Commercial watercraft gradually gave way to recreational interests and now people use sailboats, windsurfers and motorboats to travel on the lake.

Signs of the past are all around us. Tourists who visit Lake Champlain are able to visit a multitude of historical sites on land that are linked to the lake's past. School children like yourselves are part of a new generation of citizens studying the lake.

But many of our cultural resources are not on land, but underwater. The submerged vessels are on the lake's bottom for a variety of reasons. Some were abandoned after their useful life was over, some sank in battle and others sank from storms or accidents.

In the 1800s, historic vessels had to be seen from the surface at low water to be found. When they were, they were often raised. For the past 40 years, divers have explored what they could find in the lake in water up to 100 feet deep. They often searched vessels for artifacts and sometimes took wooden timbers from the boats. You may know someone who has a cane, gavel, lamp or table made from wood from one of these historic vessels. Now this kind of "treasure hunting" is against the law.

Prior to the 1970s, over a dozen historic vessels were raised from the lake. Time has taught us that this can be disastrous for submerged wooden ships because most of them cannot survive the destabilizing transition from water to air without large doses of conservation. Some vessels literally fall apart when they are exposed to the air.

Duke of Cumberland, *raised in 1909*

Nautical archeology is the archeological study of wrecks and vessels underwater. It is a relatively new science and it includes a complex process of planning, research, surveying, recovery, analysis and conservation.

We have learned that the best way to preserve a wreck is to leave it where it is. The cold, fresh water of Lake Champlain keeps the vessel from decaying. How well a wreck survives underwater depends on a number of things: salinity of the water, depth, light, temperature, and the amount of oxygen in the sediment on which the wreck sits. Much of this lake's underwater environment is clear, cold water, which is perfect for preserving ships.

Over the past 15 years, researchers have had the privilege of being able to locate and study *in situ*, or right where they are, a variety of underwater sites. Lake Champlain has vessels that represent just about all historic times: Native American dugout canoes; French and British colonial naval craft; American and British Revolutionary era ships as well as remnants from the submerged "Great Bridge;" American and British War of 1812 ships; commercial vessels of all kinds, including the *Phoenix*, the oldest surviving steamboat hull in the world, and the Burlington Bay Horse Ferry, the only known survivor of its class. As exceptional as these discoveries are, it is important to realize that as of this writing we are only beginning to scratch the surface of the size and diversity of this collection. There are more boats to be discovered!

*The use of side-scan sonar in 1988 revealed the wreck **Sarah Ellen**, a lake schooner built in 1849, which sits intact in over 300 feet of water. The state of preservation of this boat is so good that you can still read its name in white paint on the transom.*

The "Great Bridge" was constructed during the American Revolution. It spanned the lake between Fort Ticonderoga and Mount Independence.

Recently, we have seen a technological leap in the way underwater sites are located and studied. New advances in electronic remote sensing equipment have radically changed our ability to locate submerged properties. New advances in electronic technology have the potential to reveal all the lake's previously hidden secrets.

In the spring of 1994, Art Cohn directed a sonar survey with a team of historians and identified a vessel they hadn't known about. That fall the team, with archeologist Kevin Crisman, returned to the site with an ROV (Remote Operated Vehicle). They relocated the vessel and sent the remote camera down to study and record the site on videotape. After reviewing the tape, the team concluded that they had found the *L.A. Hall,* a canal boat loaded with pig iron from Port Henry. The boat had sunk in 1878.

Sometimes diving is a lot like solving a mystery. For example, until divers discovered the *General Butler* in 1981, historians didn't refer to sailing canal boats. It was commonly believed that canal boats were towed. But when divers surveyed the *General Butler,* they found mast supports and a centerboard. They thought that the vessel must have been rigged for sail. They continued research in the library and found that the boat was registered as a "schooner rigged Lake and Canal Boat." Further research determined that sailing canal boats were used on Lake Champlain.

a sailing canal schooner similar to the **General Butler**

Due to new technology, wrecks can be studied *in situ*. Divers use new electronic survey equipment to study the wreck without having to raise it to the surface.

On behalf of the citizenry, the States of Vermont and New York own the underwater heritage of Lake Champlain and no one may disturb artifacts, shipwrecks or significant sites without permission. Once a vessel is found, a team of historians, archeologists, photographers, artists and artifact handlers is assembled and a permit is issued by the Division for Historic Preservation.

*diver examining stern of the **General Butler***

Identifying and documenting a wreck is a long process. Giovanna Peebles, head of the Vermont Division for Historic Preservation, outlines the four stages of nautical archeology:

• Library research to get background information on time, place, events, technology and social and economic patterns.

*• Survey to document precise location of vessel. (Sometimes wrecks are found by accident, like the discovery of the **Phoenix**. But sometimes a group of divers does a survey of a specific area, such as the survey done of the "Ft. Ti/ Mt. I" area in 1983. A survey might be done by a group of divers or by side scan sonar.)*

• Evaluation of wreck to determine if survey information matches what is already known and if identity of ship can be determined. Evaluation involves a precise and thorough description of the property as it presently exists, including a record of its dimensions, all fittings, equipment, cargo, ballast, artifacts and other materials observed in it or nearby, and its present condition. The team produces scale drawings, photographs, video footage and historical reports.

• Data recovery, the last stage of this process. It involves physical disturbance of some or all of the artifacts. It is an incredibly time-consuming and arduous process. Even the smallest item may have significance and everything that is removed is recorded and cataloged.

The Lake Champlain Maritime Museum has recently experimented with a new interpretive process made possible by this improved archeological documentation of underwater sites. The museum began a program of building full-sized working replicas of historic vessels.

In 1987, a bateau was constructed. The bateau was a large rowboat used in the 1700s to transport troops and supplies. The crew at the Maritime Museum had to document the boat's construction, make actual builder's drawings and then plan the construction of the boat. The bateau was launched in 1987 and is now at the Maritime Museum.

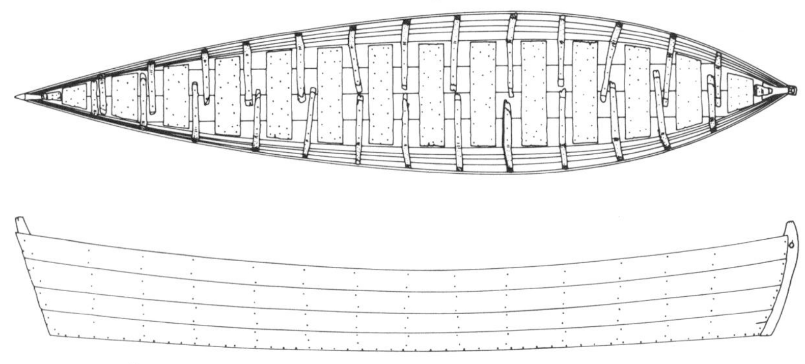

Building a replica has many advantages. People of all ages enjoy watching a boat being built. Historical information can be preserved to help people understand the story of the vessel. Launching the boat is a very exciting and festive occasion. Once launched, the completed vessel can be technically evaluated. This adds to our knowledge of watercraft. The completed vessel lets us "see history" without harming the original.

The Maritime Museum began construction of its second replica, the *Philadelphia II*, in 1989. It was launched in the summer of 1991.

The Story of Philadelphia I & II

Philadelphia I

The original *Philadelphia*, an American gunboat under the command of Benedict Arnold, was sunk at the Battle of Valcour Island on October 11, 1776. The gunboat remained underwater until 1935, when Colonel Lorenzo Hagglund raised it to the surface. There was no scuba equipment at the time. Hagglund and his crew took special care to make an inventory of the ship's location and document each artifact and part of the boat as they raised it. They also dried it out slowly, which minimized the damage of the air to the old wood.

Hagglund took the boat on a barge and toured the Hudson River and Lake Champlain for the next 25 years. In his will, Hagglund left the boat to the Smithsonian Institution in Washington, D.C. Since 1961, the *Philadelphia* has become a central exhibit at the National Museum of American History.

Philadelphia II

In 1989, the Lake Champlain Maritime Museum began construction of a replica of the gunboat *Philadelphia*. Created from plans and blueprints provided by the Smithsonian, the replica duplicates exactly the details and features of the 54-foot, 29-ton original. The crew at the museum worked for three years on the construction of the replica. Many classes and visitors saw and took part in the construction of the boat.

There were many problems that the boat builders had to solve in their efforts to build a vessel that was historically accurate. They tried as much as possible to use the tools and materials that were used to build the first *Philadelphia*, but they also made some decisions based on twentieth-century conditions.

The boat is now permanently docked at the museum and thousands of visitors board it each year and imagine what it might have been like to live, work and fight on it in 1776.

Champ's Chat with Dale Henry

Champ: Would you describe your job at the Maritime Museum?
Dale: I am a boat builder and a blacksmith. I also am an interpreter, which means I work on the site and explain the exhibits to our guests.

Champ: What was your part in the building on the *Philadelphia II*?
Dale: My official title was "boat builder's assistant." I was in charge of all the metal on board, anything that was iron, copper or lead. I also was in charge of authenticity, that's trying to make everything the way it was in 1776.

Champ: Is everything on the *Philadelphia II* exactly like the original?
Dale: No, but it's pretty close. We had to make some choices and we had a twentieth-century deadline. But there are some things that you can't do by machine. For example, the stem that holds all the planking at the bow, basically holding the front end of the boat together, has to fit exactly. It's a curved groove which can't be made by machine. So we made that and a lot of other things by hand, just for the experience of doing things like they were done then.

Champ: Why did the museum decide to build a replica?
Dale: Well, everyone can't go diving and most of the good wrecks are under the lake. Seeing a replica is a perfect way for people to get the feel of an historical boat.

Champ: What kind of decisions did you have to make when you started?
Dale: Well, we had to ask ourselves the question: Did we want to give people rides or build an exact replica? If we were going to give people rides, the Coast Guard would put so many restrictions on us there wasn't any way the boat could be authentic. So we decided to build an exact replica and the boat stays docked most of the time. If we do take it out on a sail, we have a crew of volunteers who choose to be on the boat and we don't have the same restrictions. I think we made the right choice.

Champ: How did you know where to start?
Dale: You know the original *Philadelphia* is in Washington, D.C., right?

Champ: Of course, I saw it sink during the Battle of Valcour Island and I was the only one who knew where it was until Hagglund discovered it.

Dale: Sorry, I forgot. Well, soon after the boat was brought to Washington, a man who worked there did detailed drawings of the boat. These detailed plans were like architectural drawings and they were our best resource.

Champ: What were some of the things you had to figure out?

Dale: I had to figure out how many nails were on the original *Philadelphia*. I figured that there were 250 nails on one plank. Then I counted the planks and figured out that there were about 9,000 nails on the original boat.

Champ: Did you make all those nails?

Dale: No, this was a time when we had to make some choices. The nails on the original boat were wrought iron, which is very hard to come by. It's around, but it's not made anymore, so you'd have to find things made of wrought iron and reform them into nails. That seemed like a huge task. So we bought square-cut nails. But modern nails have rounded heads and the handmade nails they used in 1776 had flat heads. So we had a blacksmith heat up the nails and flatten the heads. We only did this on the 5,000 nails that were visible. The other ones we left with the round heads.

Champ: I won't tell anyone, I promise. What were some other materials you used and why?

Dale: Well, we chose oak to build the boat. Oak was the standard wood everyone used back then because it was strong and durable. And oak was available nearby. We got our planks from a local sawmill. The mast, made of white pine, was from Bethel, Vermont, and the man that we got it from cut it down with an ax and had his team of horses carry it out of the woods, just like in the old days. He would have liked to have hewn the whole thing by hand, but again we had to finish the boat on schedule, so we did some of the hewing by machine.

Champ: Aren't there some crooked pieces of wood holding the boat together?

Dale: Yes, there are. They are called ribs because they hold the boat together just like your ribs hold you together. One of my jobs was to find trees of a special shape, with a natural crook in them, that would serve as the ribs of the boat. It was great fun, walking around the woods, looking at trees. The boat has 104 of these natural crooks and I found most of them. It used to be called compass wood.

Champ: Thanks so much for talking to me, Dale. One last question! What's the best thing about your work?

Dale: The best thing is the satisfaction I feel because I'm preserving these time-honored traditions in a modern, high-tech world!

This symbol (red and white) is used by divers in the United States to alert water traffic to diving activity.

*Zebra mussels, which currently pose a threat to underwater wrecks in Lake Champlain, were first found on the **General Butler** in the fall of 1994.*

Building replicas is one exciting way that you can learn the nautical history of Lake Champlain. But if you are a bit more adventurous and become a certified diver, there is another way you can see the boats that once traveled on Lake Champlain. In 1985, the Vermont Division for Historic Preservation created the first of five historic shipwreck sites as "Underwater Historic Preserves." This allows divers to safely locate and dive on historic wrecks.

One of the preserves is the wreck of the *General Butler*, which sank in a storm off Burlington harbor. It was manned by Captain William Montgomery, who with his teenage daughter and the crew escaped to safety. The *General Butler* is often visited by divers who can still see its remarkably intact hull and marble cargo. Bright yellow mooring buoys placed at its bow and stern make the *Butler* easy to find. Divers can follow a chain to the bottom, which connects to a yellow travel line that guides them along the lake bottom to the vessel. On the deck are the *Butler*'s anchor windlass, mast tabernacles, hatches, and dead-eyes. At the stern, divers can peer into the rear cabin where meals were served and bunks provided a moment's rest. The woodstove is still there, although it toppled on its side from the impact of the wreck. Fish congregate in schools on the stern deck and around the tiller bar that Captain Montgomery quickly lashed with a chain in his futile attempt to save his ship.

Your generation is the caretaker of this special collection of shipwrecks on the bottom of the lake. Are we to raise them, mine them, study them, recreate on them, or leave them alone? These are important decisions that you can be a part of.

Nautical Archeology
in the
Lake Champlain Basin

Activities

The activities in this section represent a sampling of the many exciting and worthwhile things you can do when studying nautical archeology with your students. Although nautical archeology and historic preservation are not subjects taught in our schools, you'll soon find out that they are incredible magnets for whatever else you are learning. The study of boats—how they were built, how and why they sunk, where they are and how they should be cared for—will add an exciting dimension to your lake study and present your students with important questions relating to the development of one's historical perspective and stewardship that they should consider.

QUESTIONS

- What is nautical archeology?
- What things are on the bottom of Lake Champlain?
- How did they get there?
- What technology is involved to survey and document them?

KEY RESOURCES

- From Sailing Ships and Sidewheelers *by Kevin Crisman (out of print)*
- Sails and Steam in the Mountains: A Maritime and Military History of Lake George and Lake Champlain *by Russell Bellico*
- Lake Champlain Maritime Museum—*field trip and educational resources*
- "Dive Historic Lake Champlain: Vermont's Underwater Historic Preserve System"—*Vermont Division for Historic Preservation*
- "Lake Champlain Dive and Historic Sites"—*Dive Research and Associates*

Word Bank

aft
amidship
archeology
artifact
ballast
barge
bateau
bow
brig
canal boat
capstan
centerboard
deadeye
draft
dugout canoe
frame
frigate
galley
gondola
gunboat
hull
keel
nautical
port
preservation
radeau
replica
rib
row galley
rudderpost
schooner
scow
ship
shipwright
side-wheeler
sloop
starboard
stern
tabernacle
tiller

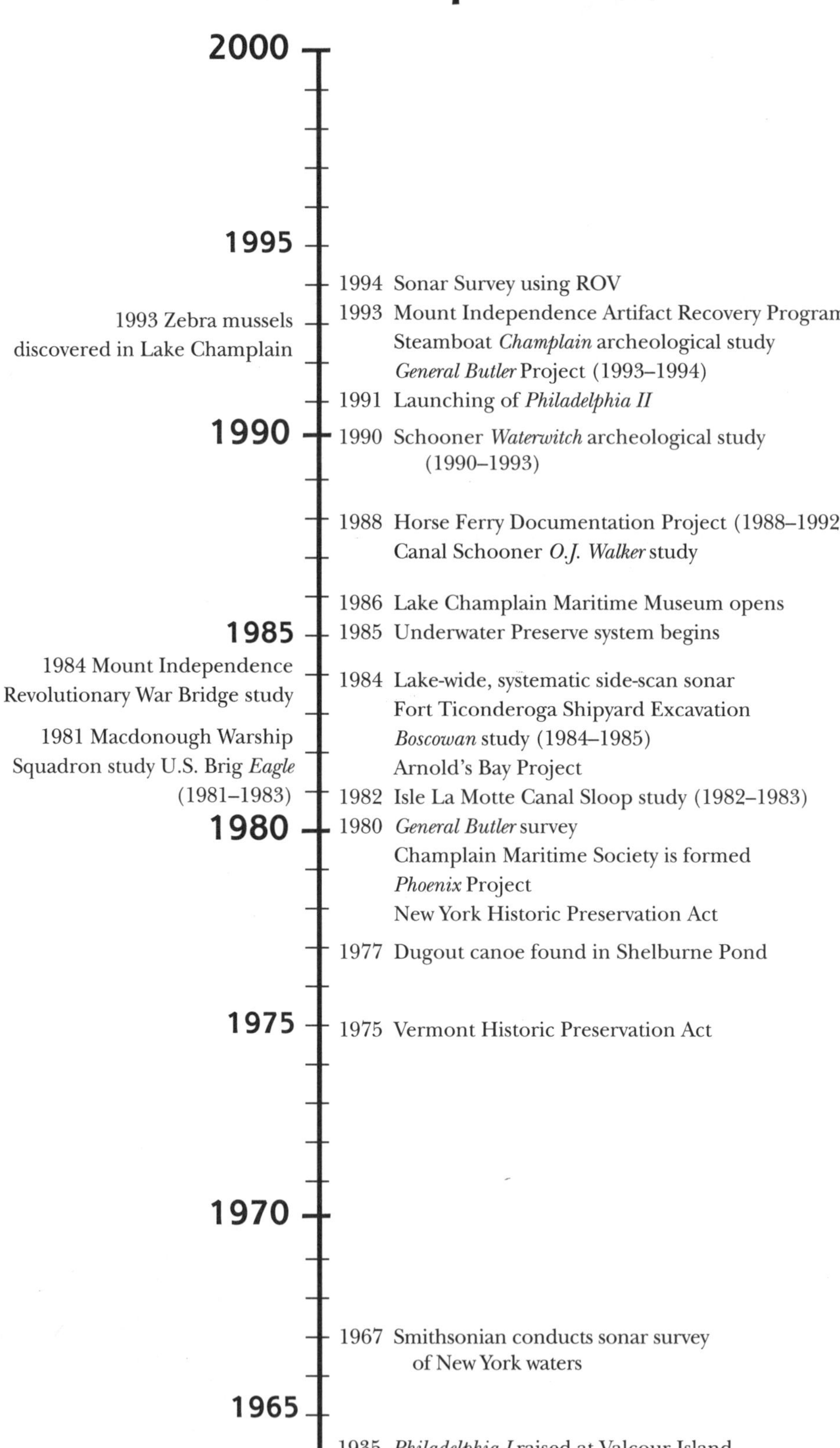

Activity: **Float a Boat**

TEACHER NOTES *and* INFO

Boats float because their weight is less than that of an equal volume of water. While boats may be made of materials that themselves will not float, such as steel or concrete, the weight of the boat hull, including its construction materials and contents (even air!), must be less than an equal volume of water—or the boat will sink.

In general, the lighter the vessel, the higher it will float in the water. For example, if you are sitting in a rowboat next to an identical empty rowboat, more of the empty boat's topsides will be visible above the water than those of your boat. The force that holds up the boat is called buoyancy. Buoyant force can be understood by imagining the part of the boat hull that's below water as a "hole" in the water that the water constantly tries to fill in. Water pushes the hull upward until the boat's weight equals the weight of the water that would fill the hole.

Most students do not expect that they can make boats from materials that do not float. The concept of buoyancy is a dynamic starting point to alter their perception of what appears to be a discrepancy in logic.

STUDENT ACTIVITY

Before beginning this activity, discuss these questions with your students:
• Why do you think boats float? Why do you think supertankers or large sailing ships float?
• What type of boat do you think was first on Lake Champlain?
• What materials can be used to construct a boat or a ship?
• Why do you think the American fleet that was on Lake Champlain during the Revolutionary War was built of oak? How do you think they came up with the designs they did for the fleet?

You will need
for each pair of students:
• a small pail with several inches of water
• oil-based modeling clay
• paper clips and other small objects that will sink

Students will arrange themselves in pairs with the necessary equipment. Instruct each pair to do the following:

1. Fashion a canoe/bateau hull from one of their balls of clay, leaving the other in a ball form.

2. Place each piece of clay, the ball and the boat, gently into the water.

3. Observe the result. Note that the boats will float. Some boats may need reshaping (higher topsides will provide a deeper "pocket").

4. Measure the load capacity of the vessels by using uniform objects as cargo. Use small paper clips or other similar sinkable objects.

This entire activity can be extended into a boat-design contest with prizes given to the designer who produces the hull with the greatest cargo capacity.

FOLLOW-UP QUESTIONS *to* Float a Boat

1. What helped your boat float?
2. What do you think is important about the design of a boat?
3. What helps a steel ship float? a wooden ship?
4. Compare data from the different hulls to initiate a discussion about buoyancy, volume and stability.

Credit: *Activity from Lake Champlain Maritime Museum. Used with permission.*

Activity: **As Time Floats By**

TEACHER NOTES *and* INFO

Carol Livingston has developed a nautical timeline activity that is a valuable way for students to comprehend the changes in nautical technology. The drawings for this activity come from a book published by the Division for Historic Preservation called FROM SAILING SHIPS TO SIDEWHEELERS by Kevin Crisman. The book, unfortunately, is out of print. We have designed this activity to be done without it, but get a copy if you can, as it contains 5valuable information about the boats and their history. The boat drawings by Kevin Crisman are included in this activity. The kinds of boats used on Lake Champlain are similar to those used other places, so you can use a general resource, such as a book on sailing ships.

Artwork by Kyle Green, Grade 5,
School Street School, Milton, Vermont

Decide before you begin how big a timeline students are going to make and prepare copies of boat drawings as needed.

Examples:

• Reduce boat drawings (p. 220-221) and have each student make a 8$\frac{1}{2}$" x 11" timeline. Use blank timeline on p. 195.
• Reduce drawings and have pairs of students make a timeline on two sheets of legal paper, taped together.
• Make one large timeline on the wall and have groups of students research a particular boat, design a way to share that information in written form and mount the drawing and the information on the large class timeline.
• Using any size timeline, have students make their own drawings using Crisman's drawings as a reference and place their own artwork on the timeline.

STUDENT ACTIVITY

Share with students basic information about the different kinds of boats on Lake Champlain. Discuss with students the changes in technology, demands of commerce and the human needs that drove this technology.

Have students make a nautical timeline.

One year we decided to put only one requirement on the students' boats: that they float. I expressed my hope that students would use the boats to process the historical information we had learned. They decided to organize the projects to cover the span of history, as well as the present and future. They wrote stories about what happened when their boats traveled the lake, then read the stories aloud while presenting their models. Their projects became a talking nautical timeline!

Credit: *Activity and handout from Carol Livingston. Used with permission.*

Activity:
Lake Champlain Boat Model

TEACHER NOTES *and* INFO

This boat model activity can be done as a culminating activity for "As Time Floats By" or by itself. Both activities are great to do after you have been to the Lake Champlain Maritime Museum.

STUDENT ACTIVITY

Invite students to make a model of any kind of boat. Carol Livingston has students make their boats at home, on their own time, using any materials that they choose.

Students working in the same time period can draw a mural background with historically accurate information. Boat models and murals can be a large three-dimensional display. Students might be able to design a mechanism for the boats to "glide by" with the mural they create!

STUDENT HANDOUT - "Lake Champlain Boat Model"

Lake Champlain Boat Model

You need to choose one type of boat that was used on Lake Champlain—between 5,000 B.C. and the present—and make a simple model of it. It may be constructed of cardboard, wood, toothpicks or other materials you have studied.

The model is due _______________, and you must complete the information below for your boat. Please learn about your boat and have fun constructing a BASIC model. Try to be accurate with your details but don't get overly concerned with how perfect a structure it is!

Name of your boat: ____

Type of boat: ____

Time period it was used on Lake Champlain: ___________________________

What was happening on the lake during this time period? ________________

____

____

Who used your boat? For what? _____________________________________

What was the real boat constructed of? _______________________________

How was the boat powered? ____

Why did you choose this boat? ______________________________________

____

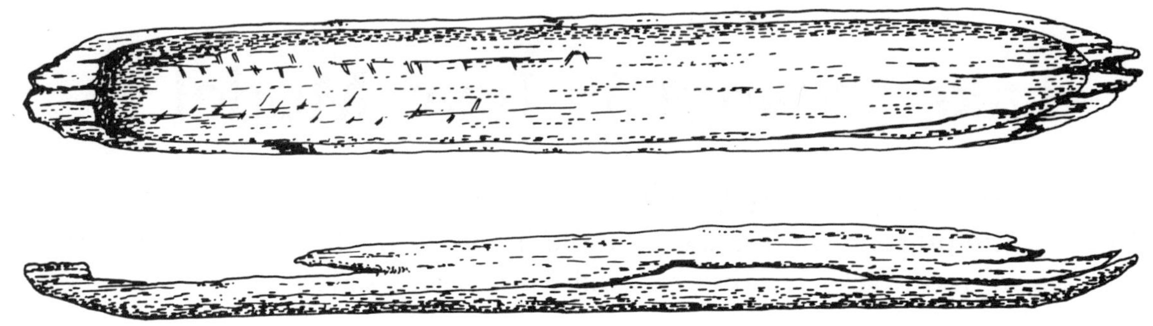

Type of boat: dugout canoe
Historical Period: Native American

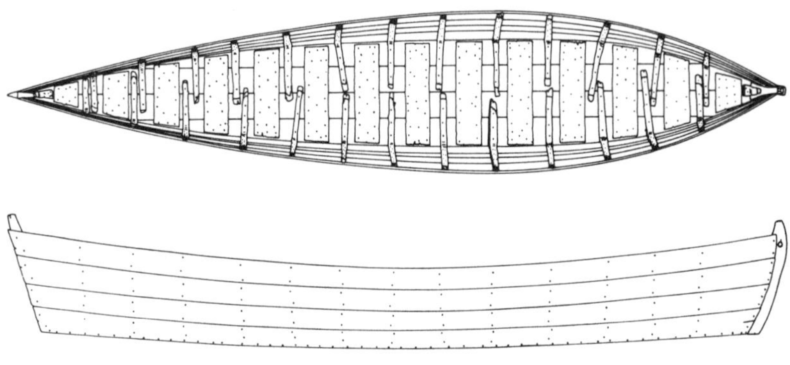

Type of boat: bateau
Historical Period: Colonial

Type of boat: sloop (British 16-gun sloop: *Boscawen*)
Historical Period: European Settlement

Type of boat: galley (Benedict Arnold's flagship: *Congress*)
Historical Period: American Revolution

Type of boat: brig (U.S. Navy's *Eagle*)
Historical Period: War of 1812

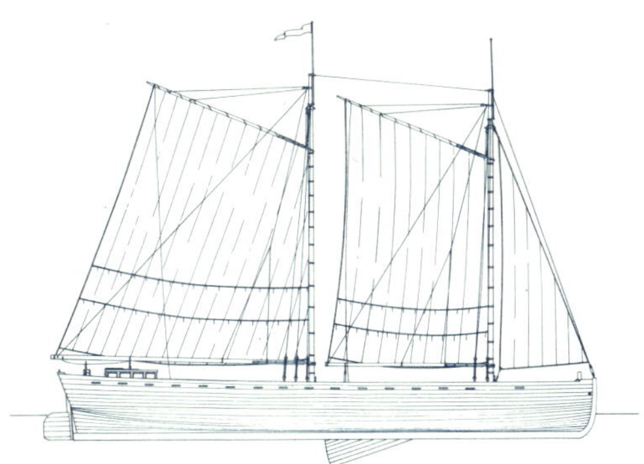

Type of boat: canal schooner (*General Butler*)
Historical Period: Commercial

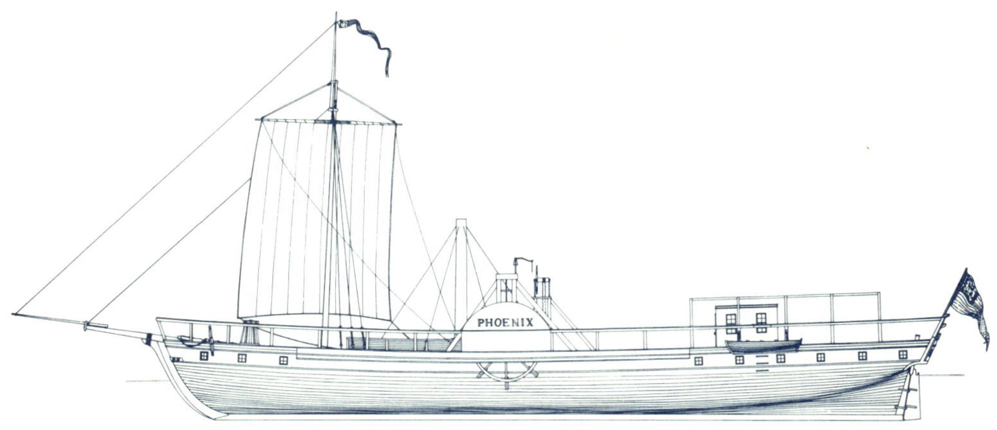

Type of boat: steamer (Lake Champlain Transportation Company's *Phoenix*)
Historical Period: Commercial

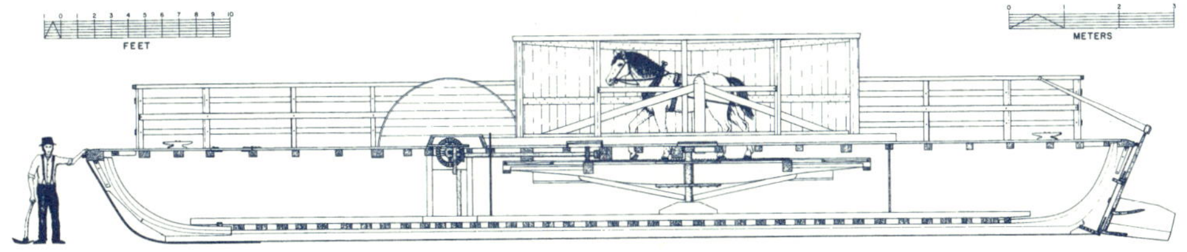

Type of boat: horse ferry; **Historical Period:** Commercial

Type of boat: commercial ferry (Lake Champlain Transportation Company's *Plattsburgh*)
Historical Period: Modern Times

Activity: **Phoenix III: Reading Interpretation**

TEACHER NOTES *and* INFO

Although the story of the *Phoenix* has been edited from the original article that appeared in the "Phoenix Project," the procedure of underwater archeology may still be hard for your students to understand. There are a variety of ways to help them. Here are a few suggestions:

STUDENT ACTIVITY

• Choose 20 nautical words from the article that you think students will need help understanding. Reference materials, including glossaries, are available from the Vermont Division for Historic Preservation or the Lake Champlain Maritime Museum. General information in the library will also help. Assign teams of students to design glossary definitions within the context of the story. Make a class "nautical dictionary" or an illustrated glossary of these terms.

• Assign your students the task of writing a manual for new divers who are participating in an underwater inventory. The manual could include diagrams, "five important things to know," a step-by-step process or safety tips.

• Assign your students a creative writing piece that tells the story of the archeological survey from the viewpoint of the *Phoenix.* Ask the students to write what the boat would be able to observe that the divers are doing.

• Paraphrase the story into one page and design a worksheet with missing information. (See "Facts About the Ticonderoga," p. 161.)

Phoenix III

For at least one hundred and twenty years, shipwrecks have been pulled out of Lake Champlain. But very few of the early salvagers showed much interest in the historical preservation of their finds. For the most part, the wrecks were brought up for their value as lumber, scrap iron or souvenirs.

The *Phoenix* Project was one of the first attempts to recover information from a sunken vessel in some kind of scientific way. This time, there was never any attempt to raise the boat.

Except for the depth, the *Phoenix* was in an excellent position for underwater exploration and study. The dark, cold water had been a perfect preservative. There were no rotten timbers or planking on the boat, and she was clean of any marine growth.

The goal of the underwater archaeological expedition was to gather enough information to be able to reconstruct the *Phoenix* on paper. This was important because there are no existing plans for the boat. Shipwrights during this period usually built boats by sight and made adjustments during construction. Historians wanted a scale drawing of the *Phoenix* so they could learn more about early steamboats. To get such a drawing, however, it was necessary to label and measure the entire wreck. This was no easy task and required some special skills. How would you have done it?

The *Phoenix* team was fortunate to have a man named Jack Chase. He began working on a technical plan to make these measurements underwater. Chase developed specific methods for taking each of the required measurements. His methods then were turned into diving tasks.

Divers had to determine, down to the last detail, exactly what was needed to complete these tasks. This demanded extreme attention to detail and a lot of ingenuity. Tools and other equipment were kept as simple as possible and all calculations were done on the surface to save time below.

How to take the vertical measurement was one of the problems the divers faced. In order for the draftsman to draw the height of the boat, he had to measure from the keelson to the ribs. The *Phoenix* team devised a way to do this. They created a series of lines by marking a plumbline at one-foot intervals (a plumbline is a line with a weight at one end). To keep the lines from entangling the divers, they tied plastic milk jugs to the lines and attached weights on the other ends. These lines were then dropped over the boat from the surface.

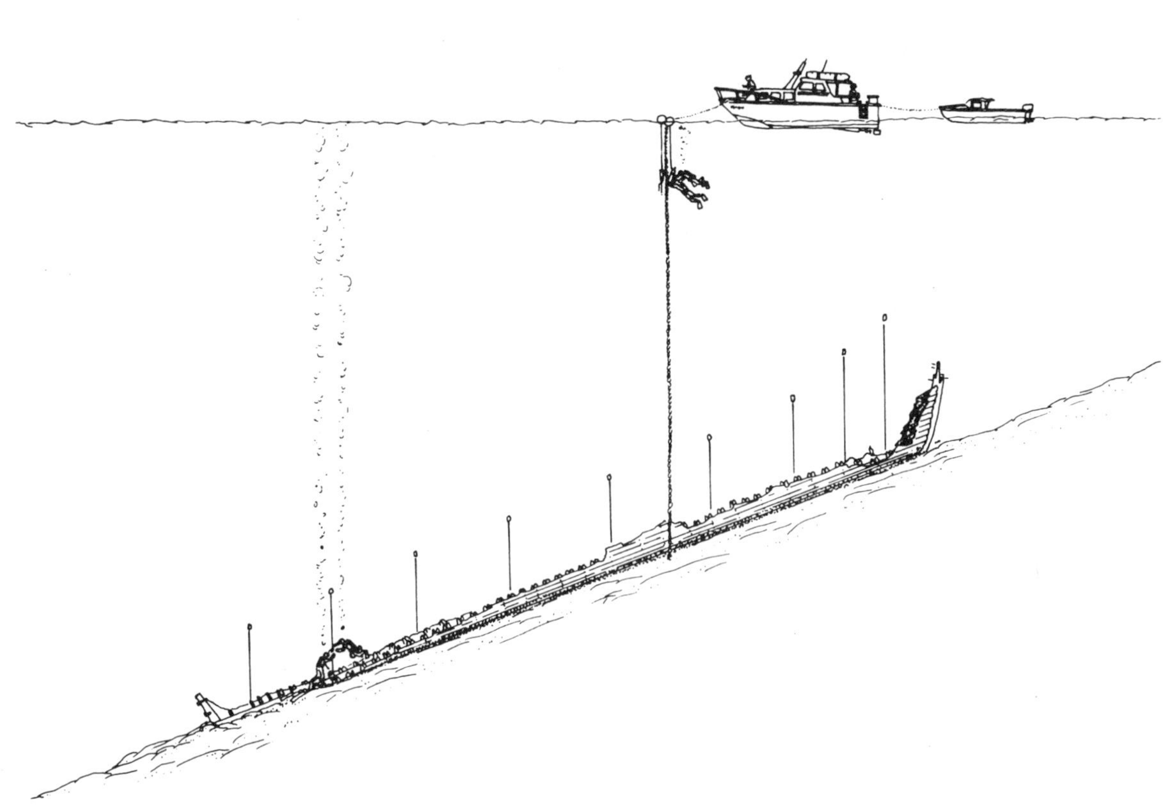

For five days the *Phoenix* team dove on the wreck with clipboards and measuring tapes. When the divers surfaced they reported their measurements to Kevin Crisman, the draftsman for the project, and he translated the mass of figures into a scale drawing. Slowly a picture of the *Phoenix* began to emerge.

Early in the diving work on the boat, the divers noticed the steamer's round bottom. This bottom, which flared up and out much like the shape of a whaleboat, differed markedly from the more traditional hull designed by Robert Fulton. After some research, the team decided that the round bottom was designed to make the boat easier to sail because it could turn easier than a flat-bottomed boat.

Although it is still open to question, the team thinks that the *Phoenix* was steered by a wheel rather than a tiller. Some clues about the wheel can be found in an account of the fire on the *Phoenix*:

> *"...the flames burst through the decks, and shrouded the pilot, the mast, and the chimney in a column of flames. The helmsman, however, held to the wheel, until his limbs were scorched and his clothes half consumed upon his back. The unusual heat around the boilers gave a double impetus to the engine. The vessel dashed madly through the waters, until she was within a few rods of land."*

From this description the team thought that the ropes leading from the wheel to the rudder were burned through, making the boat lose its steering. If the boat had been steered by a tiller, and if the accounts of the boat losing its steering are true, then when the divers studied the wreck, they would have found a burned sternpost. But, in fact, the divers found the sternpost still intact and the gudgeons still firmly attached to it.

The *Phoenix* team was able to determine the location of the engine, which was removed while the boat sat on Colchester reef before it sank. A particular problem that builders of early steamboats faced was how to make the hull strong enough to prevent sagging from the weight of the engine. The team discovered that the builder of the *Phoenix* solved this problem in two ways. First, the breadth of the boat was increased. While most steamboats of this period were eighteen feet across at their widest point, the *Phoenix* measured 27 feet. Second, the divers found a series of heavy, ten-inch-square, longitudinal timbers where the engine would have been.

With the engine located, it was a simple matter to find where the paddlewheels had been placed. Since the *Phoenix* was powered by a crosshead or steeple engine, the paddlewheels had to be in line with it.

Locating the position of the boiler was not so easy. The *Phoenix* team found two brick areas on the hull of the boat. One area was forward of the engine and one was just aft of it. Although there was some evidence that the boiler had been located forward of the engine, it was more likely that it had been located aft. The *Phoenix* team surmised that the bricks in this area were probably part of the fire box on which the boiler would have been mounted. The other brick pile was near the crew's cabin and may have been part of the cooking stove.

Divers were also able to figure out where the mast had been. They found a large square hole in the keelson twenty five feet from the bow. On one dive during the expedition, they found strips of a whitish grey substance near the engine area. They found out that it was lead. This told the researchers that the *Phoenix*, like other early steamers had trouble with a leaking engine; hot lead was used to seal engine leaks.

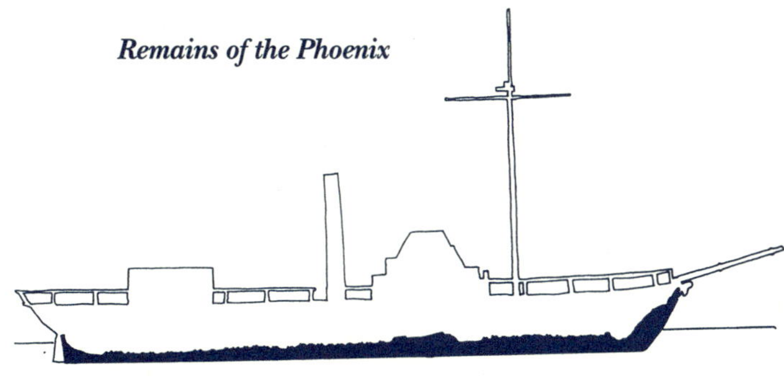

Remains of the Phoenix

Very few artifacts were found on the *Phoenix*. No pieces of hardware, such as an anchor or chain were found. Most of these things were probably salvaged when the boat lay on the Colchester reef the winter after it burned, or maybe were removed by other divers.

No artifact symbolizes a vessel more than its bell. The bell of the *Phoenix*, according to one historian, hangs in a bell tower in a Presbyterian Church in Danville, Illinois. How the bell traveled to the Midwest is a mystery!

All in all, it seems all right that some mysteries remain unsolved. Think of all the answers that were uncovered since the short time ago when no one even knew where the *Phoenix* was!

Credit: *Adapted with permission from the "Phoenix Project," a publication of the Champlain Maritime Society and the Vermont Division for Historic Preservation.*

Activity:
Zebra Mussels Be Gone!

TEACHER NOTES *and* INFO

This activity asks students to design a plan to keep zebra mussels off of ship-wrecks in Lake Champlain. It calls for students to write a detailed proposal, with drawings, action steps and costs. This activity came about while I was working on a grant related to the publication of THIS LAKE ALIVE! The process of setting out one's goals and objectives in a structured format clari-fies one's thinking and brightens one's purpose. The task of outlining a project down to the last dime clarifies one's priorities. This is one of the few activities in this book that I have not done with students. I have outlined one method; it seems it could be amended a number of different ways.

STUDENT ACTIVITY

Share with your students information about zebra mussels (see "The Latest Exotic: Zebra Mussels" and "Zebra Mussels Worksheet" in *Living Treasures*, p. 387-390 & 404), and the following article from the Lake Champlain Mari-time Museum newsletter, Spring/Summer 1995, "The Race is On!"

After you have read the article together and feel that students have enough information about the damage zebra mussels can do to shipwrecks, discuss different methods that might prevent the zebra mussels from reaching the shipwrecks.

Each group must make a proposal that includes the following:
1. A written description of their project. (Limit: one page.)
2. A diagram of the project (on one plain white paper).
3. An action plan that includes a timeline of action steps. (Limit: one page.)
4. A budget of labor and expenses.

These steps are an abridged version of a standard grant and you can get much more detailed in your requirements. It is probably a good idea to show them an actual grant proposal or invite in a person who is involved in writing grants. Be sure to have your guest write one for you to fund your Lake Champlain studies!

Note: *The Vermont Division for Historic Preservation has just published a brochure titled "Dive Historic Lake Champlain: Vermont's Underwater Historic Preservation System." It describes the location of specific underwater wrecks. If you wish, you can obtain this and have each team design a protection plan for one of the wrecks. This provides more of a challenge, since the brochure gives specific dimensions of a wreck as well as its specific location, including depth and water conditions.*

The goal of the project is for students to design a way to prevent the zebra mussels from reaching the shipwrecks. Divide the class into problem-solving teams. Have them decide on the location and dimensions of the ship, unless everyone is going to be working on preserving the same ship.

It is also a good idea to invite in a guest speaker to share information about zebra mussels.

Note: *Michael Hauser, who works for the Vermont Agency of Natural Resources, is available throughout the basin to present to school groups about the current situation regarding the invasion of the zebra mussel.*

STUDENT HANDOUT - "The Race is On!"

The Race is On!

A new and profound phenomenon has occurred in Lake Champlain: the arrival of a small mollusk known as the zebra mussel. This extraordinary invasion adds new urgency to our ongoing program to locate, inventory and document the cultural resource collection sitting on the lake bottom. We are now in a race to do this before shipwrecks are coated with zebra mussels.

We are not pausing to wring our hands or wonder why. Instead the Lake Champlain Maritime Museum is proposing what we believe is the only logical course of action: get out in front of the spreading invasion and locate and document shipwrecks before they are coated! We have the advantage of being able to learn from the Great Lakes experience and react during what we predict will be a brief window of opportunity.

A systematic approach to survey the entire lake bottom within the next five years has the potential to save a priceless body of information....We believe there are dozens—perhaps hundreds—of unlocated shipwreck sites scattered throughout the lake. If the Great Lakes experience is a guide, we predict the zebra mussels will begin by impacting shallow water sites, then migrate to sites in deeper water. Once they colonize a shipwreck they will provide an effective barrier to extracting information from the site.

We agree on the following points:
• It is a waste of time to worry about whether zebra mussels will coat shipwrecks; they almost certainly will.
• Water depth probably will not protect wrecks. In the Great Lakes, quagga mussels, which are closely related to zebra mussels, have been found coating boats in depths exceeding 200 feet.
• Nobody in the United States or Canada is looking specifically at the impact of the mussels on historic shipwrecks.
• Currently there are no practical controls available to prevent mussels from attaching to shipwrecks, and removal once they are attached will cause more damage than leaving them in place.
• We can expect a geometric increase in the numbers of zebra mussels in Lake Champlain over the next five years.

Credit: *Adapted with permission from Lake Champlain Maritime Museum newsletter, Spring/Summer 1995.*

Language Arts

Glossary

5th Grade, 1994, School Street School, Milton, Vermont

Basin - A basin is where the tributaries flow into a larger body of water. If it weren't for the basin, we wouldn't have a lake. The Lake Champlain Basin is 8,234 square miles.

Breakwater - A breakwater is built to make a long rocky line that separates rough from calm water so that it protects the harbor from big waves.

Champ - Champ is the Lake Champlain monster. He lives in Lake Champlain and he is big and long.

Crown Point State Historic Site - There are two forts at the Crown Point State Historic Site. They are Fort Crown Point and Fort St. Frederic. The remains of both forts are at the site and also a museum.

Ferry - A ferry is a large boat that carries cars, trucks, campers and people. There are three ferry crossings on Lake Champlain.

Fossil - A fossil is a rock that has been under the ground or underwater for a long time, it can be from a plant or an animal. There are lots of fossils in Lake Champlain.

Horse Ferry - A horse ferry is a ferry that is powered by horses. There is a wreck of a horse ferry that is near Burlington harbor.

Island - Islands are bodies of land surrounded by water. There are 72 islands on Lake Champlain. There are all kinds of sizes, too.

Lighthouse - A lighthouse is built on shore to warn boats about big rocks and other dangers. A famous lighthouse on Lake Champlain is the Colchester Lighthouse, which is now at the Shelburne Museum.

Philadelphia I - The first *Philadelphia* was a boat that was used during the American Revolution and sunk in 1776. It was discovered in 1935 near Valcour Island and is now at the Smithsonian in Washington, D.C.

Philadelphia II - The *Philadelphia* sunk during the Battle of Valcour Island 1776. The Lake Champlain Maritime Museum built a replica of the original in 1991 and now students can board the *Philadelphia II* at the museum.

Refuge - A place to help animals and protect wildlife. Milton has a wildlife refuge at the Sandbar State Park.

Rock Dunder - A rock point of Shelburne Bay. It has two granite bolders on it. The rock has been there for alot of years. The Abenakis call it Odziodzo.

Sailboat - A boat that has a big sail. In the 1700s they were the main way that people traveled on Lake Champlain.

S.S. *Ticonderoga* - The *Ticonderoga* is a steam boat that rode on Lake Champlain. It is now standing at the Shelburne Museum.

Sturgeon - A big fish, the biggest in Lake Champlain. Sturgeons weigh alot. They are almost extinct in Lake Champlain.

Tributary - A tributary is a stream that flows into a lake or a bigger stream. The Lamoille River is the tributary that flows through Milton, into Lake Champlain.

Whalebones - Whalebones were found in Lake Champlain. They were beluga bones. Right now there is a whale skeleton at Perkins Geology Museum.

Zebra Mussels - Small mussels that cling onto hard surfaces. They are the size of a thumb nail. They were not part of the lake until ships from Europe dumped ballast water into our region. They are dangerous to the ecology of Lake Champlain.

Introduction

No matter what the content of your Lake Champlain study is, language arts opportunities abound. There are endless ways for students to process what they are learning:

- creative stories
- factual reports
- lists of facts
- essays
- position papers
- newspaper articles
- scripts for radio or TV shows
- stories for younger children
- big books
- biographies
- folktales
- science logs
- poems
- songs
- plays
- speeches
- scientific observations
- interviews
- letters
- journal entries
- lab reports

Whatever vehicle you choose, let me add a philosophical note. Take time to let them process what they are learning, whether in formal writing, journal entries or discussion. Often, in an interdisciplinary study, when so much meaningful material gets generated, we don't stop and let the material sink in. We establish the historical chronology, rush to study wetlands, explore aquatic weeds and rush to prepare them for a quiz on the zebra mussel. More and more, I find myself braking my pace to insure that we have the

communal feeling of "Yes, we know this." The process of learners communicating what they know to another person or to the class is central to a healthy, holistic language arts component to your lake study.

Activity: **A Capital Idea!**

TEACHER NOTES *and* INFO

An interdisciplinary study can be used to teach "old-fashioned" grammar rules using worksheets!

STUDENT ACTIVITY

After reviewing common and proper nouns with the class, distribute this handout for practice or quiz.

Common and Proper Nouns

Rules: Proper nouns are always capitalized, e.g. the *Philadelphia*. Common nouns are not usually capitalized, unless they are at the beginning of a sentence or part of a title or proper name, e.g. I swam in the river, the Lamoille River.

Rewrite the following passage, in your best handwriting, with correct punctuation.

i think lake champlain is such a great place i could search all over the united states of america and never find such a lovely lake there are three ferry crossings the one that runs in the winter goes from grand isle to cumberland head in new york from the ferry you can see some islands, including valcour island, where benedict arnold escaped from the british

____

____

____

____

____

____

____

Activity: **A String of Words**

TEACHER NOTES *and* INFO

Your lake study can be used to distinguish parts of speech. Choose an activity (cluster, brainstorm, book search) to generate a list of Lake Champlain words or use word banks from this book.

Precut different colors of paper in small (3" x 5") pieces.

STUDENT ACTIVITY

As a class or in small groups, have students sort or identify parts of speech.

When students find a proper noun, write it on (orange) and hang on the "clothesline."

Examples:
• Crown Point
• Ethan Allen
• Richelieu River

When students find a common noun, write it on a (yellow) piece of paper and hang on the clothesline.

Examples:
• boat
• wave
• fort
• weed
• fossil

It will become a colorful and lengthy grammar lesson in your room.

Other Ideas

• *Use different-colored paper for adjectives and adverbs.*

• *Create a word bank on the computer of all parts of speech.*

• *Use the collection of adjectives to write a poem. Give a word (e.g. water) and ask for adjectives; continue with other words. Assemble them as a poem, rewrite on the overhead or blackboard and have students read the poem in unison. Give students time to practice sound effects and tape the reading!*

Activity: **Spelling**

TEACHER NOTES *and* INFO

Many of you may already run a spelling program that is integrated into the content of the subjects you are studying. I have included a sample of my spelling program that is completed each week. The content of the passage (or in this case, poem) is based on the science or social studies we are learning. Some questions are completed in class because they are rather extensive or require class materials. Other questions can be done easily at home for homework. Family involvement in language questions such as (6), (7) and (9) of the handout is encouraged.

STUDENT ACTIVITY

Work is handed out on Monday and completed by Friday. Students complete work in class or as assignments. A pretest is given on Monday, progress test on Wednesday and final on Friday. Some students may have only five words to learn.

STUDENT HANDOUT - "Spelling V"

Spelling V

This week, we are going to the Maritime Museum,
Pictures, artifacts and boats, you'll see them.
You'll learn about schooners, sloops and bateaux,
The tale of our history, you'll know.
*We'll row the **Philadelphia**, but not into Arnold's Bay*
Then we'll go to Crown Point Historic Site, yeah!
Where the remains of two forts remain in decay.
Then more artifacts and the world's best slide show.
Then head north to McDonald's, but not too slow.

On a separate piece of paper:

1. Copy over the whole passage correctly, in your best handwriting.

2. Write the ten key words five times each, in your best cursive.

3. Many of the events we will study this week take place in the 1700s.
What century is that? List the words eleventh through twentieth.

4. The names of specific boats are proper nouns. Find the names of eight specific boats that were on Lake Champlain. Identify what kind of boat each is.

5. The words "remain" and "remains" appear in the passage. Use the dictionary and find the two meanings of these words. Explain the use of these two words in this passage.

6. Words that are spelled the same and have different meanings are called homonyms. On your own, find three pairs of homonyms. Example: can and can.

7. Start a list of words that rhyme with Champlain. Find at least ten.

8. After our map work on Wednesday, list 10 towns that we will travel through on our way to Vergennes.

9. Write down 10 of your contributions to the Champlain alphabet. Start with the first letter of your last name. E.g. I would start with D; dugout, ecology, fish, galley, hatchery—(you may only skip a letter twice, unless it's z!).

10. Complete and decorate your thank you note to Tim Titus or Laurie Eddy by the end of L.A. class on Thursday and put in spelling box.

Activity: **Writing Journals**

TEACHER NOTES *and* INFO

The journal entries discussed in this activity are different from the thinkbook entries described in *Getting Wet.* Journal entries can be written for just about any purpose. They are helpful to put the learner "into" the material.

Many journals are based on "pretend you are..."
• a soldier stationed at Fort St. Frederic in 1734,
• a heron looking for a place to nest,
• an island in the middle of Lake Champlain,
• a girl searching for berries in the 1500s,
• a drop of water in the Winooski River...in East Montpelier,
• a cannon on board the *Philadelphia,*
• a mouse at Crown Point,
• a soldier with Arnold's fleet during the escape from Valcour Island.

Some journal entries are formal assignments that serve as the major assessment of a unit of study. Other journal entries can be written in the thinkbook as a quick response to a reading or discussion. Journals are excellent to use to process a field trip: ask the student to become an entity at the place where you visited. Students can also write journal entries that become a dialogue with another student with a similar (or different) perspective.

Carol Livingston has her students work on journals before, during and after a trip to Crown Point State Historic Site. Although you may not be able to visit Crown Point, this process is offered as a model of an extensive "pretend you are" journal assignment. The comprehensive objectives and questions serve as a model for this kind of writing.

The assessment piece for this assignment is included in the **Assessment** *chapter.*

STUDENT ACTIVITY

After reviewing some basic historical information about the Crown Point State Historic Site (see *Field Trips,* p. 285), explain the journal writing assignment to the class. Give them the handout, "Welcome to Fort St. Frederic and His Majesty's Fort at Crown Point." Students will complete first drafts of the

Other Ideas

• *Journals can also be used as a learning log or for recording specific science observations. Sue Hardin from the Frederick Tuttle Middle School in South Burlington writes:*

"Our students write a journal entry daily in their science class, so that trips to the brook to test water or collect benthic creatures are 'written up' in their journals.

On our first visit to the brook, we also have the students sit down (six feet away from anyone else) and describe the place using their senses—what they see, hear, smell, feel about the experience. Students can later transform this journal entry into a poem or return to the same spot at a different season and follow the same procedure."

• *Another science-related writing activity for outdoor environmental observations is to have students select one square foot of ground and describe everything they find there. They can also sketch one thing they see.*

journal prior to the trip (at least two entries) and work on entries and gather more information at the site, from displays, museum staff, slide show and the forts!

Give students a handout that they can use at the site that includes:

> **1. a chart to record:**
> - housing   • tools   • work   • travel
> - food   • leisure   • cooking
>
> **2. space for student, with a partner to generate ON SITE a "typical day"**
>
> **3. a timeline for students to record events of their soldiers' times at the fort, including personal and historical events.**

After the field trip, students will complete final journal entries in the classroom. They use original drafts, notes from the trip, memories and impressions, classroom resources and discussions to complete final drafts.

Final drafts can be displayed on a timeline with illustrations, read aloud or performed. Students can stage a play where they "discover" diaries or read aloud "around the campfire."

STUDENT HANDOUT - "Welcome to Fort St. Frederic and His Majesty's Fort at Crown Point"

Soldier's Journal, Samuel LaCarre, Entry #1

by Nora Sumner-Kopf, Grade 7, Camel's Hump Middle School, Richmond, Vermont

Last night we had our first frost. It killed almost all of our squash and beans. I'd like to request to go fishing today to get food. I'm afraid of the lake freezing. The fort is almost finished and I'm getting impatient. It's hard work— hauling all those stones. The barracks are finished but they do not retain much heat. My two little flannel blankets aren't enough for these cold nights. The wind is blowing and making whitecaps on the lake. As I sit here I shiver. Fort St. Frederic really catches the wind off the lake. I'm having second thoughts about fishing because it's too cold. I'd rather stand over a warm fire to help bake the bread.

Welcome to Fort St. Frederic and His Majesty's Fort at Crown Point

You are a French soldier in the French Army stationed at Fort St. Frederic during the years 1734 to 1759

OR

you are a British soldier stationed at Fort Crown Point during the years 1759 to 1784. As this soldier, you are to write a series of journal entries (AT LEAST THREE) in which you describe your daily life as a French or British soldier.

YOUR JOURNAL ENTRIES SHOULD ANSWER THESE QUESTIONS:

1. What date are you writing the entry and what place at the fort are you writing from?

2. What does the lake and the surrounding land look like? What is the plant and animal life? Describe the setting and environment.

3. What do you see, hear, smell, taste and feel as you "live" here?

4. How do you travel? Where?

5. What do you eat and how do you prepare food?

6. Where do you live? With whom? What are the furnishings? Describe the specific location of where you will live in the fort.

7. How do you spend your time? What do you do for work? What tools do you use? What do you do to relax?

8. What is on your mind? What are your concerns? your hopes? fears? What else is going on in the world that you might be thinking about?

9. What have your experiences been while stationed at the fort?

Activity: **Writing Legends**

TEACHER NOTES *and* INFO

Legends have always been important to this region. They are still used to entertain, to educate, to explain and to articulate a community's belief in what is right and wrong.

There are a number of collections of Abenaki and Iroquois legends, the most notable of which are collected by Joseph Bruchac. There are also storytellers in the region able to visit classrooms.

If you are exploring legends with your class, spend a lot of time reading different legends aloud. Only this will impart the flavor and practice of this tradition. Better yet, learn to tell the stories aloud, yourselves!

When students have heard a lot of legends from the region, spend some time identifying some common elements of all the legends. Your list may be different from mine. We identified the following elements:
- animals
- a long time ago
- a lesson or explanation of the way things are
- on the lake

STUDENT ACTIVITY

Brainstorm some story ideas and ask your students, singly or in pairs (or as a whole class) to write a legend.

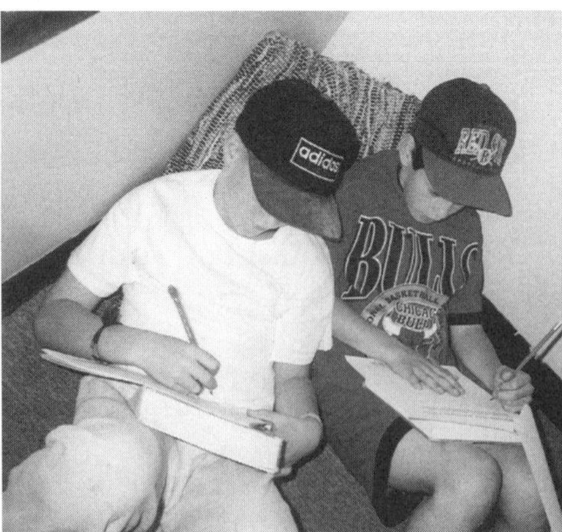

If you are collecting and grading these legends and have decided on the parts of a legend, you can assign points to the parts of a legend you agree need to be included. (See *Assessment*, p. 337.)

Give students the opportunity to read their legends aloud. That's what legends are for!

Activity: **Writing Tall Tales**

TEACHER NOTES *and* INFO

Perhaps legends and tall tales are the two story genres that have survived the longest in this region. Walk out on the ice in February and spend time with some folks telling fishing stories and you are bound to hear tales of "the one that got away."

The process of teaching tall tales is similar to that used to teach legends or any other form of writing:
• enjoy them
• practice them
• identify parts of a tall tale
• write them

For me, the trick with writing tall tales is how to help the writer make sense. Fifth graders understand exaggeration as license to stop making sense and often write stories that are jumbled, not tall. Thus, once again, the process of writing becomes an exercise in thinking and well worth our time.

STUDENT ACTIVITY

Share a "basic tale" on the overhead and have the class embellish it with exaggerated information.

Generate a list of "long tall topics" and a list of great words that will stretch a tale. Post lists during writing time.

weather
wild creatures
strange or scary animals
camping trips
amusement parks
teachers I've had...
strange people
fast runners
fishing trips
cars/boats
waves
food

Other Ideas
• *When tall tales are complete, have students devise a way to copy them over on a "tall" piece of paper. You could offer some rolls of butcher block paper or suggest making a background of a large shape on construction paper and mount the story on a large creature or thing. Tall fishing tales can be mounted on large fish, monster stories on large monsters and logging stories on huge trees.*

Activity: Aqua News—All the News That's Fit to Float

TEACHER NOTES *and* INFO

Producing a student newspaper is an excellent way for students to share what they are learning. There are levels of commitment to this kind of writing. Bill Ladabouche, at School Street School in Milton, runs his classroom as a newspaper room all year long and they use the paper to process the standard curriculum as well as many critical current events. If your class is set up as a newspaper room, you will have an editorial board, proofreaders, artists, a layout crew, etc.

A more manageable option is to use the writings as "assignments," do the proofreading yourself and choose a small group of students to help with the layout. There are lots of different ways to organize this! The activity below describes the "one-shot" approach.

STUDENT ACTIVITY

Publish an issue (or ongoing issues) related to your lake study.

1. Brainstorm with your students some of the components of a newspaper:
- news articles
- comics
- sports articles
- food articles
- headlines
- human interest
- entertainment
- comics
- weather
- advice column
- editorials
- ads

2. Brainstorm possible topics for each of these components:
- articles about our field trips
- news about water quality

- advice on preventing the spread of zebra mussels
- ads for fishing equipment
- interview with retired ferry boat captain
- "Dear Champ" advice column
- "Basin Bites" food column
- tips for boater safety
- articles about islands
- 10 important facts about the Lake Champlain Basin
- advertisements for lakeshore property, water craft, fishing equipment, aqua habitat, tourist services, ecologically-sound lake usage products
- cartoons about a "green" lake-side dweller

3. Develop a timeline with your students for completing the newspaper.

4. Assign articles.

5. Begin writing!

Our Trip to the Wetlands

by Jamie Lewandowski, Grade 5, School Street School, Milton, Vermont

Wednesday the 25th of September the Demarest/Dupont Team went to the Sandbar Wildlife Refuge! They went to study and learn new things about the wetlands. Ms. Demarest led the children on a hunt for animal prints and they found signs of Moose, Beaver, Deer and Blue Heron. As they went on a nature walk, they found a beaver lodge, duck and bird houses. Wetlands are home to many different types of animals, mammals, birds, reptiles, fish and amphibians.

On our class trip we found a deformed frog and it had one missing leg. The other leg was normal. Our teacher said that something happened to the leg, like maybe an animal bit it or something. Two days later we found out that there were a lot of deformed frogs around Lake Champlain. It was in the newspaper. Trevor Felix brought in an article from USA Today about deformed frogs in Minnesota. Scientists have had a hard time finding wetlands in Minnesota without deformed frogs. "It scares me," said Judy Helgen, a research scientist. T.J. Geraw said that he feels sad about the frogs. "I feel bad for them," he said.

The children discovered there are many different types of wetlands and this one was called a marsh. It was very wet and they fell into the mud a lot. Ms. Dupont helped the children dissect a cattail and they found the base of the stem is made up of little tiny holes. This carries oxygen to the cattail. They tasted the stem and found it tasted sweet. A lot was learned.

Activity: **Traditional Glossary**

TEACHER NOTES *and* INFO

Creating glossaries is an excellent way for students to explore vocabulary and to learn more about a content area. Students always surprise me with their insights about what is pertinent to the topic.

STUDENT ACTIVITY

Use the word bank from this book or one you have created. Have students choose a word they would like to contribute to a class glossary. I usually post a class list of names and enter the students' words as they choose. This way there are no repeats and I get to check in with each student's choice. Review with the class how a glossary definition for Lake Champlain is different from a dictionary meaning. A glossary definition must include the relevance of the word to the lake.

Have students write a glossary contribution as an assignment, then proof it and write a final draft.

Students can type their words in the computer and the glossary can be posted as a class project. (See "Glossary," p. 230.)

Activity: **Glossary (3-D)**

TEACHER NOTES *and* **INFO**
This is a more creative, three-dimensional version of a traditional glossary.

STUDENT ACTIVITY
1. Give students a long list of lake words. It could be a broad scope of words or a list pertaining to one aspect of your lake study (or you can develop a word bank of important lake words from day one of your lake study).

2. Students work in small groups; each group has a copy of the list you generated, one large piece of newsprint and four blank pieces of paper ($8\frac{1}{2}$” x 11”, or your choice).

3. Students pick four words on the list, make a cluster for each word on the large paper, and brainstorm all the associations with that word. As part of this activity, students must write a short glossary meaning (pertaining to Lake Champlain) and include it.
Example:
bateau - *large rowboat used in colonial times to transport troops and equipment.*

4. Students choose one of the words or one group of words, and using the four pieces of paper, make something to represent what they know or could learn about that word. They could:
• draw four pictures,
• make a small book with 16 pages,
• build something (e.g. model of boat),
• make a mobile.

Activity: **Know Your ABC's**

TEACHER NOTES *and* INFO

Use the spelling assignment (see "Spelling V," p. 236), to generate a large collection of Lake Champlain words. Have a small group gather all the words from each student. Make a booklet with each letter of the alphabet on one page. (Total 26 pages!)

Example: **P** *Philadelphia*
Phoenix
pumpkin seed (fish)
pollution
plankton
phosphorous
People of the Dawn
perch
pike

Words can also be collected on the computer; students can type in their own words, avoiding repetitions. Let this activity sit for a while in a visible spot and more words will appear on the list. Parents can contribute!

Precut large letters in oak tag ($8\frac{1}{2}$" x 11") for each letter in the alphabet.

STUDENT ACTIVITY

Each student gets one oak tag letter and one list of words. Fifth graders usually want the letter their first name begins with, so sometimes this process takes longer than you expect! The task is to put all the words on the corresponding letter in some artistic and legible manner and decorate it (one side). I request that no white space be left on the letters so that the colors are bold and bright, but still legible. I laminate and display the letters for Open House.

A number of other things can be done with these alphabets. You can make a book, posters or an illustrated "big book" for small children.

Activity: Crossword Puzzle

TEACHER NOTES *and* INFO

Using the word banks from the different content chapters of this book, students can generate their own crossword puzzles. If you have never done one before, play with it a bit before you start. I had one of those experiences where I thought it was a lot simpler than it was—but the students finally figured it out! Decide on what category you are going to work in, e.g. ecology, place names, nautical archeology.

STUDENT ACTIVITY

Each student (or team) needs a grid on which to place the words. The placement of the words is critical and must be done first. Advise students to make a note of what their clues might be but not to assign numbers ("3 across" etc.) until all their words have been placed on the grid. Set a minimum of words that they will need. Remind them that the words need to be ones that their audience is familiar with. If they are making one for the school newspaper or their parents, they might want to be more general. But if they want to make them for their classmates, all of whom by now are experts on Lake Champlain, they can make them more challenging.

Review with students that words cannot rest on top of each other and should not float on the page (see handout).

After the words are placed, students may number them, creating two separate categories, across and down. They are then ready to copy over the final draft of the clues. These must be written in two separate columns, across and down.

STUDENT HANDOUT - "Make Your Own Crossword Puzzle"

Other Ideas
• *A crossword puzzle would also be an excellent final exam at the culmination of your unit.*

Make Your Own Crossword Puzzle

Use this grid to make your own Lake Champlain crossword puzzle.

Your words may only be written across and down and may not rest on top of, or next to, each other.

NOT O.K.

O.K.

Write your across and down clues on a separate piece of paper. Number your words <u>after</u> they are placed on the grid.

```
        S
        E
  S     D     S
IGNEOUS       IGNEOUS
  CHAMPLAIN   M     A
        WHALE
        N
        T
```

Notes on Reading

It would be lovely if I could offer, at this point, a long list of children's literature to use in your study of Lake Champlain. The collection I know about does not cover a wide range of topics, so I have taught a unit based on books about settlement of this region in the seventeenth and eighteenth centuries. Although not all of the books suggested are specifically about life in the Champlain Valley, they describe an experience set in a similar place and time (e.g. SIGN OF THE BEAVER, one of the best depictions of the exchange between Native Americans and Europeans, is set in Maine).

Because there is not enough literature to maintain my literature program during a two-month study, we break loose after our settler unit and read books by Roald Dahl! I mention this because I think we worry that everything has to be connected in an interdisciplinary study. Although this intensity does bear fruit, my experience has been that students (and teachers!) appreciate this kind of break.

If you are set up for a literature-based social studies learning program in which students choose their own books, this unit will work easily. If you are not, you might want to read together as a class GREEN MOUNTAIN HERO, which is the tale of Ann Story and her family, who settled in Vermont prior to the Revolution. It provides an excellent look at daily life in the Champlain Valley, as well as a look at the events leading up to the Revolution (Ann was named "Mother of the Green Mountain Boys"). Parts or all of this book can be read aloud.

If your students are used to choosing their own books, here are some suggested titles and some activities to accompany the reading:

- Green Mountain Hero *by Edgar Jackson*
- Sign of the Beaver *by Elizabeth George Speare*
- Fawn *by Robert Newton Peck (out of print, but worth hunting for)*
- The Courage of Sarah Noble *by Sarah Dalgiesh*
- The Light in the Forest *by Conrad Richter*
- Calico Captive *by Elizabeth George Speare*

• The Ice Trail *by Anne Eliot Crompton (also hard to find)*
• Cave of Falling Water *by Janice Ovecka (only one third of this book deals with this time period)*

You may also want to use nonfiction books to explore this time period. There are many excellent ones, but I am not as familiar with them, as I do this unit with historical fiction.

The January 1995 issue of *Book Links*, an American Library Association publication, includes an extensive annotated bibliography on colonial times.

Some recommended titles are:
• Slumps, Grunts and Snickerdoodles: What Colonial America Ate and Why *by Lila Perl*
• Struggle for a Continent: The French and Indian Wars: 1690–1760 *by Albert Marrin*
• Going to School in 1776 *by John Loeper*
• Colonial American Medicine *by Susan Neiburg Terkel*
• Colonial Craftsmen: The Beginnings of American Industry *by Edwin Tunis*
• Giants in the Land *by Diana Apelbaum (about giant white pines felled for His Majesty's ships)*
• Hiawatha: Messenger of Peace *by Dennis Fradin*

There are many resources available for teachers on how to design a holistic reading program and I will not try to provide a comprehensive look at that here. Key elements of a successful reading program seem to be:
• the opportunity for students to develop the ability to choose books that they like and that they can read successfully,
• a system by which you and the student can communicate about and validate the reading experience,
• a multitude of ways in which the student can express what she or he is learning through reading,
• parent support of and involvement with the reading program,
• reading time at school,
• class discussions and small discussion groups that are based on how "real" people talk about books.

The reading experience can be processed via:

- reading journals, which can include lists, short answers, responses, notes to characters in books or to classmates, speculation, rewrites of the story, sequences, questions and reflections,
- projects,
- skits,
- reading letters and essays about specific topics or questions,
- oral presentations.

The year that this book was being completed, my teammate and I taught Lake Champlain history, nautical archeology and ecology in the spring. I designed an accompanying reading unit called "Children and the Earth." Each student read a book by Jean Craighead George. Many people are familiar with her famous books JULIE OF THE WOLVES and MY SIDE OF THE MOUNTAIN, but she has numerous other titles with a wide range of reading levels. Her adventure and ecological mysteries all address some aspect of a child's relationship to the earth. The books prompt lots of investigation and discussion. Each student chose a topic related to his or her book and wrote a science paper on topics such as: birds and their territory, desert plants, carnivorous plants, the Everglades and how birds communicate.

Below is a thinkbook response from Chris Sweeney, a fifth grader at School Street School. Chris read THE TALKING EARTH by Jean Craighead George.

> *"Billie Wind goes into the Everglades because she does not believe in the bad serpent, talking animals or little people that play tricks on bad children. While she was there, there was a fire that lasted all day.*
>
> *Some good things happened though. She met an otter, a panther, and a turtle. My favorite part of the book is when she meets an otter. This is my favorite part because this is when she starts to believe in the little people."*

Activity: **Wood is the Word:**
Log Cabin-Building

TEACHER NOTES *and* INFO

This is an activity where students can explore words associated with colonial times and build their vocabulary.

1. Build a log cabin frame using a cardboard box. Use the box as the walls and use two opposite flaps to construct a roof. Cover with brown construction paper.

2. Precut $2\frac{1}{2}$" x 1" "logs" of brown construction paper.

STUDENT ACTIVITY

Assign students the task of finding historically accurate vocabulary in their novels. "Good settler words," as we refer to them, are words that can help us understand daily life and make us think about things (and words) that were used at the time. Interesting class discussions take place about whether the word is a "good" settler word. An example of a "good" word is **spider pan**, which is a three-legged cast iron cooking pot used to cook food over a fire.

Trail might be considered a "good" word since trails had special importance then, even though they are used today. **Supper** probably wouldn't be chosen to help build the cabin. Every three to four days, have "cabin-building" with your class. Students contribute individually or as teams. Print words on paper with black marker and glue on the log cabin. Your cabin is built when the whole structure is covered with historically-accurate vocabulary words.

Beaver hat	Pinnacle	Rafters		
"Wattle & Doub"	Knitting	Wigwam	ax	
Ft. Crown Point	Clearing	Ethan Allen		
Birch wood	Sleigh	Squirrel	gun	cave
Blunderbust	Hunter	Abenaki		Barn door
Bark Covered Huts	Red Coat	Creek		Deerskin
Harvest	Pine Bed	Corn Cob Pipe		
Tomahawk	Ethan Allen	"Yorkers"	Saddle bag	
Game Featherbed	Schooner	Pewter	Bitawbagok	
Cottage Quilt Cornmeal	Flax Tools	Wool blanket		
Hemlock Mattress	Spear Wigwam	Fireside Torch		
Loghouse Settlement	Venison Trap	Mayflower gun		
Forest fishing	Green Mountain Boys	Chest & Settle		
Cloak firewood	Snare Indians	Skin drum		
Stockade Muzzle loader	hew logs	dugout canoe		
Wilderness Moccasins	Johnny Cakes	Ft. Ticonderoga		

Activity:
Compare and Contrast

TEACHER NOTES *and* INFO

When you are well into the cabin-building, let students compare life today with life in seventeenth- and eighteenth-century New England.

STUDENT ACTIVITY

Review some of the "great" words they've learned that describe these historical times. What if you were to assign categories? Could students come up with words for each category?

• Clothes? (*homespun, calico, moccasins, leather britches, beaver cap, fur*)

• Transportation? (*walking, wagon, canoe, trails, waterway, dugout*)

• Food? (*cornmeal, porridge, deer, stew, campfire, spider pan, pemmican*)

What about words that describe our time? What are some great words?

• neon
• electric
• pizza
• jams (shorts, not with toast!)
• rollerblades
• high-rise
• super highway
• airplane

Put these words in categories.
Use a chart to compare and contrast.

	NOW	THEN
Clothes		
Transportation		
Food		
Other		

Rubies Pearls

Activity: **Shades of the Past**

YOU WILL NEED for each student:
• 2 large (about 8-inch diameter) circles cut from drawing paper
• one large circle cut from oak tag (same size)

STUDENT ACTIVITY
Students make a NOW drawing on one drawing paper circle and a THEN drawing on the other. Mount the drawings on either side of the oak tag; punch one hole and hang them singly or as a mobile.

OTHER IDEAS
You could add ribbon, cut tissue paper, yarn, construction paper strips or a paper shape of an artifact related to the drawing.
"Now and Then Circles" could be fastened together as a pair of "shades" and displayed in the room.

Activity: **Reading Aloud**

TEACHER NOTES *and* INFO

There are two children's books about Champ to read aloud. One is THE CHAMPLAIN MONSTER by Jeff Danziger. A more recent book and my preference is LITTLE CHAMP by Jim Arnosky. Use it for those in-between moments and at the end of the day. Almost-grown teenagers succumb to the universal temptation of being read to and they love it!

Rubies Pearls

Activity: **Leaf Monster Drawings**

YOU WILL NEED:
- a large leaf (maple leaves are great) for each student
- drawing paper
- pencil and crayons or felt-tipped markers

STUDENT ACTIVITY

Trace the leaf on paper. The large shape can be any part of your Champ monster. You could trace the pattern twice and create wings. Make the large shape of the body, then the head, and then add wings, feet and tail. Add curvy lines to the outline of your monster. Make patterned designs in sections of the monster's body with lots of color!

Artwork by Mike Villemaire, Grade 5, School Street School, Milton, Vermont

Activity: **Learn All About It**

Other Ideas

• Create a station with news stories and "WWWWW" cards for students to complete independently.

• Write out worksheets with comprehension questions that correspond to specific articles.

• Establish a "lake watch" current events program in your room.

• There are always news stories about the lake. Identify five or six themes and have teams watch for different news items. Create a database of news stories. Don't forget the sports section that often has lots of information on fish and wildlife.

• Use themes to identify a "wildwatch" current events program for the United States and/or the world. Are there threats to the environment, water quality, wildlife that students have identified in their lake study that are also happening in other parts of the world? Use newspapers or the Internet to gather information on these national or worldwide issues. If you want to keep going with this idea, telecommunicating with students in other areas of the world that are also learning about these issues gives students a great opportunity to learn and share data.

TEACHER NOTES *and* INFO

Newspaper articles collected by you or your students are a great way to build skills of reading comprehension and citizenship. I usually have a lot of articles on the wall and/or in a scrapbook. Sometimes I mount them on construction paper and hang them on the "clothesline." Mounting them makes it a lot easier to pass articles around the room and reuse them.

STUDENT ACTIVITY

Practice reading an article with students.

Many teachers use:

Who

What

When

Where

Why

to decipher news stories. It is a great method to interpret the main idea in a story and it helps them separate the facts from the commentary. News isn't written for kids and they need help understanding most of it.

Practice "WWWWW" by placing a news story on the overhead and going through it together as a class.

When students are familiar with this process, let them each try their own articles. Since reading levels vary so much, I usually hand out articles myself and try to match the story to the student's reading level and interest. I make little "cards" that students complete, attach and display to help other students interpret the news stories. Each student has one story and one card.

Who _______________________________

What ______________________________

When ______________________________

Where _____________________________

Why _______________________________

____

Summarize the main idea of this news

story. ____________________________

____

____

Option: Create an illustration to go with
this news story.

Who _______________________________

What ______________________________

When ______________________________

Where _____________________________

Why _______________________________

____

Summarize the main idea of this news

story. ____________________________

____

____

Option: Create an illustration to go with
this news story.

Who _______________________________

What ______________________________

When ______________________________

Where _____________________________

Why _______________________________

____

Summarize the main idea of this news

story. ____________________________

____

____

Option: Create an illustration to go with
this news story.

Who _______________________________

What ______________________________

When ______________________________

Where _____________________________

Why _______________________________

____

Summarize the main idea of this news

story. ____________________________

____

____

Option: Create an illustration to go with
this news story.

ORAL PRESENTATIONS

Sometimes I think we get carried away with designing such creative ways for students to process information that we forget how important it is for them to have time to just tell each other what they are learning (doing, feeling, planning). Being able to tell a story about what is happening to them is the very basis of the art of language (*pronounce "language arts"*). This is a very important part of the culmination of a large interdisciplinary experience, but it is also important in the day-to-day process of learning. It helps you assess where they are and where you need to get to. It sometimes can unearth a critical missing piece in your study and often develops a sense of camaraderie. Why did we ever stop Show-and-Tell in third grade?

"Today we had our first Reading Circle. Each kid was asked to bring in something to read aloud. It could be their own writing from their thinkbook, their interview, their tall tale. Or it could be something they'd found in the newspaper, or a source (we're just beginning the I-search) or another student's writing.

Students made all different selections. It was a really sweet day. Chairs were in a circle and students listened hard to each other's reading. Maureen (reading teacher) and I got good opportunities to give feedback. The kids got into it...telling each other:
'It was really funny when...'
'I really liked the way you described the waves...'
'It was neat how you made it sound.'

A reading circle. A peaceful end to a hectic week."

ABD Teaching Journal

Math

T his chapter was written by Kris Kenlan, a math teacher at the Frederick H. Tuttle Middle School in South Burlington, Vermont.

Her purpose was to provide the classroom teacher with a sampling of math activities to use in conjunction with an interdisciplinary study. Kris designed activities that employ a variety of math skills—basic computation as well as higher level problem solving—which of course will entice you to design more math activities. There is so much data now available about the Lake Champlain Basin and new standards invite teachers to use this "real world" data with students. The possibilities are endless!

In choosing these activities, Kris sought to:
• provide students the opportunity to use a variety of math skills,
• use math as a bridge to help students understand the many different features of the Lake Champlain Basin and to see these features in new ways,
• provide the practical application of math skills to the "real world" of the basin.

Activity: **Count the Boats!**

TEACHER NOTES *and* INFO

A survey of boat use and activity was undertaken during the summer of 1992. The data obtained were the result of aerial photographs taken on one clear weekend day in July, 1992. The photographs were then analyzed. Boats were divided into categories of type, size, distance from shore and activity. I wanted to use pictographs as a way of showing this data.

The pictographs included here represent the count for Shelburne Bay. Each boat represents 25 boats and is an approximation, to the nearest 25, of the actual data. I left out data on commercial vessels and boats larger than 54 feet; their low numbers would have been hard to represent. Categories are organized according to type, size and activity.

Note: The data for this activity was taken from the "Lake Champlain Boat Study," by Susan Bulmer, a report published by the Lake Champlain Basin Program in 1993.

STUDENT ACTIVITY

First have students study the pictographs, then have them interpret the data.

QUESTIONS *for* STUDENTS

1. Estimate the number of boats in each category.
2. How many more sailboats were there than motorboats?
3. What was the most common boat size in Shelburne Bay?
4. What was the most common activity?
5. How many more boats between 0 feet and 21 feet were there than between 33 feet and 54 feet?
6. How many boats of all types were in Shelburne Bay at the time of the count?

STUDENT HANDOUT - "Boat Count Data for Shelburne Bay (July, 1992)"

Boat Count Data for Shelburne Bay
(July, 1992)

= 25 boats

Boat Type

Motorboats

Sailboats

Other

Boat Size

0' - 21'

22' - 32'

33' - 54'

Boating Activity

Docked

Moored

Moving

Fishing

Waterskiing

Anchored

Activity: **Let's Dive!**

TEACHER NOTES *and* **INFO**

The following activity is designed to look at one of the ways that money is spent on recreation and to review some basic math skills.

STUDENT ACTIVITY

Hand out the worksheet "Take a Dive!" to your students. Let them determine how much it would cost them to "suit up" for scuba diving in Lake Champlain. The list of equipment and costs can be used in various ways for more complicated math problems.

STUDENT HANDOUT - "Take a Dive!"

Jon Eddy of the Waterfront Diving Center often visits classrooms and shares slides and artifacts. Sometimes students have a chance to put on scuba equipment—as you see in this photo.

Take a Dive!

Scuba divers need many pieces of equipment in order to dive safely and comfortably. They need equipment to provide warmth, a source of air, a way to control their buoyancy and a way to measure their depth and direction, among other things. How much would it cost to "suit up" for a summer dive in Lake Champlain?

EQUIPMENT *and* COSTS

1. Wetsuit $289.00
2. Standard tank $119.95
3. Regulator $249.50
4. Buoyancy compensator $269.00
5. Mask $ 62.95
6. Fins $ 69.95
7. Diving boots $ 34.45
8. Wetsuit hood $ 32.95
9. Diving gloves $ 28.95
10. Three-gauge console $209.95
11. Underwater light $ 49.95

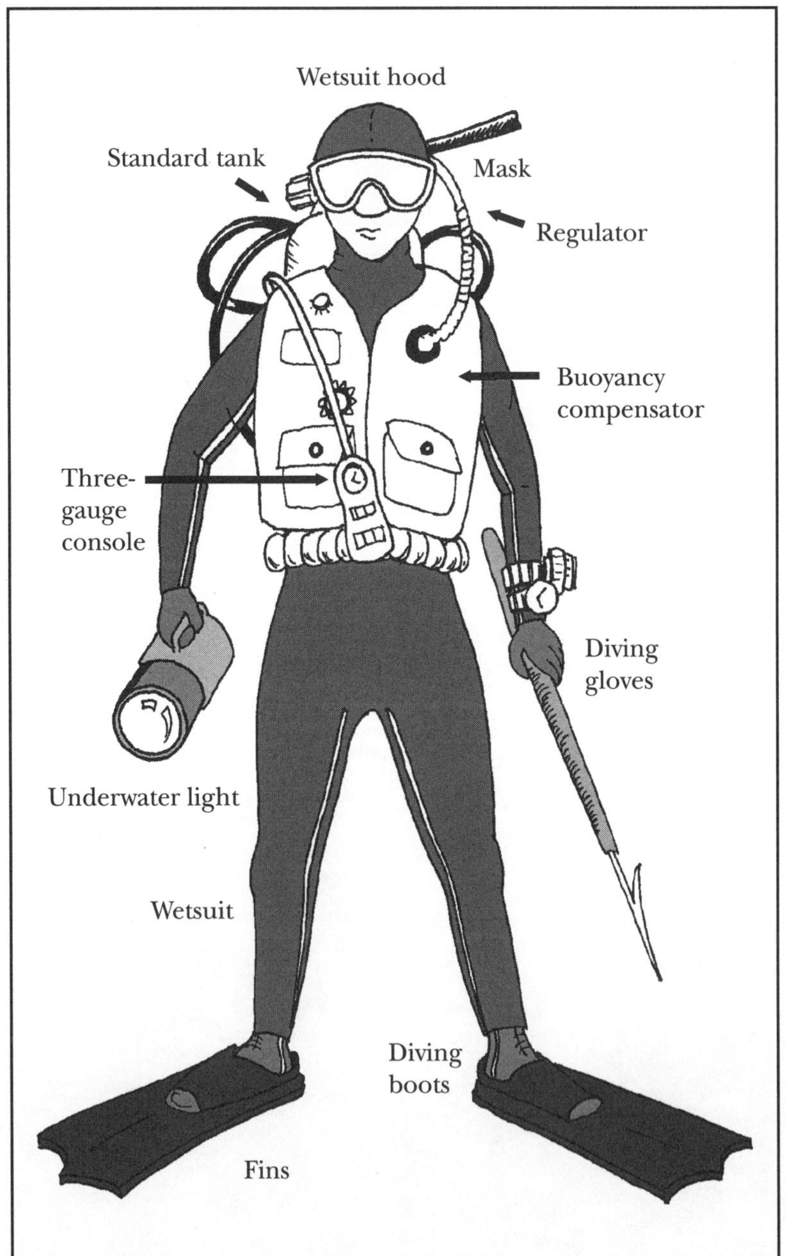

Activity: **Lake-Level Learning**

TEACHER NOTES *and* INFO

The level of Lake Champlain (above sea level) is published daily in the *Burlington Free Press* weather section. It is expressed in decimal notation (i.e. 96.2 feet). During spring runoff, the lake level often shows dramatic daily increases. Students can create a bar graph showing the daily lake level and then use it to calculate daily and/or weekly increases or decreases.

They will need to be able to read and interpret a bar graph and perform addition and subtraction of decimals. A large wall graph could be created for the classroom as well.

STUDENT ACTIVITY

The x-axis represents days of the month. The y-axis represents the lake level in feet above sea level.

1. Collect and graph daily information during spring runoff (late March to mid-April).

2. Have students calculate the overall increase in lake level, largest single daily increase, smallest daily increase, etc.

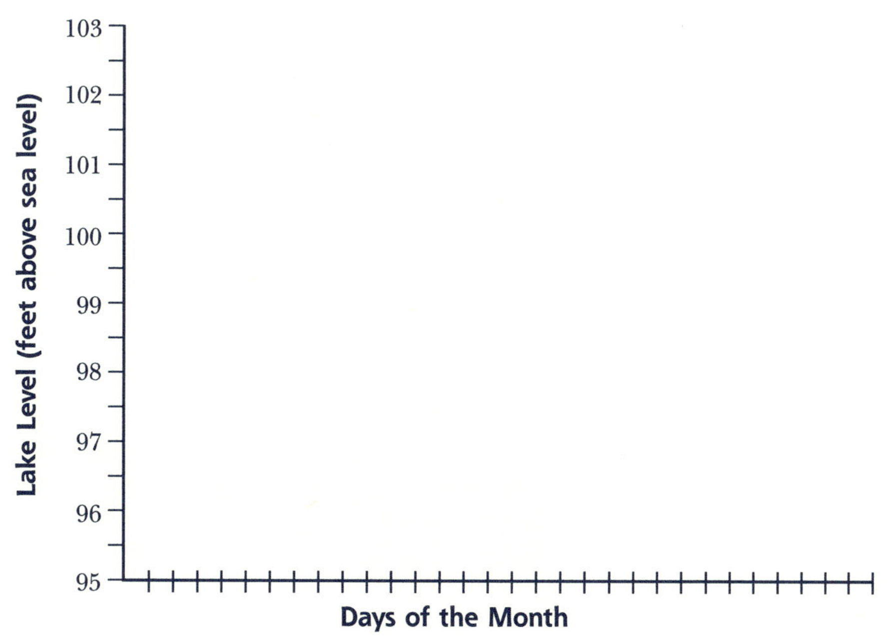

You will need:
• graph paper or prepared blank graph form
• daily lake-level data available in the *Burlington Free Press* or in the *Press-Republican* (Plattsburgh)

Other Ideas

• *Compare changes in the lake level with temperature and precipitation patterns.*

• *Information on snow depth at the stake on Mt. Mansfield is also printed in the weather section of the* **Burlington Free Press** *(expressed as inches). Compare snow melt with lake level.*

• *Challenge students to calculate the volume of water it would take to raise the level of the lake one foot. You will need to know the surface area of the lake in square feet in order to perform the calculation. The surface area is 415 square miles. One square mile = 5,280 feet x 5,280 feet.*

• *Calculate the volume of water it would take to fill your classroom.*

Activity: **River Jigsaw**

TEACHER NOTES *and* INFO

This activity requires students to work together to identify and solve a problem. Each person in a group is given a card with several pieces of information on it. Some of the information is useful and some is not. One of the cards includes the question to be answered or problem to be solved. Since each person holds some useful information, the group must work together to solve the problem.

This activity has students calculate average stream flow or discharge. This is a measure of the amount or volume of water passing a point within a specific amount of time. It is easy to calculate based on stream width, depth and velocity.

If you look at a stream in cross-section, you can see that the cross-sectional area at one location is the stream width times the stream depth. This area is multiplied by stream velocity and the result is the volume of water passing through that cross section in a given amount of time. The diagram and example below illustrate how to calculate discharge.

Make copies of the cards for each group (see next page).

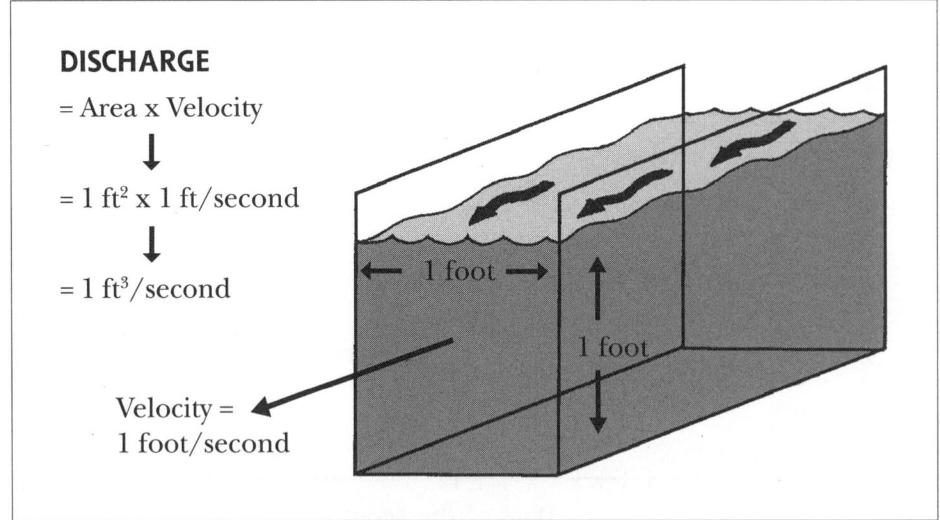

STUDENT ACTIVITY

Divide the class into groups of four and have each group appoint a leader, timekeeper, recorder and reporter. Give each member of the group one of the four cards. Together, the group will have all the necessary information. Group members may not show their cards to other members of the group. They need to explain the information. Through quiet discussion, the group will identify the question to be answered and decide which information is useful. The group then solves the problem. When all the groups are done, the reporter will share the process and the solution with the class.

Card 1

1. Velocity is a measure of distance covered over a period of time.
2. The average stream depth is 4 feet.
3. Discharge is measured in cubic feet per second.

Card 2

1. The average width of the stream is 30 feet.
2. You figure out discharge by multiplying the area by the water velocity.
3. There is a hydro-dam 1/4 mile upstream.

Card 3

1. It took an orange 10 seconds to float 20 feet downstream.
2. Area = Length x Width.
3. Calculate the stream flow or discharge.

Card 4

1. Discharge can change quickly as a result of the hydro-dam.
2. Discharge is the amount or volume of water passing a certain point within a given period of time.
3. Water is flowing at a rate of 2 feet per second.

Activity: **Gigantic Geography**

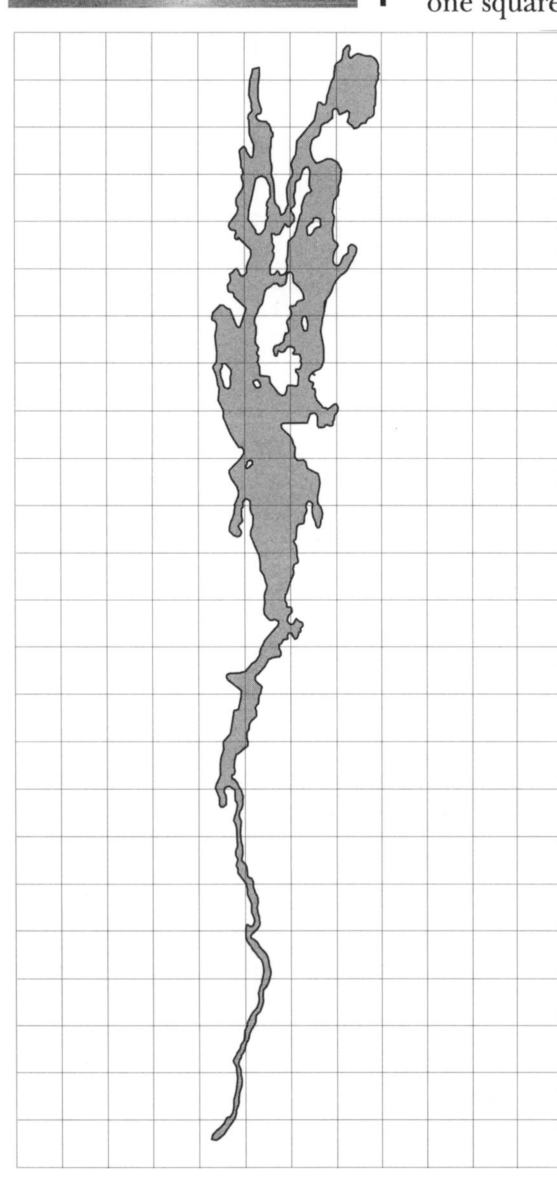

TEACHER NOTES *and* **INFO**

This activity uses the concept of scale to create a room- or hall-sized floor map of the outline of Lake Champlain.

Trace a map of the lake onto standard graph paper. If you have floor tiles, one square on the graph paper can equal one square tile on the floor and you have a built-in scale enlargement, with one-to-one correspondence. If you don't have floor tiles, you will have to calculate a scale that corresponds to the size of your map.

The map is laid down, square by square, using colored floor tape, which is available at sporting goods stores. It familiarizes students with lake features, is visually striking, relatively simple and requires few materials. Students, both those involved in the mapping and observers, enjoy watching it grow. Once the lake outline is mapped, points of interest can also be marked with tape.

This project works best with pairs of students working together on a given map section.

STUDENT ACTIVITY

1. Trace a 12- to 18-inch map of Lake Champlain onto standard graph paper. If the map is taped to a window and the graph paper is taped over it, it's easy to trace.

2. Once you trace the map, determine the length and width of the lake in squares. This will be the number of floor tiles or floor area that you will need to transfer the map accurately.

3. Divide the lake into sections and assign a pair of students to each section. Make copies of the map so each team will have its own map.

4. Mark off the floor space that will be used, with a starting and stopping place for each team.

5. Have students lay floor tape according to the pattern on the

graph paper. They must follow the pattern square-by-square. It is a good idea to have them cross off squares as they do them.

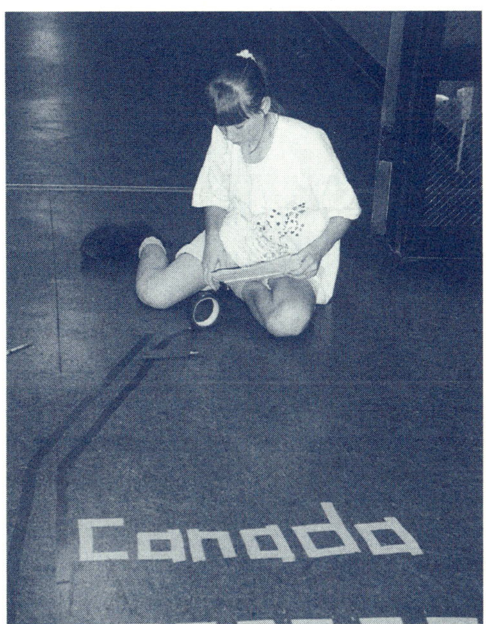

Tips for laying tape
• The floor beneath the tape should be clean.
• The tape should be laid smoothly, without bubbles or rough edges. This is especially important in a high-traffic hallway.
• Cut the tape with an Exacto knife or razor blade. Use caution!
• The tape will curve, but sharp turns require cutting and piecing.

You will need:
• page-sized map of Lake Champlain (see p.viii)
• floor tape
• Exacto knife or razor blades (one per team)
• graph paper
• one copy of the traced map per team

Other Ideas
• *Map a section of the lake instead of the entire lake.*

• *Mark and label points of interest on the floor map with tape.*

• *Determine the relative surface area of the lake by counting tiles, estimating parts of tiles, etc.*

Activity: **Ferry Tales**

TEACHER NOTES *and* INFO

This activity requires students to read and interpret the Lake Champlain Transportation's (LCT) ferry schedule in order to solve word or "story" problems. An answer key is not provided because the schedule changes!

STUDENT ACTIVITY

Hand out copies of the ferry schedule and spend some time interpreting it together as a class. Hand out "Story Problems" and let students answer questions.

STUDENT HANDOUT - "Story Problems"

You will need:
- copies of the LCT Ferry Schedule

You can order them from:
Lake Champlain Transportation Company
King Street Dock
Burlington, VT 05401
802-864-9804

Activity: **Do the Data!**

TEACHER NOTES *and* INFO

This activity requires students to perform basic math operations using large numbers. They need to pay attention to operation signs and the placement of parentheses. The calculations lead them to interesting and less well-known facts about the Lake Champlain Basin.

STUDENT ACTIVITY

Distribute the handout "Do the Data!" to your students, along with some scrap paper where they can work out each problem.

STUDENT HANDOUT - "Do the Data!"

Story Problems

1. School is out for the summer. You and your family would like to cross the lake by ferry and have lunch at a restaurant in Essex, New York. The restaurant is a 5-minute drive from the ferry dock in Essex. Your reservations are for 12:30 p.m. What ferry do you need to catch from Charlotte in order to get to the restaurant on time?

2. Your family is made up of 2 adults, one 11-year-old child, one 8-year-old child and one 5-year-old child. What will the round-trip fare be for your family to travel from Charlotte to Essex in the car?

3. If the speed of the ferry averages 6 miles per hour and the trip takes 20 minutes, about how far does the ferry travel on a one-way trip between Charlotte, Vermont, and Essex, New York?

4. You are biking with a friend and plan to bike from Burlington to Grand Isle, Vermont. From there you intend to cross the lake on the ferry to Plattsburgh, New York, bicycle from Plattsburgh to Port Kent, New York, and then return to Burlington by ferry. How much will you each have to pay for ferry transportation? Figure this out for the age you are now.

5. Which ferry runs throughout the year?

6. When (date and time) is the first possible ferry of the year you can catch from Essex, New York to Charlotte, Vermont?

7. If you miss the 8:30 a.m. ferry from Port Kent, New York, during the summer, what time is the next ferry you can take?

8. How much time will you need for a round-trip ride between Burlington and Port Kent if you turn around and take the next ferry back?
Hint: There is a wait while the ferry unloads and reloads. Read the schedule.

9. For a family of four traveling by car (2 adults, 2 children ages 6–12), what is the difference in the cost of 1 round-trip between Grand Isle and Plattsburgh and 2 one-way trips?

10. If you leave Plattsburgh on the 9:00 a.m. ferry, what time will you reach Grand Isle?

Do the Data!

Calculate the following:

1. The number of people who drink water drawn from Lake Champlain.

61,352 + 4,578 + 12,910 + 109,160 = ___________

2. The number of fish species in Lake Champlain.

(443 - 200) ÷ 3 = ___________

3. The approximate number of people living in the Lake Champlain Basin.

500 x 8 x 5 x 15 x 2 = ___________

4. The record high-water level (feet above sea level) for the lake [as of 1996].

231.75 - 129.86 = ___________

5. The record low-water level (feet above sea level) for the lake [as of 1996].

38,808 ÷ 10 ÷ 14 ÷ 3 = ___________

6. The year of the record high-water level.

(60 x 40) - (250 +157) = ___________

7. The year of the record low-water level.

(425 + 763 + 1209 + 12) - (227 + 274) = ___________

8. The number of acres of wetlands in the Lake Champlain Basin.

(47 + 63 + 36 + 54) x (350 + 614 + 236 + 124 + 176) =

____

9. The number of amphibian species found in the Lake Champlain area.

649,740 ÷ 52 ÷ 35 ÷ 17 = ___________

10. The number of reptile species in the Lake Champlain area.

(342 + 117) + (25 + 619) - (628 + 455) =

____

11. The approximate number of years that humans have inhabited the Lake Champlain Basin.

10 x 10 x 10 x 10 = ___________

12. The year zebra mussels were first discovered in Lake Champlain.

3 x 5 x 7 x 2 x 9 + (61 + 42) = ___________

13. The number of mammal species in the Lake Champlain area.

(112 + 35) - (57 + 34) = ___________

14. Speed limit (in m.p.h.) for boats within 200 feet of shore.

2,880 ÷ 24 ÷ 8 ÷ 3 = ___________

15. The number of miles of Lake Champlain shoreline.

(214 x 58) - (473 x 25) = ___________

16. Up to this number of ducks and geese use the Lake Champlain Basin during migration.

12,423 + 16,004 + 7,998 + 3,575 = ___________

17. Number of boats observed on Lake Champlain on one summer day in 1992.

(25 x 3 x 497) ÷ (651 - 648) = ___________

18. The amount of phosphorus (in metric tons) that enters the lake each year.

936,000 ÷ 45 ÷ 32 = ___________

19. The number of islands in Lake Champlain.

2,045,009 - 2,044,939 = ___________

20. Adult zebra mussel colonies can have this many individuals in one square meter.

3,126 + 12,009 + 648 + 24,217 = ___________

Answers: 1. 188,000, **2.** 81, **3.** 600,000, **4.** 101.89 ft., **5.** 92.4 ft., **6.** 1993, **7.** 1908, **8.** 300,000, **9.** 21, **10.** 20, **11.** 10,000, **12.** 1993, **13.** 56, **14.** 5, **15.** 587, **16.** 40,000, **17.** 12,425, **18.** 650, **19.** 70, **20.** 40,000.

Field Trips

Introduction

Opportunities for fun and educational field trips abound in the Champlain Valley. This section will offer some general advice on field trips, review some of my favorites and list some other possibilities.

Field trips can be a valuable part of your learning if you view the site as an integral part of your classroom experience. In order to maximize the field experience, remember **P.O.P.**:

- Pre-visit learning activities
- On-site learning
- Post-visit assessment

A note like this can be on their desks when they arrive in the morning, as well as a copy of the schedule and their name tag.

PRE-VISIT LEARNING ACTIVITIES

It is important for your students to know what they will be doing (develop the schedule together, if possible) and what they will be expected to learn. Often this involves showing slides of the site, or maps of the area. If students will use a worksheet, scavenger hunt list, or guide while there, show this to them before they go. Develop clear expectations of what you want your students to get from the trip and what kind of behavior you expect. The more they know about the tasks and expected outcomes, the more they will be able to process information while at the site. They won't be spending time trying to figure out what's going on!

Field trips should not be a "test" of students' knowledge, but an opportunity for them to integrate what they know and develop a better understanding of the topic.

Examples:

If students visit Crown Point, they will need information about the chronology of the two forts. Share timelines, journal entries, maps and outlines of the fort. Discuss with them why forts were built in a star shape and why Crown Point was considered a good site for a fort. When students see the two sites and walk the span of the ramparts that frame Crown Point and look from its high point, up the stretch of the lake to the north and south, they will learn more about military strategy than you can ever teach them at school, and everything you do in the classroom will make sense!

When you spend time in class doing "Wetlands Metaphor" (see *Ecology*, p. 465), which lets students compare the qualities of a wetland to those of tangible objects, they will "get it" when you visit the wetland. They bounce on the springy ground and exclaim, it *is* like a sponge!

ON-SITE LEARNING

The three most important words of advice I can offer for a successful visit are plan, plan and plan. Plan it as you would a lesson, not an outing. I always plan our schedule down to the minute, especially for a long day. Figure travel time, eating time, gift shop time and snack breaks, as well as educational time. Once on site, you can adjust the schedule as needed.

Ask yourself, "What kind of learning experience can I design to connect the kids to their surroundings?" Find ways to get students into smaller groups and a more intimate learning circle. Think of ways to bring in parents and experts who can teach your children "on-site."

Examples:
At the Shelburne Museum, my teammate and I—and one year, the guidance director and a student teacher—stayed at four different stations and taught small groups of kids while parents did an amazing job of getting kids from one site to the next. At my station, in the Colchester Lighthouse, students sat around me on the rug in one of the upstairs rooms and I read aloud from the book LIFE IN THE COLCHESTER REEF LIGHTHOUSE about the jobs of a lightkeeper. Students then completed a scavenger hunt of the lighthouse.

On a wetlands walk, we split the kids into two groups. Judy Elson from Shelburne Farms led half the kids through a "muck walk," while a parent took the other half on a scavenger hunt.

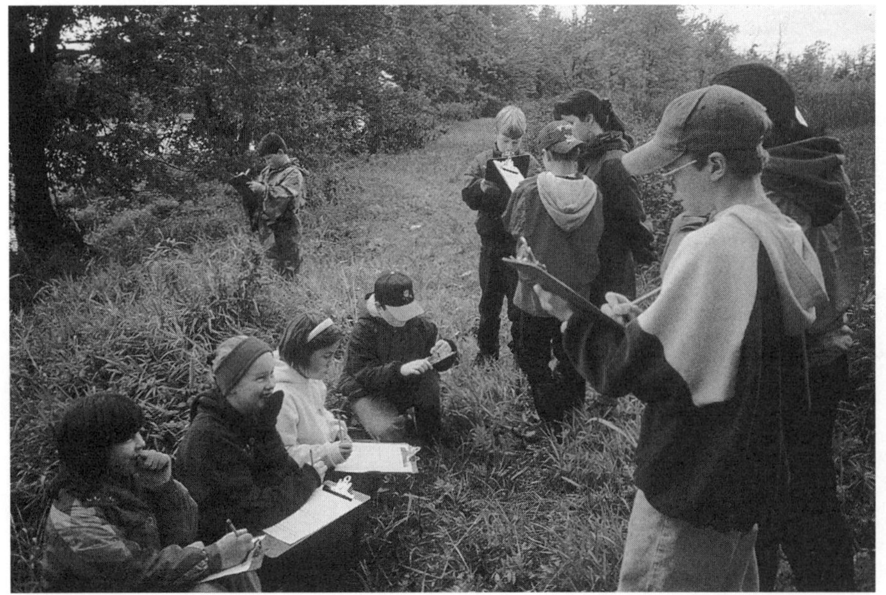

Luckily for us, the Champlain Valley is full of qualified educators who will help design a successful visit. Always clarify with museum staff your needs and expectations. Scheduling a field trip involves more than telling a museum what time you will arrive; discuss with personnel what your students can learn at the site.

POST-VISIT ASSESSMENT

The day after you return from a field trip, devote a lot of time to acknowledging and processing what the kids have learned. In my experience, they sometimes aren't aware of all that they know until they are given a chance to express it. By stating what they have learned, students learn more. They can write what they liked best or what they learned, draw pictures, hold class discussions or make presentations. Bill Ladabouche writes a "listening quiz" of basic information learned on the trip for students to take when they return.

Sometimes the learning happens in their thank you notes! Students can write thank you notes or postcards to museum staff and chaperones. This is a letter a student wrote to Frank Lowenstein who, at the time, worked for the Lake Champlain Committee and took the class on a wild and wet walk into a part of the Sandbar Wildlife Refuge. One of the things he wanted to teach them was the pattern of vegetation created by changing water levels.

> *Dear Frank,*
>
> *Thank you for giving us a tour of the Sandbar Wildlife Refuge. It was fun to walk in all that mud and water! I was fascinated about how you told us about how the wetlands was created how the trees are on higher ground and the water is on the lower ground. The pattern was neat how it went trees water trees water and so on. Please write back!*
>
> *Sincerely,*
> *Austin Barber, Grade 5, Milton*

The field trips can often be the incentive for a larger writing assignment or a culminating project. It makes sense that the best time to work creatively with the material is when the images are fresh in students' minds. For example, because they see so many visual pictures of the past on our visit to Crown Point and the Lake Champlain Maritime Museum, I use this time to launch our major writing project, "Trip Around Lake Champlain" (see *It's About Time*, p. 191).

Processing the trip is also important because you need to communicate the importance of the day and credit their work. The expression "what you give is what you get" is very true on field trips in terms of behavior, attentiveness and learning. I often have a note on students' desks when

they come in the next day that says: "Thanks for a great day, I am proud to be your teacher!"

Stamp

To: _______________

Other Ideas

When they return from a trip, use postcards for students to write about their trip. They can draw on the blank side and write a note to a real or imaginary character on the back. They can also be used as thank you notes. One year, after visiting the Shelburne Museum, I bought real postcards of the S.S. ***Ticonderoga*** *and the students wrote postcards as if they had actually been on a boat ride.*

ABD'S FAVORITE FIELD TRIPS

TOUCH LAKE

Ask all students to touch the lake during the lake study. They are encouraged to arrange a trip with their families, if possible, to share the lake's beauty. It's okay if everyone can't do this with families, because they will have an opportunity to touch the lake on field trips.

Educational material available prior to visit? No.
TOPIC: Appreciation of Lake Champlain.
Pre-planning activity: Brainstorm possibilities.
On-site activity: It's up to them!
Post-visit assessment: Journal entry, class map with sites visited.

SATURDAY "HASSLE-FREE" FERRY RIDES

Just for fun! If your energy holds, a really nice thing to do in the fall or the spring is to invite your students and families for a Saturday ferry ride. You can try to arrange a discount price and hope to get a good showing, but you don't need permission slips because students come with families and there is minimal cost, other than your loss of a free Saturday! Families provide transportation to the ferry, the cost of a ticket and their own bag lunches.

Educational material available prior to visit? No.
TOPICS: Geography, fun!
Pre-planning activity: "Ferry Tales" (see *Math*, p. 270).
On-site activity: Socialize and enjoy the ride!
Post-visit assessment: Thank you notes to families
and a report to the class on anything of interest.
Contact person: Lake Champlain Transportation Company
Address: King Street Dock, Burlington, VT 05401
Telephone: 802-864-9804

"I did a 'touch lake' experience with my mother. It was on the Sandbar at around 5:30-6:00 p.m. We had bought grinders and soda. We watched the sunset while eating our supper. Almost forty-five minutes later I went down and touched the freezing lake."

thinkbook entry, grade 7

The ultimate "touch lake" experience is offered in the summer by the Lake Champlain Maritime Museum. A group of teenagers travel to the museum each day for three weeks and each person builds his or her own kayak. They then set off on a two-week kayaking odyssey on Lake Champlain. What an experience!

SPIRIT *of* ETHAN ALLEN

It is important, lest you lose sight of the real reason why you are studying Lake Champlain, to spend some time just enjoying the lake! This tour boat is a great introductory field trip. The captain of the boat gives an extensive narration of history, geology and local lore. Students may miss some of this while on deck, so clarify with your students how much you are asking them to absorb. You will be able to see part of the Champlain Thrust Fault north of Burlington harbor. I tend to let them enjoy the ride; it's pretty exciting on a wavy day!

Educational material available prior to visit? No.
TOPICS: Geography, geology, fun!
Pre-planning activity: Be familiar with the basic geography of the lake and the Ojihozo myth.
On-site activity: Enjoy!
Post-visit assessment: Review sights, Ojihozo, Champlain Thrust Fault, rock formations, weather and Burlington waterfront. This is a good time to start a word bank with all their impressions of what they saw!
Contact person: Mike Shea
Address: P.O. Box 605, Burlington, VT 05402
Telephone: 802-864-9804

SHELBURNE MUSEUM "LAKE CHAMPLAIN" TOUR

Educational material available prior to visit? Yes. A printed Museum Guide about Lake Champlain is available with lots of information to help you plan your tour.

TOPICS: Maritime history, nautical archeology.

Pre-planning activity: Complete fact-finding about the S.S. *Ticonderoga* and do activity: "Beacons of the Future" (see *History*, p. 165). Discuss steam travel, the commercial use of the lake and the chronology of the lake's nautical history.

On-site activity: Divide into groups to see the lighthouse, the S.S. *Ticonderoga* and the exhibit on nautical archeology. Other exhibits outlined in the tour are also relevant to the lake.

Post-visit assessment: Write postcards from their "trip on the Ti." Review facts learned on site. Write stories about the lake.

Contact person: Garet Livermore

Address: Shelburne Museum School Programs, Shelburne, VT 05482

Telephone: 802-985-3346 EXT 396

LAKE CHAMPLAIN MARITIME MUSEUM

This is the place to go if your main focus is history or archeology. It is perhaps the most single valuable educational field trip that your students can take while studying Lake Champlain. The Maritime Museum currently offers four educational "field study" programs that range from an introduction to watercraft for students in K–3, to regional history and nautical archeology for students in grades 4 and up. You can arrange for your students to see a slide show that reviews this history in clearly defined, well-described historical periods. Make sure to clarify with the museum staff exactly what your tour will include. There is now so much to see at this site that each tour cannot cover everything. If school budgets were different, I'd visit this site twice a year.

Field study programs include:

"Boats, Boats, Boats" about how boats operate and what boats were used on Lake Champlain.

"Digging, Diving, and Documenting" about nautical archeology that includes a hands-on investigation of a shipwreck.

"1776: American Revolution in the Champlain Valley" and **"History and Heritage: An Overview of Historic Lake Champlain"**

Educational material available prior to visit: Yes. Curriculum materials are available to complement most programs.

TOPICS: History, nautical archeology, American Revolution.

Pre-planning activity: Establish familiarity with, but not mastery of, historical chronology, vocabulary, and nautical archeology. It is helpful to know the story of the *Philadelphia* (I and II) and sailing terminology. For me, this field trip works best mid-way into our study, when students have enough knowledge to absorb all the visual material at the museum. The trip will spur as many questions as it answers, so don't leave it to the end; it will energize your further study.

On-site activity: The educational staff conducts the field study programs. Teachers and chaperones are enlisted to participate as needed.

Post-visit assessment: Creative writing and timeline illustration (see *It's About Time*).

Contact person: Laurie Eddy, Education Director

Address: Lake Champlain Maritime Museum at Basin Harbor, RR 3, Box 4092, Vergennes, VT 05491

Telephone: 802-475-2022

CROWN POINT STATE HISTORIC SITE

I guess if I had to say which is my favorite field trip, I would have to say Crown Point. If you are studying early white settlement in the Champlain Valley, you have to come here. Although a visit to Fort Ticonderoga offers students a view of a period fort, reconstructed exactly as it was, there is something about the ruins of Fort St. Frederic and Fort Crown Point that challenges students' imaginations. The site has a wonderful museum with a collection that is easily understood and "the world's best slide show."

Educational material available prior to visit? Yes.

TOPICS: History, American Revolution, European Settlement.

Pre-planning activity: Every year, I spend more and more time getting my kids ready to visit this site. There is a new teacher's guide, which clearly outlines the historical periods relevant to this site and also includes illustrations, maps and primary documents. I show slides of the site and review eighteenth-century fort construction. I also think it is important to read journals of how soldiers and settlers spent their time there.

On-site activity: Scavenger hunt (available from museum); time to explore and to tour the museum. One year, when I visited with a class that had done a lot of research, students did skits portraying the different historical moments at the fort at the appropriate spots. Carol Livingston, a teacher at Camel's Hump Middle School, has students write soldiers' journals at the site.

Post-visit assessment: Writing, discussion and drawing (see *It's About Time*).

Contact person: Greg Furness

Address: Crown Point Historic Site, RD 1, Box 219, Crown Point, NY 12928

Telephone: 518-597-3666

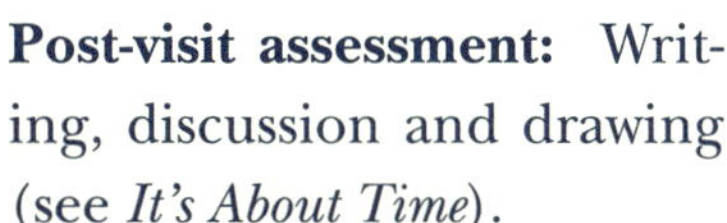

MOUNT INDEPENDENCE

This is an important site if you are leading an in-depth study of the American Revolution. As one wanders from crumbling rocks to a lookout point, one can see its value as a strategic station during the American Revolution. There have been archeological digs there for quite a few summers. It is unclear how I might describe this incredible site if I were writing this in five years. The site currently offers seven miles of hiking trails that lead you past the archeological remains of this once-bustling fort. The State of Vermont built an interpretive center, which opened in 1996 and it offers exhibits and other programs.

Educational material available prior to visit? Yes.
TOPICS: Camp life, military strategy during American Revolution.
Pre-planning activity: Review maps, camp life and military strategy of American Revolution. Read "Mount Independence" (see *History*, p. 138–139).
On-site activity: Explore grounds with an interpreter if possible. Tour museum.
Post-visit assessment: See *It's About Time.*
Contact person: Audrey Porsche
Address: Chimney Point Historic Site, RD 1, Box 3546, Vergennes, VT 05491
Telephone: 802-759-2412

Bill Murphy and the Mount Independence Coalition can be reached at:
Address: P.O. Box 28, East Middlebury, VT 05740
Telephone: 802-388-7577

A history buff who has been involved in the site for many years and is currently co-president of the the Mount Independence Coalition is Bill Murphy, a retired high school teacher. Bill often tours sites with school groups.

BURLINGTON WASTE WATER TREATMENT PLANT
and BURLINGTON WATER TREATMENT PLANT

These two plants, run by Burlington Public Works, are important stops for a study of human impacts on the Champlain Basin. The chief plant operators at both plants are extremely knowledgeable and they understand the importance of educating the public about the issues of water. The Waste Water Treatment Plant is located just south of the Perkins Pier entrance at the foot of Maple Street at the Burlington waterfront. The tour begins with an explanation of the rationale for treatment plants and then a description of the process step by step, using visuals and water samples. Students see each step of the process at the plant. The Burlington Water Treatment Plant is located next to the Coast Guard station on the northern end of the waterfront. This tour begins with the room housing the huge computer that monitors the operation. The chief operator explains each step of the process as he leads students through the different sections of the plant.

Educational material available prior to visit? Yes. Pamphlet from Waste Water Treatment Plant.

TOPICS: Water treatment, waste water treatment, ecology of the lake, human impact.

Pre-planning activity: Review geography and ecology.

On-site activity: Tour plants with chief operators. Students can complete flow charts and questions about processes.

Post-visit assessment: Discussion; debate about residential, commercial and industrial development, residential water use and farm runoff (see *Ecology*).

Contact: Steve Roy, Project Engineer
Address: Waste Water Treatment Plant, 53 Lavalley Lane, Burlington, VT 05401
Telephone: 802-865-7258

Contact: Tom Dion, Chief Plant Operator, Water Treatment Plant, Lake Street, Burlington, VT 05401
Mailing Address: P.O. Box 878, Burlington, VT 05402
Telephone: 802-863-4501

ETHAN ALLEN HOMESTEAD

If your Lake Champlain study includes a close look at how people lived on the lake from 1500–1800, this site can offer a wealth of possibilities to fuel your study. The settler unit that I teach (see "Notes on Reading" in *Language Arts*, p. 249), focuses on the exchange and contrast between native peoples and Europeans. The museum offers tours and activities that do an excellent job giving kids a hands-on feel for life in the wilderness and how different people experienced it.

Educational material available prior to visit? Yes. Flyer available that outlines tour themes and activities.

TOPICS: Native American relationship with the land, European settlement.

Pre-planning activity: Read children's literature of this time period. Become familiar with the chronology of the colonial period and the geography of region.

On-site activity: Design with museum staff.

Post-visit assessment: Creative writing and evaluation.

Contact person: Scott Stevens

Address: Ethan Allen Homestead Trust, 1 Ethan Allen Homestead, Suite 2 Burlington, VT 05401

Telephone: 802-865-4556

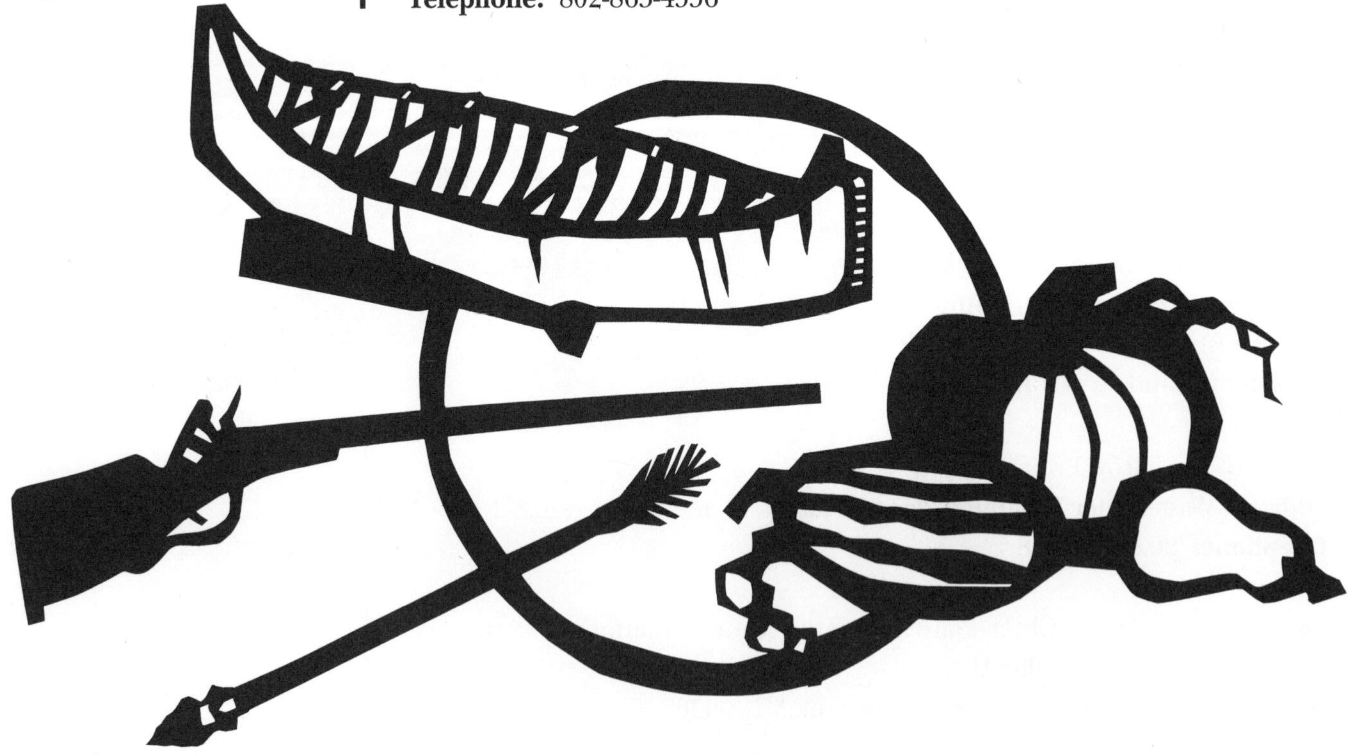

OTHER FIELD TRIPS

I have outlined some of my favorite trips, but the list of possibilities is long. The following sites here are no less important; I am just not as familiar with them.

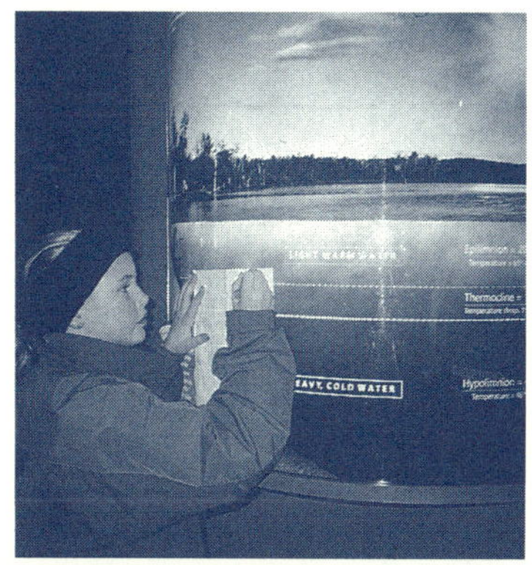

Ed Weed Fish Culture Station (Grand Isle Fish Hatchery)
There is a self-guided walking tour of this state-of-the-art fish hatchery. You can visit the visitor's center, which has a video and excellent graphics on the life cycle of fish and lake ecology. Walk by the fish in the raceway enclosure and tour the grounds to gain an understanding of how the whole facility works.
TOPICS: Fish, ecology, zebra mussels.
Contact: Hatchery Supervisor
Address: 14 Bell Hill Road, Grand Isle, VT 05485
Telephone: 802-372-3171

Button Bay State Park
This state park contains a large natural area and nature center (staffed seasonally). It is very close to the Maritime Museum so it's possible to combine them into a full day of activities, either to view the geology or just to have fun!
TOPICS: Geology, natural history, ecology.
Contact: Raelene Emerson
Address: RR 3, Box 4075, Vergennes, VT 05491
Telephone: 802-475-2377

Lake Champlain Basin Science Center
This exciting new interdisciplinary museum is still brand new as this book is being completed. The museum is open to school groups and offers a multitude of exhibits and programs.
TOPICS: All topics. Exhibits on nautical archeology and wetlands.
Contact: Julie Silverman
Address: 1 College Street, Burlington, VT 05401
Telephone: 802-864-1848

Boat ride on M.V. *Carillon* to Fort Ti
The *Carillon*'s narrated $1\frac{1}{2}$-hour tour goes to Hand's Cove, Chapman's Point, Mount Independence, Catfish Bay, Masting Rock and Fort Ticonderoga.
TOPICS: History, geography and ecology.
Contact: Mahlon Teachout
Address: Teachout's Lakehouse Store and Wharf, P.O. Box 64A, Shoreham, VT 05770
Telephone: 802-897-5331

Skenesborough Museum

The Skenesborough Museum, located in the 1917 canal terminal building on the Champlain Barge Canal, offers exhibits, artifacts and photographs that tell the story of Whitehall's part in Lake Champlain's history, specifically canals and railroads.

TOPICS: History, nautical archeology, canals, commerce and railroads.
Contact: Carol Greenough
Address: P.O. Box 238, Whitehall, NY 12887
Telephone: 518-499-1155

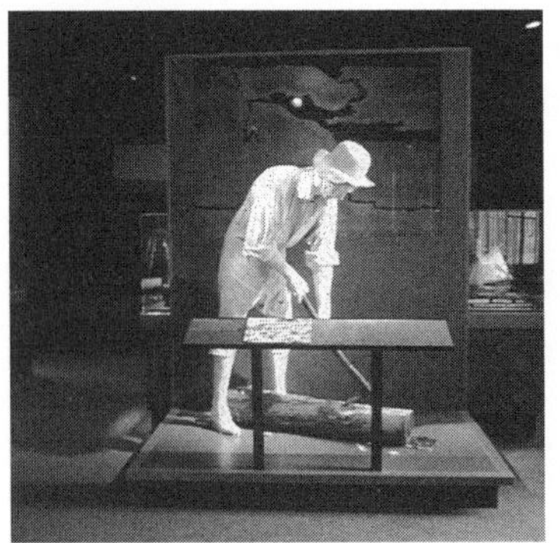

Shelburne Farms

Shelburne Farms, 1,400 acres of land and buildings formerly owned by the Webb family, is now an educational center and working farm. Field trips are based on seasonal events in the natural world and on the farm.

TOPICS: Water quality, ecology, natural history, local history of the Farms.
Contact: Field Trip Coordinator
Address: Shelburne Farms, Shelburne, VT 05482
Telephone: 802-985-8686

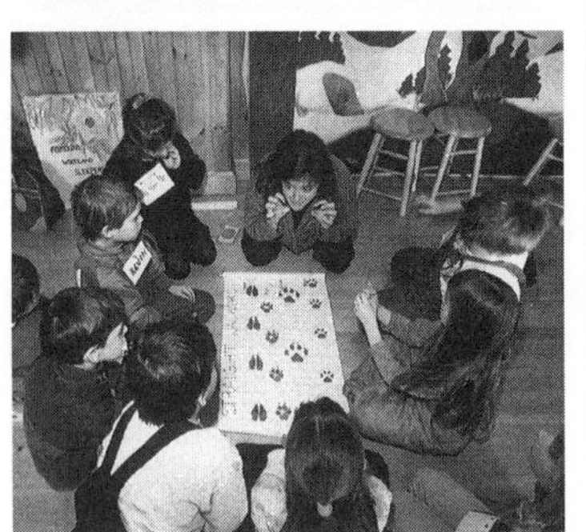

Melosira

The *Melosira* is UVM's research vessel and is operated by the School of Natural Resources. It will take groups of students (max: 24) who are prepared to participate and observe the latest in scientific monitoring techniques. Trip should be planned in conjunction with class activities.

TOPICS: Water quality, fisheries, electronic navigation and scientific research.
Contact: Dick Forbush, captain of the *Melosira*
Address: Lake Studies Center, George D. Aiken Building, University of Vermont, Burlington, VT 05405
Telephone: 802-656-4057

Perkins Geology Museum

The Perkins Museum houses a large collection of rocks, gems, minerals and fossils, including a collection specific to the Champlain Valley. The Museum has the Charlotte Whale as well as graphics depicting the glacial history of the Champlain Valley.

TOPIC: Geology.
Contact: Geology Department - Staff/Students
Address: Perkins Geology Museum, c/o Geology Department, University of Vermont, Burlington, VT 05405
Telephone: 802-656-3396

Chimney Point Museum

Chimney Point was a seasonal campsite for Native people beginning 7,000 years ago and later the site of the French settlement, Hocquart, in the early eighteenth century. Exhibits tell the story of our Native American and French heritage.

TOPICS: Native American history, French settlement, archeology.

Contact: Audrey Porsche

Address: RD 1, Box 3546, Vergennes, VT 05491

Telephone: 802-759-2412

Mt. Philo

The State Park on top of Mt. Philo offers spectacular views of the Champlain Valley and the geologic layering of marine life and fossils. Walking up the mountain and looking out over the Champlain Valley, students will be able to identify important elements of Champlain's geologic history.

TOPICS: Geology, geography.

Contact: Russell Mace, Park Ranger

Address: Mt. Philo State Park, RD 1, Box 1049, North Ferrisburgh, VT 05473

Telephone: 802-425-2390

KAREN MURDOCK'S
FAVORITE FIELD TRIPS

Karen Murdock is principal of Cumberland Head Elementary School in Plattsburgh, New York, and has been active in the Lake Champlain Basin Education Initiatives.

ADIRONDACK MUSEUM

This museum is noted for its exhibits depicting the work and leisure of people in the Adirondack region—explorers, fur traders, lumberjacks, artists, mothers, hermits, boat builders, guides and entrepreneurs. Exhibits are housed in 22 exhibit buildings in a scenic setting. The "Woods and Water" exhibit houses collections of recreational activities including fishing, hiking, camping and early Olympic bobsledding. The Boat Building houses an unbelievable collection of canoes from early times, as well as racing boats and pleasure boats. The Mining Building depicts the actual mining of iron ore and includes a vast collection of tools that were used. One building contains a pictorial history of logging. On a hill overlooking Blue Mountain Lake are several Adirondack Camps furnished as rustically as they were in the 1800s.

Educational material available prior to visit? Yes. Numerous videos, worksheets, slide sets, books and traveling trunks with artifacts.

TOPIC: Social and natural history of the United States and the Adirondack region.

Pre-planning activity: Students need to understand the diverse aspects of the Adirondacks, local culture and folklore. Discuss natural environment and global links to issues about logging and recreation industries and environmental politics.

On-site activity: Guided tours, demonstrations, classes and overnight program with area nature center are available.

Post-visit assessment: Creative writing, artwork, journal writing.

Contact person: Michelle Pierson

Address: P.O. Box 99, Blue Mountain Lake, NY 12812

Telephone: 518-352-7311

FORT TICONDEROGA

This is a must for every student within the basin. Originally the French fort "Carillon," the fort played an important part in the development of the Champlain Valley. Costumed guides lead school group tours of the fort and students can visit an extensive museum of eighteenth century artifacts and graphics.

Educational material available prior to visit? Yes. Kits include artifacts and information on museum displays.

TOPICS: History, Native Americans, colonial settlement, Seven Years' War and American Revolution.

Pre-planning activity: Read all or parts of THE BRAVE BOYS OF TICONDEROGA by Carroll Lonergan. This is a great book that brings events at the fort alive.

On-site activity: Guided or self-directed tours, Fife and Drum Corps.

Post-visit assessment: Creative writing, artwork, journal writing.

Contact person: Linda Edson

Address: P.O. Box 390, Ticonderoga, NY 12883

Telephone: 518-585-2821

STATE MUSEUM *of* NEW YORK

This museum has an extensive collection and incorporates the historical, cultural and environmental development of New York. The section of the museum that is my favorite is the Iroquois exhibit. There is a life-sized longhouse, original clothing, bead work, art work, and wampum. Dioramas show people doing daily tasks.

Educational material available prior to visit? No.

TOPICS: Iroquois culture and history, natural history, logging, commerce.

Pre-planning activity: Students should study Iroquois culture and their daily life.

On-site activity: The museum provides guided tours. There is a "museum search" that helps students discover parts of the museum in small groups.

Post-visit assessment: Writing activities, projects, artwork.

Contact person: Pat Whalen

Address: New York State Museum, Cultural Education Center, Albany, NY 12230

Telephone: 518-474-5843

Note: This Albany experience is wonderful. Plan for a full day and pack your lunch. There are places to eat outside on the Mall and view the skyscrapers. Take a ride on the large escalators and tour the top of the Education Building and see the panoramic view of Albany. I suggest a tour of the Capitol if there is time.

COLLEEN CARTER'S FAVORITE FIELD TRIPS

Colleen Carter is a science teacher at Richelieu Valley Regional High School in Masterville, Quebec and has been active in the Lake Champlain Basin Education Initiatives.

IROQUOIS INDIAN MUSEUM

This new museum, housed in an exciting building that evokes a longhouse, used to be the Schoharie Museum. The museum has contemporary Iroquois artwork, an archeology collection, performing arts and nature trails.
TOPICS: Iroquois culture and history, art and natural history.
Contact person: Colette Lemmon, Director of the Children's Museum
Address: Caverns Road, Box 7, Howes Cave, NY 12092
Telephone: 518-296-8949

ECOMUSEUM

The Ecomuseum is a wildlife interpretation center that has over ninety species of fish, frogs, salamanders, snakes, turtles, birds and mammals that are native to the St. Lawrence Valley. Guides plan trips with you and offer sleepovers with a nocturnal tour of some of the animals.
TOPICS: Natural history, ecology.
Contact person: Sylvie Matte
Address: 21,125 Chemin Ste-Marie, Ste-Anne-de-Bellevue, Quebec 89X3L2
Telephone: 514-457-9449

MUSEUM AT CHAMBLY, CANADA

The Chambly Fort, fully reconstructed, stands near the Chambly rapids. School programs relate the history of the fort, living conditions of its inhabitants and various archeological projects.
TOPICS: History, archeology.
Contact: Danielle Bruneau and Kevin Robinson
Address: 2 Richelieu Street, Chambly, Quebec, J3L 2B9
Telephone: 514-658-1585

Research and Inquiry (and Action!)

The Year 3000

by Becky Martell, Grade 5, School Street School, Milton, Vermont

It is the year 2012. A beautiful lake, Lake Champlain, is becoming polluted and full of garbage. The *Spirit of Ethan Allen* does not sail on Lake Champlain anymore because the propeller got clogged with garbage. It is in an old garage, rotting in decay. No one cares. The last ride on the *Spirit of Ethan Allen* was in 1998.

No one pays attention to what they are doing to the lake, because they all have million-dollar pools. And they are too busy partying and having a good time and throwing trash all over which ends up in the lake. There is a low population of fish and only a few people still eat fish from the lake.

No one has seen Champ since 1996. Scientists say he or she has died. That is all they said so they could go home and watch the NFL on a new channel called "Football Only."

No boats go on the lake anymore; they are all locked up like the *Spirit of Ethan Allen.*

One summer the clean water supply was low, then it was gone. No one could fill up their pools so they decided to go to the lake. When they got there they had a big surprise. The lake was full of garbage and it was sick. No one wanted to swim in that, so they went home.

As the days went by, it got hotter and hotter and there was no water. The people were getting hot and mad at each other and they were getting mad about what happened to the lake.

Then on the hottest day of the whole summer, they decided to clean it up. It took six weeks with all the people helping.

Now they had to fix the *Spirit of Ethan Allen.* After four months and two days, it was able to sail again on Lake Champlain. Champ has been seen again and Lake Champlain is still beautiful in the year 3000.

Introduction

Although not in my original plans, the need for this chapter grew as the book evolved. I found myself writing: "depending on how you structure your classroom" numerous times. I didn't want to start philosophizing every time I wrote that, but it started to make sense to write about such things in a separate place.

Learning about Lake Champlain is different from studying the pyramids of Egypt and invites new methodology. Here are some of the ways that teaching and learning could and should be different when studying a local resource.

I want to note that much of the research that I did with students was when I was teaching seventh grade in Milton Junior-Senior High School. At that time, I taught Social Studies to 110 students, in a junior high setting. Suggestions for amending research for the lower grades are included here.

There are many excellent sources to help you do nontraditional research:
- Sometimes a Shining Moment *by Elliot Wigginton*
- My Backyard History Book *by David L. Weitzman*
- Our Town: Recording and Presenting Local History and Folklife (Teacher Handbook) *by Greg Sharrow*
- Many Cultures, One People: A Multicultural Handbook about Vermont for Teachers *edited by Greg Sharrow*
- "Legacy of the Lake" (video)—*Vermont Folklife Center*
- You Hear the Ice Talking: The Ways of People and Ice on Lake Champlain *by I. Sheldon Posen*

Also, here are three books I recommend regarding stewardship:
- Come Back Salmon *by Molly Cone*
- It's Our World, Too! *by Philip Hoose*
- Letters from the Earth *by Schim Schimmel*

How the World Works

HOW CAN I LEARN ABOUT HOW THE WORLD WORKS?

ASK

1. of an explorer

curiosity

imagination

organization

WHERE CAN I FIND OUT HOW THE WORLD WORKS?

SEARCH

2.

books

people

nature

articles

music

encyclo-pedias

posters

legends

maps

artifacts

computers

radio

stories

news-papers

animals

I'M STARTING TO FIGURE THINGS OUT!

ORGANIZE

3.

List

brain-storm

cluster

categorize

listen

talk

think

read

partner

write

interview

draw

4.

SEE HOW MUCH I KNOW ABOUT HOW THE WORLD WORKS?

COMMUNICATE

graph

chart

form

report

speech

artwork

film

replica

diagram

categories

brochure

essay

poem

story

5.

HOW CAN I HELP CARE FOR THIS WORLD?

STEWARDSHIP

team-work

actions

persuade

decide

educate

problem solving

life-style

publicity

learn more!

Research and Inquiry (and Action!)

Getting students excited about learning about the lake is central to everything this book is about. Research and inquiry, whether structured or informal, is at the heart of an interdisciplinary study.

I believe our job is to help students:
- learn to ask questions about what is around them,
- identify ways that they can find answers to these questions,
- use skills of reading, observation, experimentation and dialogue to obtain answers,
- organize answers in a way that is meaningful to them,
- design a way that they can communicate what they have found.

This chapter is based on how to design classroom research that is tied into the life-long skill of self-directed learning. Whether you and your students want to do a large, ongoing research project or whether you do a short inquiry about boater safety, you are engaged in finding out how to find things out. I will outline some of the possibilities for a large research project as well as for a variety of shorter projects.

I call the large in-depth research project an "I-search." I will describe the parts of an I-search. Keep in mind that any one of its components may be set up individually as a shorter inquiry project.

This chapter will explore a "redefinition of sources" and a variety of ways that kids can learn from these resources. Unless you're in a very unique situation, turning them loose in the library is not an option. Even if your library has a good collection of local history material or freshwater science books, much of it is not fit for kid consumption. So let's think beyond books! The study of Lake Champlain is a very "happening" thing and students need to learn how to access information in new ways.

What kind of inquiry do you want to do?

Decide (with your class as much as possible) what sort of research you want to do. You may decide to devote two or three weeks to a major research project or to enhance your ecology study with some oral interviews about land development.

How much time will you devote to the research?

Many factors determine how extensive the research will be. I have had the experience of thinking we would spend a long time doing research and, for one reason or another, discovering my plans didn't "take." I have also (in general science, not with Lake Champlain studies) organized a snappy little research/reading inquiry and had the class turn it into a four-week study, including my first-ever and most wonderful science fair. Although we have a multitude of things dictating our time, sometimes it's good to "go with the flow."

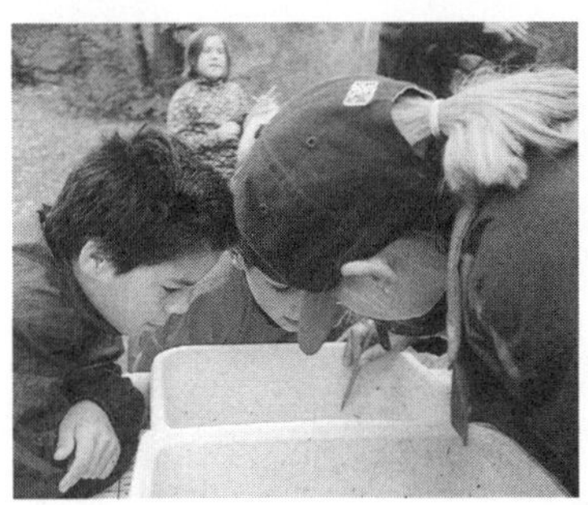

Can I do this with all ages?

I am not currently doing this extended I-search project with fifth graders. Even when I did this in seventh grade, the reading level of much of the information, as well as the availability of much of the material, was a constant challenge. That doesn't mean it isn't possible. I made up three-ring binders and folders on various topics. I collected newspaper articles, flyers, newsletters, maps and diagrams—I scrounged! I also collected a lot of books and pamphlets, some of which are unfortunately out of print. But that was in the "old days" of lake studies and you now have available to you a number of other resources that you can collect for your classroom. I had to steer some kids to topics that they could handle, like fishing and species of fish, geography and Native American artifacts. Other students got carried away with underwater archeology, biographies, ecological issues and life at Crown Point.

What is it?

The "pieces" of an extensive research project are outlined below. They can also be used separately for shorter inquiries.

The I-search project includes:
1. setting clear expectations,
2. choosing a topic,
3. investigating sources,
4. using people as sources,
5. keeping in touch,
6. finding out about current research.

SETTING CLEAR EXPECTATIONS

Before you officially begin your I-search, discuss with your students the main parts of the project. Depending on how you run your room, you may or may not have this worked out ahead of time. Usually, I "cheat." I have a pretty good idea of what I'm hoping to do, run it by them and hope they buy it. Sometimes they don't, as I mentioned before, and it's worth adjusting your plans if they don't. But if they do, and hopefully you've created enough build-up so they will, work out with the class the pieces of the research. For example, I find it a lot easier to discuss how long a paper they think they can write and reach a consensus than to say "I will require a 10-page report." Communicate your expectations. You may have in mind a three-page minimum. They might lobby for two; that's when you make really clear that, in your opinion, you can't successfully communicate enough information in two pages and if they are really going to put a lot of time into this, they need to proceed with higher expectations.

It is also important to discuss what work you expect students to do on their own and what work might be done collectively. I remember that I originally introduced the non-written project as an individual project. My students quickly communicated that they really wanted the option of doing their projects together. Being able to present together, even if they had made projects separately, was also important.

It's a question of balancing your standards as a teacher and the need as a human being to be responsive to the other 20-plus human beings that you are working with. In our profession, it's an issue we face all the time and it's important for each teacher to figure out her philosophy in this regard.

When we have finished our discussion, I write on the board the agreements that we have made. I will type this up and hand it out the next day. It's a good idea to send it home for a parent signature since parents can be a significant source of support.

Consider the power that their full agreement has brought to the research compared to handing them a worksheet with the decisions all made!

The handout might look something like this (see next page):

"The most interesting thing about my I-search is that I'm working with friends and we're doing a play."

thinkbook entry, Grade 7, Milton

Lake Champlain I-Search

The I-Search has three main parts:

1. Research Paper

- Each student writes his or her own paper, three-to-five pages.
- Includes the following: introduction

                                           information

                                           sources

                                         conclusion

Rough draft due: ________________

Final draft due: ________________

2. Non-Written Project

- Students may work in groups.
- The student-designed creation should illustrate some aspect of the student's research.
- It can be a map, diagram, model, skit or play, timeline, video, collage, poster, or ....

Projects must be completed by ________________

3. Presentation

- Students may present together.
- Each student will present his or her research and project to the class.

Presentations will be given ________________

The grade for the I-Search will be based on the completion of all parts described above, as well as on the ability to be on time and on task with daily responsibilities.

CHOOSING A TOPIC

The most critical part of the process is choosing a topic. It is also the most difficult. Students don't always make up their minds, how and when you want them to. I believe firmly that, in this kind of inquiry, it is their job to decide what they want to learn about; I am here to help. Allow plenty of time for this process and find different ways to keep in touch with what they are thinking. When I have a special-needs student who does much of the class work with a paraprofessional, I try to alert both student and helper that this is coming up so that they can get a jump on the process. Many children have difficulty taking this first step. As often as I can, I try to have an early conversation with a student, if his or her interest was piqued by a guest speaker or field trip. Strike while the iron is hot!

Explore topics with cluster
Brainstorm all the possibilities for topics in a cluster. Post the cluster in the room and add topics as they come up. Students can also use this as a way to sign up for their topics. It is important for them to be familiar with each other's topics, so they can share information as they proceed in their research.

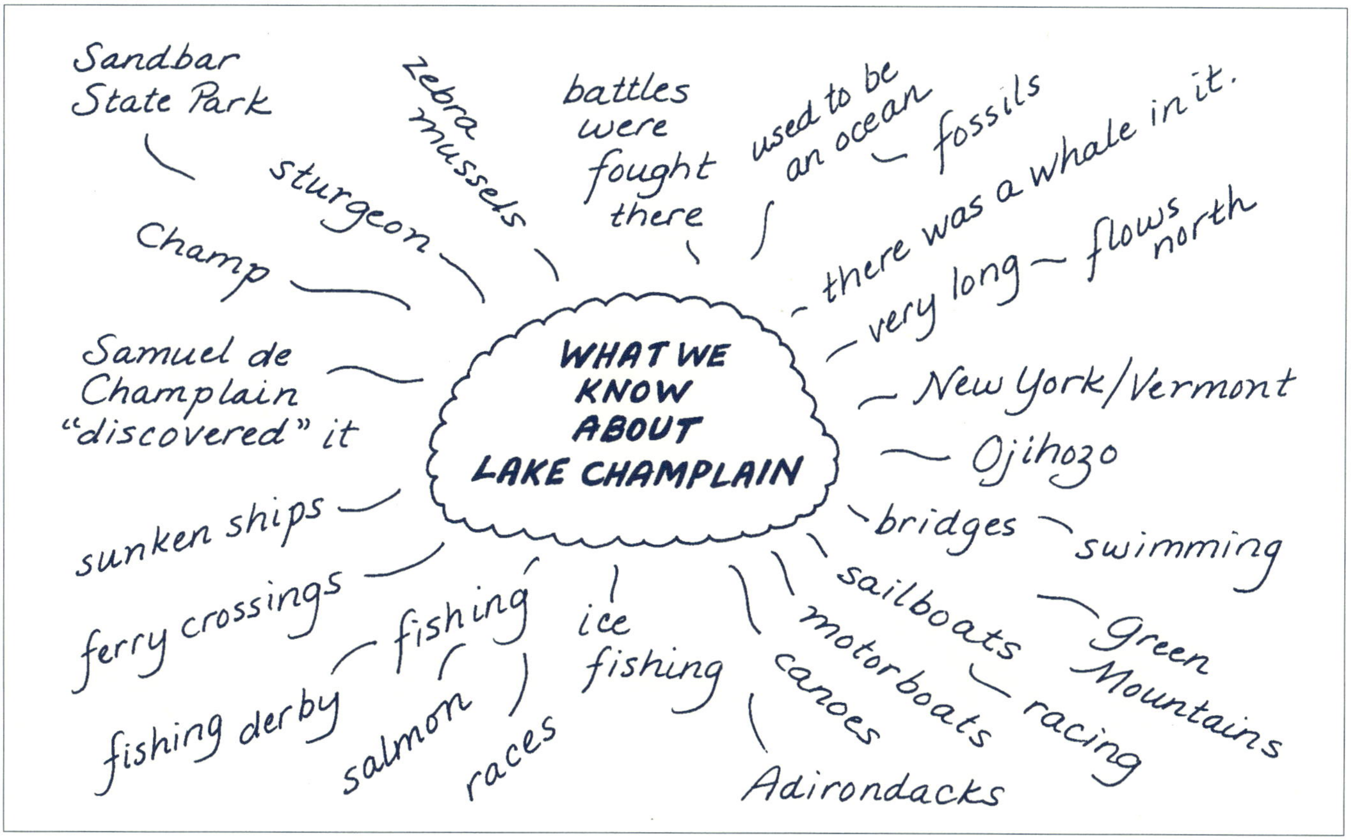

Keep in mind available resources as students make their choices, but don't underestimate the detective skills of middle-level students when they get going. I had one student my second year who was bound and determined to study toxins in fish. At the time, I knew next to nothing about it and had few resources to offer. I think he ended up making use of the Lake Champlain Committee and their newsletters and the local game warden. He was very proud of his final work.

When the student has ownership of and a vested interest in the topic, the results multiply. Much of the success of this kind of inquiry rests on students' knowing the reason for the inquiry and wanting to go digging. They may have a reason for choosing a topic that you don't understand, but that is very clear to them.

When a seventh grader chose to research "Champ's Chips," I must admit I had doubts about the worth of the project. "Potato chips?" I asked myself. Her final project was outstanding. She arranged a trip to the factory and observed the process and workings of the technology necessary to make potato chips. She conducted interviews and conducted a taste preference survey. Her paper and accompanying diagrams outlined the process and her classmates were enthralled. When she wrote in her thinkbook, she explained the potato chip to Samuel de Champlain! She was an expert on potato chips and proud of it. Heaven forbid if she had listened to her teacher!

Self-directed research requires the ♥ of an explorer, wanting to go looking and seeing and learning in different ways. I think it is necessary to talk about this directly and not hope that it happens. Encourage your students to go digging. Shout a loud hurrah when they do. How you model that in your room is critical to the integrity of this kind of work. I know that my "crazed passion" for learning about Lake Champlain had a lot to do with the success of my students' research. You can't sign up for that, but hopefully you will be teaching about it for a reason that you, yourself, believe in.

When students have chosen their topics, it is important for them to communicate with you early on in the process. (See "Keeping in Touch," p. 312-315.)

INVESTIGATING SOURCES

What is a Source?

Brainstorm with your class "What is a source?" Encourage them to think of how they get information and from where:

• people
• television
• newspapers
• artifacts
• photographs
• artwork
• telephone
• encyclopedia
• nonfiction books
• fiction books
• atlas
• computers: data base, internet, CD-ROM

Brainstorm what you have to do to get information from these sources. What sources do they feel the most confident about? Which ones will they need some help using?

OR

You can use a source brainstorm as a way to have students start to think about topics for a major research project, or a shorter inquiry.

• What are students interested in?
• What kinds of things might they like to find out?
• What kinds of skills are necessary to find information from different sources?

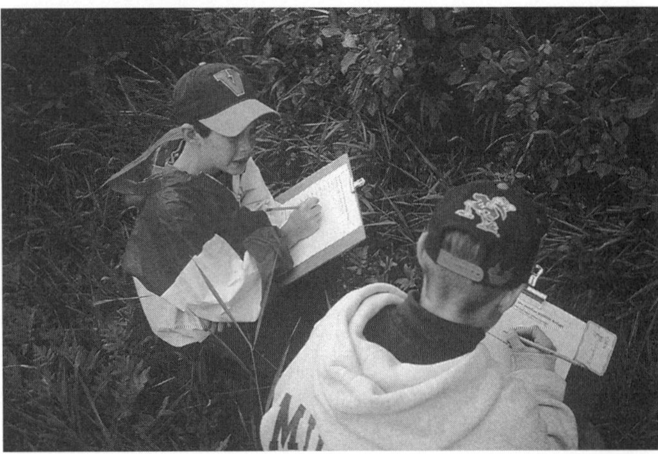

There are a number of organizations that publish information. As adults we use agencies as sources all the time. Many agencies have charts, graphs and maps that are difficult to decipher. It makes sense to me to bring these "real" sources into the classroom and practice using them.

For example, interpret a Fish and Wildlife Department fact sheet on muskrats or a diagram on the water cycle from the Agency of Natural Resources. Sometimes this can be done informally by just having students review

material together. It can also be done as a reading comprehension assignment with a teacher-designed worksheet.

When you are doing research, you may choose to make a requirement that expands a student's use of sources. I require that one source be a person. Bill Romond, at Colchester High School, requires that his students use the telephone to acquire information. I think we often equate research with the printed word. Formalizing the use of different sources helps the teacher and the student!

Source Search

I mentioned earlier that much of the information available about Lake Champlain is difficult for students to read. A "source search" can be used to get students familiar with the resources that are available and expand their choices for topics. It will also help students feel more comfortable with the sources, since many of them are "grown-up" books.

Assemble as many books as you can about Lake Champlain. (See "Get the Picture" in *Getting Wet*, p. 13.) After you have spent some time enjoying and sharing the information, explain the source search. You may choose to pick one book and do a source search together on the overhead.

After all students understand the source search, I usually let them complete one at their own pace, perhaps during reading time or study hall. This is helpful because several students may want to complete a source search on the same book and this way they can take turns. Set a due date for all source search papers to be complete.

Source Search

Write down three things you learned from looking at this book.

1.____

2.____

3.____

Write down one thing that you learned from a picture in this book.
Explain what you observed in a short paragraph.

____

____

____

____

Write down one interesting fact that you found in this book.

____

____

Write a note to your classmates about how you think this book might be helpful to them.
Try to be specific. Your "review" will be posted.

____

____

____

Use the back side to make a sketch of something that you learned from looking at this book.

USING PEOPLE AS SOURCES

The lake provides a rich opportunity to interview people about their experiences. Students need a lot of preparation to do successful interviews. On the other hand, talking about the past is a natural human activity. No matter how involved you get teaching the interview process, be sure to include interviews in your local study.

How to use a person as a resource
Interviewing is a skill for students to learn. It can be incorporated into a larger research project, as one of several ways to get information, or it can be an inquiry project of its own. In either case, the interviewing skill needs practice.

Sometimes the simplicity of children learning to talk to and learn from adults (and vice versa) makes an oral history project worthwhile all by itself, even if they don't find out anything about Lake Champlain! Here are a few tips:

1. Educate your class about people as sources. You can do this by reading journals, oral histories, old and new newspapers or by bringing a volunteer to talk to your class about a topic of interest. An interview is not just an assignment for class. It's an important life skill that involves:
- sharing history,
- preserving history,
- collecting stories,
- learning about your neighborhood,
- learning to talk to people,
- sharing and hearing opinions.

2. Give students time to prepare questions (and get feedback) and time to practice asking questions. They can practice on each other and if you have time, they can "warmup" by going through the whole process (preparing questions, practicing, interviewing, write-up, and final draft) using each other as sources. Each student can choose something he or she would like to be interviewed about.

3. Coach students on designing questions that:
- make the interviewee feel comfortable,
- establish the basic facts about the person and the topic,
- dig more deeply for information,
- clarify or rephrase.

People who:
- ice fish
- work on ferries
- make duck decoys
- dive
- make canoes
- go boating
- go duck hunting
- observe birds
- shoot pickerel
- found artifacts
- smuggled during prohibition
- saw Champ
- conduct scientific research
- can carve
- can sail
- worked on an old ferry
- danced on S.S. *Ticonderoga*

Devote some class time to practicing follow-up questions.

4. Help your students find sources. Find a few people (maybe who work in your building) who will be available for interviews for the few students who will have a hard time finding a neighbor or relative—or who are unable to structure the time to interview someone.

Choosing a topic for your interview

The scope of topics to interview people about is broad. Start a list with your students of possible topics. If you post the list in the classroom, you and your students can post names and addresses of people who are willing to be interviewed.

You can also base a class-wide inquiry, where all students pursue the same topic but interview different people, on some general categories such as:
• Find someone who remembers a cold winter on or near Lake Champlain.
• Find someone who is doing research on or near Lake Champlain.
• Find someone who has an opinion about....
OR
Base your inquiry on general questions:
• What does the lake mean to you?
• What do you remember about the lake from when you were young?

"The interview is perhaps the hardest thing in the unit. But I never doubt its worth. Some students feel discouraged that they'll never find anyone. I tell them that perhaps they could find a student in school that has done a lot of fishing.

I knew things were picking up when Laurie J. asked me if it would be all right if she interviewed her grandmother who used to go to dances on the **Ticonderoga** *when it was still afloat. Could she! I exclaimed. What a wonderful idea.*

Many kids found out that their parents knew more about the lake than they thought —'and that it was really fun to ask Dad questions.'

Mrs. Fitzgerald, an aide at school, took three kids to interview her father, Mr. Manley, who has an extensive arrowhead collection. That was a treat for the kids who went, and, I suspect, for Mr. Manley.

Mrs. Fitzgerald, a member of the Milton Historical Society, also uncovered other interviewees, one of whom fished for his food and livelihood during the Depression."

ABD Teaching Journal

Interview Tips

Before your interview:
1. Make an appointment.
2. Explain the purpose of the interview.
3. Agree on a mutually convenient time and place.
4. Arrange your transportation ahead of time.

Be prepared:
1. Bring your questions and an extra pen or pencil.
2. Group your questions so the interview makes sense.
3. Write out your questions and leave space for answers. Practice!
4. Bring a tape recorder (optional). (You will need permission to tape.)

At the interview:
1. Introduce yourself.
2. Make the interviewee feel comfortable.
3. Find ways to get longer, more detailed answers.
4. Follow an interesting topic—even if it wasn't one of your questions.
5. Have the interviewee sign a statement allowing you to use information in your final paper or project.
6. Thank the person for his or her time and help.

After the interview:
1. Take time to go over your notes and fill in any gaps.
2. Go somewhere quiet where you can write up the main part of your interview.
3. If you missed something important you may need to call up your source.
4. Send a thank you note—and follow-up questions if necessary.

Your interview write-up should include the following:
1. The person's name, and the date and location of the interview.
2. Information that you learned.
3. What you found most interesting.
4. Additional information of your choice.

KEEPING IN TOUCH

When students have chosen their topics, it is important for you to know that they have a clear understanding of the topic and the beginnings of a plan. This is especially true in a long-term research project, but also true in a shorter inquiry.

During the early stages of research, it is important to check in with each student and see how each is doing. This can be done informally, through class discussion, thinkbook entries and individual conferences, but another way to assess uniformly where each person is at is to have "checkpoints."

Students should know ahead of time when these "checkpoints" will be. The first one should be done early enough that you can still "save" a student who is floundering. Don't be upset with yourself if you didn't anticipate this problem. Sometimes floundering is good! But it is to help the occasional flounderer that you need these pre-established check points. It may be a case of:

"I know you want to research the General Butler but we've been working for two weeks now. You have four days to see if you have adequate information. When we do our "Fact Finding and Communication" on Friday you'll have to be able to show me you are all set or you will have to change topics."

Fact Finding and Communication

Write 10 facts that you have learned from your research.

1. _______________________________   6. _______________________________
2. _______________________________   7. _______________________________
3. _______________________________   8. _______________________________
4. _______________________________   9. _______________________________
5. _______________________________   10. ______________________________

In the space below and on the reverse side, write a well-organized paragraph using at least one fact from your research. You may use more, but remember, the point is to explain what you learned in your own words. When you are done, underline the parts (facts) that you borrowed. Try a rough draft on a separate piece of paper first. _______________________________

____

____

# WHEN STUDENTS NEED MORE DIRECTION

As already mentioned, self-directed research is not for everyone. Some students have a very hard time. Maureen Saunders, when working in my classroom as a Chapter One paraprofessional, demonstrated a particular knack for directing students who were floundering. It takes a graceful touch, because you don't want to take away the student's choice. However, it is important to step in when you are needed. How do you know when a student needs you to sit by her side and say, "Here, how about doing this?"

Stepping in does not mean deserting your open inquiry goals. Some students can't handle too much exploration and need the safe confines of teacher direction. Maureen had some ready-made possibilities that the student could choose from. Within the confines of the discussion with the teacher, the student had many opportunities to choose.

> *"Your topic is ferry crossings; let's look at your plan. What is one thing you have learned about the ferries? You've learned that there are three crossings? Okay, let's write a paragraph about each crossing here. Is there one ferryboat that you learned about? Okay, let's write about that here."*

Examples of topics:
- **Geography:** Make a map and locate shipwrecks, or historic sites or ferry crossings.
- **Fish:** Research different kinds of fish and make a poster of five fish with captions. Add a diagram of a fish and label the parts.
- **Zebra mussels:** Research and make a poster with five facts and a diagram of the life cycle of the zebra mussel.
- **Wetlands:** Write about five important things that wetlands do; draw a picture and make a wetlands tape of wet, mucky noises.

When discussion centered around the structure of a research paper, Maureen had in mind some ways to structure the paper so it didn't seem so huge. In a writing conference, she sat down and outlined the parts of the paper, then the student had smaller spaces to fill in.

It is important for us to remember what a momentous thing it is to make a choice and commit yourself to creating something. An important aspect of our job is to facilitate this process whenever possible and make it a safe and successful experience for every student.

Research Plan

Topic: ____

Define your topic in a well-organized paragraph. You should have a focus.

Think about the things you want to learn and communicate.

____

____

____

____

Identify at least three sources (title and author, name of person and address, etc.)

1. ____
2. ____
3. ____
4. ____

Do you have any questions about topic or process? ___________________________

____

____

What are you planning to do for your presentation? ___________________________

____

____

What do you want to teach the class about your topic? ___________________________

____

____

DOING RESEARCH WITH STUDENTS IN LOWER GRADES

Doing self-directed research with students in lower grades is more of a challenge when many of the sources are hard to interpret. Still, it is worthwhile.

There are many ways to structure research to make it a successful experience for all of your students. Cooperative groups, a limited choice of topics, smaller research projects and different levels of projects help. An example of a "mini-research" project is a well-defined science paper for fifth-graders with a choice of three topics and outlines for each topic.

Science Paper
Possible Topics

A FISH

1. Pick a fish.
2. Identify characteristics (size, color, weight).
3. Identify habitat, life cycle.
4. Find other interesting information.

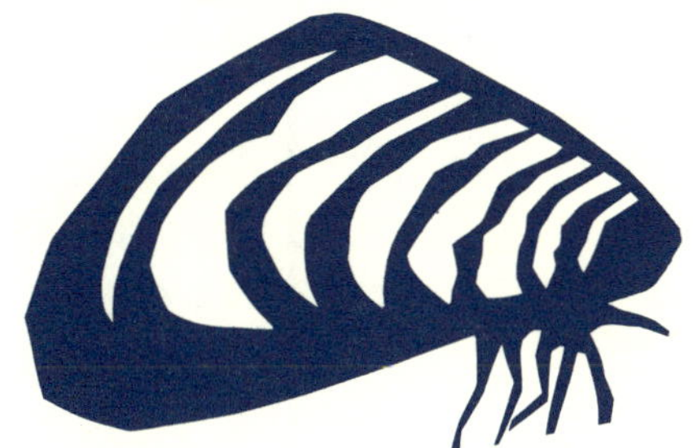

AN ENVIRONMENTAL ISSUE

1. Identify issue or problem.
2. Identify cause or problem.
3. Suggest possible solutions.

THE LAKE AS AN ECOSYSTEM

1. Identify topic.
2. Include meaning of important science vocabulary.
3. Give an example.

FINDING OUT ABOUT CURRENT RESEARCH

An amazing amount of data is currently being collected about Lake Champlain. Millions of dollars are spent on scientists, data collecting, and equipment. When I ponder in 1995 what wasn't known about the lake in 1985, it is staggering. What resources will children have in 2005 as they learn about this precious resource?

One thing is for certain, somehow attaching your study to other studies in the basin gives your students a sense of community with other learners and an awareness that science and inquiry are alive!

River Watch and other citizen monitoring programs use data collected by students, another excellent way to get students involved in their area. Colchester High School students conduct water sampling in Mallett's Bay and do research that must be shared with the community when completed.

Here are some ways to connect your students to some of the ongoing research and activities in the Lake Champlain Basin:

Classroom Activities
• Bring in guest speakers who will share their research (sometimes graduate students have more time).
• Bring in guest speakers and encourage connections with people in your community that are involved with environmental action.
• Conduct an oral interview with a scientist or river monitor.
• Find a way to update some data on an "old" flyer.
• Offer telecommunications opportunities. Mountain Lake Broadcasting arranges on-line telecommunications with schools and researchers. Students can use the Internet to research up-to-date data on the lake and communicate with other learners.
• Read up-to-date newsletters and brochures such as those currently published by the Lake Champlain Committee, the Lake Champlain Basin Program, the Lake Champlain Maritime Museum, and state Fish and Wildlife agencies.

Field Trips
• Visit the *Melosira,* the University of Vermont's research vessel.
• Visit the Lake Champlain Basin Science Center.
• Visit laboratories that are conducting research such as Miner Institute in Chazy, New York, or the School of Natural Resources at UVM, in Burlington.

Going to the Lab

by Bachir Yahi, Grade 6, Frederick H. Tuttle School, South Burlington, Vermont

Bachir Yahi, Brian Costello, Joe Leonard, and Andy Griggs went to the State Health Department Laboratory to test the water from Potash Brook. We met Senior Chemist Carla White who gave us a tour of the facilities.

During the tour we tested the water that we had brought from Potash Brook. We first tested for turbidity. Turbidity is the test for visible solids, for example, if the turbidity is high, the water is cloudy.

After that we tested for pH. The pH is how acid or basic the water is. For example a pH of 7 is neutral while 14 is very basic and 1 is very acidic. We also tested for things like alkalinity and sodium.

To test for sodium we put the water through a pump that sprayed it into a very, very hot fire! If it turned white the sodium was high. If you have high sodium, the water will taste foul.

We also learned that the State Lab tests for AIDS and tuberculosis. They keep the tuberculosis in a "hood" that keeps the bad stuff out of the air. They also test for rabies, so they get dead animals to test. The way that they test for rabies is to smash the animal's heads open to test. They call the room the bat cave because once a bat that people thought was dead started to fly around the room!

In conclusion, the State Lab is an interesting place to visit.

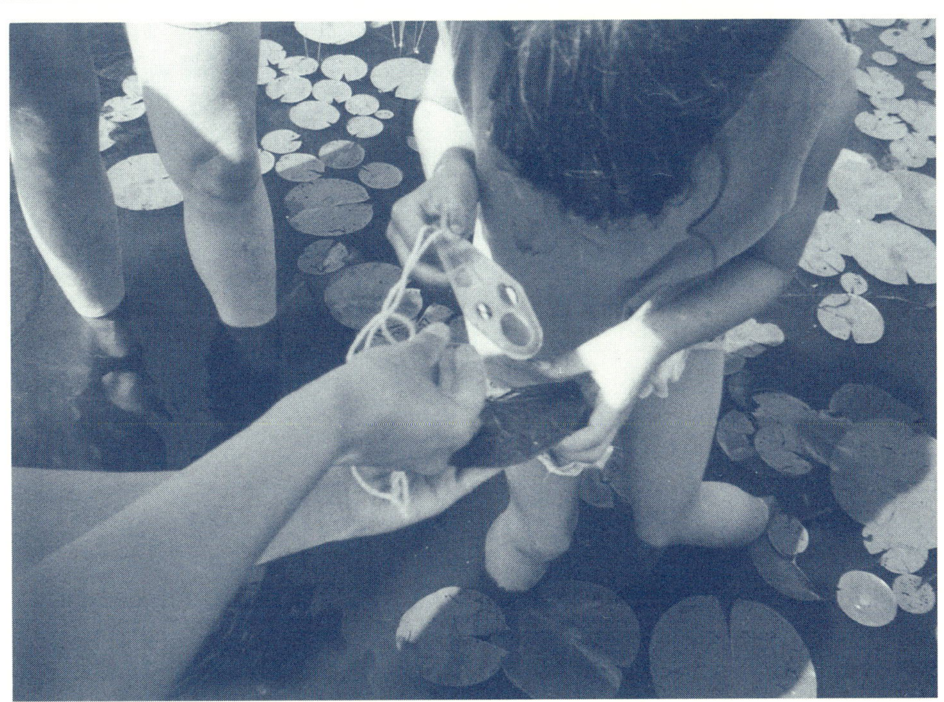

Mentors/Lake Heroes

Perhaps one of the most important things you can do is bring them in touch with people who are working to preserve the lake. Guest speakers who share their knowledge always inspire students to learn more about the lake. Lori Fisher, head of the Lake Champlain Committee, is one of the lake's heroes and students can meet her in "Champ's Chat with Lori Fisher."   Below, she shares her vision for Lake Champlain.

"Not a day goes by that I am not moved by Lake Champlain's beauty and power and fragility. We are less than half a decade shy of a new millennium. Many of the people in this room will live out half their lives in the new century. In our actions today, we need to ensure that the Lake Champlain of 2000 and beyond is a lake with edible fish, and drinkable, swimmable waters. That people will have access to the lake without having to own shoreland property. That when residents and visitors look to the shoreland from the lake the view will still be dominated by swaths of sand, rocky precipices, floodplain forests, fertile pastures, and stands of cattails and wild rice. That the children of tomorrow will still have the opportunity to see and be moved by the lake's unique and wild places—to see the snow geese lifting from Dead Creek in the fall and great blue heron fledglings learning to fly at the rookery on Shad Island. That they will be able to stroll along the waterfronts in Plattsburgh, Port Henry and Burlington and find that the built landscape embraces and reinforces Lake Champlain's culture, history and economic and environmental vitality."

Lori Fisher, closing statement
to Lake Champlain Committee,
Annual Meeting, 1996

Champ's Chat with Lori Fisher

Champ: Hi Lori! I've heard that you are a great resource. Mind if I ask you a few questions?

Lori Fisher: It's my pleasure to be interviewed by a lake creature.

Champ: You know, I'm concerned about the lake. I've lived there my whole (very long) life. How do you think our lake is doing?

Lori Fisher: Well, Lake Champlain is aging faster than it should. All lakes go through a natural aging process called eutrophication. Over hundreds of thousands of years, lakes slowly change from cold and clear water to green, swampy, and warm water and eventually fill in with marshland and become solid land.

Champ: Yikes! What will happen to me?

Lori Fisher: Well, you won't have to worry about that for a very long time, but there is a problem. Because of the things that humans do, the lake is aging faster than it should. Runoff from farms and parking lots, sewage treatment discharges, and erosion made worse by development all add more nutrients to the lake than it needs. That's why we see more algal blooms. It makes the water less healthy for aquatic creatures like you! Lake Champlain is a beautiful lake but it's not as healthy as it should be and it will be in serious trouble if we don't take care of it.

Champ: Is that what the Lake Champlain Committee is doing, trying to take care of the lake?

Lori Fisher: That's exactly what we're doing. We began in 1963 and have worked for over three decades for a clean Lake Champlain. We prevented a nuclear power plant from being built near Charlotte, Vermont, led the lake-wide effort to ban phosphate detergents, and helped pass a law that prevents boats from dumping sewage into the lake. We've been involved in numerous educational efforts that help make people aware of how their actions affect the lake.

Champ: That's great! I remember talk about a nuclear power plant. That really scared me. How did you become involved in the Lake Champlain Committee? What is your job?

Lori Fisher: I started working at the Lake Champlain Committee when I was a college student at the University of Vermont. I fell in love with the lake. I used to study on its shore and swim in it often. I wanted to do something to help it. My job as executive director means that I'm responsible for managing the day-to-day operations and carrying out the policies set by the board of directors. I'm involved with drafting legislation and water-quality policy to help clean up the lake, and arranging educational programs. I want people to understand how the lake functions.

Champ: That's a very important job. Are young people involved in the things that the Lake Champlain Committee does?

Lori Fisher: They can be; we welcome help from everyone. Young people can volunteer time at the office. In the field, we've had students stencil storm drains to prevent people from dumping waste oil into them, kids have put in plants along stream banks to lessen erosion, and they have helped clean litter and debris off the beaches. There's so much work to be done! Kids taught their parents to recycle; I think they can get their parents involved in the clean-up of Lake Champlain.

Champ: What are some important things young people should know?

Lori Fisher: They need to know that what they do in their lives will affect the lake. We use the lake every day; most of the people who live in the Lake Champlain Basin get their drinking water from the lake. When we flush the toilet, our wastes go through a septic system or a wastewater treatment facility before being discharged back into the lake; when we drive a car some of the pollutants that come out of the tailpipe end up in the lake. Young people, and adults, need to know how their actions affect our lake.

Champ: Next time a young person asks, "How can I help?" what should I tell them?

Lori Fisher: You can tell them that they can help clean up the lake by limiting their own family's impact on water quality. A few quick tips include: buy or make nontoxic household cleaning alternatives, avoid spreading pesticides on your lawn and garden, dispose of pet waste in a landfill or toilet, and walk, bike or take the bus when traveling short distances. Don't waste water. Although Lake Champlain contains about 6.8 trillion gallons of water, the more we use, the more we need to pump and treat with chemicals.

If they want to do more, they can volunteer for the Lake Champlain Committee or a local action group or write a letter to a government official stating concern about the lake's health. They can do research in their town to find out about local water issues and what political decisions affect the health of the lake. The more kids learn, the easier it becomes to participate in important decisions. If everyone does a few things to improve water quality, we'll be able to clean up the lake!

Champ: Thanks, Lori! Keep up the good work! The lake is lucky to have people like you who really care.

Assessment

The General Butler

by Jason Pariseau, Grade 5, School Street School, Milton, Vermont

The *General Butler* was a canal boat on its way to Burlington carrying tons of granite. It went out in a storm which is now called the storm of the century. Captain William Montgomery was the owner of the boat. There were two teenage girls on the boat, one which was his daughter. There was also an injured sailor aboard. His eye was injured. The boat was hitting waves ten feet tall. All the passengers had to jump off the boat onto the breakwater. A man in a row boat went and brought them to shore. The *General Butler* sank on December 9, 1876.

Introduction

L earning is a human activity. I would like to discuss assessment in this context. There is a tremendous amount of valuable information available to educators on assessment but the discussion often fails to put education in its human context. At the risk of sounding too simplistic, I believe educators are people who choose to communicate with children and be part of children's emotional, social and intellectual development. Who we are as individuals greatly affects the choices we make and these choices drive the structure and content of this human experience. Equally, the personalities, learning styles and emotional and social needs of the students we teach affect this experience.

Mary Dupont contemplates a writing piece with a fifth-grade author.

People communicate in different ways. When you are telling a friend a story and she says, "What do you mean?" you may decide to give an example or draw a picture. As teachers, we constantly use and adjust our communication skills to tell stories and present information. As we teach, as we tell the story, we assess whether students are "getting it"—are excited and engaged— and make adjustments on the spot and over time about how the story should be told.

Think how many times you have been explaining something to a room full of blank faces and run to the board, grabbed a globe, asked students to get out of their seats and make a motion. All of these choices we make are part of assessment. Think how many times you have been driving home realizing you need to adjust a lesson, bring in some graphics, talk with group A. All of these decisions that you make are part of assessment.

Teachers are responsible for planning approximately 20 hours of learning time for students each week. The choices we make every day, the material we choose, how we structure the time, the way in which we design learning activities are driven by assessment. All this has to do with who we are as teachers, what it is we want to teach and how well we keep in touch with the people

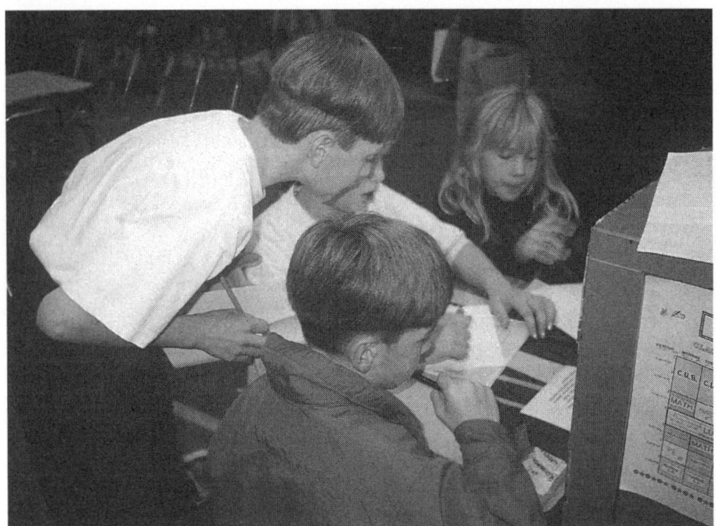

we are teaching. When you piece together a large interdisciplinary unit, all these factors will drive the choices you make and become part of your ongoing assessment.

Assessment involves a multitude of assessment techniques, both formal and informal. There are many models currently under discussion in education and this chapter will not try to present them nor will it pretend to provide any final answers. Whatever hook you are hanging your hat on, whether it is Howard Gardner's theory of multiple intelligences, or Vermont's Common Core, it is you the teacher who has to decide what it is that you want to accomplish and how you will know whether you have met your goals. Thus your personal teaching philosophy is central to assessment. How you play it out in your classroom also depends on what model of change your district is following and how much that impacts you and your classroom.

In environmental education—or in the study of anything that is as REAL as Lake Champlain is—the task of teaching and learning is more complex. The story is more complex, so the task of ascertaining whether the story is understood is more complex. A great deal of the learning task is the sharing, comprehending and mastery of material—facts, dates, statistics, dimensions of change. Some of this material is relatively straightforward to measure. But an added dimension of mastery involves decision making and an involvement of one's self and the material. Communities are currently disagreeing over whether content or values should be taught. It's not an issue of either/or—it's both. When we teach about something as important as the Lake Champlain Basin, real learning takes place and this involves the student as a whole person—not just as a recipient of information. *Learning is a human activity.*

In order to effectively assess what students are learning, I believe the following things are necessary:
• clear educational goals and philosophy
• an ability and willingness to respond to your students
• a commitment to ongoing assessment
• clear, measurable unit objectives

CLEAR EDUCATIONAL GOALS *and* PHILOSOPHY

Mary Dupont, my teammate at School Street School, while writing her master's thesis, "The Development of a Curriculum Designed to Enhance Television Literacy and Critical Thinking Skills in Middle Level Students," stated one of her philosophical goals:

> *"Knowledge should not be delivered by the teacher but discovered by the student, together with the teacher and peers. Students should be allowed to construct meaning through hands-on experience, research, exploration, collaboration with peers, dialogue, reflection and discussion."*

A clearly stated philosophy such as this serves as a guidepost to designing learning activities. When Mary and I plan together we know this is one of our goals and we can more easily plan learning time to correspond to it. When this philosophy is clearly articulated to students and their families and apparent in the workings of the classroom, then the learners know what they are about. Clear goals facilitate the learning process because teachers and students can work together on a commonly understood purpose. It is much easier to examine whether goals have been accomplished when everyone knows what they are.

AN ABILITY *and* WILLINGNESS *to* RESPOND *to your* STUDENTS

In order to stay in touch with your students, the people to whom you are telling the story, you must be willing to change. You will have to adjust lessons to the many learning styles of your students. This involves continually reassessing your program and your teaching.

Is there a way for you to communicate with your students so you are able to know how they are doing? When you talk to a friend, you might say, do you know what I mean? In education we rarely take time to really listen to our students. When we do listen, we must be willing to pay attention and make the necessary changes.

A COMMITMENT *to* ONGOING ASSESSMENT

Assessment is ongoing and begins with planning. Planning the variety of learning experiences and allowing time for learning to happen are integral to the assessment process.

"These days, I learn in my classroom. What happens there has changed; it continually changes...and the curriculum unfolds now as my kids and I learn together. My aim stays constant—I want us to go deep inside language, using it to know and shape and play with our worlds—but my practices evolve as eighth graders and I go deeper. This going deeper is research, and these days my research shows me the wonders of my kids, not my methods."

Nancy Atwell
IN THE MIDDLE: WRITING,
READING AND LEARNING
WITH ADOLESCENTS

If one of your goals is to provide fun and exciting learning opportunities, the first step is to plan those activities. If one of your goals is for students to discuss with each other and share opinions about the material that they are learning, then it is important, and often challenging, to plan that time into your school day. We often get to an end of a unit and wonder why the students didn't grasp part of what we thought we were doing. Then we realize that we didn't provide ample time for them to process that particular aspect of the study. We may have an amorphous goal that we hope "happens as we go along" but realize too late that we have to carve out time for our priorities. This is especially true as expectations for what teachers should accomplish in the school day increase.

Have you planned in time when you will assess your progress? Do you have time to talk to students about what they are learning? To me, this is one of the more challenging aspects of our job. Planning for dialogue and interaction is critical.

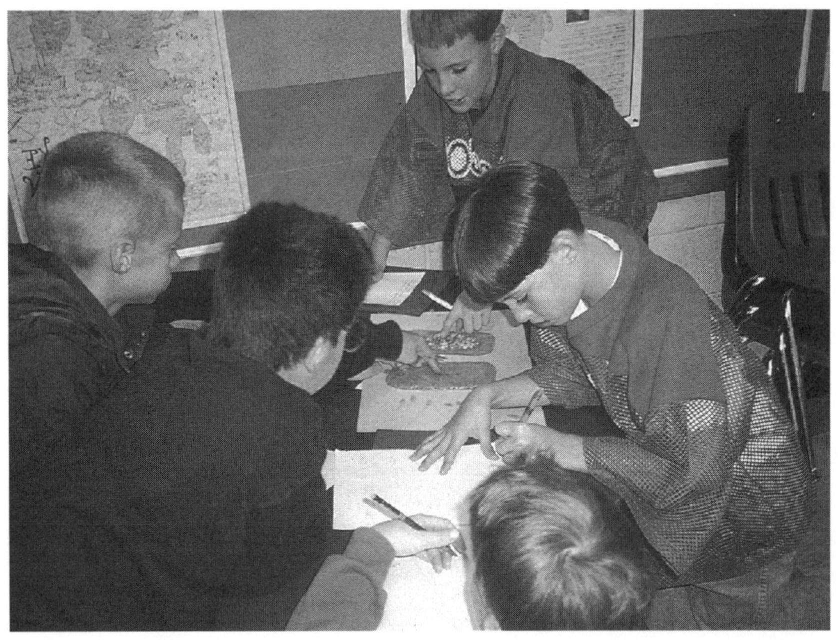

CLEAR, MEASURABLE UNIT OBJECTIVES

Mastery Learning, an educational philosophy that has come and gone, left me with one important lesson that has stayed. It's so obvious yet somehow ignored: always tell your students what you intend to teach them and why. Never hold them accountable for information you haven't collectively declared. Oftentimes in interdisciplinary studies, new material is generated as you proceed. This need not "break the rules." Many times on a field trip or with a guest speaker, we generate new material. This is good—and it's okay to learn together. Be sure to acknowledge this material together and include it in your classroom bank of information.

METHODS OF ASSESSMENT

An interdisciplinary study based on such a rich resource as Lake Champlain offers a multitude of ways for you to assess what your students are learning.

During the course of an eight-week unit, I might use any or all of the following:

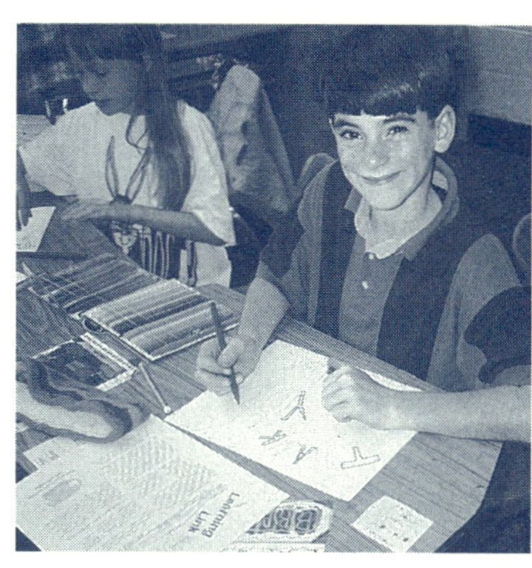

- a test
- a short quiz
- factual writing
- a thinkbook response to a speaker, field trip, reading or activity
- class discussion
- homework
- essays
- creative writing
- oral presentations
- artwork
- theater
- a project for history day or science fair
- simulation
- portfolio

FORMAL ASSESSMENT

Formal assessment includes tests, quizzes and other activities that ascertain student mastery of specific material. Formal assessment allows the teacher to stop at a designated point and ask the students whether they have retained certain information and met specific unit objectives.

Identifying what this information will be is an extremely important part of formal evaluation. It is especially important with a self-designed unit of study when you can't say: "The test on Friday will be on chapters two and three." I usually have a class discussion on what students can expect on a quiz or cumulative test. Often students will surprise you by claiming responsibility for information you hadn't planned on, such as material gathered during a field trip or student presentation. The information that the class agrees on should be posted in the classroom or handed out to each student in writing. This is best done at the beginning of the unit, although important things come up during the interdisciplinary study that may be necessary to include.

Another way to guarantee a clear understanding of what learning is to be assessed is to design a study sheet with questions. Cooperative groups can then work together and use student folders and classroom resources to check and record the answers. We can then review as a class and confirm all the things that will be on the test. There shouldn't be any surprises! The process of students' claiming the material they have learned is a critical element of their success at mastery.

In the book, ASSESSING STUDENT OUTCOMES, the authors illustrate a variety of questions that can be used on a cumulative test. I borrowed the categories and wrote Lake Champlain questions, which are listed on the facing page.

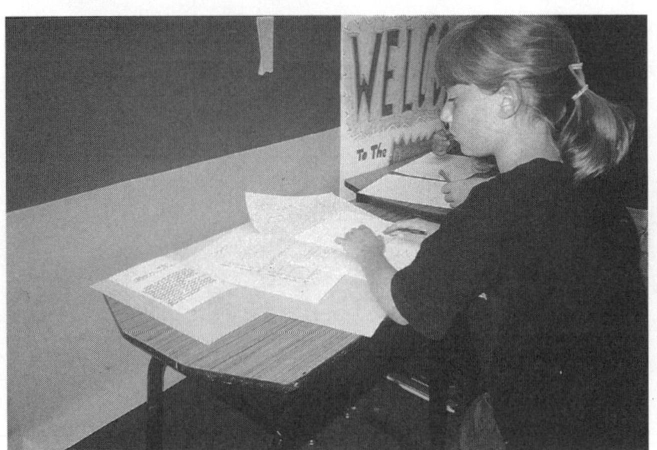

Matching Questions: Choose the best answer and write the correct letter in the left-hand column.

_____	**1.** Lake Bitawbagok	A. first inhabitants of western shore
_____	**2.** Iroquois	B. escaped from British at Valcour Island
_____	**3.** Benedict Arnold	C. Lake Champlain in 1500
_____	**4.** Otter Creek	D. southern tributary
_____	**5.** Plattsburgh Bay	E. famous naval battle, War of 1812

True or False: Circle T or F.

1. T   F   Golf courses can be a source of pollution in Lake Champlain.

2. T   F   The Champlain Canal was completed in 1860.

3. T   F   Plankton are microscopic plant and animal life.

4. T   F   Zebra mussels were first found in Lake Champlain in 1988.

Completion Questions

1. The Lake Champlain Basin is ____________ square miles.

2. The ____________________ is a tributary that flows through Milton.

3. There are ________ species of fish in Lake Champlain.

4. The __________, Benedict Arnold's gunboat, is on display at the Smithsonian in Washington, D.C.

Multiple Choice Questions

1. _____ The ________________ River drains Lake Champlain into Canada.

     a. Connecticut   **b.** Lamoille   **c.** Richelieu

2. _____ Many of the boats built during the American Revolution were built at ______________.

     a. Burlington   **b.** Skeenesborough   **c.** Shelburne

3. _____ A tributary of Lake Champlain that runs through Milton is the __________________.

     a. Missisquoi   **b.** Winooski   **c.** Lamoille

Short Essay Question

Explain to Samuel de Champlain at least three changes that have taken place on the lake since he traveled on it. Be specific and give good examples. Describe the changes so that your answer shows how much of Lake Champlain's history you have learned.

Open-ended Question

In the space below, list as many things as you can think of that you could do to protect the water quality of Lake Champlain.

Name that Fact! Write in correct information. There may be more than one right answer!

1. One famous battle fought on Lake Champlain: ________________________

2. One tributary in New York: ____________________

3. Three fish that live in Lake Champlain: ____________ ________________ ______________

4. Two problems that face Lake Champlain: __________________ ____________________

INFORMAL ASSESSMENT

Informal assessment, which happens more frequently, is your way of keeping in touch with students. This is integral to your success as a teacher. Knowing how your students are processing the information is the only way you are going to know whether you have accomplished some of your most important learning goals. The following categories of informal assessment are taken from an excellent book titled: ENVIRONMENTAL EDUCATION IN THE SCHOOLS: CREATING A PROGRAM THAT WORKS by Judy A. Braus and David Wood. I borrowed the categories and wrote about how I use these learning activities in the study of Lake Champlain. The different kinds of informal assessment identified by Braus and Wood are:

- listening and recording,
- homework,
- journals and notebooks,
- research and reports,
- discussions and debates,
- peer and self-evaluation,
- portfolios.

The book, ENVIRONMENTAL EDUCATION IN THE SCHOOLS: CREATING A PROGRAM THAT WORKS, was written for use by the Peace Corps in Africa and is a wonderful resource. Judy Braus is the person who created the NatureScope science series when she worked at the National Wildlife Federation. Braus now works for the World Wildlife Fund.

LISTENING *and* RECORDING

Listen for, observe and record the following things happening in your classroom:

- **questioning**

"How does the water go underground and then end up in the lake?"

- **planning**

"Meghan and I were talking about the Open House and we really want to make a display on wetlands and make some really neat creatures out of cardboard. Could we look at that book you showed us yesterday with the pretty photographs?"

- **sharing**

"Do you think it would be all right if I brought in some pictures of my grandfather's camp on St. Albans Bay? He even said he'd come to class if you want....He's lived there since 1932."

- **speculating**

"What if the zebra mussels hurt all the other fish and water creatures in the lake and it wasn't the same?"

Note: *These are approximations of students' comments that I've heard during the study of Lake Champlain.*

- **communicating**

"I went home and told my sister about the wrecks in Lake Champlain and she told me that Sheri's mother was a diver and she had found a pot that was thousands of years old and it is now on display at the Maritime Museum."

- **expression**

"I really liked what we did in class yesterday when we built a watershed. Wasn't it cool when the water turned colors?"

- **listening**

It's silent, but you can see it when they are listening to each other!

- **behavior**

"Weren't we great on our field trip yesterday! We are awesome!"

- **participation**

"Everybody worked hard in the cooperative groups today, even ___ who hardly ever listens!"

Aside from the many ways that you can watch to see if your students are learning, you can also measure this systematically if you have a particular objective. Below is a chart that Braus and Wood suggest:

	participates in discussion	gives creative responses	works well with others
CARLA			
TOM			
JOEY			
SARAH			

There are a multitude of other ways that we keep in touch with our students and assess how they are doing. These are the many learning activities that we plan into our program to meet our goals.

HOMEWORK

Homework is an important indicator of your students' involvement in the work and the success of the program. It is important to assign it consistently and check it thoroughly. It can help you understand what they are learning and what they are interested in.

I am sure that there is a mathematical correlation between the effort students spend on homework and the time the teacher takes to review it. Whenever I feel homework slacken, I look at myself first. Time in class to share and acknowledge what was done is important. Too often we move onto the next task or topic.

I include homework success as part of the grade. Ten percent of their grade in every subject reflects homework completion. This is particularly important in the middle grades when students are adjusting to the amount of homework that they are given.

JOURNALS *and* NOTEBOOKS

For me, the thinkbook (see *Getting Wet*, p. 5) is an important tool for keeping in touch with how students are processing the material. One of the ways I can tell when we are really "cooking" is when we have 100% completion of thinkbook entries. I make a big deal of this when it happens.

Since I cannot collect and grade 24 thinkbooks every day (maybe in my next life!), I take a few minutes of class time each day to check for completion. I ask students to open their books to last night's homework, then proceed around the class (no time for conversations, it's done or it isn't—if someone has a good reason, he or she knows to talk to me before the day begins) and make a star or a frowny face on the page. I collect and read them once a week to make comments and assess the content of their writing. This is a wonderful time for me to have those "conversations" that there is never time for! Their homework completion grade is averaged in with the final thinkbook grade.

RESEARCH *and* REPORTS

Doing research and reports is an important way for students to learn research skills. Learning to analyze information, document facts, distinguish facts from opinions and organize information are important critical thinking skills for middle grade students.

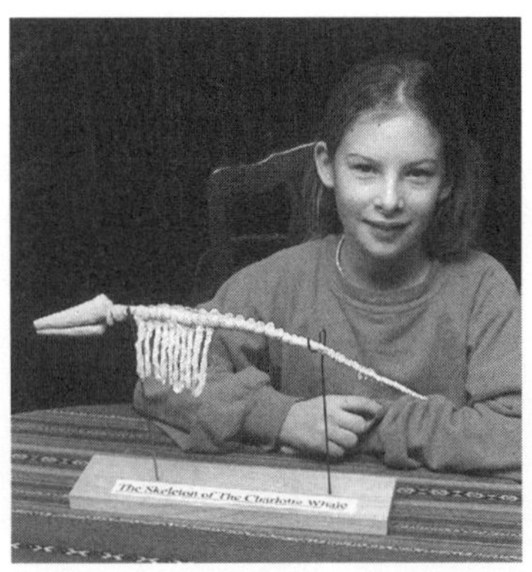

Projects that are linked to research and inquiry are valuable ways for students to express their learning. Tai Dinnan, author of "Our State Fossil," displays her model of the Charlotte Whale.

I have emphasized what I believe are key ingredients for successful research projects in the *Research and Inquiry* chapter, in a section called "Keeping in Touch." (See *Research and Inquiry*, p. 312.)

DISCUSSIONS *and* DEBATES

An essential element of the development of stewardship is not only learning information about the lake but developing opinions and learning to express them. Students need opportunities to practice formal and informal expression. Role plays, skits, debates, class discussions, and problem solving in small groups can give students chances to think about and form opinions on the complex issues surrounding the lake.

PEER *and* SELF-EVALUATION

Students should have the opportunity to talk about their work and get support and feedback from their peers. It is important to deliberately create time for this. Sometimes it is as simple as: "*Turn to the student next to you and tell him or her five things you just learned from our discussion.*" It can be done more systematically at the end of an important learning activity. It is a main ingredient in cooperative groups and can also be used formally in evaluating writing.

On the next page is a sample of a formal peer evaluation used for a student's write-up of an interview.

PORTFOLIO

As with all units of study, I find it valuable to have students organize their final work into a finished folder. The process involves organizing and reviewing the work, making choices about what to include and evaluating one's own learning. My students make a small book with a table of contents and a decorated cover. For those of you involved in the Vermont portfolio process, a Lake Champlain study offers a wealth of work to include. Students' written evaluation of the unit and their work should be included in the final portfolio.

"I am very proud and surprised at all the work I have done this year. I never thought that I could improve my writing. I never thought that I could write so much. I am very happy with myself."

Colleen Robie, Grade 5, Milton

AUTHOR_____________________________________ EDITOR_____________________________________

Interview Write-up Conference Sheet

Did the author include the following:

Introduction to report
_____ Name of interviewee
_____ Date of interview
_____ Location of interview
_____ Explanation of what the interview was about

Main section of report
_____ Clear presentation of information
_____ One or two quotes, or some way to get an idea of the character of the interviewee.
_____ Good organization of the information

Conclusion to report
_____ Opinion, what they liked best about the interview, or what they found interesting
_____ Other method of wrapping up your topic

G.U.M. (Grammar, Word Usage, Mechanics)
_____ Complete sentences
_____ Capital letters at beginnings of sentences and with proper names
_____ Correct spelling
_____ Correct punctuation marks
_____ Words used correctly
_____ Are you able to read the work without guessing what it says?
_____ Is the report the student's best effort in grammar, usage, mechanics?

Other comments
_____ Did the author give enough information?
_____ Did you learn anything?
_____ What else would you like to tell the author?

ASSESSING WRITING

In addition to the categories identified by Braus and Wood, I am adding my own emphasis on the assessment of writing. This section will briefly outline some aspects of assessing writing that I think are important.

When I assign an extensive piece of writing, I do the following:
• design the writing assignment with the class,
• identify key elements to the writing piece we are undertaking,
• assign scoring points to the different elements of the writing piece,
• establish deadlines for the first and final drafts.

Below is an example of a scoring sheet that I will develop with my class; the same scoring sheet will be used to evaluate the first and the second draft with higher expectations on the second draft.

On the next page is an example of a scoring sheet that is a self-evaluation process, which Carol Livingston uses when students complete the soldier's journal. (See "Writing Journals" in *Language Arts*, p. 237.)

Any rubric that will be used to score a piece of writing should be shared at the beginning of the writing process.

Trip Around Lake Champlain

First Draft   Due: __________
    Historically accurate (*includes historically-accurate details*)   50 pts __________
    G.U.M.: Grammar   10 pts __________
           Usage   10 pts __________
           Mechanics   10 pts __________
    Good story (*makes sense, is about Lake Champlain, fun to read*)   20 pts __________
    100 pts __________

Final Draft   Due: __________
    Historically accurate   50 pts __________
    G.U.M.: Grammar   10 pts __________
           Usage   10 pts __________
           Mechanics   10 pts __________
    Good story   20 pts __________
    100 pts __________

Lake Champlain Soldier's Journal Evaluation Form

Content And Details (50 pts)

You have accurately completed three journal entries that show what life was like for a French soldier stationed at Fort St. Frederic or a British soldier at Fort Crown Point. You have included:

___ dates and locations of entries,

___ setting: fort, land, lake, wildlife,

___ what you see, hear, smell, feel,

___ how and where you travel,

___ what, how, where you eat and cook,

___ where, with whom you live, furnishings,

___ how you spend time: work, leisure, use of tools,

___ what worries, hopes, concerns you have.

______ **pts**

Organization (20 pts)

Your entries each have some form of introduction and conclusion that help the reader follow your purpose listed above. You have connection between paragraphs.

______ **pts**

Voice/Tone (10 pts)

Your entries show your character's "voice." We can "hear" the opinions, feelings and viewpoint of this character.

______ **pts**

Editing (10 pts)

Your entries have been edited for: spelling, punctuation, correct verb tense, capitalization, complete sentences, I-topic paragraphs.

______ **pts**

On Time (10 pts)

All drafts were turned in on time. The final is neatly written in cursive or is typed.

______ **pts**

______ **TOTAL POINTS**

Evaluation: I believe my Soldier's Journal merits a grade of ____ because ________________________

____.

Teacher comments: ____

____

The scoring sheets are cover sheets for any drafts that are handed in, and they serve as a basis for writing conferences. It greatly facilitates the writing process.

If you are exploring a particular genre with your students and wish them to include the specific elements of this genre, such as a folktale, assign points to each element. For example, if you are writing folktales, you might include:

- animals,
- a long time ago,
- a lesson or explanation of the way things are,
- on the lake.

A rubric is a particular kind of scoring sheet that is now used more frequently by educators. A rubric clearly defines levels of competence. Below is the rubric used in the Vermont writing process. It can be used successfully with any piece of writing as it includes the key elements of good writing.

WRITING	RARELY	SOMETIMES	FREQUENTLY	EXTENSIVELY
Purpose	*Purpose and focus not apparent*	*Attempts to establish a purpose; focus is not clear*	*Establishes a clear focus and purpose*	*Establishes and maintains a clear focus and purpose*
G rammar U sage M echanics	*Errors interfere with understanding*	*Numerous errors*	*Some errors*	*Few or no errors*
Voice or Tone	*Numerous errors*	*Attempts personal expression or tone*	*Established personal expression or effective tone*	*Distinctive personal expression or tone enhances writing*
Organization	*Writing difficult to follow*	*Lapses in unity and coherence*	*Few lapses in unity or coherence*	*Logical progression of ideas; fluent*
Details	*Few details; random or inappropriate*	*Details lack elaboration, merely listed or unnecessary repetition*	*Details are elaborated or develop ideas or information*	*Details are pertinent, vivid or explicit and provide in-depth information*

ASSESSING ENVIRONMENTAL EDUCATION

In addition to the elements of assessment mentioned already, environmental education invites some particular methods of assessment. Teachers in the basin are designing many new ways to assess student learning that takes into account the many dimensions of environmental education.

The XStream, a seventh-grade interdisciplinary team at Missisquoi Valley Union Middle School, uses a Water Log to document their year-long study of water. This Water Log is an ongoing assessment of student work. A three-ringed binder has sections that include:
• pre-study information—pretests on opinions, values, facts and predictions,
• journal entries—observations, poems, short stories,
• reference and unit materials.

On "Water Friday," which occurs every other week, students are divided into small groups and engage in water-related activities and water testing on the Missisquoi River.   Students enter information in their Water Log as part of the day's activity. Each student is responsible for organization and mainte-nance of his or her Water Log. Once a month, students evaluate the order and contents of the materials in their own Water Log. A brief checklist and narrative evaluation are com-pleted by each student and are placed in the Water Log and read by each teacher. At mid-term exam time, students com-plete a written evaluation of their Water Log and it is at-tached to their report as an ad-dendum item. During a culmi-nating event, "Water Day," stu-dents participate in an oral in-terview as a review of the year.

In 1995, the XStream Team consisted of Gary LaShure, Alan Fletcher, Monica Kelly and Dale Paul.

One of the tools the XStream Team uses is a Pre/Post Test. On the first/last Water Friday of the year, the students are given the Pre/Post Test and results are compared.

Pre/Post Test

Values

1. If a sewage treatment plant was going to be built in your neighborhood, would you fight it or accept it?
      a. fight   **b.** accept

2. If you caught a 10-inch trout, would you eat it or let it go?
      a. eat   **b.** release

3. Water is
      a. an important resource,   **b.** a great danger sometimes,   **c.** an important historical factor.

Predictions

1. At the end of October, the temperature of the Missisquoi River is about _____ ˚C.

2. If you were to walk out to the middle of the river near Marble Mill, how deep would it be?

3. (MORE or LESS) than half of the community is concerned with water quality. (Underline your answer.)

4. Do you think that (MORE or LESS) than half of the community thinks that the Missisquoi River is in good shape? (Underline your answer.)

True or False

1. _______________ Dissolved oxygen is not important.
2. _______________ You can tell the quality of water by the amount of insects in it.
3. _______________ You can tell the quality of the water by its temperature.
4. _______________ The pH is an indicator of the acidity or alkalinity of water.
5. _______________ A liquid with a pH of 7.0 indicates an acid.

Opinion (Answer Yes or No)

1. ______ Is water quality an important issue to you?
2. ______ Is water quality an issue that should concern everyone ?
3. ______ Should people like yourself be active participants in preserving water resources?
4. ______ Should all types of people help preserve our water resources?
5. ______ Is water our most important natural resource?

End Note
from a Lake Lover

In the introduction, "Why Teach Kids About Lake Champlain," I stated that the primary objective of this learning experience is stewardship. How then do we teach stewardship? And a question that is even more difficult to answer—how do we know if we have succeeded? I can't honestly say that I can answer that question! But I do know that stewardship is fostered by a child's knowledge of the lake. In knowing many things about the lake, one learns to appreciate it.

When Robbie wrote in his letter, "*I love the lake. If people loved it as much as I do, the lake wouldn't have all the pollution,*" he suggests that a love of the lake will spur a desire to take care of it. That's stewardship! My goal as an educator is to generate the learning of information and hopefully make it possible for students to build a personal connection to the lake. This connection, I believe, is what will ensure the lake's protection for generations to come.

Most students already know something about Lake Champlain or have a connection to lake-related activities. Most students have been there, or you will hopefully get them there. While students are learning about it they will be able to imagine it and relate to it in ways not possible with many of the things we teach.

In my introduction, I said that teaching about the lake has been fueled by my own passionate love of the lake. It is not a requirement that all my students feel this way, but a lot of excitement, pride and interest is generated by learning about THEIR lake.

Understanding its historical importance, its ecological vulnerability, its role of providing homes for waterfowl, its importance in maintaining the diversity of life forms—this grows from information that they have learned in the classroom. A rich interdisciplinary study of Lake Champlain gives the student a chance to develop respect for the lake and all its complexities.

Part of the task of assessment is to ascertain whether they have mastered information. They will know more than most residents of the basin and be proud of it. The mastery itself generates a lot of excitement.

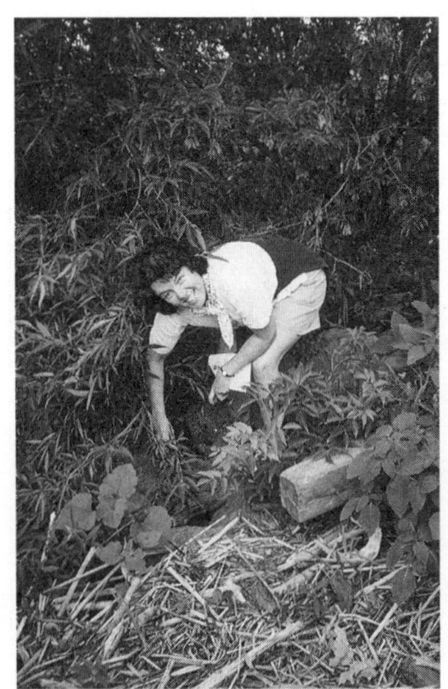

author exploring for fossils at Button Bay State Park

EXCITEMENT is a pretty important thing. It is the glue between the information that students master and what they might do with that material as concerned citizens. (What exactly is being glued together? The information and the SOUL!)

• Shall the town build a 600-slip marina that will destroy wetlands?
• Will they respect the nesting needs of birds that build their homes on the shores of Lake Champlain's islands?
• Will they make the effort to clean boat propellers to ward off further infestation of exotics?
• Will they vote to fund historic preservation efforts as Lake Champlain becomes an historic corridor?
• Will they work to protect a farmer's pasture in Isle La Motte that contains ancient marine fossils?

You have no control whether your students will vote in 15 years or whether they will remember that zebra mussels filter feed. But you do have tremendous control over the learning activities you choose for your students and how much excitement those activities might generate. How do you create a classroom where kids learn a lot and are excited? I think it has a great deal to do with the extent to which you offer them the opportunity to make a connection. Hopefully this book has given you some ideas! When students are allowed to make a real connection, that connection stays with them and can influence the kind of citizens they become.

In the late 1980s, Ann Swanson, who ran the Chesapeake Bay Commission, spoke to a group of environmentalists, scientists, citizens and officials who were meeting to create an interstate system to manage the cleanup of Lake Champlain. Swanson decided to skip her opening remarks about the logistics of how things worked for the Chesapeake Bay and said what it was she believed would secure a future for Lake Champlain:

> *"'In the end, people's love of the lake will make it or break it,' she said, saying her Chesapeake Bay Commission relies on these same grassroots stirrings to build the political base for its stewardship of the great estuary between Maryland and Virginia. 'It has to be more than an ecological commitment,' she said. 'It has to be a gut-level commitment. It has to be people who love the lake....'"*

It is, after all, the love of the lake that is central to what this learning experience is all about. Have a wonderful time!

*Quote from **Addison County Independent**, November 9, 1989.*

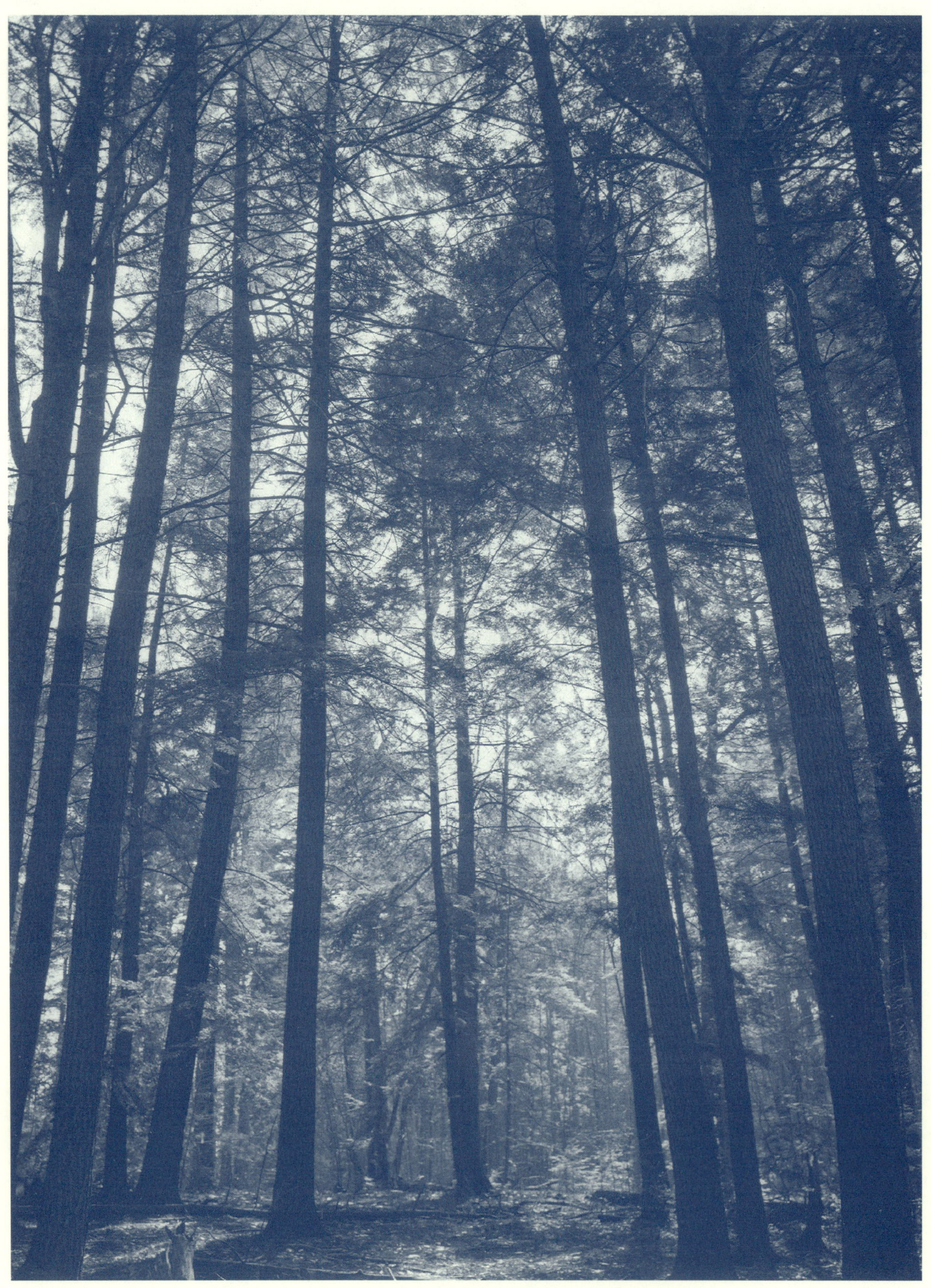

Gluskabi and the Game Animals

as told by Joseph Bruchac

Long ago Gluskabi decided he would do some hunting. He took his bow and arrows and went into the woods.

But all the animals said to each other, "Ah-hah, here comes Gluskabi. He is hunting us. Let us hide from him." So they hid and Gluskabi could not find them. He was not pleased. He went home to the little lodge near the big water where he lived with Grandmother Woodchuck.

"Grandmother," he said. "Make a game bag for me."

So Grandmother Woodchuck took caribou hair and made him a game bag. She wove it together tight and strong and it was a fine game bag. But when she gave it to Gluskabi, he looked at it and then threw it down.

"This is not good enough," he said.

So then Grandmother Woodchuck took deer hair. She wove a larger and finer game bag and gave it to him. But Gluskabi looked at it and threw it down.

"This is not good enough, Grandmother," he said.

Now Grandmother Woodchuck took moose hair and wove him a very fine game bag indeed. It was large and strong and she took porcupine quills, which she flattened with her teeth and she wove a design into the game bag to make it more attractive. But Gluskabi looked at this game bag, too, and then threw it down.

"Grandmother," he said, "this is not good enough."

"Eh, Gluskabi," said Grandmother Woodchuck, "how can I please you? What kind of game bag do you want?"

Then Gluskabi smiled. "Ah, Grandmother," he said, "make one out of woodchuck hair."

So Grandmother Woodchuck pulled all of the hair from her belly. To this day you will see that all woodchucks still have no hair there. Then she wove it into a game bag. Now this game bag was magical. No matter how much you put into it, there would be room for more. And Gluskabi took this game bag and smiled.

"Oleohneh, Grandmother," he said. "I thank you."

Now Gluskabi went back into the woods and walked until he came to a large clearing. Then he called out as loudly as he could, "All you animals, listen to me. A terrible thing is going to happen. The sun is going to go out. The world is going to end and everything is going to be destroyed."

When the animals heard that, they became frightened. They came to the clearing where Gluskabi stood with his magic game bag.

"Gluskabi," they said, "What can we do? The world is going to be destroyed. How can we survive?"

Gluskabi smiled. "My friends," he said, "just climb into my game bag. Then you will be safe in there when the world is destroyed."

So all of the animals went into the game bag. The rabbits and the squirrels went in and the game bag stretched to hold them. The raccoons and the foxes went in and the game bag stretched larger still. The deer went in and the caribou went in. The bears went in and the moose went in and the game bag stretched to hold them all. Soon all of the animals in the world were in Gluskabi's game bag. Then Gluskabi tied the top of the game bag, laughed, slung it over his shoulder and went home.

"Grandmother," he said. "Now we no longer have to go out and walk around looking for food. Whenever we want anything to eat we can just reach into my game bag."

Grandmother Woodchuck opened Gluskabi's game bag and looked inside. There were all the animals in the world.

"Oh Gluskabi," she said, "why must you always do things this way? You cannot keep all the game animals in a bag. They will sicken and die. There will be none left for our children and our children's children. It is also right that it should be difficult to hunt them. Then you will grow stronger trying to find them. And the animals will also grow stronger and wiser trying to avoid being caught. Then things will be in the right balance."

"Kaamoji, Grandmother," said Gluskabi. "That is so." So he picked up his game bag and went back to the clearing. He opened it up.

"All you animals," he called, "you can come out now. Everything is all right. The world was destroyed, but I put it back together again."

Then all of the animals came out of the magic game bag. They went back into the woods and they are still there today because Gluskabi heard what his Grandmother Woodchuck had to say.

And so the story goes.

The Living Treasures
of the
Lake Champlain Basin

The Great Journey

by Colin Brady, Grade 5, School Street School, Milton, Vermont

One day in 1993, a fish named Colin had a huge fight with his parents and decided to run away. "I'm going to run away," yelled Colin to his parents.

So Colin gathered up his supplies like: scales, extra fins and food. He went to his best friend's house to see Brian, a small little perch.

"Will you come on a journey with me?" asked Colin.

"Sure," answered Brian.

They left the next morning. They traveled about a mile north and then met their first kind of trouble of being alone, a mean gang of northern pikes. That doesn't really sound like such a big problem but when their leader's name is Butch and another guy's name is Spike, you would be pretty scared.

Brian screamed, "We're in their territory, we're dead now!"

"How do you know?" yelled Colin.

"Because that sign back there said Northern Pike Territory!"

But you couldn't count these guys down yet. Colin wasn't fish of the year for nothing. He had a plan. The plan was to swim for their lives! So they started swimming as fast as they could.

"Swim faster, you slowpoke!" yelled Brian.

"I'm trying," yelled Colin.

They swam a few more feet and then Brian said "YES! We're out of their territory!"

"How do you know?" asked Colin.

"Because there was a sign back there that said you're out of their territory," answered Brian.

That night, after their adventure, they spent the night in the sunken ship, the *Phoenix*. In the middle of the night, a skull fell on Brian's fin. He woke up instantly and screamed, "AAAAA!"

Colin woke up after Brian's scream and asked what was the matter.

"There's a skull!" yelled Brian.

"Oh" said Colin and went back to sleep.

Two seconds later Colin screamed, "A skull!" and they swam off and spent the night in an old beer can.

The next day, they were swimming along when they met some northern pikes. Instantly they swam away. By then they were in the Champlain Canal. They had been resting a little when Brian noticed a little minnow floating around. He went up and grabbed it.

The fisherman yanked up and caught Brian. But the fisherman said, "aw, too small," and he threw Brian back in.

Those two got out of there pretty fast. They swam into the St. Lawrence Seaway and then swam for days and days into the Atlantic Ocean. They found partners and mated. They each have eight kids and are about to go on their great journey back to Lake Champlain.

EPILOGUE: This will probably go on and on forever. With that I will leave you. Have a safe trip back, young fish.

Introduction

The *Living Treasures of the Lake Champlain Basin* was not in the original plans for THIS LAKE ALIVE! It became a need as we worked on the ecology chapter. We felt that what we wanted to say about the natural world needed its own space, although much of the contents in *Living Treasures* are intertwined with key concepts of the ecology chapter and the chapters should be regarded as "cousins."

I began with a short essay by William Countrymen and Judy Elson and I wrote what you see here. It soon took on a life of its own as it became important to include all living things, as well as how humans have interacted with the natural world. Even so, it falls short of exploring all aspects of the basin as an ecosystem, as it does not fully deal with interactions among nonliving things, such as soils and climate. The *Geology, Ecology* and *Geography* chapters can be used to expand the meaning of this chapter.

Mostly, we wanted this chapter as part of this book because of the profound lessons the natural world can teach us about living on earth. Children are already linked to this world; our only job as teachers is to make sure that this link stays intact as they go through school.

Many people contributed to this chapter. Don Jarrett, Laura Eaton, Mark Scott and Nick Staats reviewed this chapter; Steve Faccio and Madeleine Little read parts. Deb Parrella wrote the section on plants. Mary Watzin, Lou Borie and Mark Labar contributed short pieces.

Judy Elson and I had many conversations about whether the piece on exotics belonged in *Living Treasures* or *Ecology* . We didn't disagree; we just couldn't decide. So we decided to let it sit in this chapter, but place it separately so you can use it however you choose! It's an important part of both chapters. Exotics, by telling their own tale, tell the larger tale as well. Also, like any topic that deals with the management of natural resources, it has a lot of timely information. For example, at the moment, everyone is alarmed about zebra mussels and there is, at present, no plan to protect the shipwrecks in Lake Champlain from these invaders. What zebra mussels will do to the native mussel population is a huge concern.

William Countrymen's article, "Plant, Fish and Wildlife Communities in the Champlain Basin," appears in a publication of the Lake Champlain Committee: ESSAYS ON LAKE CHAMPLAIN.

The monitoring and management of nuisance species is constantly being revised. This is important to share with students, but it also means that this piece will be outdated sooner than others. If I had written it without information about management plans, it would not be very useful. New information is readily available from Departments of Fish and Wildlife in your area. I hope you agree that it was still helpful to write the piece this way.

The Living Treasures of the Lake Champlain Basin

The Lake Champlain Basin is an ecosystem. An ecosystem is a combination of interactions over time among living and nonliving things. Ecosystem is really a term that represents an idea more than a place or set of things. An ecosystem includes living organisms, nonliving components, and a source of energy. Defining the Lake Champlain Basin as an ecosystem helps us to understand the relationships between all the living things in the basin and how they affect each other.

The basin is home to a variety of creatures, all of whom reside in a web of interdependence. This essay will explore some of the ways that the natural world of the basin operates. It will also look at some of the ways that humans have had an impact on the fragile balance among creatures and relate the story of some of the interesting inhabitants of this region as we slip into the twenty-first century. If you ever feel lonely, you won't after you find out how many winged, furred, leafed and scaled creatures share this world with you.

THE BASIN *is* HOME *to* MANY LIVING THINGS

There are six major groups of living things that live in the basin: fish, invertebrates, amphibians and reptiles, birds, mammals and plants. We cannot look at all the creatures, but by telling the story of a few, we will learn the story of many. Nor can we review all of the relationships that function in this amazing ecosystem—that would take a whole book, maybe one that you will write.

WHAT LIVES *in the* LAKE CHAMPLAIN BASIN ECOSYSTEM ?

Just to give you an idea, check out these figures:

- fish - 81 species identified
- birds - 318 species breed or live
- mammals - 56 species
- reptiles - 20 species identified
- amphibians - 21 species identified
- countless invertebrates
- vascular plants - over 1,900 identified

All of these living things interact in numerous complex relationships. The major relationship between living things is the process of transferring energy from one species to another via a simple food chain or a more complex food web. These species depend on one another because many of them eat one another. Plants are considered the producers. Animals and plants that eat other plants or animals are called consumers. The graphics below display a simple food chain, a food pyramid and a more complex food web. At each feeding stage or trophic level, energy is transferred to the consumer. Approximately 2 to 40% of the energy at one level of a food pyramid gets passed on to the consumer at the next level. Therefore, the animal at the top of the food chain has progressively less available energy.

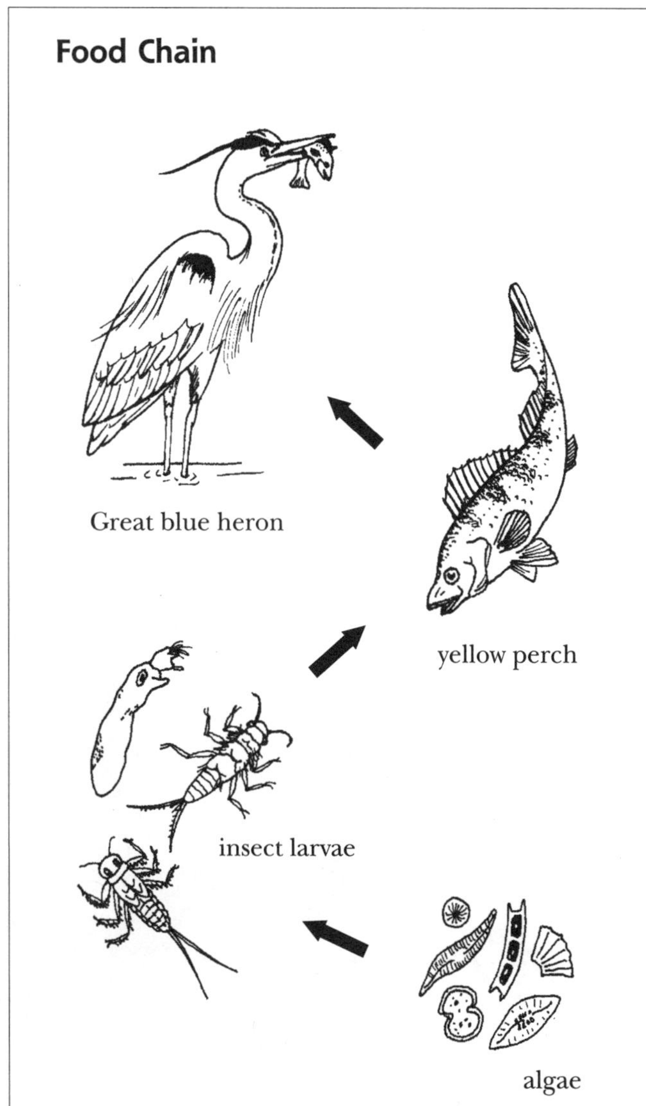

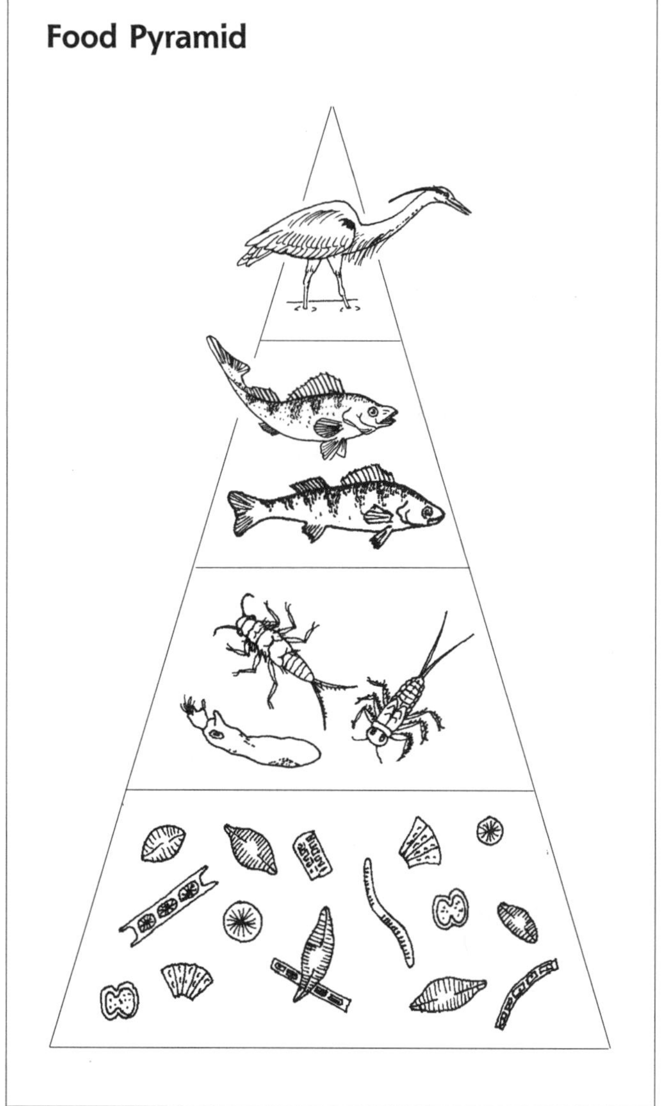

Food Web

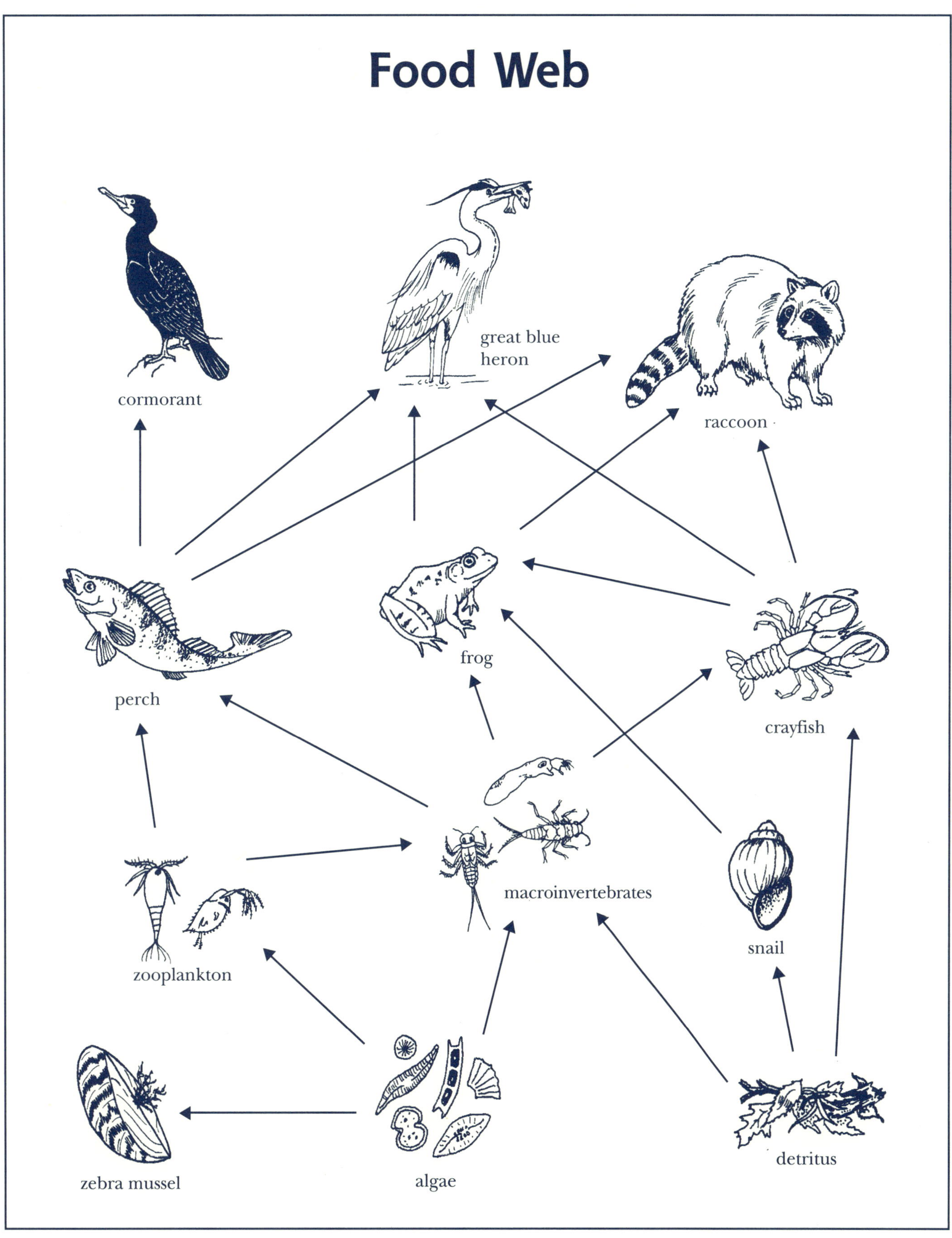

THE BASIN CONTAINS MANY HABITATS

Habitats are places where plants and animals live, where they feed, find shelter and reproduce. Some habitats are relatively small, like a nesting and feeding area of a largemouth bass, which may encompass only one-half of an acre; some are quite large, such as that of an osprey, which may fly miles in search of food. Some habitats vary according to the season, and animals may change their habitats for many reasons, some of them natural, and some not.

Habitats are defined by their different physical features. In the Lake Champlain Basin you will find many distinct habitats: woods, rivers and streams, open meadows, wetlands and lake waters. All land and water is classified according to the type of habitat it provides. Each of these habitats is divided into zones. Let's just look at the different parts of the lake.

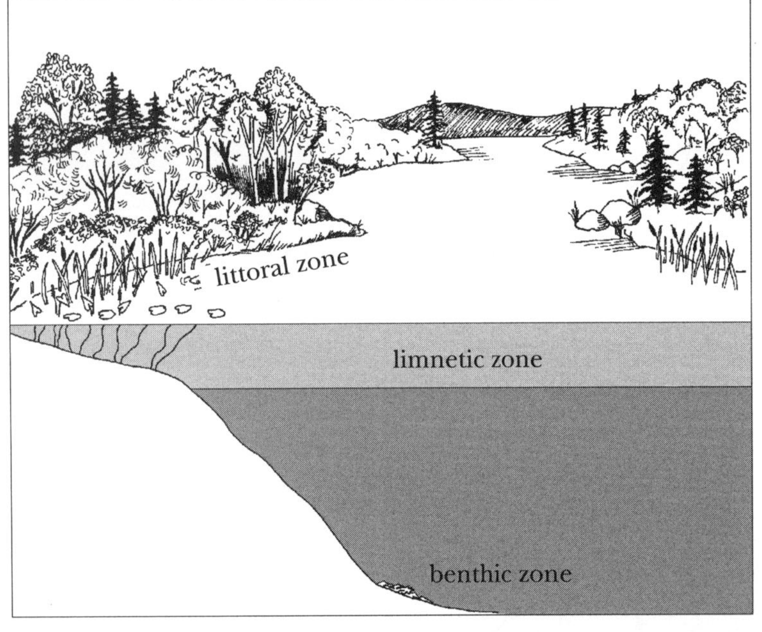

The lake itself, home to many aquatic creatures, contains a variety of habitats. By definition, a lake is a body of water that is deep enough to have layers. The layers that exist in a lake as deep as Lake Champlain are called littoral, limnetic and benthic. These zones have different characteristics that determine what variety of fish and other aquatic creatures live there. Some fish like the layer where the water is cold and deep; others like warm, shallow water. Some creatures can tolerate water with low amounts of oxygen and others cannot.

While aquatic animals such as fish live in the lake, other animals such as otter, muskrat or red-winged blackbird depend directly on the lake but don't live in it. Some other animals live nearby. Wildlife species such as snow geese, great blue herons, double-breasted cormorants, ring-billed gulls and common terns depend on the islands in the lake and wetlands around it for feeding, breeding, wintering and migration habitat. Other animals live on the land surrounding the lake and in the wooded forests in the mountains. They depend on the tributaries in the lake's watershed. Even though a moose's habitat is the forest, for example, it depends on wetlands for many meals. Many creatures travel from one place to another and live in many kinds of habitat.

It is natural for migrating birds to change habitats according to the seasons. But sometimes habitats become unsuitable for some species. If wetlands are filled, or too many trees that grow near water are cut down, birds that prefer a rotting tree overlooking a wetland full of food will nest somewhere else. If land is overdeveloped and soil erodes and turns a gravelly river bottom into a murky and silty river bottom, the fish that usually spawn there will not return. If many habitats are destroyed over time, a population of a species will decline or disappear.

Wetlands are an especially important habitat in the Lake Champlain ecosystem. Wetlands are defined as areas that have a certain amount of moisture and thus provide a unique environment for specific plants and animals. They are spawning and nesting areas, resting places and safe hideaways as well as a nutrient-rich feeding ground for many animals. They benefit the entire basin as they also perform critical cleansing and purifying duties.

Where have all the species gone? Habitat destruction, pollution and hunting are the major reasons why species are disappearing. Humans are the main cause for species becoming **rare, threatened, endangered, extinct and extirpated.** Some species have very specific needs in order to survive. For example, the black sedge is a plant that only grows on certain mountains in Vermont. A species that is "picky" about its food or habitat limits its ability to survive in a changing world.

• A **rare** species has a small population due to natural reasons or human impact. The pale painted cup is designated as rare because it has a specific habitat located in Smuggler's Notch in Vermont.

• **Endangered** animals and plants are in immediate danger of becoming extinct or extirpated if they are not protected. The small whorled pogonia is endangered in the Lake Champlain Basin and also is listed as a federal endangered species.

• **Threatened** species are those with declining populations, and they may become endangered if they are not protected. The spiny softshell turtle is a threatened species that lives in the shallow, sandy areas in Lake Champlain.

• **Extinct** means forever. If all the animals of a certain species die, they are extinct—gone forever. The passenger pigeon is an example of an extinct species. The last passenger pigeon died in a zoo in 1914. You will never be able to see a living passenger pigeon.

• When a species disappears from a specific area, but is not extinct in the world, it is said to have been **extirpated.** An example of a species in the Lake Champlain Basin that has been extirpated is the wolf. Wolves are not extinct throughout the world, but they no longer live in the basin.

ABENAKI *and* IROQUOIS *were* STEWARDS *of this* LAND

The Abenaki and the Iroquois were the first people who lived, fished and hunted in the Champlain Basin. Their survival depended on knowing the land and the rhythms and habits of the plants and animals that lived here. In order to safeguard the supply of food, the people had to protect the bounty of the earth. Through the centuries, people saw themselves as part of a community of living creatures, not the dominant force. The first lake dwellers believed that humans were stewards of the land and waters.

In the late summer, when women gathered plants to use for medicine, they left a family of a plant behind and scattered seeds from the mature flower so that new plants would grow. The food they ate depended on what was available during each season. They would often make seasonal camps so that a whole village could live near a food supply. In the spring, they lived near the rapids of the rivers and caught fish; in the winter, they moved to the mountains where the larger game lived.

There was a plan for what parts of the land were hunted. The native people rotated areas where they hunted, choosing a new quarter each season. This gave the plants and animals a chance to replenish. Hunters also tended to seek out the slower and older members of a herd, leaving the younger animals to mature.

Although people hunted and fished to sustain themselves, they paid respect to the animals that provided life-giving sustenance. For example, when one killed beaver, muskrat or waterfowl, one did not just throw away the bones. To show respect, the bones were returned to the water, with a request that the species be continued. Wasting food was considered an offense to the animals. If the animals felt they were not respected, they would not continue to give themselves to the people.

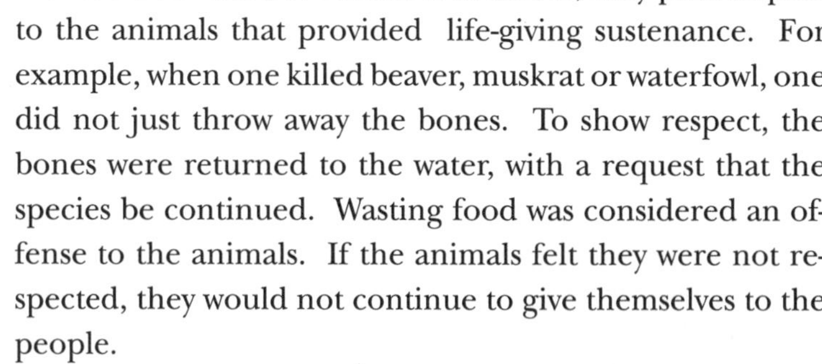

Although agriculture was not central to the survival of native people, it was practiced and followed similar principles of conservation. The soil was fertilized and crops were rotated so that the soil could replenish itself. Crops were used to supplement fishing and hunting and the harvest was stored for the lean months of winter.

THE EUROPEANS COME *to the* CHAMPLAIN BASIN

When the Europeans came to this land in the 1600s, most of them did not recognize the system of stewardship that had been in place for thousands of years. They thought of the land as an uninhabited wilderness, using the Old English "wild deer ness," which meant "lonely empty, undeveloped and un-touched."

Samuel de Champlain was the first European to visit the Lake Champlain Basin. He came in 1609 with a group of Algonquins to make war against the Iroquois. He also recorded the natural resources of the region. The Algonquins brought Champlain a strange-looking fish, the long-nose gar. Champlain wrote:

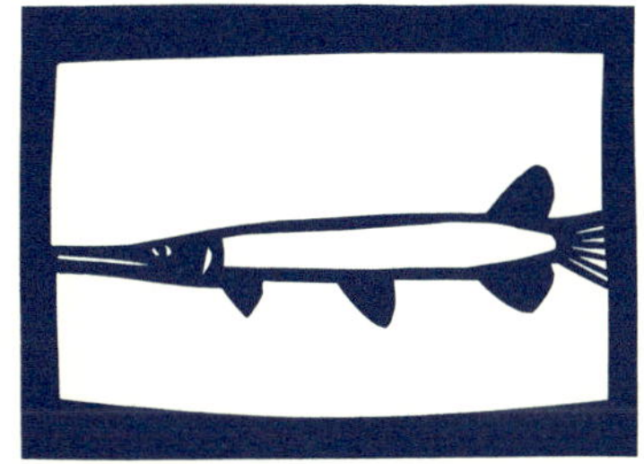

> *"The largest of them, as these tribes have told me, are from eight to ten feet long. I have seen some five feet long which were as big as my thigh, and had a head as large as my two fists, with a snout two feet and a half long, and a double row of very sharp, dangerous teeth....When the birds come and light on its snout, mistaking it for a stump of wood, the fish is so cunning, that shutting its half-open mouth, it pulls them by their feet under the water. The natives gave me the head of one of them, a thing they prize highly, saying that when they have a headache, they bleed themselves with the teeth of this fish at the spot where the pain is and it eases them at once...."*

Another person who wrote early recordings of the area's resources was a Swedish scientist named Peter Kalm, who, in 1749, was sent here to gather seeds and plants. Kalm traveled from one end of the lake to the other. He was especially interested in the laurels: mountain laurel, sheep laurel, and pale laurel. He sent specimens of these species to Linnaeus, who, in honor of Kalm, named that genus of plants after Kalm. The genus is called Kalmia.

Kalm's journal contains many interesting observations of the natural wealth of the region:

> *"Bears are plentiful hereabouts, and they kept a young one about three months old at the fort. He had exactly the same shape and qualities as our common bears in Europe, except the ears, which seemed to be longer in proportion, and the hairs were stiffer; his color was deep brown, almost black. He played and wrestled every day with one of the dogs. A vast number of bear skins are annually exported to France from Canada.*
>
> *The Indians prepare an oil from bear's fat, with which in summer they daub their faces, hands, and all naked parts of their body, to secure them from*

*Linnaeus was a Swedish natural-ist for whom Kalm was working. Linnaeus developed our modern system of binomial nomenclature where each species has a two-part name. The first name identifies the group (or genus) that similar species belong to. The second name is the specific species name. Think of it like your own family: you may all share a common last name but you are given specific first names. Linnaeus grouped all Laurel plants in the genus **Kalmia**, so sheep laurel is known as **Kalmia angustifolia**. **Angustifolia** is the species name.*

EUROPEANS BRING CHANGES *to* LAND *and* WILDLIFE

Europeans induced native people to trap vast quantities of mammals to sell in Europe to make fashionable European clothing. Beaver, bear, marten, fisher, lynx and others were hunted in huge quantities. Caribou, deer, elk and wolverine were also hunted.

In addition to the huge impact Europeans had on the animal population, many other things changed. Native people who had lived in harmony with the creatures of the forest and woods were enticed to hunt year-round and go further from home. Time-honored practices were sacrificed as the fur trade brought more pressure on native society. Who owned the land that provided the fur- bearing animals became important. Relationships between family groups changed when it began to seem as if there wasn't enough to go around.

The very heavy, unregulated, year-round trapping, by both native peoples and whites, was only part of the change that was happening. New lifestyles and a different kind of relationship with nature affected the land in various ways.

The settlers who followed the fur trade were farmers and brought with them their own outlook on land. They practiced an age-old custom of planting the same crop in a field year after year, regardless of the slope, without fertilization. These practices had exhausted the soils in southern New England; farmers came north looking for new soil and kept the same practices. Farmers were self-sufficient and used wood to build everything. Trees were burned to clear thousands of acres for agriculture.

The logging industry and sheep farming also accounted for much of the habitat loss, seriously depleting the land. By the 1850s, 75% of Vermont's land was open. It had been cleared for timber, pastures or crop lands. This destruction of habitat caused a significant decline in the populations of many species.

Burned trees yielded potash, one of the area's first export crops. It was used as fertilizer and a raw material for soap. It was also one ingredient for gunpowder.

The dominant rule of the land became private ownership. There were still small enclaves where Native Americans preserved their way of life. Along the Missisquoi, for example, a community survived and maintained fishing and hunting practices that they have maintained until today. These native people came into increasing conflict with the existing government, but have fought to preserve practices that they believe protect the land and the winged and furred creatures that reside here.

For over a hundred years, no notable white voices spoke against this destruction of land and habitat.

George Perkins Marsh, who wrote MAN AND NATURE in 1864, was one of the first exceptions. One of the first environmentalists, Marsh spoke in favor of land conservation and species preservation. Another person who spoke out was Rowland Robinson, an author and naturalist who criticized the deforestation and loss of wildlife.

The presence and the practices of the Europeans brought many changes to the Lake Champlain Basin in a short period of time. The following section will look at some of the species that survive and thrive in the region today.

WILDLIFE *of the* LAKE CHAMPLAIN BASIN

Animals are divided into two large groups, vertebrates and invertebrates. Vertebrates get their shape from an endoskeleton also known as the backbone. You have a backbone and so do all other mammals, birds, fish, amphibians and reptiles. Invertebrates do not have backbones. Invertebrates such as earthworms, snails and insects use other bodily adaptations to create their body structures: segmented bodies, a hard outside shell or mucous skin. You are part of a very diverse group of creatures that live on this planet. Let's explore some of the local vertebrates and invertebrates of the Lake Champlain Basin.

FISH

All fish are cold-blooded animals that spend their whole lives living in water. Most fish have fins to help them move through the water. Fish are separated into two large groups: those with a skeleton made of cartilage (like your nose) and those with skeletons made of bone.

There are over 81 species of fish that have been identified in Lake Champlain, which provides one of the largest assortments of freshwater fish of any lake in the world. Some of the many fish in Lake Champlain are the lake sturgeon, bowfin, freshwater drum, mooneye, northern pike, walleye, largemouth bass, smallmouth bass, rock bass, bluegill and muskellunge.

Fishing is an important part of our region's economy. Anglers are mostly interested in 20 species of the lake's fish. The lake has excellent warm-water fisheries for largemouth bass, smallmouth bass, walleye, northern pike, chain pickerel, brown bullhead, channel catfish and yellow perch. Cold-water fisheries are home to lake trout, landlocked Atlantic salmon, rainbow trout, brown trout and rainbow smelt.

Lake Champlain has the only New England population of mooneye, an unusual freshwater fish. The mooneye inhabits the waters off Port Henry, south to Whitehall, New York, and is usually not seen elsewhere. This fish belongs to a special group called the bony tongues (osteoglossomorpha). As you might guess from the name, the mooneye has large pointed teeth on its tongue! It also has large eyes and a short snout.

The scientific name for cold blooded is ectothermic. Ectothermic animals cannot regulate body temperature. Their body temperature is determined by the temperature of their surroundings.

Fish have scales that cover their body and help protect them. Some fish, however, do not have scales; they have a leathery outer skin instead. Scales help us age a fish. As a fish's scales grow in size, the number of rings per scale indicate the age of the fish. This is similar to counting the rings on a tree.

In 1988, $31.7 MILLION was spent on fishing in Lake Champlain.

The bowfin is a primitive, hard-headed fish that can live in water with little oxygen. It can actually absorb atmospheric oxygen by coming to the water surface and using its swim bladder as a lung. Bowfin spawn in shallow, weedy areas of the lake. The males clear away vegetation to build a nest about three feet in diameter. After the eggs are hatched, the young attach to the vegetation around the nest. The young fish form a school around the male who guards them for several weeks. They begin by feeding on plankton and small insects, then switch to fish. Adult bowfin feed on aquatic vertebrates and occasionally will eat a shrew or a duckling.

The freshwater drum is a fish that can grow to a tremendous size. The drum is also called the sheepshead because it resembles the face of a sheep. It has two funny-looking bones in its ears, called otoliths, which can be carved out of its skull. Known as "lucky bones," they are considered good luck; keep one in your pocket if you ever find it. From the size of the lucky bones in some Native American graves, we now assume that the sheepshead can reach a weight of 75 pounds or more. The freshwater drum makes a strange grunting noise that can be heard from shore.

Historically, salmon and lake trout were abundant in Lake Champlain. Both fish were an important food source. By the late 1800s, however, they were nearly, if not completely, eliminated from Lake Champlain. Native communities who still practiced ways of preserving fish populations had the only "regulations" on fishing practices. Otherwise, there were no laws about when or how many fish could be harvested. The biggest problem was that dams built to power the growing industries blocked the migratory routes of the salmon on their spawning runs. The dams also allowed easy harvest. Great numbers of fish would gather near the dam and people would harvest them, further speeding their disappearance. The sea lamprey also contributed to the problems of the lake's fisheries.

Heavy logging in Lake Champlain's watershed also hurt the salmon and trout. Logging caused erosion and silt to enter the rivers. This suffocated the incubating salmon eggs. The loss of the tall trees, which had provided shade, also caused the sun to warm the water in the streams so that the temperature became too high for the young salmon.

All bony fish have otoliths, but the ones in sheepshead are unusually large. A bony fish has three otoliths in each side of the head, one large and two small. Each set of three bones is encased in a liquid-filled pouch that helps the fish maintain its balance.

The Lake Champlain Restoration Program, which began in 1973, has restored landlocked Atlantic salmon and lake trout to Lake Champlain. The sea lamprey was an obstacle in the success of this program because it threatened the survival of the fish. In February of 1996, a 23-pound lake trout was caught in Button Bay. This was the first salmonid over 20 pounds caught in Lake Champlain since the restoration program began.

No one can even imagine how many smelt there are in the lake, but they certainly number in the millions. They provide the food base of many other fish species, such as lake trout and salmon. For many years their breeding spots in Lake Champlain were unknown, and there was no evidence that they were breeding in the tributaries. Scientists only found out recently that smelt can breed in fairly deep water, about 40 to 90 feet down.

The common carp is the largest minnow in the lake. It was introduced to the United States from Europe in the late 1800s because people thought it was a good eating fish and adaptable to different habitats. Now it is considered a pest. Carp reproduce plentifully.

Yellow perch is considered to be an important food fish. It can be caught easily at any time and is most popular in the winter as the cold seems to improve its taste. It is also an important feed fish for other, larger fish in the lake and used as an indicator for the health of other fish populations. Perch populate shallow areas near the side of the lake.

The eastern sand darter is one of the lake's smallest fish. It matures to three inches long. It lives in the sandy river bottoms of Lake Champlain's tributaries but is threatened because its habitat is changing. Soil erosion has covered river bottoms with silt. The fish will disappear when there is no habitat for them. The eastern sand darter is one of the five fish listed as threatened or endangered in the state of Vermont.

THE IMPORTANCE *of* KNOWING *about* FISH

Fishing has continued to be an important part of the culture of our region. Although we sometimes think of fishing as just a relaxing sport, there are many important issues to look at when studying the lake's fisheries.
- Fish can be an indicator of water quality and the status of a habitat.
- Species that are introduced, even if they are a welcome guest like the rainbow or brown trout, may alter the aquatic ecosystem.
- The traditional practices of Native Americans are in conflict with existing fish and wildlife laws. The Abenaki have held fish-ins to spotlight their claim to aboriginal rights.
- Mercury levels in fish have become a concern and scientists monitor levels of chemical contaminants in fish flesh. Dietary guidelines have been issued by the Vermont and New York Departments of Health for moderate fish consumption.

THE LAKE STURGEON: Giants of Lake Champlain

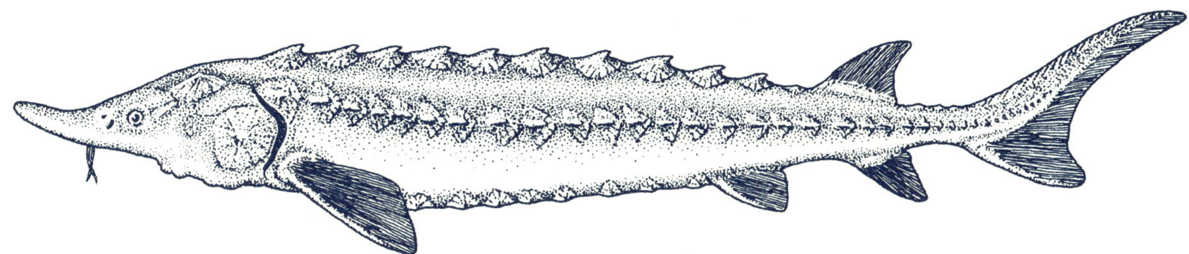

Over the years, people who don't believe in Champ have claimed that the creature must have been a sturgeon, not a sea monster. One can understand the confusion when you consider that sturgeon can be over six feet long and weigh over two hundred pounds. Some sturgeon live for 150 years! It is the largest freshwater fish in New England.

Sturgeon like to live where there is a clean sandy bottom. They eat clams, snails, crayfish and insects. Young sturgeon have teeth but adult sturgeon do not. Adults find their food with sensory barbels or whiskers and suck up their meal like a vacuum.

Sturgeon populations have declined over the years due to overfishing. Their meat and roe, which was used to make caviar, was in demand. Even their skin was once used to make leather. Also, dams built on rivers stopped sturgeon from swimming upstream to lay their eggs. Some areas where the sturgeon could have laid their eggs were buried because of soil erosion.

The lake sturgeon breeds in the tributary streams of Lake Champlain. Sturgeon are not able to reproduce until they are about 20 years old and then only spawn every 3 to 4 years. This makes their survival even more precarious. Although once nearly extirpated, a few still survive.

Although this species is in peril, it also has proven itself over time. Sturgeon inhabited the earth before dinosaurs. Those that do survive have a long and active life. One sturgeon was tagged in 1942 in the St. Lawrence River, recaptured in 1944 in Lake St. Clair and recaptured 28 years later in Lake Michigan.

Currently, Fish and Wildlife officials are considering ways to restore sturgeon populations, such as placing spawning habitat below stream barriers and researching methods of cultivating sturgeon in hatcheries. The University of Vermont did a study in 1994 to see if it would be possible to restore sturgeon to Lake Champlain. The Lake Sturgeon is threatened in New York and endangered in Vermont. Their status in Lake Champlain is described as rare.

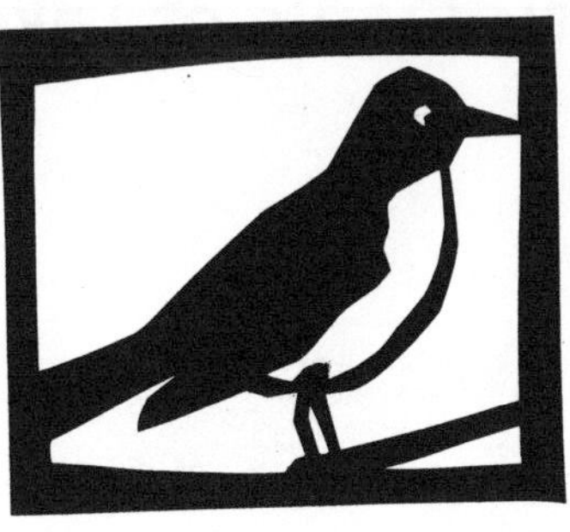

BIRDS

Birds live on land, in trees and on water, but most birds fly. Some birds, such as penguins, do not fly. All birds have four general characteristics. They have wings, feathers, beaks and scaly legs. Birds also lay hard-shelled eggs. Bird bones are hollow, which makes birds lightweight. The main difference among the 8,500 species of birds in the world is their beaks.

It is difficult to estimate accurately how many species of birds there are in the Champlain Basin. Some breed in the region, some are blown in by storms, and others migrate through the area. The total number of species that has ever been observed is 318.

The loon, or great northern diver, is a magnificent bird with bright red eyes and a glossy black head. The Abenaki called the loon "The Spirit of Northern Waters." The French called it "The Diver with the Necklace." Since its legs are situated very far back on its body, the loon finds it awkward or impossible to walk on land. Hence, it spends most of its time in the water, diving with great ease. It catches meals of fish, insects, crayfish and special aquatic plants. The loon's water takeoffs are characterized by a lot of wing flapping—it needs a long "runway" to become airborne. Loons are currently not nesting on Lake Champlain but use the lake as a resting spot during their migrations. Non-nesting singles may stay for an extended time.

Many people think the wood duck is the most beautiful of all the waterfowl. Its Latin name, *Aix sponsa*, means "water bird in bridal dress." It almost became extinct in the late 1800s when people cut down large amounts of forests, which is an important habitat for the wood duck. The wood duck especially likes to nest in the cavities of dead or dying trees. After the young chicks hatch they are moved to the marshes to feed and mature. The Migratory Bird Treaty of 1918 set up protection of the species and its recovery is seen as one of the success stories of modern waterfowl management.

Osprey are the only birds of prey in North America that feed almost entirely on live fish. They are acrobats of the skies, plunging to the water to catch fish with their feet. The claws of an osprey have special serrations to hold the slippery catch. Imagine the energy it takes for an osprey to become airborne from the water carrying its prey! Osprey populations were decimated in the 1960s because of the use of the pesticide DDT. The pesticide entered the

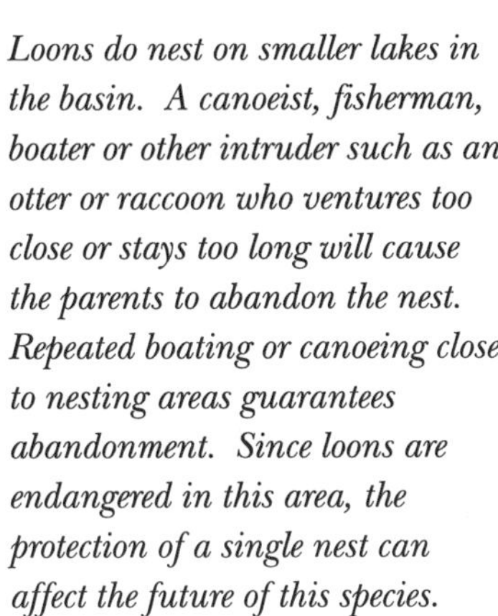

Loons do nest on smaller lakes in the basin. A canoeist, fisherman, boater or other intruder such as an otter or raccoon who ventures too close or stays too long will cause the parents to abandon the nest. Repeated boating or canoeing close to nesting areas guarantees abandonment. Since loons are endangered in this area, the protection of a single nest can affect the future of this species.

It is no longer against the law to hunt wood ducks, as their numbers have reached a healthy population. Wood ducks are omnivores. They eat vegetation and invertebrates, fish and amphibians. They provide a link in the food chain between herbaceous plants and invertebrates and higher predators such as raccoon, foxes, great horned owl and mink.

food chain and was eventually consumed by birds of prey. This caused the birds' eggshells to be thinner than normal and the chicks could not survive.

The peregrine falcon was extirpated east of the Mississippi River in the 1940s. Efforts to reintroduce the species have generally been successful. Vermont and New York have some breeding birds. Birds are hatched in captivity and placed on ledges. Their natural nesting sites are cliffs. This falcon is one of the fastest of birds; it can fly at speeds close to two hundred miles per hour.

Herons are many people's favorite birds. It is a wonderful thing to witness the patience of a heron as he awaits his dinner, standing on one leg in a marsh until the moment is right. Herons love to eat small fish and frogs, which fit down their gullets whole. Herons use their very sharp beaks to stab their prey.

Herons winter in the southern United States and South America and travel to Lake Champlain to spend the summer raising their young in wetlands or any wet, quiet place.

There is a special rookery on one of the Lake Champlain Islands where a colony of black-crowned night herons live. Black-crowned night herons are small with short necks and legs. This species is dark on the back and the top of the head and snowy-white beneath, which makes them easy to identify. They hunt at night and sleep during the day.

Bald eagles do not nest in the basin but do use the lake during spring and fall migrations. They will even stay the winter if the water on the lake stays open. Bald eagles eat fish, live or dead and other carrion. They always live near water and need undisturbed shoreline and large trees, such as those that grow in old forests, to nest in and perch on. Like the osprey, bald eagles were harmed by DDT but also are making a comeback.

The Lake Champlain Basin is home to many songbirds. Many songbirds migrate south during the winter to find food. Due to habitat destruction in both their winter and summer homes, many songbird populations are declining. Organizations such as the Vermont Institute of Natural Science in Woodstock, Vermont, study songbird populations and habitats to keep a pulse on the health of songbird populations.

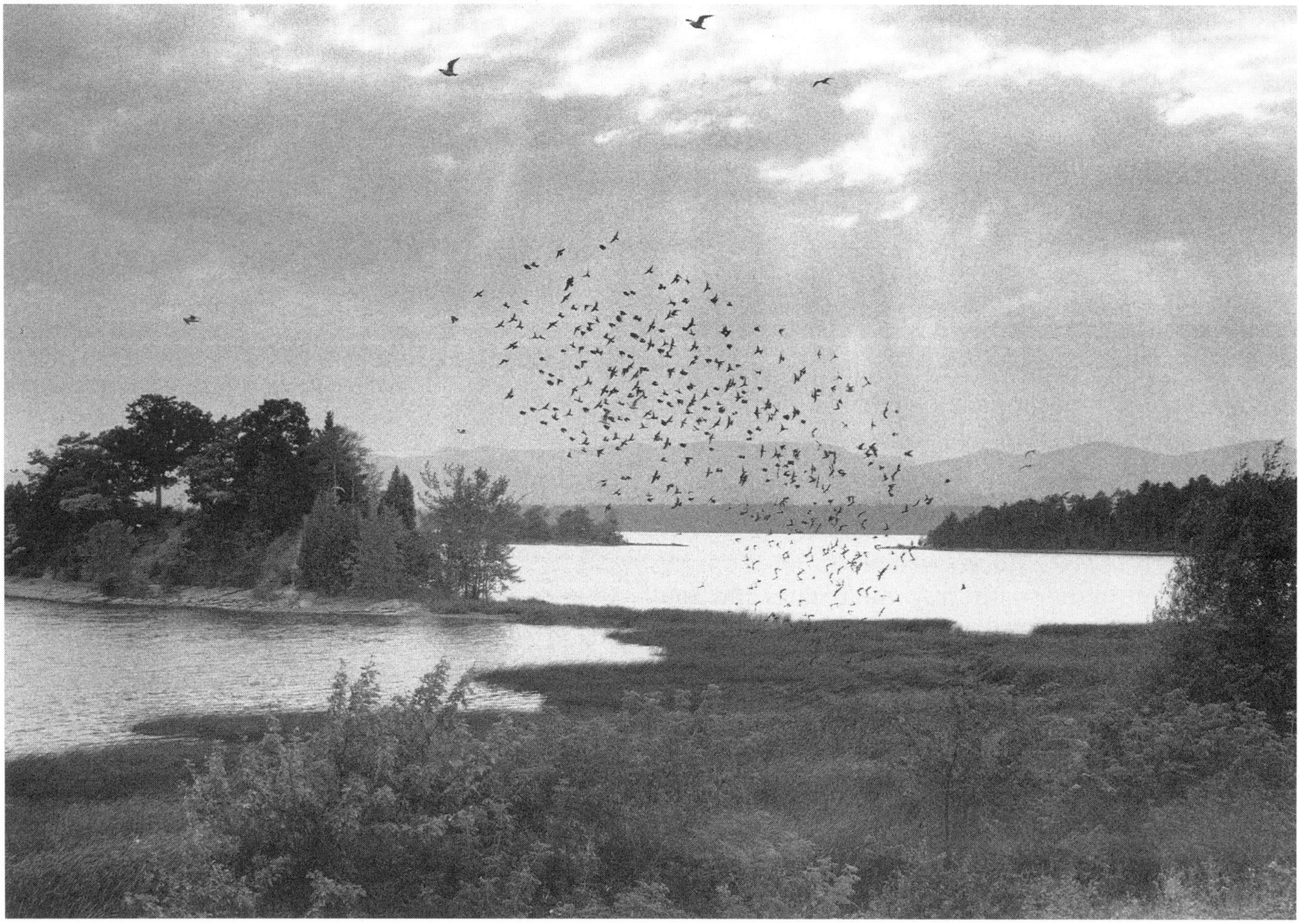

THE IMPORTANCE *of* KNOWING *about* BIRDS

Although we sometimes think of birds as just a lovely addition to the natural world, there are many important issues to look at when studying the birds that live in the basin.

• Birds have a particular role in an ecosystem and perform many specific tasks, such as carrying seeds and facilitating pollination. Raptors are important for controlling rodents and many birds eat insects.

• Birds have particular habitat needs and are sensitive to development.

• Birds are long-distance travelers and link issues concerning the health of the basin to the health of the planet.

• Birds depend on the basin for breeding grounds and stopovers on migration routes.

• There are many federal and state programs to protect and restore birds' habitat and nesting sites.

Bob Spear: Bird Lover

by Lou Borie

One day, when Bob Spear was eighteen, he captured a stray parakeet that had flown into the woodshed of the family farm in Colchester. The bird became a family pet, and it also became the model for Bob's first bird carving, whittled from a piece of white pine with a jackknife by the light of a kerosene lamp. That was more than fifty years ago and Bob Spear has been carving birds ever since. More than two hundred and fifty of his bird carvings can be seen at the Birds of Vermont Museum in Huntington.

The parakeet carving opened up the world of living things to Bob, who had been encouraged by his mother to explore the world of nature. Bob began to carve other species of birds, sometimes working late into the night in his shop. *"I used to get the chores done and eat, and then I'd go out and work until 11 or 12 o'clock and sleep out there on a cot,"* Spear remembers.

Many years later, when he was director of the Green Mountain Audubon Nature Center in Huntington, Bob used his carving skills to develop a set of bird carvings he could take to schools to illustrate his talks on Vermont's birds.

Bob discovered that students could focus on the bird carvings better than on live birds. It was hard for students to concentrate when he led them on walks through the nature center.

"When you take a group of school kids out on a field trip, the birds fly overhead or you hear them sing— occasionally you get a glimpse of them nearby. Kids don't really get a good look at them. The carvings are great for teaching because you can form the birds any way you want, and you can create a scene that would be almost impossible to see in the wild. The kids really get interested in the carvings."

In 1970, someone donated a collection of bird nests to the nature center. Bob thought of creating displays with the nests and a pair of carved birds to go with them. He started to think about a complete collection of wood carvings of Vermont's birds. Now, more than twenty years later, the Birds of Vermont Collection is a reality.

To make a bird carving, Spear starts with a block of native Vermont basswood, a relatively soft wood with a fine, straight grain. He uses photographs in books and mounted specimens as guides. He roughs out the bird's shape with carving knives and chisels. He then uses a power carving tool with ruby-tipped bits to contour the bird and to outline individual feathers. When the body of the bird is finished and painted, Bob fashions legs and feet out of solid wire and plumber's solder and inserts glass eyes.

For the display, Spear starts with a real nest, which he collects after it is abandoned by a pair of birds in the fall. Songbirds don't use the same nest twice, and Spear has both federal and state permits to salvage bird nests. If a bird nests in a tree cavity, the way woodpeckers do, Spear tries to find a section of a tree with an abandoned nesting cavity in it.

Eggs for the nest are made from sections of hardwood dowels, shaped to exact dimensions and painted. Spear makes remarkably lifelike leaves and flowers using thin-gauge aluminum, the kind used for pie pans, then scribes them with veins and other tiny details.

When Spear's artistry is complete, each display is mounted on a pedestal and enclosed in a Plexiglas case. Walking through the rows of display cases, you see the birds as if they had been frozen in time, captured at one instant of their lives in the wild. A screech owl, wings and talons extended, comes to rest on a tree limb with a just-captured beetle in its mouth. A cliff swallow wheels in towards its mud nest that is tucked up under the eaves of a house. A bluejay lands with outspread wings while its mate sits secretively by the nest.

Bob has been captivated by the endless variety of the natural world his whole life. He's carved hundreds of birds since the parakeets he crafted as a teenager, but he never tires of his task.

At times, he still works late into the night, sitting at his carving bench, applying the techniques which make his carvings so unique. Most would consider Bob Spear's collection a lifetime achievement, but for Spear the carvings are simply the culmination of his many years spent studying the natural world and encouraging others to appreciate its wonders.

AMPHIBIANS

Amphibians are cold-blooded animals that are adapted to live part of their life in water and part of their life on land. In order to live their lives like this, most amphibians go through metamorphosis—a process whereby their bodies change. For example, a frog starts its life as a tadpole with only a head and a tail. As the tadpole grows to be an adult, its body changes. First the back legs grow, then the front legs grow, then the body forms and the head becomes large and more defined. Most amphibians have moist, smooth skin and lay their eggs in the water. The eggs in the water are surrounded by a jelly-like substance that helps to nourish the young amphibians as well as protect them. Amphibians are split into two groups, those with tails (salamanders) and those without tails (frogs and toads).

The mud puppy is an aquatic salamander with a "collar" of odd-looking clusters of external gills. It is a creature that keeps some of its larval characteristics, such as its gills, its whole life. Because it has both gills and lungs, it is often used in comparative anatomy courses to show the transition from gills to lungs. Up to a foot in length, it is mostly nocturnal and likes to feed on aquatic insects, crustaceans and small fish. Not entirely true to its name, it lives in clear or muddy water, but spends much of its time along the muddy bottom of streams and wetlands.

The red spotted newt is a small salamander about three to four inches long. Its tail has a fin with a fleshy keel on the top and bottom. Newts are green with little spots like speckled trout. Red efts, the terrestrial stage of the red-spotted newt, are juveniles that sometimes live on land two to seven years before returning to water to transform to adults. You might think that their bright orange color would mark them as easy prey, but Mother Nature was looking out for the red eft. Their orange skin is toxic and discourages predators.

A bullfrog has a familiar call that you can hear near water. It is the largest frog in North America and is sometimes hunted for its tasty legs. Male bullfrogs have an eardrum that is bigger than its eye; females have an eardrum that is the same size as the eye. Tadpoles overwinter for one or two years and won't reproduce until up to five years. Bullfrogs spend the winter buried in the bottom of a pond or wetland.

REPTILES

Reptiles are cold-blooded animals with thick, dry, scaly skin. This skin helps to protect the reptiles. Reptiles can live in water or on land and they have lungs for breathing. Most reptiles lay tough leathery eggs usually on land. When young reptiles hatch from their eggs, they resemble their adult parents. There are four types of reptiles: lizards, snakes, turtles, and alligators and crocodiles.

The northern water snake can often be seen swimming in or near the water's edge of ponds, streams and lakes. These snakes are often confused with the venomous water moccasin and are often killed by fearful humans. If you are ever fortunate enough to observe one of these beautiful and graceful creatures, take a minute to sit back and observe its behavior. The water snake may be seeking its favorite prey of tadpoles, small fish or salamanders; it may be seeking refuge from a predator such as a heron, raccoon or fox, or it may be seeking a safe location to leave the water and bask in the sun along the shore. Water snakes are one of the reptiles that have live young. A female water snake will give birth to 12 to 60 baby snakes. The mother snake does not care for the babies, and they eventually slither away to fend for themselves.

The American toad is slow-moving and easy to catch. Toads have two large glands behind the eyes that secrete a bad-tasting milky fluid, so even though they are slow, they are not that appealing to predators. American toads breed in the early spring and females lay thousands of eggs.

The map turtle is named because its green shell is etched with lines like a map. It is a Great Lakes species that occurs only in Lake Champlain and nowhere else in New England. It lives in shallow rivers and lake shores and likes to hibernate in muddy river bottoms. You might see a map turtle sunning itself on a log. The map turtle nests on sandy beaches and since there are so few quiet sandy beaches in the springtime, scientists are concerned about the survival of this species.

A stinkpot is a very small turtle. Its carapace, or top shell, is only three-and-a-half to five-and-a-half inches in length. It is dark brown, high-domed, and sometimes covered with algae. Young stinkpots do stink; they have two glands that emit a smelly, yellowish liquid. They eat plants and animals and some-

On North Hero Island, scientists are trying to keep people from disturbing nests in June when map turtles come to lay their eggs.

times carrion. If the carcass is large, a stinkpot will hold onto it with its front feet and tear off large pieces of meat that make its little throat bulge as it swallows its meal.

Perhaps the most interesting turtle we have in the lake is the eastern spiny softshell. Its "shell" is leathery in texture and it has a long, snake-like head with a snout on it. These turtles like shallow, sandy areas in lakes and prefer to lay their eggs on sandbars. They cannot tolerate any kind of pollution. They like to eat tadpoles, frogs and sometimes plants. The eastern spiny softshell turtle is threatened. It is what is called a distinct species in Lake Champlain: its small population is isolated in this region and is found no-where else nearby. Lake Champlain is the furthest east this species is found.

THE IMPORTANCE *of* KNOWING *about* REPTILES *and* AMPHIBIANS

Athough you may think they are slimy, scaly and potentially dangerous, reptiles and amphibians have many characteristics that help people understand the diversity of life on earth.

• Amphibians, because of their permeable skin cover and dependence on both land and water, are vulnerable to pollution and other changes in the cnvironmcnt.

• Reptiles (like some snakes) are thought to be harmful, but usually are not.

• Both groups play critical roles in transferring energy along the food chain. They are effective predators of a wide range of animals (and plants) from invertebrates to fish to small mammals, and in turn, are preyed upon by many other animals.

MAMMALS

Mammals are warm-blooded with fur or hair on their bodies. All mammals feed milk to their young. Mammals can be grouped according to what they eat.

• Carnivores eat meat.

• Omnivores eat meat and plant material.

• Herbivores eat only plant material.

Mammals also can be separated into three groups based on how their young are born:

Monotremes: Young hatch from eggs. (The duck-billed platypus is a monotreme but not a resident of the basin!)
Marsupials: Young are born live in an immature stage. The young crawl into the mother's pouch on the front of her abdomen and live there and drink her milk until they are fully developed. The only North American marsupial is the opossum.
Placentals: Young stay inside their mother's body until they are fully developed and then they are born. Most mammals, including yourselves, are placentals.

For many different reasons, mammals are vulnerable to human predation. They are sought after for food, furs and killed as sport. In addition, mammals suffer from loss of habitat. Some animals such as cougars and wolves were extirpated because they threatened people. Today, these two species are no longer found in the basin. The range of habitat that they depended on is gone.

The last catamount, or mountain lion, was shot in the region in 1881 near Barnard, Vermont. It can be seen at the Vermont Historical Society Museum in Montpelier. Recent reported sightings of the catamount in the Adirondacks and Vermont may signify a return of the catamount to the region. In December of 1994, Vermont Fish and Wildlife officials confirmed that scat found in Craftsbury, Vermont, was from a catamount.

An animal that survived longer in this region was the timber wolf, always an enemy of sheep and cattle farmers. Samuel Williams, a Vermont historian, wrote in 1794:

"One of the most common and noxious of all animals is the WOLF....His eyes generally appear sparkling; and there is a wildness, and a fierceness, in his looks....This animal is extremely fierce, sanguinary, and carnivorous. When a number of them assemble, it is not for peace, but for war and destruction. The animal at which they...aim, is the sheep....They attack the deer, foxes and

Big cats such as the catamount, need a large territory in which to roam and that expanse of land is no longer present in the basin.

The last wolf in Vermont was killed in 1900.

The wolf was bountied in 1779 and from then until 1820, wolf hunts were a popular sport. These hunting raids and continued land development destroyed the territory of the wolf. By 1900, the wolf was gone from the region.

The wolf and the cougar were the top of the food chain, and now both are extirpated from the region. The disappearance of these animals is used to justify the hunting of deer. As the deer's natural predators are gone, people must serve as predators.

Beginning in the 1940s, the coyote has taken some of the place of the wolf in the food chain.

Historically, white-tailed deer were abundant and an important food supply for Native Americans. The arrival of the white settlers and loggers soon changed that. The deer were hunted year-round, supplying commercial meat markets; their forest habitat dwindled and no laws protected them. The first laws to protect them were issued to the New Hampshire grants in 1741, but early efforts did not succeed in restoring the deer population. By 1800, deer were nearly extinct in the east. It became illegal to hunt deer in Vermont.

Deer were imported to Vermont from New York in the 1870s. Things improved. Wolves and catamounts, the natural predators of the deer, were being hunted and were less of a threat. Also, forest habitats in the 1860s and 1870s were making a comeback so the region became more hospitable to deer. An open season on deer was reestablished at the turn of the century. By the 1960s, populations were large. Hunting is the major wildlife management tool used today to keep the deer population in balance with the natural habitat.

The beaver was the most sought after mammal by the first Europeans, and was hunted primarily for its fur. The beaver is the largest North American rodent. Fur-trading companies hired Native Americans to supply them with beaver and other skins. The beaver population was close to extinction from the Atlantic to the Mississippi River by the middle of the nineteenth century.

The story of the restoration of the beaver population is similar to that of the deer. Biologists sought protective laws and brought in beavers from out of state. Now, if you're a farmer in the basin who has lost your fields to beaver ponds you may wish these out-of-staters would return to where they came from!

The story of the fisher and the porcupine is interesting. The fisher, or fisher cat, is neither a cat, nor is fish its favorite food. It is omnivorous and eats fruits, berries and a variety of animals, including porcupines. The fisher is actually a weasel. Fishers and porcupines were abundant in the region but the fisher had a prized pelt that sold for a large sum of money in the seventeenth century. By the mid-1800s, they were extirpated from the region. Then, there started to be an overabundance of porcupines. Porcupines were a big problem to loggers because they gnawed through trees and destroyed good timber. The fisher, a good hunter, was a predator of the porcupine, being strong and agile enough to knock the porcupine from the tree and attack its soft underbelly without getting quilled. Biologists decided to bring back fishers and in 1959 began a program that restored fishers to the region. Now the fishers are established and loggers no longer have problems with porcupines. Surely the porcupines don't think this was a good solution!

Insectivores are a group of insect-eating mammals that includes the mole and the shrew. They don't hibernate in winter and have to work hard to find their food. Because they have high metabolisms, they have to eat almost constantly or they will starve to death. In winter, they live under the snow.

The starnosed mole works underground in the moist soil of river bottoms and near lakes. It goes deeper in the winter than in the summer as it moves down below the frost line in search of prey. It uses its fleshy, tentacle-like nose to sense the movement of earthworms and grubs, then digs furiously with its spade-like front paws to reach them.

A smaller relative, the short-tailed shrew, scours higher up either in the humus and leaf litter of the soil or in the low vegetation. Even though it is small, it is a fearless hunter, day and night. Weighing about as much as a toothbrush, it will attack mice and other prey twice its size. It also eats earthworms, insects, land snails and other terrestrial animals.

The moose used to be present in large numbers in the Champlain Basin. It became scarce in the 1800s. Now moose can be seen in their natural habitat,

roaming in the thickets around remote ponds or lakes, browsing on water-side plants or wading to uproot aquatic weeds.

Sometimes a moose causes quite a commotion when it wanders into populated areas. Although it may just be lost or in search of a mate, it may be suffering from "moose sickness." This disease is caused by a parasitic worm that bores into the brain tissue of the moose and causes it to be disoriented and clumsy. The worm gets into the moose's body from a snail that hosts the worm. The moose might eat the snail while munching on aquatic plants, where the snail may be living. The worm leaves the snail and works its way into the moose's central nervous system and then into the brain.

The Indiana bat is one of the few mammals we have that is on the federal endangered species list. It has been found in Brandon, Vermont, and several south-central areas. The bats prefer limestone caves for hibernation.

The brown bat, a resident of the basin, can consume as many as 600 mosquitos in an hour. Some people are scared of bats, but lately, more people are aware of how helpful bats can be. People are even putting up bat houses nearby so the bats can eat bugs. Scientists also are protecting caves where bats live by placing gates over the entrances to keep people out.

THE IMPORTANCE *of* KNOWING *about* MAMMALS

Although we may only see the mammals that have gotten used to living around humans, such as squirrels, chipmunks and even deer, there are many important issues to look at when studying all of the mammals of the basin.

• Our ancestors living tens of thousands of years ago depended on mammals for their survival. They hunted mammals for their food, clothing and weapons. Today, we continue to depend on mammals in many ways by eating their meat, making clothes from their hides, drinking their milk, and using them in scientific research.

• Some mammals are highly visible and "part of the scenery." Other mammals, like the shrew, are rarely visible and remain hidden to the human eye.

• The hunting of mammals—deer, moose, bear—is an ancient tradition of native people in the basin. Their age-old traditions are in conflict with current fish and game laws.

• There are numerous other issues surrounding the practice and regulation of hunting.

Rabies Alert!
All mammals can get rabies. Bats are tolerant to the virus so they live to pass it on. Raccoons and skunks are also relatively tolerant to the virus and often live in human-occupied environments. You should never go near any animal that is acting oddly or appears unafraid of you.

If a person is bitten by any wild animal, the animal should be captured, destroyed and tested for rabies. Whether the animal is captured or not, the wound should be cleaned immediately and a doctor contacted.

In general, it's a much better idea to watch wildlife than to touch it—as it may pose a risk to you or to the wild animal.

PLANTS

Flowering plants are in the kingdom Plantae. They are characterized by having cells containing chloroplasts and rigid cell walls. The chloroplasts are filled with the green pigment chlorophyll, which allows plants to convert sunlight energy into food. The Lake Champlain Basin, with its diverse bedrock geology and long growing season, supports a variety of natural communities and rich flora.

One of the common plants growing along the wooded bluffs of Lake Champlain is northern white cedar. Cedar is a long-lived evergreen tree with aromatic scale-like leaves and tiny cones. To the Native Americans it was canoe wood. They discovered that cedar logs pounded on one end split easily along the growth rings. These strips were then fashioned into ribs and frames of canoes. Additionally the wood is lightweight and resistant to rot, perfect for water travel.

Growing beneath cedar on lakeshore bluffs are two rare plants that are protected in Vermont. Golden corydalis is related to bleeding hearts and dutchman's breeches. It has yellow, spurred flowers and finely cut leaves. Ram's head lady slipper is a small delicate orchid that is also state-protected. The inch-long purple flower has a lip petal that points downwards and early botanists compared its unusual shape to a ram's head.

In big river corridors and along the lake, you are sure to see cottonwood. This tree's large sticky buds leaf out into triangular leaves with large fuzzy catkins. But it is probably best recognized in spring when its seed pods burst, sending forth a mass of white cottony seeds floating everywhere.

Shagbark hickory is another characteristic tree of the basin. It is easily recognized by its smoke-grey bark, which warps and peels away from the main trunk in strips one foot or more long and 6 to 8 inches wide. These loose curling strips make the tree look shaggy in profile or silhouette. Its nuts were collected in the past and its wood prized for its high fuel value. Today its green wood is unmatched for the flavor it imparts to meats smoked over its coals.

The herb layer of floodplain forests is often composed of ostrich fern, known as the fiddlehead fern. This wild edible is commonly collected and sold in grocery stores as a gourmet spring delicacy.

Many people are familiar with jack-in-the-pulpit but few have seen its close relative, the rare green dragon, which can also be found growing in these wet woods. The green dragon is threatened in the State of Vermont. The green dragon has a compound leaf composed of 5 to 15 leaflets. The so-called flower is actually composed of a spathe, or leaf covering. A spathe is made up of modified leaves that encircle the actual flowers. The floral structures are borne at the base of a fleshy spadix, or floralspike. In a green dragon this spadix is prolonged into a long, pointed tail that extends well beyond the enclosing spathe. This is quite unlike little jack who remains inside his pulpit.

In springtime, carpets of white trillium are a familiar sight in the Champlain Basin. As the name implies, the flower has its parts in threes—three leaves, three sepals and three petals. These showy flowers in the lily family put on quite a display turning from white to pink as they age.

Growing on the dunes and sandy beaches of Lake Champlain are three Vermont state-listed plants that are most commonly found along the Atlantic seacoast. Beach pea has typical pea foliage, lovely purple pink flowers and arrowhead-shaped stipules. Beach heather is low-growing with fuzzy grey-green foliage and star-shaped yellow flowers. Champlain beach grass forms cones and is one of the few grasses well adapted to shifting sands. It is excellent at stabilizing the dunes where it grows. These plants are post-glacial relics from the time when Lake Champlain was part of a great inland sea.

Everyone is probably familiar with cattails, which grow in marshes throughout the Champlain Basin. The brown sausage you see is the female flowering structure composed of thousands of brown hairs connected to seeds, which are still attached to the central stalk. Protruding above this sausage is a bare spike, which originally held the male flowers. They die back after they shed their yellow pollen, which pollinates the lower female flowers. Cattails are well-adapted to life in the water. Their leaves and stalk are filled with special open cells that transport oxygen down to the saturated roots. Cattails and other wetland plants provide many vital ecological functions. They recharge groundwater, provide flood protection, and filter water. Cattails are able to take up excess nutrients and pollutants in water. Through complex metabolic processes, nutrients and pollutants are transformed into less harmful substances and/or incorporated into tissues of the plants. Tests have shown that water leaving a cattail marsh is remarkably cleaner than that entering it. Cattails are also an important food source.

trillium, the sign of spring

The beach pea is a threatened plant. Beach and heather and Champlain beach grass are endangered in the state of Vermont.

THE IMPORTANCE *of* KNOWING *about* PLANTS

The Lake Champlain Basin is fortunate to have both a variety and an abundance of plant species. Even where humans have tried to stop plant growth, such as by paving an area of land for a parking lot, often the plant prevails. The pavement gets a small crack where a seed can lodge—add water, sunlight, a few nutrients and up pops a plant!

• Plants are considered the producers in the food chain. This means that they can produce their own food. This happens through a process called photosynthesis. Basically, the plant combines carbon dioxide with water and sunlight to produce oxygen and carbohydrates (food).

• Plants are used by humans as a source of food, clothing, shelter, and medicine. The Native Americans taught the settlers in the basin about the medicinal properties of some of the native plants. Witch hazel, a common shrub within the basin, was and still is used today as an astringent (a medicine that stops bleeding). The Native Americans showed the settlers how to turn the leaves, bark and twigs of the witch hazel into usable remedies.

• Plants help to keep the earth from falling apart! The roots of plants hold the soil together and stop the soil from eroding into our streams and rivers. When lots of soil gets into the water it causes trouble for the aquatic species. It clogs the gills of fish, for example. Shoreline restoration is a popular project in the basin: people plant species such as willow trees along eroding riverbanks. As the willows take root and grow, the soil is held into place, decreasing the amount of soil eroding into the river.

INVERTEBRATES

The Lake Champlain Basin is home to many invertebrates. These invertebrates have a very important job in the basin. They are an important food source to other larger invertebrates and vertebrates.

There are eight major groups of invertebrates in the world: sponges, hollow-bodied animals, flatworms, roundworms, segmented worms, mollusks, spiny-skinned animals and arthropods. Invertebrates are the largest group of animals on the earth.

Due to the fact that invertebrates are so small, many of them are very sensitive to changes in their environment. Scientists can use invertebrates as indicators of environmental health. Invertebrates can be found on land and in the water throughout the basin. Let's take a closer look at the small critters who share our ponds, lakes and streams.

Sponges are the simplest kind of invertebrate. They live in water and do not have heads, mouths or other separate body parts. Their bodies are like sacks. The cells of a sponge take on various body jobs like breathing and eating. The next time you are wading in a body of water in the Lake Champlain Basin, look closely at the rocks. If you are lucky, you may see areas of green and brown slippery or bumpy "stuff" attached to the rocks. This material can be removed easily from the rocks, but please be careful not to disturb its habitat. You have found a freshwater sponge! Some larger invertebrates live in and feed on the sponges.

Hollow-bodied animals, such as jellyfish and sea anemones, have a hollow center lined with digestive cells, tentacles dangling from the hollow body and a mouth. Most of these animals live in the ocean or freshwater. The green hydra, a close relative to the jellyfish, is an example of a hollow-bodied animal that can be found in the Lake Champlain Basin. It can grow to be four inches tall and has six or more dangling tentacles that catch tasty morsels such as water fleas as they float by in a clump of zooplankton.

Flatworms live in fresh or salt water or in plants or animals. Flatworms have one body opening where food and waste enter and leave the body. Many flatworms are parasites; they feed on the cells of another plant or animal. The tapeworm, for example, is a human parasite. A parasitic relationship

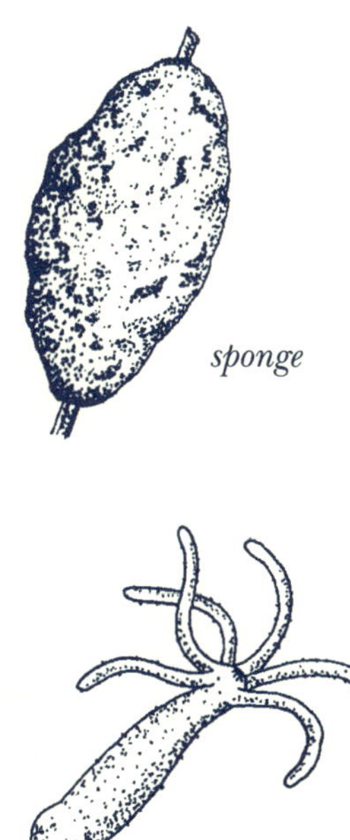

sponge

hydra

flatworm

means that one species benefits while the other is harmed or sometimes killed. A human tapeworm lives in the intestines of humans and can grow to be ten feet long! This can cause a human to become very sick. Underneath a flatworm's body are many hair-like structures, called cilia, that help the flatworm to glide along surfaces such as rocks. Can they see where they are going? Flatworms have two eyespots located in the head region that are sensitive to light. So if you were about to step on a rock that had a flatworm on it, the flatworm might detect a decrease in light produced by the shadow of your foot. Watch where you step!

Roundworms or nematodes are similar to the tapeworm except they have two body openings. Many roundworms are also parasites and are more commonly found living in the soil or in plants or animals. Nematodes are the smallest of all the worms. You will need to look closely to see them with the naked eye! Good luck.

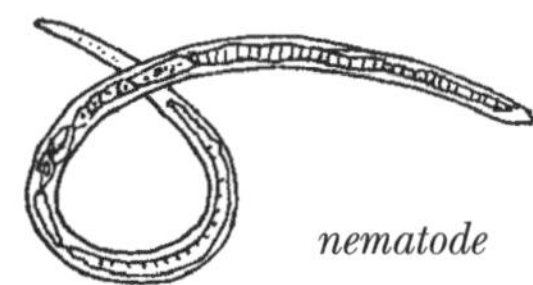

nematode

Segmented worms are more complex than the tapeworms or roundworms. They have a digestive system with two openings as well as a nervous system with a small brain. Their bodies are made up of small ring-like segments. An earthworm is a segmented worm. Although we may be more familiar with the terrestrial earthworm, it has an aquatic counterpart that also likes to eat soil. Another common segmented worm is the leech. Depending on the species, leeches can range in size from 3 to 18 inches. Believe it or not, leeches can fly, with a little help from some feathered friends. A leech uses its well-developed sucking mouth to attach to the legs of certain waterfowl species. When the bird decides to move to another pond or lake, the leech gets a bird's-eye view of the world below and a new home!

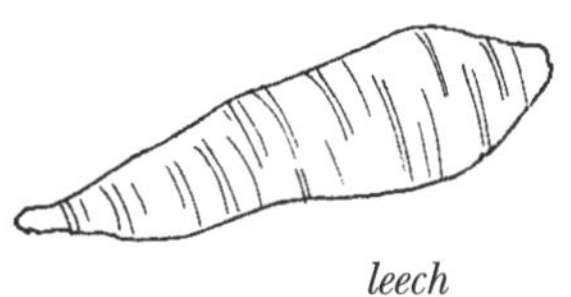

leech

Mollusks also have two body openings but they also may have small eyes, a shell or a foot. There are three major groups of mollusks: the one-footed mollusks such as a garden snail, the scallop, which is a mollusk with two shells hinged together like a clam or mussel, and the octopus, which has tentacles instead of a single foot. Mollusks are found in freshwater, saltwater and on land. The zebra mussel, first found in Lake Champlain in 1993, is an example of a mollusk that is not a native of the Lake Champlain Basin.

freshwater mussel

Spiny-skinned animals have hard outside coverings, such as seen with the starfish or sea urchin. Spiny-skinned animals are only found in the ocean. They once lived in the Champlain Sea. Fossils of these animals can be found in the Lake Champlain Basin.

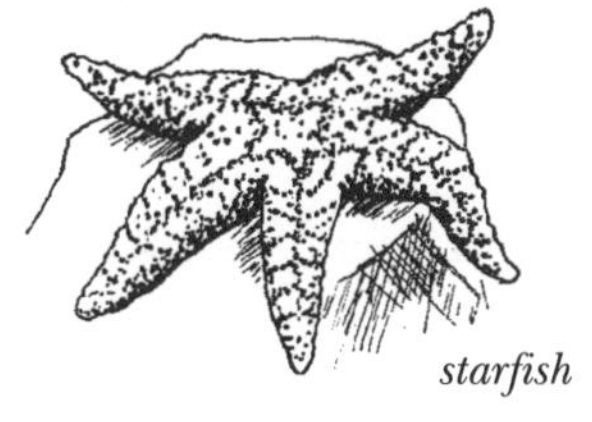

starfish

Arthropods are known as the joint-legged animals. This group is made up of insects, spiders, centipedes and millipedes, and hard-covered crustaceans such as lobster, shrimp and crayfish. Arthropods can live in water, on land or in the air. They have segmented bodies and often jointed legs. Arthropods have a hard outside covering called an exoskeleton that gives them structure and protection. A favorite insect to all who love to explore water environments is the caddis fly. The caddis fly is an insect that spends its youth in the water in a larval stage and then goes through metamorphosis, changing into an adult with wings and emerging from the water to fly and mate. The larval stage of the caddis fly is great fun to find. In a stream, look for moving sticks or small rock tubes. Caddis fly larvae spin silk around their bodies and then stick pond material to these silk cases and live inside the case for protection from predators. The caddis fly is one of nature's true sculptors.

crayfish

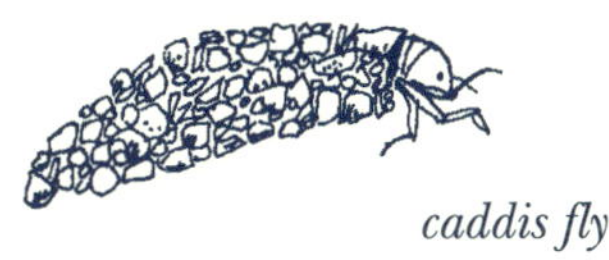

caddis fly

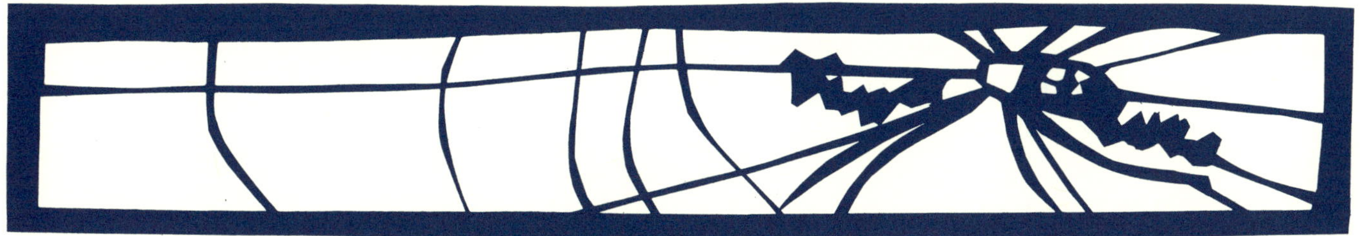

THE IMPORTANCE *of* KNOWING *about* INVERTEBRATES

Invertebrates, because they tend to be small, may not be noticed by many basin residents. However, these creatures are very important in the natural world.

• The soil beneath our feet is full of invertebrates. Earthworms may be considered the star of the soil show! They help to keep the soil healthy by wiggling around and putting air into the soil and by decomposing organic matter through their digestion process. They are nature's plows and fertilizers! Some farmers in the basin use worms as an indication of healthy soil—the more earthworms the better the soil.

• By studying aquatic macroinvertebrates (invertebrates you can see with an unaided eye), we can determine the quality of the water. A stonefly nymph can only live in healthy water while a leech can live in both healthy and polluted water. By surveying the macroinvertebrate populations in a local body of water, you can help your community learn more about the water quality.

• Invertebrates sit at the base of the food chain—they provide a strong and healthy foundation for all other animals to stay alive. You may think that mosquitoes are a pain in the neck as they buzz in your ear or bite you, leaving a welt on your skin, but mosquitoes are important food for many other animals, like the brown bat.

Champ's Chat with Mary Watzin

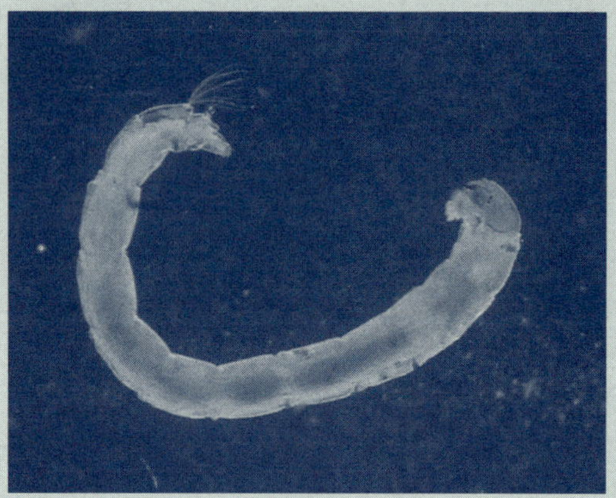

midge larva

Champ: What are midges?

Mary Watzin: Midges are small insects. As larvae, they live in the mud at the bottom of the lake. They look like little worms and they are a favorite food of some fishes like yellow perch. When a midge larva is a couple of months old, it pupates, metamorphoses and emerges from the water as a flying adult. The adults look very much like mosquitoes, but they don't bite. The adults only live a few days; they mate, the females deposit the eggs in the water and then they die.

Champ: Why did you start to study them?

Mary Watzin: I started to study midges because I wanted to know how important the larvae were in the diet of yellow perch. It turns out, they are a pretty important prey item for these fish when the fish are 2 to 5 years old and feeding on the bottom of Lake Champlain. Midges are also eaten by other fish and by insects, frogs and birds.

I also study midges because they are a good test species to see if there are toxic substances, or poisons, in the mud in polluted parts of the lake. In lakes, toxic substances tend to accumulate in the bottom sediments so those organisms that live there, like midges, are often most vulnerable to the pollution. Studying midges can help us decide where we need to focus our pollution-prevention activities before the problem gets so bad that the entire ecosystem is in jeopardy. I study the teeth of midges. Midge teeth get deformed when the insects are exposed to some contaminants. We can sometimes use deformed teeth as an early warning of a pollution problem.

Champ: How do you study midges?

Mary Watzin: I study midge larvae in the laboratory and out in Lake Champlain. To see if midge larvae were being eaten by yellow perch, we collected perch and looked at their gut contents. We found lots of midge larvae in perch guts. We also sampled the sediment in places where yellow perch like to feed, like the weedy areas along the shores of the lake, to see how many midges were available as fish food.

The midges we use in pollution studies we grow in the lab. We have little midge aquaria where we grow large numbers of larvae. We bring mud from areas where we think pollution may be a problem into the laboratory, and let the midges live in this mud. After several days, we look to see how well they are doing.

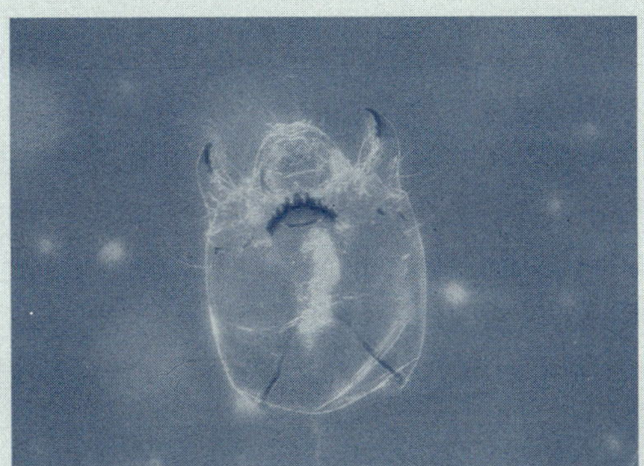
midge head larva

Midge larvae are pretty tiny creatures. You could lay about 10 of them on a penny. To look at the teeth of midges, we must mount the midges on a slide and look at them under the microscope so we can see their head capsules. It's pretty amazing to see how these little creatures look when the microscope makes them 50 or 100 times bigger than they are in the natural world. They have antennae, and mouth parts with teeth, and segments, and little clusters of setae (spines) on their tails. You can't see any of this with the naked eye.

Champ: Why are midges important?

Mary Watzin: Midge larvae are very important in the food web of Lake Champlain. They are eaten by a variety of fishes, and help to break down dead plant material in the sediment. Adult midges are eaten by other insects and by frogs and birds.

Midges are also important because they can help us understand where contaminants might be a problem in Lake Champlain and other lakes.

Champ: What is important for scientists to think about when doing this kind of research?

Mary Watzin: There are a lot of reasons that ecosystems change. Some change is natural, but some change is the result of human activities. Scientists studying pollution have to be very careful to design their experiments so they can distinguish one environmental problem from another. It sometimes seems harsh to expose organisms to materials we think may be toxic just to verify that a poison is there, but unfortunately, sometimes that's the only way to do it. We can't see chemicals in the environment. Once we know what the problems are, we can begin to look at ways to clean them up.

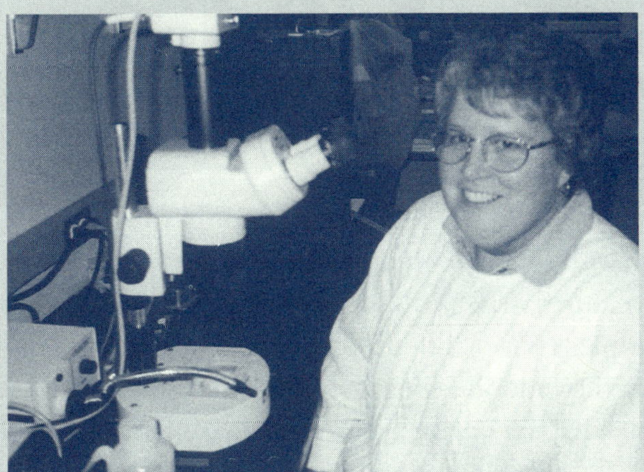

"Being an environmental scientist is a little like being a detective. I apply scientific methods to read the clues about how nature works. I apply the information I gather to help solve pressing environmental problems, like pollution, and to work for better management of our aquatic resources."

Mary Watzin

GOOD NEWS!

This essay has told some of the stories of creatures of the basin. Many of these stories tell of the harm that humankind has done by overhunting, habitat destruction or planned eradication. Yet there is a lot of good news when one looks at the relationship between people and creatures. Here is some of the GOOD NEWS! On the next page you can read about one of the basin's success stories: "The Common Tern Returns."

Humans share the earth with so many wonderful and unique plants and animals. Every day these creatures struggle to survive in an ever-changing world. Those in the Lake Champlain Basin are no exception. The Lake Champlain Basin was designated by the federal government as a Biosphere Reserve in 1989. This decision confirms that we live in a very unique environment. Due to the fact that species in the basin and everywhere do not speak our language, it is up to all of us to act and protect this precious place.

The Common Tern Returns

by Mark LaBar

For at least 100 years, the common tern has returned to nest on the same small, rocky islands on Lake Champlain. This graceful, robin-sized waterbird is white and gray with a black cap, pointed red bill and forked tail. It eats small fish that it catches by diving into the water from the air above.

The common terns nest in dense groups, called colonies, which enable them to team up for defense against predators. These colonies can range in size from several pairs to thousands of pairs. The largest colony of common terns on Lake Champlain is on Popasquash Island, near St. Albans, where 100 pairs nested in 1993.

In 1988, only 50 pairs of common terns nested on Lake Champlain. Their numbers were so low that the common tern was put on the Vermont Endangered Species list. People began to wonder what was causing the decline in the number of adult terns and soon realized that if something wasn't done, the common tern might become extinct on Lake Champlain.

In 1987, biologists from the Vermont Institute of Natural Sciences and the Vermont Department of Fish and Wildlife began studying the common tern on the lake to find out what was happening to the terns and what could be done to protect them. After doing their studies, biologists realized that very few chicks were surviving. Without young terns to replace the older terns, the population was getting smaller and smaller.

Biologists found three reasons why the chicks were not surviving. First, many chicks were being eaten by predators, primarily great horned owls and black-crowned night herons. Second, ring-billed gulls were forcing terns off their traditional nesting areas. And third, humans were disturbing the terns by landing their boats on the terns' nesting islands.

After pinpointing these problems, biologists explored different solutions to help the terns. The biologists started by putting floating signs around the islands, stating that the terns were endangered and asking people not to disturb them. Next, the biologists built wooden and rock shelters for the chicks so that they could hide from hungry predators. And finally, ring-billed gulls were prevented from nesting in the traditional tern nesting areas.

All this work paid off. Since 1989 the number of surviving chicks has increased dramatically and the number of breeding adults has doubled. Although things are looking better for the common tern on Lake Champlain, predation continues to be a problem. Still, biologists are hopeful that the populations will continue to increase and that the common tern will remain part of Lake Champlain's bird community.

Credit: *"Casin the Basin," newsletter of the Lake Champlain Basin Program. Used with permission.*

EXOTICS AFFECT *the* ECOSYSTEM *of the* BASIN

In the natural scheme of things, species exist in a balance. Each organism in the food chain has a particular role or "niche" and together the links in the chain form a closed circle. Of course, all kinds of things upset this balance. A disaster, like an early blizzard or hard winter, may kill off or weaken a species. Humans may destroy a habitat or overhunt a species. Or humans may, without realizing the impact, bring a new species to an area, which can cause havoc to the existing order of things.

The "existing" food web is the one that is in a region naturally. The species that were there originally are called indigenous or native. When a species is introduced to an area from somewhere else it is called nonindigenous, non-native or exotic. Exotics are generally considered harmful. Species that intrude on an area and cause trouble are called invaders or "nuisance" species. Nuisance species upset the natural balance in the existing ecosystem.

Every new species introduced has an impact, but sometimes the damage is minimal. Some exotics have been introduced to an area with no serious consequences to the existing ecosystem. Brown trout were not originally in Lake Champlain but have been stocked by Fish and Wildlife biologists. Although they do have an impact on the food chain of the fishery, they are generally considered welcome guests!

Some of the most common non-native nuisance species that we see are Eurasian milfoil, water chestnut, purple loosestrife, flowering rush, common reed, and sea lamprey. White perch, European rudd, and gizzard shad are recent non-native fish introductions that also could become nuisances. Great watercress, slender-leaved naiad, yellow floating heart and curly pondweed are plant species that may become a nuisance.

At the time this book is being written, zebra mussels are an exotic that is causing great concern. The zebra mussel was discovered in Lake Champlain in 1993 and has quickly established itself in many parts of the lake. Scientists are designing management plans to protect native mussels and important water intake pipes from zebra mussel infestations.

The management of nuisance species that have not yet done significant damage is a tricky one for scientists. It is hard to predict how a new species will impact a food chain and the variety of habitats within the lake's ecosystem. Scientists have to develop plans for every non-native species; it's complicated!

The European water chestnut is a nuisance plant. The plant produces one seed that has a hard shell. The shell has four points so that however a seed sits, one point sticks up. The four points also have spines, each containing small, curved teeth. If you have ever stepped on a water chestnut shell at the beach, you know all about those little teeth!

The water chestnut, like other nuisance aquatic plants, is easily spread by boat trailers. Infested areas are now posted with notices requesting people to pick the weeds off their gear to avoid extending the noxious plant to uninfested waters.

In the northern and southern ends of Lake Champlain, Eurasian milfoil has become a serious problem. The long stringy plant gets wound up in the propellers of boats. St. Albans Bay has been infested with the plant for more than 20 years; some years the milfoil has been raked out of the water and loaded onto trucks in order to clear the waters sufficiently for recreation and navigation.

Because the water chestnut and the Eurasian milfoil are the most troublesome nuisance weeds in the lake, the Departments of Environmental Conservation in both Vermont and New York, in conjunction with the U.S. Army Corps of Engineers, conducted a mechanical harvesting program for several years to stop the spread of the water chestnut in the southern part of the lake and to control the Eurasian milfoil in St. Albans Bay. Scientists have discovered an aquatic weevil that eats milfoil and are testing the effectiveness of using the weevil to control the spread of the milfoil.

In the southern part of Lake Champlain you are also apt to find floating heart, an attractive plant with a yellow flower. It is even possible to buy it from water plant nurseries, which is probably how it was introduced to the lake.

Purple loosestrife is another European plant that can be found in the basin. It often grows in highway ditches and can now be found across the United States. This plant invades wetlands and displaces native wetland plants. Many people find the weed pretty and it used to be sold in nurseries. The plant has little value to wildlife, however, unlike the native plants it's displacing. Scientists at Cornell University are doing experiments with an insect that eats the roots of this plant.

The seed of the water chestnut will sink to the bottom of the lake but sometimes can remain at the bottom of the lake for 12 years before producing a new plant.

The mechanical harvesting of Eurasian milfoil was stopped when researchers found that plant fragments would fall to the bottom of the lake and re-root, resulting in new plant growth.

The sea lamprey in Lake Champlain is a strange-looking, parasitic fish. It is eel-shaped and has a sucker-like mouth and a rasping tongue. It attaches to fish and bores into the flesh of its hosts. Sea lamprey attacks have been documented on virtually all of Lake Champlain's larger fish species. It prefers smooth-bodied fish like salmon and lake trout, however, because it can penetrate such fine-scaled species more easily than it can fish with heavy, thick scales such as the northern pike. Each sea lamprey will consume 40 pounds of fish blood in its lifetime. Their impacts on the Lake Champlain fisheries are enormous.

Prior to the efforts of Vermont and New York agencies to re-establish land-locked salmon and lake trout in Lake Champlain, the lamprey was not much of a problem. When the salmon and trout were stocked in the lake, however, the lamprey population suddenly increased because more host fish were available.

The lamprey has a curious life cycle. It spawns in tributary streams. What hatches from the egg is a little wiggly thing called an ammocoete. The ammocoete buries itself in the sand and feeds by filtering microscopic organisms out of the water. Eventually the ammocoete metamorphoses, grows eyes, leaves the sand, becomes parasitic and then attaches itself to a host fish. The lamprey control program, which began in 1990, is aimed at reducing the numbers of ammocoetes produced in Lake Champlain tributaries.

Lampricide programs involve placing toxic material in the stream. Although scientific evidence supports the claim that the damage to the river ecology is minimal, some people are concerned that placing toxins in the streams is not an acceptable risk. Other nonchemical methods of controlling lamprey populations include small barrier dams, electrical barriers and adult trapping. In general, however, the lampricide programs have popular support because of the extensive damage that lampreys have inflicted on the Lake Champlain fisheries.

THE LATEST EXOTIC: ZEBRA MUSSELS

Zebra mussels were discovered in Lake Champlain in 1993:

On July 24, 1993, 13-year-old Matt Toomey and his sister were fishing off their dock in Benson Bay in Orwell, Vermont. As Matt began to reel in what he thought to be a big fish, he recruited the help of his sister to pull up what turned out to be just an old brick. But attached to the brick was a zebra mussel, the first to be found in Lake Champlain. Matt encouraged his mother to call the Lake Champlain Hotline and report his find.

The next day, the specimen was taken to the Vermont state biology lab for identification. James Kellogg, aquatic biologist with the Vermont Department of Environmental Conservation, positively identified the specimen as a zebra mussel. Since that time, zebra mussels have been found as far north as Rouses Point.

Why are people so upset about the possible invasion of zebra mussels? To understand that, let's learn more about them!

Matt Toomey

Zebra mussels were first identified in North America in 1988 in Lake St. Clair, Michigan, near Detroit, and they have spread quickly through the interconnected waterways of North America to the Mississippi and Ohio river systems. It is believed that the zebra mussels, native to the fresh surface waters of southeastern Europe were unknowingly transported in the ballast waters of transatlantic freighters.

Biological Impacts

The specific impacts of zebra mussels in Lake Champlain are not yet known. However, because zebra mussels are not indigenous and reproduce quickly, it is feared that their population will rapidly grow out of balance with the lake ecosystem.

Zebra mussels filter-feed on phytoplankton and detritus, main elements of the aquatic food chain. If zebra mussels are present in large numbers, they could:
• alter established food chains so that the survival of some species is threatened,
• harm or kill fish and wildlife that consume zebra mussels containing high concentrations of toxic materials,
• starve or suffocate native mussels.

Exotics travel all over the world! A jellyfish, native to the east coast of the United States, found its way to the Black Sea in the ballast water of ships. It is thriving there because it has no natural predators and it is devastating the ecosystem. In 1996, the jellyfish reached an estimated mass of 900 million tons—equal to 10 times the world's annual fish catch!

*Zebra mussels are thumbnail-sized freshwater mussels whose D-shaped shells are often striped with alternating light and dark bands—similar to a zebra's. The common zebra mussel is also known by its scientific name: **Dreissena polymorpha**.*

Economic Impacts

Zebra mussels can quickly foul human-made water systems by attaching to solid, submerged surfaces and rapidly forming dense colonies. They also:
• clog water intake or outflow pipes,
• disrupt sensitive, water-dependent systems
    a) boat motors
    b) municipal water facilities
    c) industrial facilities,
• harm tourism
    a) litter beaches with sharp shells and emit a foul odor
    b) cover and therefore damage historical treasures: shipwrecks, etc.

Zebra Mussel Life Cycle

The typical zebra mussel lives 2 to 5 years on average. Despite its seemingly short life, the zebra mussel is able to multiply rapidly. In each seasonal reproductive cycle, a mature female zebra mussel can release 40 thousand to one million eggs while the mature male zebra mussel can release more than two hundred million sperm. Fertilization of the eggs occurs in the water outside of the female zebra mussels. In approximately two days, the fertilized eggs develop into free swimming larvae known as veligers. The veliger stage lasts 2 to 3 weeks. Veligers are active swimmers and they can be dispersed though the water by currents. The older veligers seek and attach to solid surfaces underwater.

Zebra mussels cling to surfaces by using thread-like strands called byssal fibers, which are tipped with a strong, sticky substance. As many as 700,000 mussels have been reported to occupy a square meter area. Once attached, zebra mussels generally remain on the solid surface but they can detach, crawl slowly and move about. It is possible for zebra mussels to be transported by "hitchhiking" on fish, crayfish, waterfowl or on vehicles such as boats, boat trailers, barges or seaplanes. Adult zebra mussels feed by filtering water and removing the available zooplankton, phytoplankton or detritus to use as a food source. A mature, thumbnail-sized zebra mussel is known to filter one liter (approximately one quart) of water each day.

Zebra Mussel Life Cycle

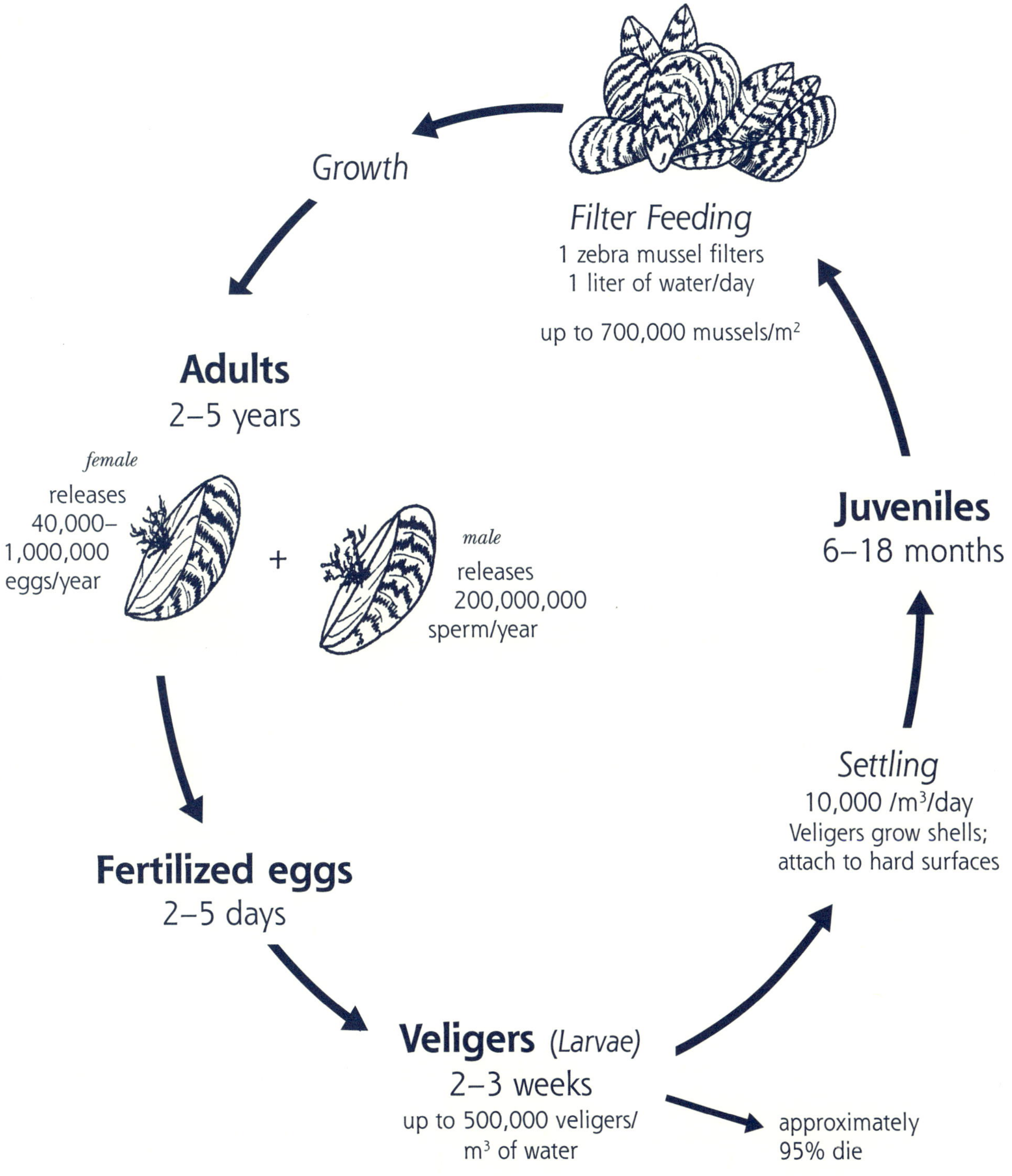

Credit: *Zebra mussel information from Lake Champlain Basin Program, "Fact Sheet Series," Number 1. Used with permission.*

Zebra Mussel Habitat

The ideal habitat for zebra mussels is directly related to the filtering mechanism that mussels use to obtain food. Zebra mussels prefer water that contains enough phosphorus to support healthy populations of phytoplankton. Because zebra mussels rely on filtering nutrient-rich water, water intake (or outflow) structures can be ideal habitats for the zebra mussel. Such structures generally provide a steady flow of water, which brings food to the mussels and removes waste. These structures also protect mussels from predators, severe weather and environmental changes.

Taking Action

- Learn to identify the zebra mussel.
- Use the Zebra Mussel WATCH Card available from Lake Champlain Basin Program. It explains how to identify a zebra mussel.
- Attend zebra mussel workshops and ongoing information sessions in Vermont and New York.
- Monitor for the presence or absence of zebra mussels.
- Collect samples of zebra mussels if you find them.
- Preserve the samples in containers filled with rubbing alcohol.
- Record the precise location of the collected sample.
- Contact the Lake Champlain Basin Program immediately at 1-800-468-LCBP.
- Educate others.

Actions for Boaters and Anglers

Anglers and recreational boaters may accidentally transport zebra mussels from infested Lake Champlain waters into other areas of the lake and to inland lakes and waterways. Mussel larvae, which are invisible to the naked eye, can be carried in boat bilge water, live in wells, bait buckets and engine cooling water systems. Juvenile and adult mussels can also attach to boat hulls, engine drive units and boat trailers.

Help prevent the spread of zebra mussels by taking a few precautionary steps after boating or fishing:
- *Inspect your boat and trailer carefully for mussels and aquatic vegetation. Remove any mussels or vegetation and discard them in the trash.*
- *Drain all water from the boat, including the bilge, live well and engine cooling system.*
- *Dry the boat and trailer in the sun for at least two days or if using your boat sooner, rinse off the boat, trailer, anchor, anchor rope and chain, bumpers, engine, etc. with tap water or at a car wash.*

The Living Treasures of the Lake Champlain Basin

Activities

Y ou will see that there are noticeably fewer activities in this section than in other chapters. There are so many activities for teaching about the natural world in other resources that we felt teachers could easily access these. (See "Key Resources" in this chapter and in *Ecology*).

I recommend reviewing some of these sources so that you can sprinkle some study of living creatures into whatever else you are doing. The world of living things is such a strong learning connection for kids that it will add fuel to any study.

Before I began teaching science, I always marveled at teachers who got their classes outdoors. It seemed like you had to know so much before you went and it took a tremendous amount of planning. Well, it does take a lot of planning but the payback is enormous. I learned that Mother Nature is a very forceful teacher and wonderful teammate. Get outside as often as you can and you will see!

QUESTIONS

- What fish and wildlife live in the Champlain Basin?
- How is their health?
- How do humans impact the lives of fish and wildlife?
- What animals are threatened or endangered?
- What is being done and what more can be done to protect these species?

KEY RESOURCES

- Vermont Fish and Wildlife Department
- New York Department of Environmental Conservation
- U. S. Fish and Wildlife Service–Lake Champlain Fish and Wildlife Resources Office—*publications and educational resources*
- Vermont Threatened and Endangered Species Education Guide—*Vermont Fish and Wildlife Department*
- The Nature of Vermont *by Charles Johnson*
- Opportunities for Action—*Lake Champlain Basin Program*
- NatureScope Series—*National Wildlife Federation*
- Project Wild—*Western Regional Environmental Education Council*
- Aquatic Project Wild—*Western Regional Environmental Education Council*
- The Original Vermonters: Native Inhabitants, Past and Present *by William Haviland and Marjory Power*
- Keepers of the Animals *by Michael Caduto and Joseph Bruchac*
- The Stokes Nature Guide Series *by Donald Stokes*

Natural History
of the Lake Champlain Basin

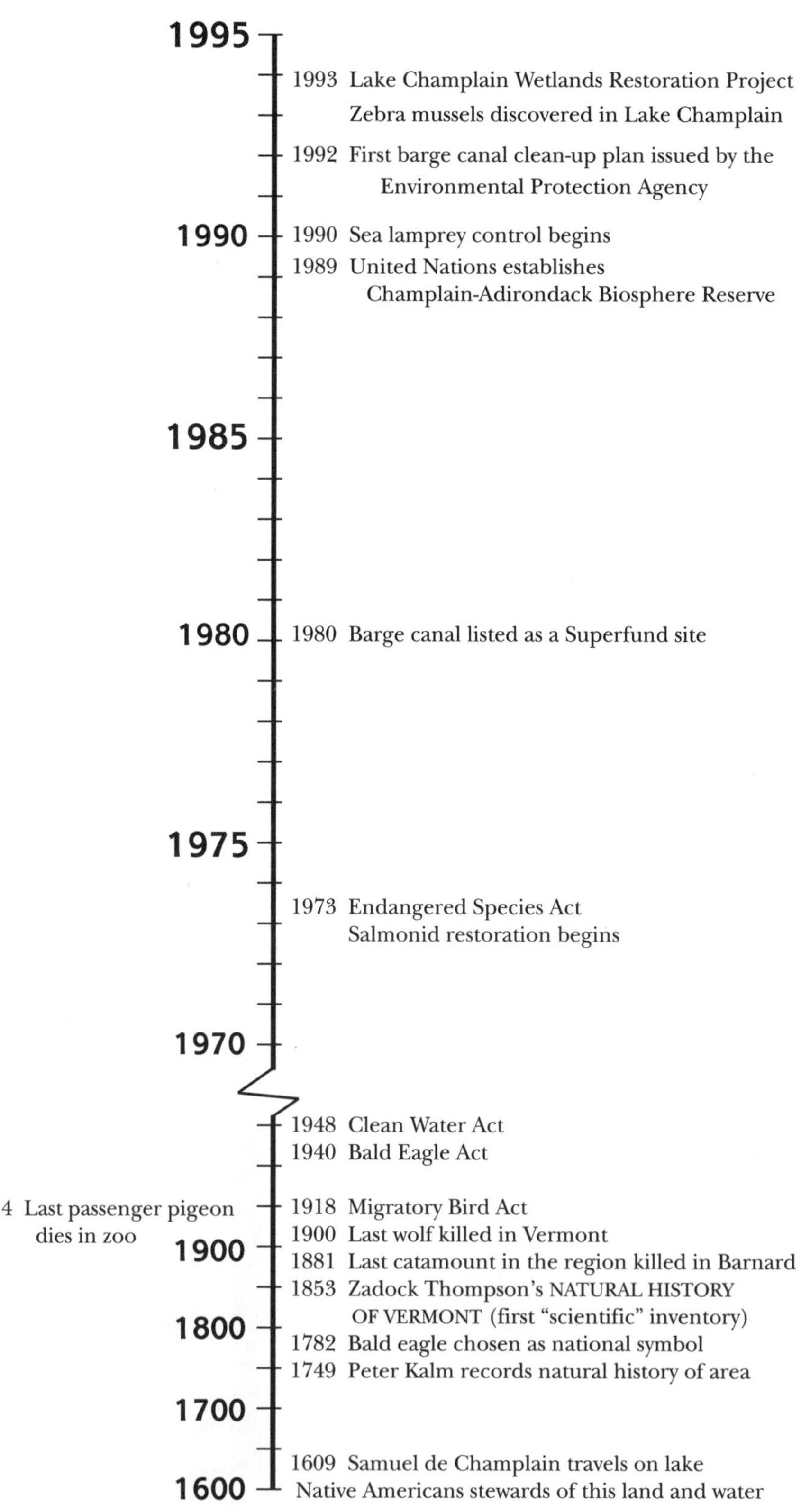

Activity: **Food Sources Calendar**

TEACHER NOTES *and* INFO

The graphic in this activity, created by Peter Thomas, shows how Native people gather food according to the seasons. This activity allows students to interpret a unique "picture chart." Interpret the chart with your class. Ask them to make true statements about traditional food gathering. For example:

- *"In May people hunted…."*
- *"In March, _________ were not hunted."*

Observe that no animals were hunted year-round. What would be the reasons for that? (*Spawning, nesting, hibernating, mating habits*)

Could such a chart be made for most students today? Some foods are eaten seasonally—but pizza is consumed year-round! What other things do we do seasonally? Discuss what parts of our lives are tied to the seasons. Discuss the technology that was used to obtain food at different times in history.

Understanding seasonal customs, which some Vermonters practice today, sheds light on the controversy between Native Americans' claim of aboriginal fishing rights and fish and wildlife laws that limit harvesting. What are the similarities and differences between the two points of view?

STUDENT ACTIVITY

Have students, individually or in groups, design a calendar. Decide whether it will be about one theme, such as sports, or an open choice. There are many ways to organize production. How you do it depends on what you want to do with the final product. You, or a creative student on the computer, will have to provide the bottom part of the calendar with the days of each month.

Ruby Thibault, of School Street School, has successfully used calendars designed by the school as fundraisers. Each of the eleven classes created one page, plus one page from the faculty. Each individual contributed a miniature pen-and-ink drawing around a common theme and these were joined together as one graphic.

You could have partners design one illustration (2 x 12 = 24) and copy all

twelve for a class project. Students could create their own during the year (starting in September with their summer memories), complete them in June, and you could assemble them over the summer (with all the money left over in your classroom activity budget!) and present them in September as a "Welcome back to school" gift! I have never done this, but I like it!

Food Sources

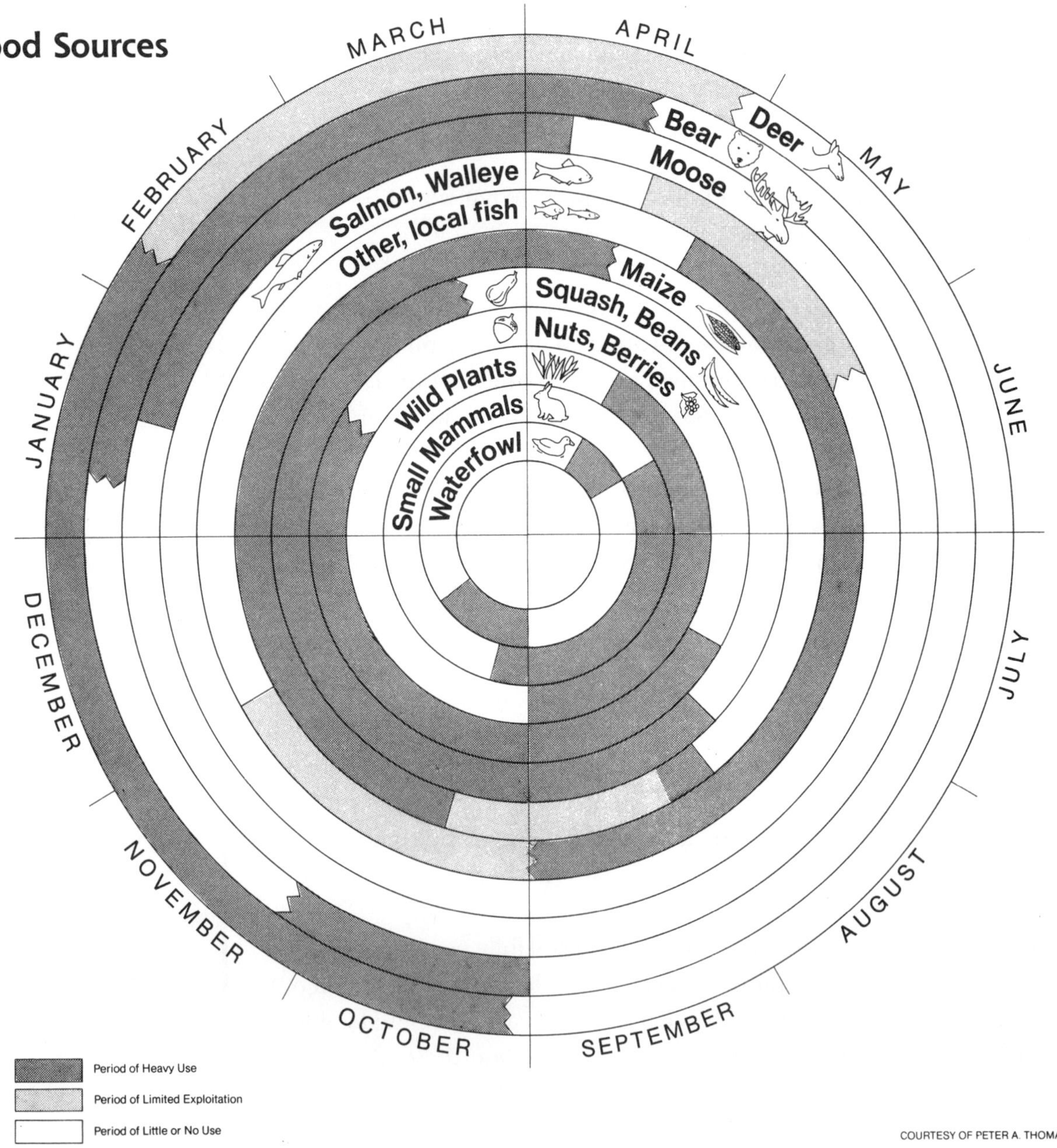

COURTESY OF PETER A. THOMAS

Activity: **Food Chain Game**

TEACHER NOTES *and* INFO

The Lake Champlain Basin harbors a wealth of interconnecting food chains called food webs. Taking a closer look at food chains helps students understand how we are all connected and how energy travels from one species to another. Students also become more aware of predator and prey relationships. Students can research their own food chain relationships to play the following game or you can utilize the one below as a model. This is an active game that requires a large open space where students can move around and be loud. (There is a lot of laughter and excited screams as predators move in on and eat their prey!)

STUDENT ACTIVITY

Designate the playing area or pond and spread the phytoplankton (popcorn) around the pond. All critters should be outside the pond at this time. While handing out the cards, explain the food chain the students represent. The caddis fly eats the phytoplankton, the minnow eats the caddis fly and the bass eats the minnow. Hand out the bags, which represent the stomachs or the place where food will be collected. Explain that the critters will enter the pond, a species at a time, with their bags to collect food.

Caddis flies enter the pond first; they must crawl on their hands and knees to collect the phytoplankton in their bags. After 20 seconds of caddis fly feeding, the minnows enter the pond. Their goal is to tag the caddis flies. The caddis flies must hop on one foot. When a caddis fly is tagged, it hands over its stomach contents to the minnow, crawls out of the pond and sits quietly along the edge to view the food chain in action. All other un-eaten caddis flies can continue to eat the phytoplankton and dodge their predators. Next enter the bass. Bass must walk heel-to-toe while in the pond as they try to tag the minnows. A tagged minnow must give its stomach contents to the bass and hop on out of the pond. Yell "freeze" after a minute of food chain action. Make observations as to who remains alive and who is sitting along the edges of the pond.

You will need:
cards for a class of 25
(with string to hang cards
around students' necks):
- 2 with a picture of a
  bass (or some other
  local carnivorous fish)
- 8 with a picture of a
  smaller fish such as a
  minnow
- 15 cards with a picture of a caddis fly larva
- popcorn to serve as
  phytoplankton
- 25 bags as "stomachs" to
  collect food

After the food chain chasing ends, discuss the following questions with students:

• Why did the game start out with more caddis flies than minnows or bass?

• What did it feel like to be tagged?

• If you wanted to extend the food chain, who would eat the bass?

• How is this game different from the real life of critters in the pond? How is it the same?

Students are great at coming up with variations to this game. Have fun!

Activity: **What Can You Do?**

TEACHER NOTES and INFO

This book offers many opportunities to discuss with students how their lifestyles affect our natural world. The information here is from the Vermont Threatened and Endangered Species Education Guide. It is a succinct summary of the many possibilities students might consider.

STUDENT ACTIVITY

Brainstorm with your students the negative and positive impacts that humans have on the natural world. Ask them to identify which impacts they might have control over. You may choose to use the handout as a reference for yourself as students create their own "guide" or hand it out and have them share it with others.

STUDENT HANDOUT - "What Can You Do?"

What Can You Do?

If you are interested in creating more good news, you may want to think about things that you can do to help the natural life of the basin. Here are some ideas from the Vermont Department of Fish and Wildlife. *You* can have an impact and save wild species from extinction.

1. Examine your lifestyle.

Habitat loss is the greatest danger to animals. Practice minimum impact. This means decrease your influence on wild species and their habitats. You can apply this to all parts of your life.

Transportation
• Walk or bike or use a bus whenever possible.

Energy consumption
• Find out what type or types of energy your family uses for heating, cooking and lighting.
• What impact does each energy source have on wild species? Think of its origins. How is it taken from the earth? How does it get to your home and does it cause pollution?
• Think of ways you can cut back on energy use in your home. Turning off the lights when you leave a room is one way to conserve energy.

Food
• Organically-grown food is more healthful for you and for wildlife. Because chemical pesticides and weed killers are not used in organic foods, chemical residues do not get into your food, the soil, the water or other animals through the food chain.
• Reduce the amount of food waste and garbage you produce by:
> - *eating everything on your plate,*
> - *avoiding the use of individually packaged foods and plastic bags,*
- *recycling egg cartons, cereal boxes, glass and plastic bottles, and aluminum cans,*
- *learning about composting food scraps so that organic wastes can be put back in the soil.*

Household Chemicals
• Find out what poisonous and hazardous chemicals you have in your home. These could include chlorine bleach, drain cleaner, cleaning chemicals, car polish, paint and paint thinner, weed killer and pesticides. If a chemical is poisonous to people, it is probably poisonous to wildlife (and vice versa!)

• Don't pour chemicals down the drain. They will eventually pollute rivers and lakes. Find out how to safely dispose of toxic chemicals.

• Learn how you can use fewer hazardous cleaning products in your home and in your school.

Recreation

• Certain sports and recreational activities have high impacts on wildlife. For example, snowmobiling in a deeryard may frighten deer.

• Examine the environmental impact of your favorite pastimes. Consider the noise, pollution, land use and energy use of each activity.

Recycling

• Recycling can benefit wildlife habitat by reducing the need for more landfills, and by reducing the need to take raw materials from the land.

• Recycle these substances: paper, glass, aluminum, copper, steel, plastic, rubber, wood, food and yard waste.

2. Get involved in government.

• Find out who your state and federal legislators are. Write letters to encourage the protection of habitat, to stop pollution and to protect endangered species. Support elected persons who support environmental protection.

• Learn how local, state and/or federal laws are passed. Find out who the people are in your area responsible for the enforcement of these laws.

• Go to town meetings and learn how you can help shape the future of your town. Support issues that will help protect habitat and insure the survival of native species.

3. Do something wild!

• Volunteer for a state or private agency that is directly working with threatened and endangered species.

• Do a report or project about an endangered or threatened species or some aspect of wildlife that interests you. Share it with a school, scout or church group.

• Feed birds during the winter.

• Set up bluebird nest boxes at home or at school.

• Set aside some land for wildlife habitat on your property.

Activity: Lake Champlain Yellow Perch Problem

TEACHER NOTES *and* INFO

Explain the simulation to the class.

STUDENT ACTIVITY

You are a fish biologist working for the Vermont Department of Fish and Wildlife.   One of the tools you use to gain information to manage a lake fishery is the creel survey. Creel surveys are designed to obtain estimates of fishing pressure, the amount of fish harvested from a body of water, and other items of interest. A creel survey is done by going out on the lake at predetermined time periods, and counting and talking to anglers. You ask them what they are fishing for, what they have caught, and how long they have been fishing. If they have fish, you might measure them and take a fish scale off each. Fish scales, when studied under a microscope, will show the age of the fish.

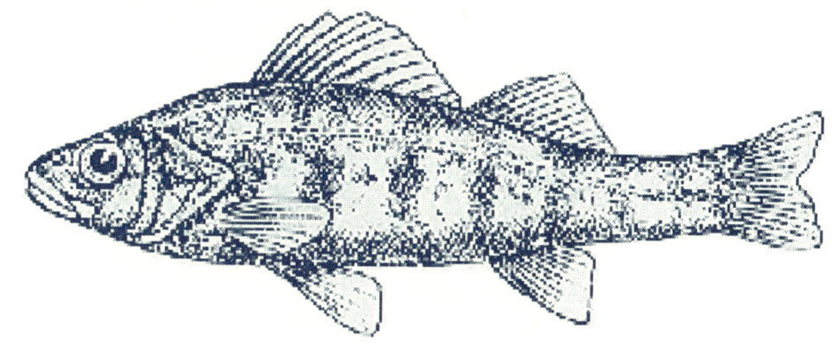

While doing a survey in the northern part of Lake Champlain, you hear complaints that the perch fishing has declined. The anglers tell you:

> *"All I catch are small perch."*
> *"People are overharvesting the perch; they're taking all the big ones."*
> *"We need to put a limit on the numbers of perch you can keep in a day."*
> *"There needs to be a length limit to protect the small perch."*

You, the fish biologist, head back to your laboratory to determine what the problem is and how to solve it. After analyzing your angler count and interview data, you find that:

1. The estimated perch harvest is high.

2. Catch rates (the number of fish caught per hour of fishing) are also high here, compared to other areas of the lake.

Nick Staats visits School Street School

Credit: *Activity from Nick Staats, Fish Biologist, U.S. Fish and Wildlife Service. Used with permission.*

After analyzing the perch scales you collected and fish lengths, you find:

3. The perch vary in age from four to eight years old.

4. The size of the perch for each age differs only a little. (In other words, they are growing slowly.) For example, seven-year-old perch are not much bigger than six-year-old perch.

As a scientist, you have learned from other scientific studies that:

1. As fish populations become more abundant, competition for food increases, which tends to cause them to grow slowly.

2. Overharvested fish populations have good or fast growth rates. This is because there are less fish competing for the same food source.

3. When perch populations are overharvested, there will be more younger fish (two-to-four-year-olds). This is because when there are fewer perch, they mature earlier to reproduce more fish.

4. Walleye fish eat perch and the walleye population has declined.

5. Perch feed on minnows, which feed on small water animals that survive on the nutrients in the water. People have been trying very hard to clean up the lake's water by reducing the amount of nutrients entering the lake.

Compare this information with what you have found out about the perch in northern Lake Champlain. What can you determine is going on with that population?

• Are the perch being overharvested?
• Would putting a limit on the number of fish you can catch in a day help solve the "problem"?
• Would a length limit help?
• Do you create a new perch-fishing regulation to satisfy the anglers even when it may or may not help the perch?
• Could the walleye population have an effect on the perch?
• Could the amount of nutrients entering the lake have an effect on the perch?

You realize now that the perch problem is more complicated. It may not be solved in a week, year, or even five years. What you do know is that there are anglers disappointed about the perch fishing and want something done—now. What will you do?

Activity:
Zebra Mussel Information

TEACHER NOTES *and* INFO

There is a wealth of information available on the zebra messel—the current "villain" in the story of Lake Champlain. The Lake Champlain Basin Program has generated a lot of information in recent years. There is also material available from the Great Lakes region. The story of how an exotic affects an ecosystem is a fascinating one to explore with children. The story of the zebra mussel is so current and important that discussion takes on a special significance. Students must understand a great deal about the life cycle of a zebra mussel in order to comprehend the impact it can have. For example, the juvenile—called a veliger—is microscopic and cannot be stopped by conventional screens or barriers.

As the story unravels, students engage in higher level thinking:
• What will happen to the native mussel population?
• What if the native mussels were put in a "zoo" to be protected until we solve the problem?
• What if veligers from the water in the fish hatchery are transported to all the small lakes in Vermont?

STUDENT ACTIVITY

Read the essay section, "The Latest Exotic: Zebra Mussels" (p. 387–390). Complete the worksheet after reading the information.

STUDENT HANDOUT - "Zebra Mussel Worksheet"

Taking It Home

Design with your students a system to share information with family and friends.

The process could be posted as an exponential math problem: If one student tells two people and each person agrees to tell two people how many people will your class have informed? How many could they inform if every person who was told, told another?

Zebra Mussel Worksheet

1. Describe what a zebra mussel looks like.

2. Zebra mussels were first found in 19 ___ in St. Clair, _______________ .

3. How did zebra mussels come to North America?

4. The scientific name for zebra mussel is: _______________ _______________.

5. What are the potential **biological** impacts of the zebra mussel?
   A. alter _______________ _______________
   B. harm or kill _______________ and _____ _______________
   C. starve or suffocate _________ _______________

6. What are the potential **economic** impacts of the zebra mussel?
   A. clog _______________ or _______________ pipes
   B. disrupt systems that need water:
      a. _______________________________
      b. _______________________________
      c. _______________________________
   C. harm _______________________

7. Please draw the life cycle of a zebra mussel—with labels!

8. Write short meanings for these words:
   A. **indigenous** _______________________________________
   B. **plankton** ____
   C. **veliger** ____
   D. **detritus** ____

9. What are three things you can do to protect our lake from zebra mussels?

Answers: 1. *answers will vary,* **2.** 1988, Michigan, **3.** ballast of ships from Europe, **4.** Dreissena polymorpha, **5A.** food chains, **5B.** fish, wildlife, **5C.** native mussels, **6A.** intake, outflow, **6Ba.** boat motors, **6Bb.** municipal water facilities, **6Bc.** industrial facilities, **6C.** tourism, **7.** *answers will vary,* **8A.** native, **8B.** microscopic plant growth, **8C.** microscopic young zebra mussels, **8D.** base of food chains, **9.** *answers will vary.*

Rubies Pearls

Activity: Fish Prints

YOU WILL NEED:
- the total body of a fish that doesn't move; if it is
  frozen dry it off with a paper towel. Frozen fish are best.
- speedball printing ink
- styrofoam meat trays (washed and disinfected)
- soft sponge brayer (available from an art supply catalog)
- newsprint or thin drawing paper (thin copy paper is good)

brayer

STUDENT ACTIVITY
1. Place two tablespoons of printing ink in a styrofoam tray.
2. Roll ink all over the inside of a tray with the soft sponge brayer. This will place a nice thin coat of ink on the sponge roll. When the ink covers the roll with a nice layer, it is *ready*.
3. Take the brayer and roll up, down, and side-to-side, *all over* the fish. When a nice thin layer of ink covers the textured body, you are ready to print.
4. Place newsprint paper over the fish—try to hold still. Rub on top of the paper—gently but firmly.
5. Pull off the paper: You have a great print! You can take two prints before you need to re-ink the fish with the brayer.

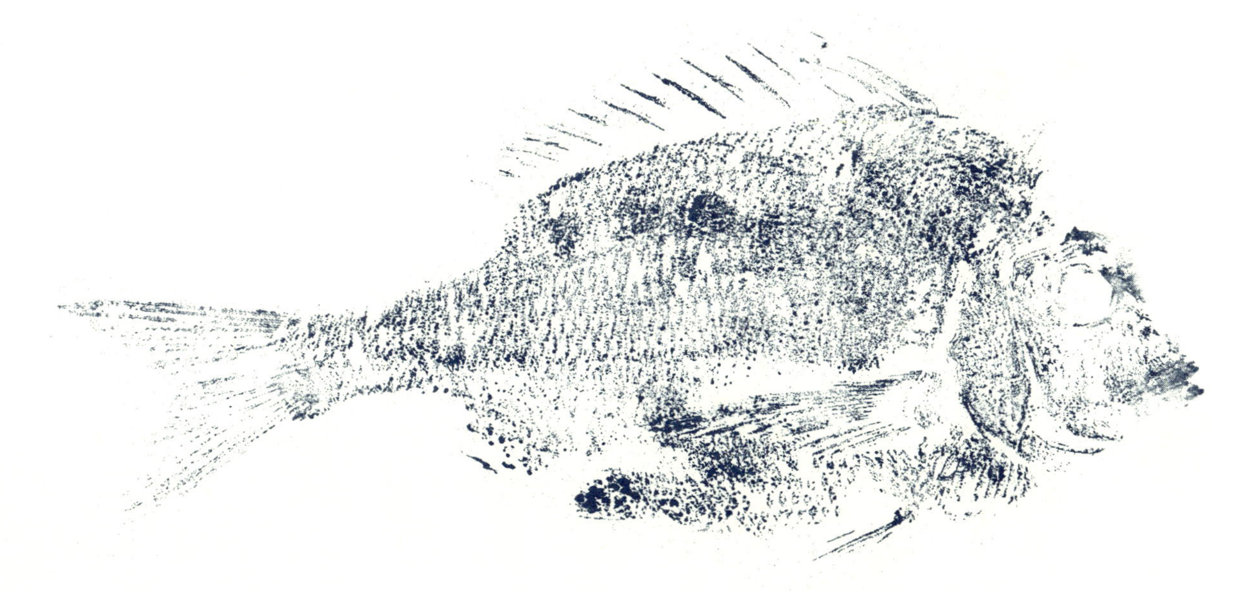

Koluscap and the Water Monster

as told by Joseph Bruchac

Once there was a great drought. The rain stopped falling and the Earth became dry. Finally the streams themselves stopped flowing. There was a village of people who lived by the side of the stream, and life became very hard for them. They sent someone upstream to see why the stream had stopped. Before long, the man came back.

"There is a dam across the stream," he said. "It is holding back all the water. There are guards on the dam. They say their chief is keeping all the water for himself."

"Go and beg him for water," said the elders of the village. "Tell him we are dying without water to drink." So the messenger went back again. When he returned, he held a bark cup filled with mud.

"This is all the water their chief will allow us to have," he said.

Now the people were angry. They decided to fight. They sent a party of warriors to destroy the dam. But as soon as the warriors came to the dam, a great monster rose out of the water. His mouth was big enough to swallow a moose. His belly was huge and yellow. He grabbed the warriors and crushed them in his long fingers, which were like the roots of cedar trees. Only one warrior escaped to come back to the people and tell them what happened.

"We cannot fight a monster," the people said. They were not sure what to do. Then one of the old chiefs spoke. "We must pray to Gitchee Manitou," he said. "Perhaps he will pity us and send help." Then they burned tobacco and sent their prayers up to the Creator.

Their prayers were heard. The Gitchee Manitou looked down and saw the people were in great trouble. He decided to take pity and help them and he called Koluscap. "Go and help the people," Gitchee Manitou said.

Koluscap then went down to the Earth. He took the shape of a tall warrior, head and shoulders taller than any of the people. Half of his face was painted black and half was painted white. A great eagle perched on his right shoulder and by his side two wolves walked as his dogs, a black wolf and a white wolf. As soon as the people saw him they welcomed him. They thought surely he was someone sent by the Creator to help them.

"We cannot afford you anything to drink," they said. "All the water in the world is kept by the monster and his dam."

"Where is the monster?" Koluscap said, swinging his war club, which was made of the root of a birch tree.

"Up the dry stream bed," they said.

So Koluscap walked up the dry stream bed. As he walked he saw dried-up fish and turtles and other water animals. Soon he came to the dam, which stretched between two hills.

"I have come for water," he said to the guards on top of the dam.

"GIVE HIM NONE, GIVE HIM NONE!" said a big voice from the other side of the dam. So the guards did not give him water.

Again Koluscap asked and again the big voice answered. Four times he made his request, and on the fourth request, Koluscap was thrown a bark cup half full of filthy water.

Then Koluscap grew angry. He stomped his foot and the dam began to crack. He stomped his foot again and he began to grow taller and taller. Now Koluscap was taller than the dam, taller even than the monster who sat in the deep water. Koluscap's club was now bigger than a great pine tree. He struck the dam with his club and the dam burst open and the water flowed out. Then he reached down and grabbed the water monster. It tried to fight back, but Koluscap was too powerful. With one giant hand, Koluscap squeezed the water monster and its eyes bulged out and its back grew bent. He rubbed it with his other hand and it grew smaller.

"Now," Koluscap said, "no longer will you keep others from having water. Now you'll just be a bullfrog. But I will take pity on you and you can live in this water from now on." Then Koluscap threw the water monster back into the stream. To this day, even though he hides from everyone because Koluscap frightened him so much, you may still hear the bullfrog saying, "Give him none, Give him none."

The water flowed past the village. Some of the people were so happy to see the water that they jumped into the stream. They dove so deep and stayed in so long that they became fish and water creatures themselves. They still live in that river today, sharing the water, which no one person can ever own.

The Ecology of the Lake Champlain Basin

Zebra Mussel Attack

by Stephanie Bushey, Grade 5, School Street School, Milton, Vermont

Hi. My name is Karen. My brother and I are going to the beach. Daddy is going to bring us. We begged him. It's a beautiful day so he said yes!

"Karen! Tommy! Come on! We're not staying there all day," Daddy yelled.

So we ran downstairs and went outside and got in the car.

On the way there, Tommy and I played copy cat. When we got there, Daddy said, "Oh man."

Karen said "What?"

"It's closed!" my dad said. He got out of the car and read this sign. Then he came back.

Karen said, "What is it?"

"Zebra mussels are everywhere on the beach," he said.

"What are they?" Tommy said.

On the way home, Daddy explained what they are. He didn't seem to even care what the mussels were doing.

So when we got home I said I was going to the library. I had heard about them before in school. I know that they cluster together and stick to things. And are shaped like a D. But nobody thought they would get this bad in Lake Champlain.

When I got there I got some books on zebra mussels. I sat down and started reading. I looked for the section on how to get rid of them. I found out there's an acid that gets rid of them in pipes. And some kind of chemical that you can put in the water. But it harms other animals. There's one thing they could do but it cost so much money. It's a certain thing you can put in the water and they will die. And it doesn't harm other animals.

So when I got home I explained to my parents about it. They said, "We should start a club and do fundraisers."

So they got a group of people together. So the club started having fundraisers and yard sales and car washes. We also put allowance money in. The club did so much work.

One night Karen, Tommy and their parents counted up all the money. They had 500 dollars. They needed 700 more. So Karen's mom said, "We should go to the state!"

So the next morning the whole club went to the state. They explained about their problem.

The state said, "Well, if you care this much for the lake, well then yes."

So they ended up doing the treatment. The next time Karen and Tommy went to the beach it wasn't closed.

THE END

P.S. You should have learned that zebra mussels are a problem and they're getting worse. So something needs to be done.

Introduction

The Lake Champlain Basin is truly a rich and wonderful resource. This chapter is designed to take you through the ecology of the basin one drop at a time, starting with "Water as a Universal" to "Water Naturally," then exploring issues of "Human Impact." From the bottom of Lake Champlain to the tops of the Green and Adirondack Mountains, there is an amazing variety of habitats containing numerous complex interrelationships that you can explore with your students.

The ecology of the basin is a huge topic. As Judy Elson and I began to write this chapter, we felt as if we were trying to unravel a ball of yarn. Where was the beginning of the story and how could we lay it out in relatively simple terms so it would be useful to science and non-science teachers? Tom Hudspeth and Bill Romond had some initial conversations with us that helped us begin to unravel the yarn. Tom advised us to "define water, say how it behaves in the natural world and then describe what happens when humans interact with it." This became the framework for the three sections in this chapter.

However you structure the ecology portion of your study, you will soon discover, if you haven't already, that using real data with kids and exploring the natural world with them is a free ticket to meaningful learning—and besides that it is really fun!

Tom Hudspeth, Bill Romond and Pat Straughan reviewed this chapter. Fred Magdoff and Nancy Bazilchuck wrote short articles.

The Ecology of the Lake Champlain Basin

WATER AS A UNIVERSAL

Just look around you. Water is everywhere! It might be raining, or you might be having a glass of juice. Perhaps your town is covered with a blanket of snow, or you can see a sunset sparkle on a nearby lake or river. How does this water move? Where does our water come from? Contemplate the adventures of a water droplet!

A single droplet of water may evaporate from Lake Champlain, travel in a cloud over the Atlantic Ocean and precipitate as rain in a reservoir in France. The local town in France gets its drinking water from that reservoir. That same droplet is taken from the reservoir and sucked into a water pipe heading for the town. It is forced out of a faucet into a dog dish and slurped up by a French poodle, Pierre! What happens next? You can continue this story for as long as you like, but it is a story without an ending. The water droplet cycles around the earth forever and ever!

WATER *is* EVERYWHERE!

Welcome to the water planet! Water, this life-giving resource, covers about 70% of the earth's surface. Does all this water look, feel and smell the same? Absolutely not. Water takes many different forms on this planet:

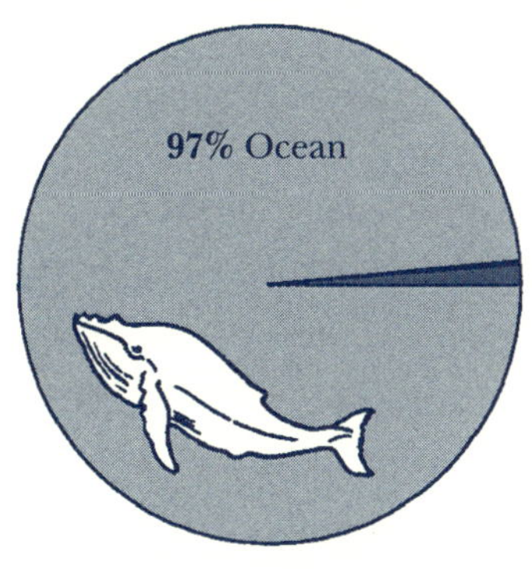

0.003% Fresh water available to living things
(*streams, lakes, groundwater, soil moisture, water vapor*)

2.997% Fresh water unavailable to humans
(*glaciers, water too far below earth's surface*)

Water makes up part of every living thing on earth. It is part of many nonliving things, too. Your body may contain as much as 70% water. A loaf of bread contains as much as 35% water! Stop for a moment and look around you. Count how many things you can find that have water in them, need water to be alive, or used to have water in them. Water is everywhere!

Many living things can use salt water to survive, but others, like humans, freshwater fish and most plants, need water with low amounts of salt (fresh water) to survive.

What is a hydrologist?
The prefix "hydro" means water. The suffix "logy" means to study. Put the two together and you've got a person who studies water—a hydrologist.

WATER *has* MANY FORMS!

Water in all its forms—as a puddle, as part of a plant or absorbed in a paper towel—behaves like no other substance. A water molecule is formed when two atoms of the gas called hydrogen join one atom of the gas oxygen. Covalent bonds join the atoms within each molecule of water. A covalent bond simply means that atoms share electrons. Together, these two gases make a molecule called water—also known as H_2O. A water molecule has a strong pull, or attraction for other molecules. This attraction is why water mixes so well with other substances—including pollutants!

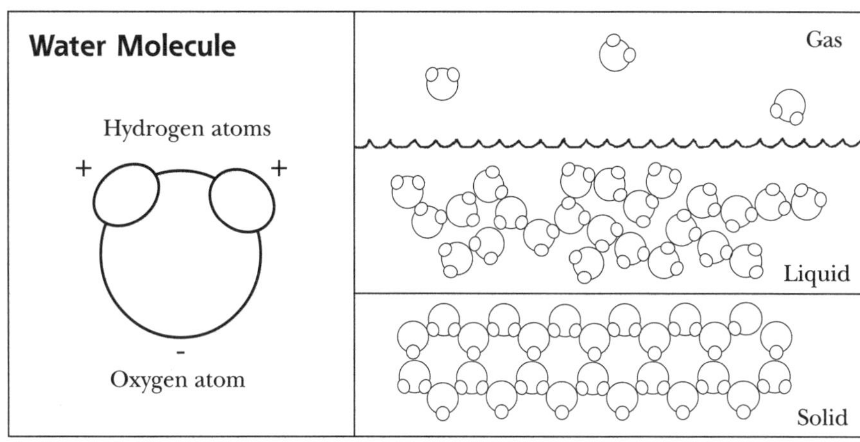

Water has a few other intriguing properties.
• Water can transform from a solid to a liquid to a gas.
• Some aquatic insects can walk on the tense skin of the water's surface.
• Many substances dissolve completely in water. Water is called a universal solvent!
• Water becomes less dense when it becomes a solid (ice).

THE WATER CYCLE!

Water circulates around the earth as the main component of the "hydrologic," or water cycle. Some parts of the world have more water than others. Although water may gush from your faucet, we can't assume there's an endless supply. Why? Go to the faucet and slurp down a handful of water. That gulp may have been the same water the dinosaurs used, and the same water that your grandchildren will use. Water is a precious and limited resource.

When water comes in contact with dry air, it evaporates from lakes and other bodies of water to form water vapor. This vapor can remain a gas, contributing to humidity in the atmosphere, or it can cool and condense to form water droplets. Moisture is carried into the basin in air masses from other regions. As the air cools, it holds less water and the excess moisture falls as rain, snow or fog. This is called precipitation. Precipitation falls on the land and returns to the lake as surface runoff. It can also infiltrate the soil and be taken up by plants or become groundwater. Groundwater is water stored under the earth's surface in underground reservoirs or aquifers. As water moves into the soil (infiltration) and through the soil (percolation), it can be purified.

WATER NATURALLY

GO *with the* FLOW!

We live in a watershed. If we could walk around the whole Lake Champlain Basin and attach a string to all the highest points as we went, the string would mark the outline of the watershed. All the water that fell within the string would end up in Lake Champlain. Any water that fell outside the string would contribute to another watershed such as the Connecticut River Basin.

A watershed is all the land that contributes water to a lake, a pond, a river or a wetland. Another term for a watershed is a drainage basin. The Lake Champlain Basin drains about 8,234 square miles of land. 56% of this land is part of Vermont, 37% of this land is part of New York and 7% of this land is part of Quebec. The Lake Champlain Basin is made up of a series of smaller watersheds or sub-basins.

When water falls from the sky and onto an area of land, it seeks the lowest point and may eventually end up in the bottom of its watershed, which in our area is Lake Champlain. For example, let's say a drop of rain falls into Upper

Gravity is the force of attraction between matter in proportion to its mass. Gravity is the force that holds us on the ground and holds the Moon in orbit around the Earth.

How does Lake Champlain compare with other lakes of the world? Locate these three lake regions on a world map.

• *Lake Baikal in Russia contains the world's largest volume of fresh water. It is also the world's deepest body of fresh water, measuring 5,315 feet (700 kilometers). The lake is home to approximately 1,700 species of plants and animals, 1,200 of which are not found anywhere else on earth.*

• *Lake Hozgol in Mongolia is perhaps the second oldest lake in the world and is still in pristine condition. This lake has never been commercially fished or the surrounding area logged. The lake is clear enough to see fish 30 feet below the surface.*

• *The Great Lakes are made up of five interconnected lakes that contain at least 20% of the world's fresh water. Approximately 26 million people drink this water. About 40% of U.S. industry and 50% of Canada's industry is in the Great Lakes watershed.*

Ausable Lake in St. Huberts, New York. If that drop of water stays in liquid form, it will flow down to the Lower Ausable Lake, then into the Ausable River, and eventually will flow into Lake Champlain at the mouth of the Ausable River in Port Kent, New York. The force of gravity causes the water to find the lowest point!

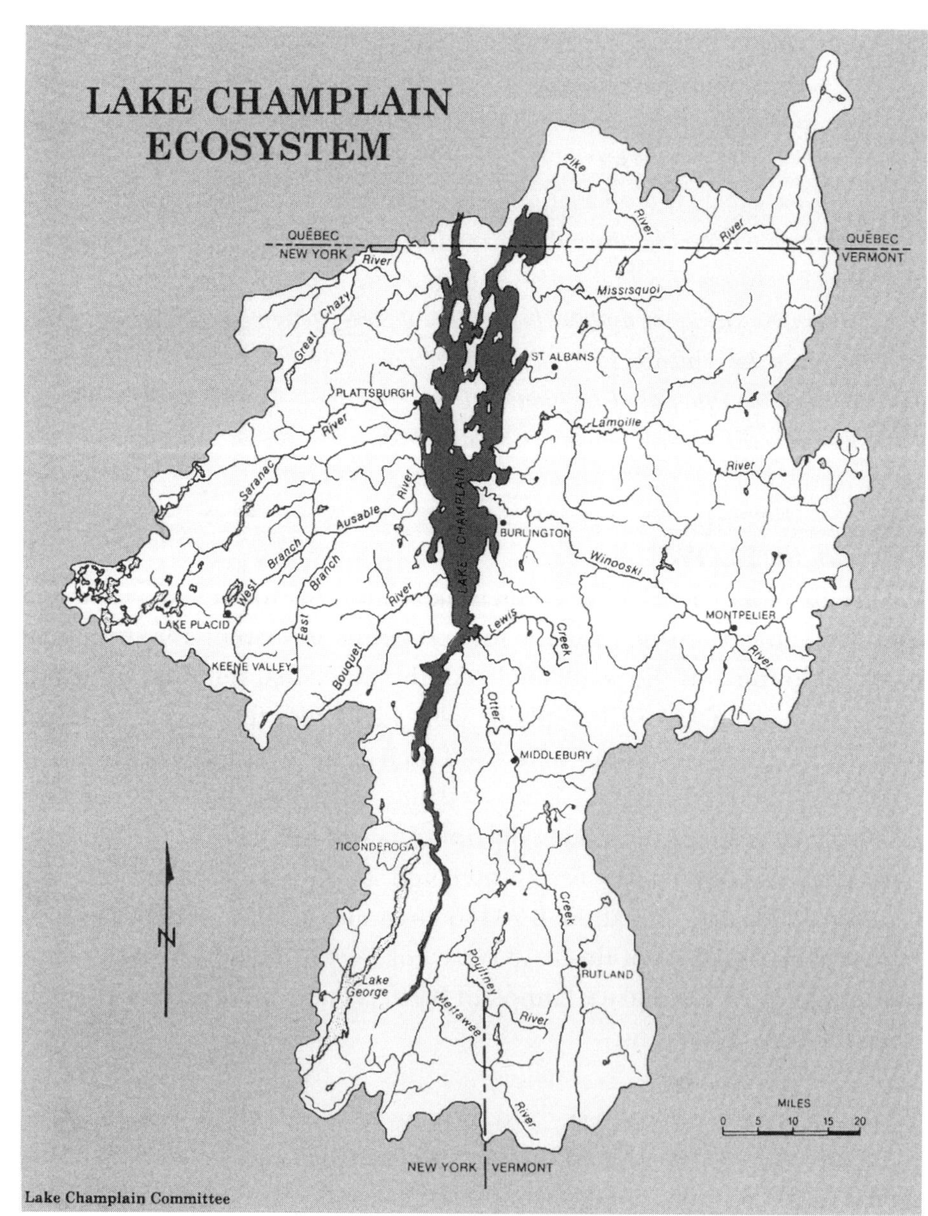

GEOGRAPHY *of* LAKE CHAMPLAIN

Lake Champlain is one of the largest freshwater lakes in North America. We are fortunate to have such a beautiful and valuable resource in our backyard. It is 120 miles long, starting near Whitehall, New York, and flows north to Ash Island, Quebec, where it drains into the Richelieu River. It is a narrow lake, only 12 miles across at its widest part, and it has over 70 islands. The average depth of the lake is 64 feet, but some parts are 400 feet deep. Lake Champlain is bordered by mountains on both sides—the Adirondacks on the west and the Green Mountains on the east.

Only 10% of the water that reaches Lake Champlain falls into the lake directly; the other 90% of the water flows through the watershed first.

Due to the shape and size of Lake Champlain, it is divided into five distinct areas or lake segments. Each segment has different physical and chemical characteristics:

• **Missisquoi Bay** is very shallow with warm water. Water flow in and out of the bay is very slow.

• **South Lake** is a very narrow and shallow section of the lake and acts much like a river.

• **Main Lake** holds 81% of all the water in the lake. This includes some of the deepest and coldest water in the entire lake.

• **Mallett's Bay** is the smallest of the five segments. Bordered by causeways on the north and west, this section of the lake has very poor water circulation.

• **The Inland Sea** has water flowing south from Missisquoi Bay and north from Mallett's Bay. From here the water flows past the many islands in the Inland Sea through the Gut and Alburg Passage.

Most of the water that flows into Lake Champlain comes from 12 major rivers. Five of these rivers are on the Vermont side. They are from north to south: the Missisquoi, the Lamoille, the Winooski, the LaPlatte, Otter Creek, and the Poultney/Metawee River. On the New York side the lake is fed by the Great Chazy, the Saranac, the Ausable, the Boquet and Lake George. Rivers and streams that flow into a larger body of water are called tributaries.

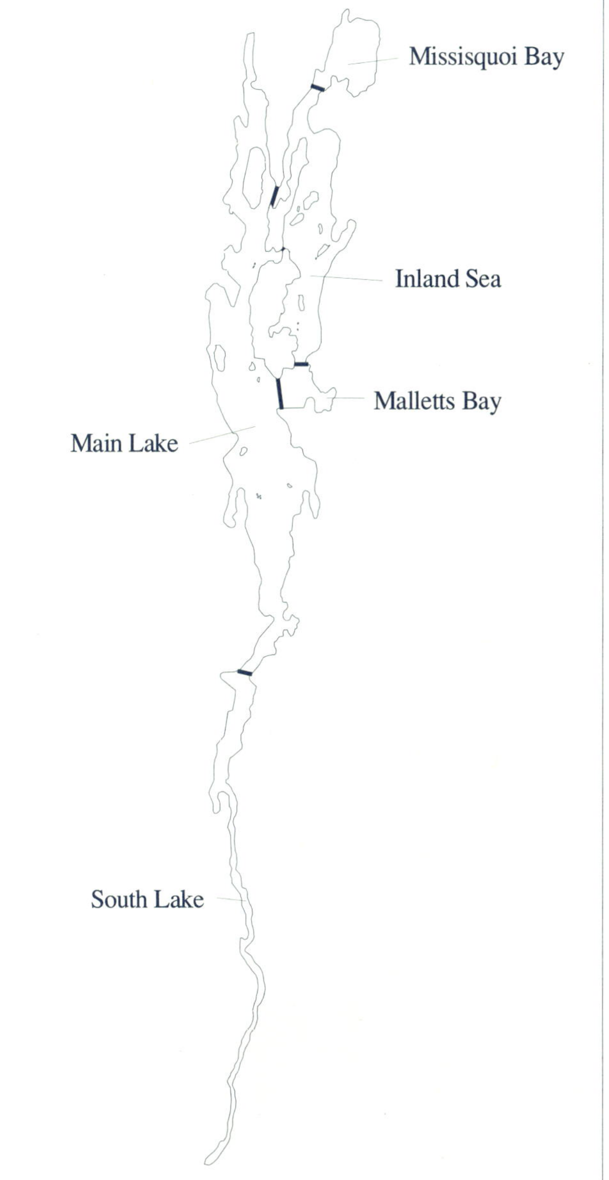

Riparian refers to the area near a stream and can refer to plants, animals or soils that are connected to the stream or riverside.

These fast- or slow-moving and meandering bodies of water we call rivers, brooks and streams are also known as lotic waters. Lotic means "washed." On the other hand, lentic waters are the calm waters such as ponds, lakes, swamps, marshes and bogs. Lenis means "calm."

RIVERS *and* STREAMS

Streams and rivers are home to many plants and animals. Along the edges of the stream, you may discover riparian vegetation such as willows, alders, ferns, liverworts and water plantain. Otters, muskrat, moose and maybe a black bear might come to feed and drink along the shore. While exploring a river, you may discover a mayfly nymph, crayfish or the various forms of algae. All these forms of life make up the ecology of rivers and streams.

The Lake Champlain Basin can be viewed as a network of rivers, brooks and streams. Every river is part of a larger system, which includes all of the other rivers, streams and brooks that contribute to it. Rivers generally go through three phases as they flow downward from the mountain tops, as shown below.

Rivers and streams, although very similar, also have marked differences. The table on the following page shows how the two environments can be different from one another.

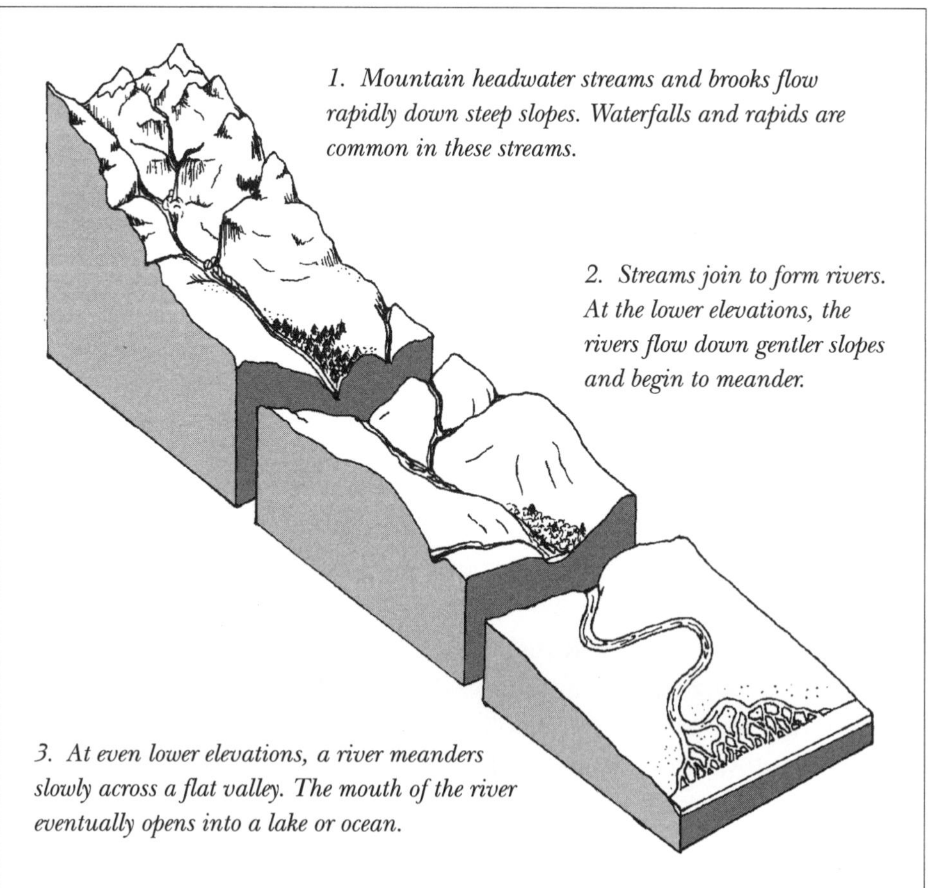

<table>
<tr><td>

STREAM ENVIRONMENT

- *Cooler water throughout the stream*

- *Good amounts of dissolved oxygen in the water*
- *Normally clear water*
- *Narrow channel*
- *Shallow*
- *Gravel or rock bottom*
- *Swiftly flows in v-shaped valleys in a series of riffles, pools and runs*
- *Fully shaded by stream bank vegetation*

- *Water level may fluctuate greatly*

</td><td>

RIVER ENVIRONMENT

- *Warmer water, can even see some thermal stratification like in a lake*
- *Good amounts of dissolved oxygen*

- *Water can be turbid or cloudy, murky*
- *Broad meandering channel*
- *Shallow to deep*
- *Muddy, silty, sandy or clay bottom*
- *Swiftly or slowly flows or meanders in u-shaped valleys*
- *Only shaded by stream bank vegetation along the edges of the river. The middle of the river is unshaded.*
- *Water level is more stable*

</td></tr>
</table>

Rivers and streams tend to be rich environments with a diversity of life. They frequently contain a lot of dissolved oxygen due to the constant movement of water. There may also be a large supply of nutrients for many different organisms. Nutrients enter the streams and rivers in many different ways:

- by plant matter falling into the water from overhanging trees and shrubs,
- by dead plants and animals washing downstream, settling into a pool and decomposing,
- from phytoplankton (small aquatic plants) drifting in the sunny upper levels of the river or stream,
- from flooding—when large amounts of water are washed into the rivers and streams (nitrates),
- by being attached to eroding soil particles (phosphorus).

LIVING THINGS DEPEND *on* CLEAN RIVERS *and* STREAMS

Many species depend on varying levels of oxygen and nutrients to survive in streams and rivers. For example, a stonefly nymph prefers to live in a stream with good water quality—high in oxygen, just the right amount of nutrients and a fairly fast flow rate, or velocity. A midge larva, on the other hand, can tolerate poor water quality—lower levels of oxygen, many nutrients, and a slow water velocity. Scientists study these macroinvertebrates to determine the water quality in streams and rivers. If a scientist finds only those species that tolerate poor water quality then there may be a pollution problem.

damselfly nymph

Artwork by Jodi McQuillen, Grade 6, South Burlington

Macroinvertebrates are invertebrates you can see with the naked eye.

A larva is the immature stage of development in animals that go through complete metamorphosis. Larvae usually look very different from the adult. A nymph is the immature stage of development in animals that go through incomplete metamorphosis. Nymphs look very similar to the adult.

LAKE CHAMPLAIN *through the* SEASONS—
A YEAR *in the* LIFE *of a* LAKE

Nature controls the many changes in Lake Champlain. The changing seasons bring variations in temperature, winds, and forms and amount of precipitation. These factors all affect the movement and amount of water in the lake.

The water in a lake is always changing. Although the water in Lake Champlain naturally flows from south to north, there are many other factors that control the movement of water within the lake.

The water in the lake has different temperatures at different times of the year. Spring graciously brings warmer weather, and the sun heats the surface of the lake while the deeper parts of the lake stay cool. This layering of the lake is called lake stratification.

Imagine the lake as being a huge cake. The warmer surface water of the lake is less dense than the cold water. Therefore, the warmer water floats on top of the cold water, forming the top layer of the cake known as the epilimnion. Below this layer, there is a thinner layer called the metalimnion (the icing between the two cake layers) which separates the warm water on top from the cold water below. The bottom layer of the cake is called the hypolimnion. This water is very cold and still.

When the water moves, so do all the things suspended in the water, such as microscopic plants and animals. The movement of the water re-supplies parts of the lake with nutrients and oxygen for aquatic species. This helps to balance the system and keep the lake healthy.

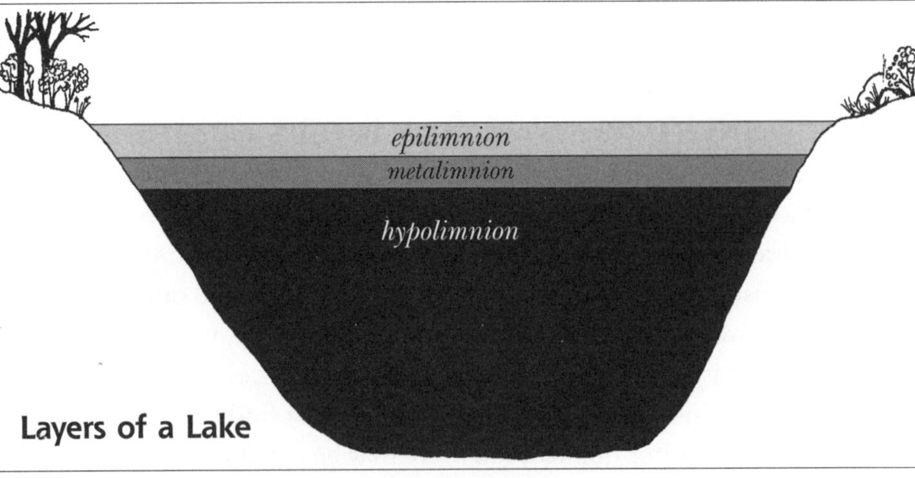

SPRING

Spring brings warmer temperatures. The warm weather begins to melt the snow on land. Every spring the water level of the lake rises due to the melting snow and the spring rains. These changes cause the water level to be highest during the spring and early summer. Stones, silt and other debris (logs, solid waste, organic matter, chemicals and manure, to name a few) are washed into the lake by this new rush of water. The height of the lake can vary about six feet during this time of year.

The changes in water level can be seen as good or bad, depending on whether you are a person or a fish! Many fish depend on the changing water levels to survive. Annual flooding in the spring replenishes and nourishes the wetlands, which provide fish spawning habitat. But when the lake floods, there can be stormy, high winds and shoreline erosion. Flooding often occurs where development along the shoreline has damaged soil, altered wetlands or destroyed vegetation—all things that nature provided to protect shorelines from natural flooding. Excessive erosion causes the water to become murky with silts and sands, making it hard for some aquatic species to survive.

SUMMER

As spring slowly gives way to summer, the lake's layers become more defined. Changing wind speeds and directions control an internal wave called a seiche. This wave is continually active from early spring to late fall. For example, a strong north wind may blow for a few days pushing some of the warm surface water (epilimnion)

down to the southern part of the lake. At the same time, this wind action pushes the colder, deep water to the north end of the lake. When the wind stops, there is no longer any force keeping the water piled up on the southern section of the lake, and it moves back north. Natural momentum allows the water to oscillate back and forth, forming the internal seiche or wave. This sloshing motion can cause mixing of the water and sands and silts.

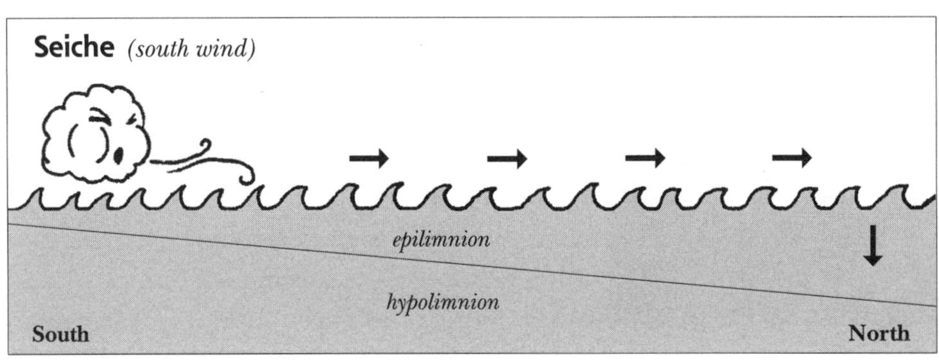

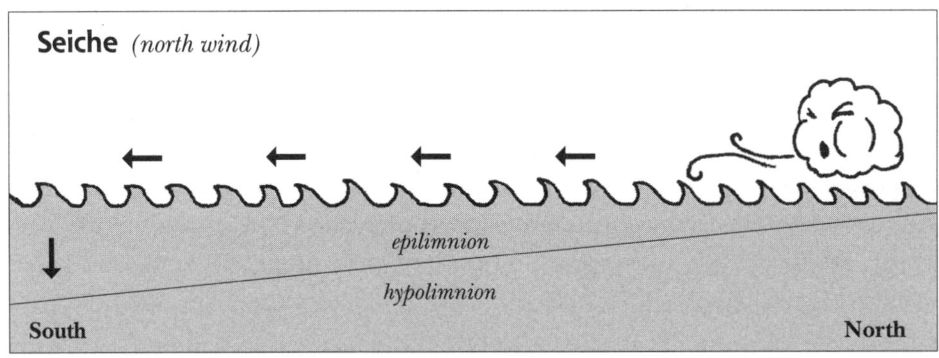

Because it rains more in the summer, you'd think that the lake level would rise. In fact, lake levels are lower in the summer. Because it is warmer, more water evaporates from the surface of the lake. Also, plants are growing on the land and they consume a lot of the water that would have drained into the lake. As the soils dry out in the summer, they hold more water after a rainstorm. Because more water is retained by the soil, less water is available from the rain to enter the groundwater or surface water.

FALL

The surface waters cool in late fall, making them more dense or heavy than the water below the surface. The cooler water sinks to the bottom and flushes the warmer water below up to the surface. This is known as lake turnover. Lake turnover also occurs in late winter and early spring. As the air temperature remains cooler, the lake holds the warmth from the summer. Therefore, the air temperatures near the lake stay warmer later in the season. This helps some of the local farmers extend their growing season later into the fall.

The fall is a very active time for wildlife. Birds are passing through on their way south for the winter, and year-round residents are preparing for the long winter. The Lake Champlain Basin is part of the Atlantic Flyway. This is a route that migratory birds follow as they move back and forth between their winter and summer habitats. In the fall, some of the basin's birds move south along the Atlantic coast and winter in the southern United States or continue on to Central America. At the same time, the basin is welcoming birds from farther north in Canada. These birds overwinter in the basin where it is warmer and where there's more food.

WINTER

During the winter, the temperature of the lake averages 39°F. The surface waters may or may not freeze depending on the harshness of the winter. The whole lake does not freeze every winter. However, the bays do freeze most winters. As the long winter comes to a close, the surface ice begins to melt. This melted ice is colder and more dense than the water below, so it sinks to the bottom, forcing the water that was below the ice all winter to the surface. The lake water has "turned over" for the second time in one year.

What happens to all the animals during the winter months? It depends on the species. For example, some fish, such as the bass, spend their winters at the bottom of lakes in a dormant state. In other words, they take long naps hiding under rocks. Some fish, such as bullheads, actually bury themselves in the mud at the bottom of the lake and remain dormant all winter. Other fish, such as the pike, perch, walleye, smelt and lake trout, remain active in the winter and spend time swimming in deeper, warmer water. These are the fish that the ice-fishing folks catch on those blustery days. Amphibians and reptiles burrow in the mud at the bottom of the lake and hibernate. Their heart rate slows down and their body temperature is very cold, and they breathe through their skin. Aquatic insects also borrow down into the mud and lie dormant. Some aquatic insects overwinter as eggs laid in the mud.

THE LAKE CHAMPLAIN BASIN *as an* ECOSYSTEM

Ecosystems are communities of organisms that interact with each other and their nonliving environment. The Lake Champlain Basin is an ecosystem. When we look at the basin as a whole, we are looking at all living things on land and in water. Human beings are part of this ecosystem. The Lake Champlain Basin ecosystem is made up of a variety of habitats including woods, rivers and streams, open meadows, wetlands and lake waters.

The sun provides the fuel for this ecosystem. The sun's energy warms the earth, water and air, causing wind currents, and activates the hydrologic cycle. The light energy from the sun also fuels photosynthesis.

AN AQUATIC FOOD CHAIN

Plants grow by using the sun's energy to make many different types of chemicals. In water, small aquatic plants, including algae and other types of phytoplankton, are consumed by tiny floating animals or zooplankton. Next in the chain are larger organisms that feed on these tiny animals, including small crustaceans and forage fish. Larger fish and other animals are the next link in the chain, and they are eaten by birds, mammals (including humans), reptiles and amphibians. The step that completes the cycle is decomposition. When plants and animals die, decomposers, organisms that eat dead plant and animal matter, break down the material into basic components. These elements can then be cycled back through the food chain.

Each link in the food chain represents the transfer of energy through the ecosystem. Since each species is usually part of more than one food chain, the food chains in an ecosystem are interconnected. These connected food chains form a food web. Pictures of food chains and food webs show how the energy that creates life moves from one trophic level to another. These pictures also show how harmful pollutants can be passed along through an ecosystem.

Photosynthesis is the process of green plants turning water, light and carbon dioxide into oxygen and glucose. The oxygen is released to the atmosphere and the glucose is used by the plants to grow.

Photosynthesis

$12H_2O + 6CO_2$ + chlorophyll *(acted on by sunlight)* leads to $6O_2 + C_6H_{12}O_6$ (glucose)

There are approximately 487 vertebrate species of fish and wildlife in the basin.

Important organisms such as fungi, bacteria and worms are the decomposers that feed on the dead animal and plant materials.

What will happen to this food web if one of the species' population declines due to poor water quality? Will anything else be affected by this change in the web?

Food Web

cormorant
great blue heron
raccoon
perch
frog
crayfish
zooplankton
macroinvertebrates
snail
zebra mussel
algae
detritus
Food Chain
cormorant
perch
macroinvertebrates
algae

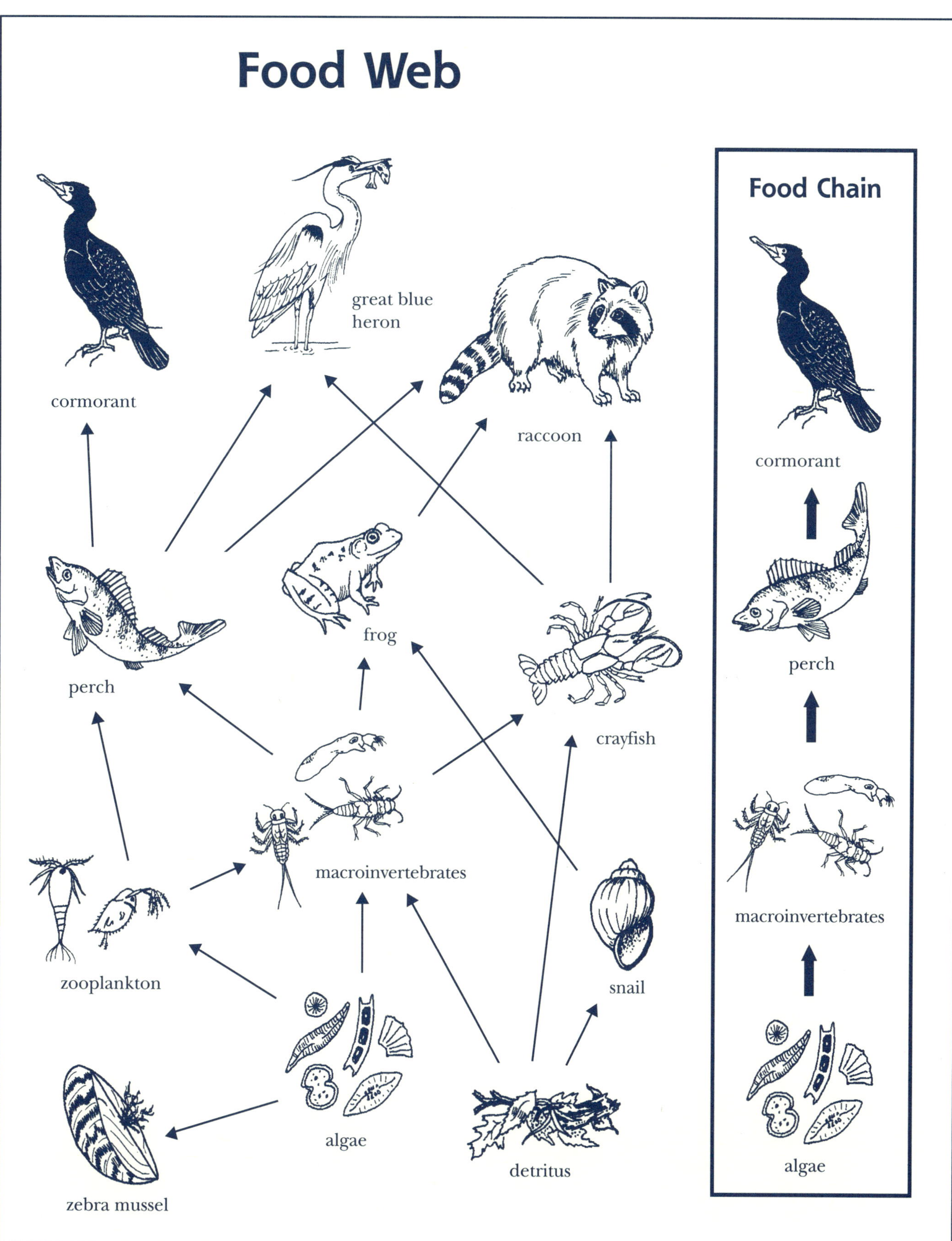

Habitat Highlight

Wetland habitats are wonderful places to visit and they are especially fun if you are a curious person. Awaken your five senses while exploring the wonders of the wetlands. Wetlands are full of many plants and animals.

The characteristics of a wetland help us to understand why so many species depend on wetland habitats for their survival. For example, if you are a fish, the calm and nutrient-rich waters of the wetlands are a perfect place to spawn and raise your young. Birds love wetlands because of all the delicious bugs for eating and the trees and tall grasses for nesting. Turtles can find lots to eat in a wetland, as well as fallen logs protruding from the calm water for sunning and mud for burrowing into during the winter months. Unique plants such as cattails have a special design that allows them to get oxygen to their roots. Roots of plants that don't have this design will die if the soil becomes too wet, because the soil below the surface of wetlands does not contain oxygen.

What is a wetland? A wetland is an area of land covered all or part of the year with water. The U.S. Fish and Wildlife Service more specifically defines wetlands as "lands where saturation with water is the dominant factor determining the nature of the soil and what grows on its surface." There are many kinds of wetlands including: swamp, marsh, bog, open water and wet meadow.

WHY ARE WETLANDS IMPORTANT *to the* LAKE CHAMPLAIN BASIN?

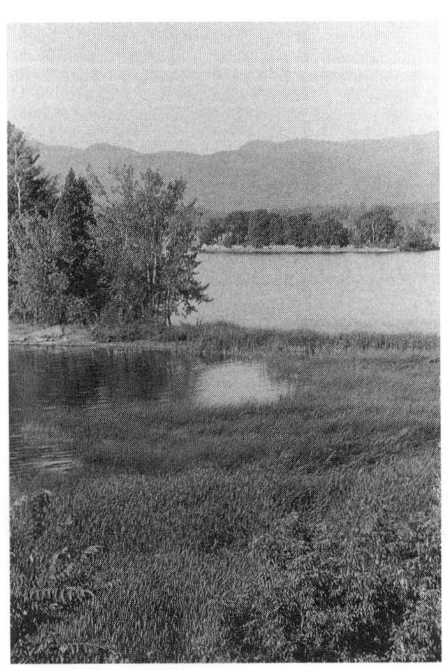

• The Lake Champlain Basin wetland habitats provide: nesting sites, food, shelter and protection for wetland species such as migratory birds (ducks, geese, gulls and songbirds), beaver, moose, insects, amphibians, silver maples, cattails, water lilies and tall grasses to name a few!

• Wetlands help to improve water quality by acting as large filters. As water travels through a wetland, the soils of the wetland filter out sediments, pollution and excess nutrients.

• Wetlands are full of plants with strong roots that help to stabilize the soil and prevent erosion.

• Wetlands are like huge sponges that soak up lots of water. During the flood seasons, wetlands help to absorb the excess water that enters the basin. This can help protect the basin from damaging floods. During drier times of the year, wetlands slowly release the water back into the water table.

• Some wetlands in the Lake Champlain Basin are Wildlife Management Areas, which provide wonderful recreational activities and educational opportunities including fishing, canoeing and bird-watching.

Due to increased land development pressures, introduction of non-native aquatic species, and pollution, wetlands are in danger. The State of New York regulates wetlands under its Freshwater Act passed in 1975. The State of Vermont passed a Wetland Act in 1986. Both New York and Vermont follow the national guideline that states there should be "no net loss" of wetlands. The Lake Champlain Basin has approximately 300,000 acres of wetlands.

And now for some good news! The Lake Champlain Wetlands Restoration Project began in 1993 to provide funding and technical support to willing landowners who want to restore wetlands on their property. The project hopes to restore 100 to 525 acres of wetlands.

Wetlands are exciting places and lots of fun to explore. If you visit one, remember you are a guest in the home of many other species. Be polite and you'll be invited back!

A LAKE GROWS UP!

All lakes go through a slow, natural aging process called eutrophication. Over very long periods of time, perhaps hundreds to thousands of years, all lakes eventually fill with plant matter and debris and become a marsh or a bog and then fill in completely and become land. This will eventually become the fate of Lake Champlain. Although this is many thousands of years away, it is important to understand how human activity is linked to an increasing rate of eutrophication, which affects the quality of our water today.

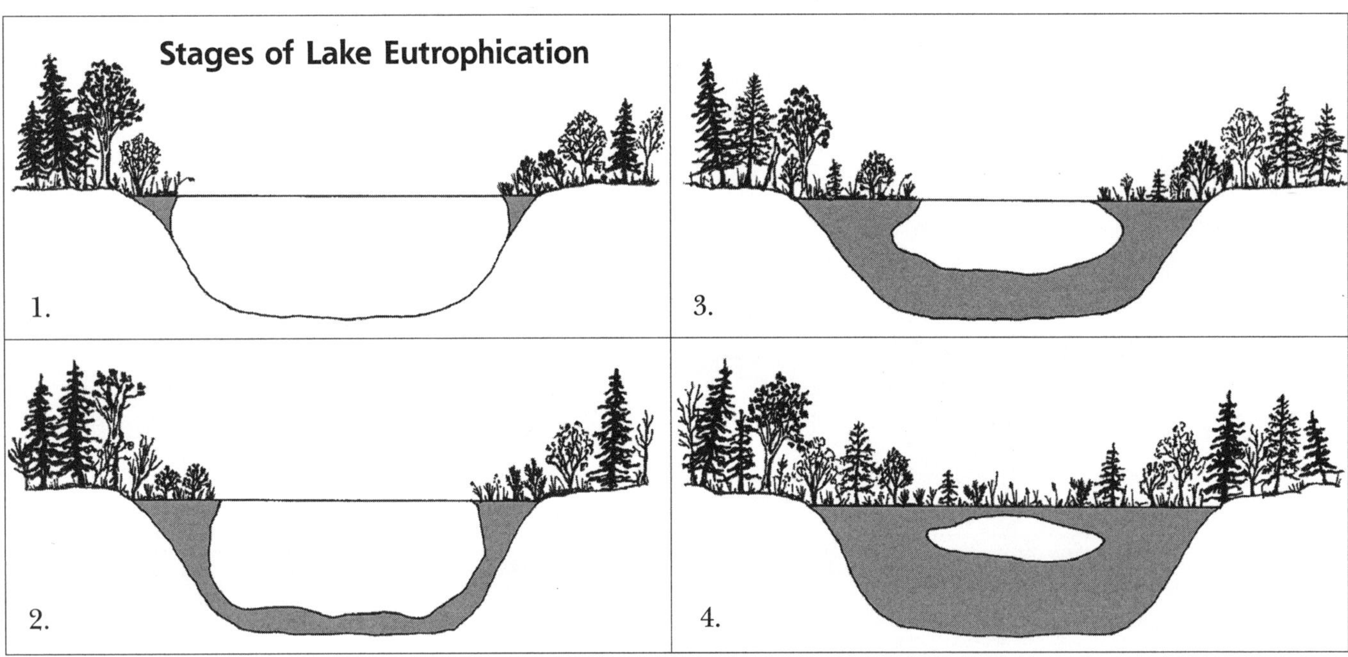

The rate of eutrophication depends on the amount of nutrients that enter the lake. What are nutrients? Nutrients are elements that sustain the lives of every living thing. Among humans, healthy eaters choose certain foods that are particularly rich in specific nutrients. You can eat broccoli for Vitamin C, milk for calcium, and potatoes for potassium. In order to maintain life in a lake, nutrients also must be present. Some of the common nutrients found in the lake are: potassium, magnesium, iron, calcium, nitrogen and phosphorus.

When a nutrient, or any other essential need such as light or oxygen, is lacking it is known as the limiting factor because it inhibits the growth of plants.

Most lakes are naturally low in nutrients, which leads to little plant and algae growth. This keeps the water clear. Lakes at this stage in their lives are called oligotrophic, meaning poorly nourished. Lakes that have medium levels of nutrients and plant growth are called mesotrophic. Lakes that contain high nutrient levels that cause excessive amounts of plant growth are called eutrophic. Overall, Lake Champlain is categorized as mesotrophic to eutrophic.

Sometimes, one or two nutrients are present in relatively small amounts compared to what plants need. This limits the plants' ability to grow. Phosphorus, which naturally cycles through lakes, is one of these "limiting nutrients." Aquatic plants and algae use what phosphorus is available to survive and grow. In Lake Champlain, as in other freshwater ecosystems, phosphorus is usually the nutrient that limits plant growth.

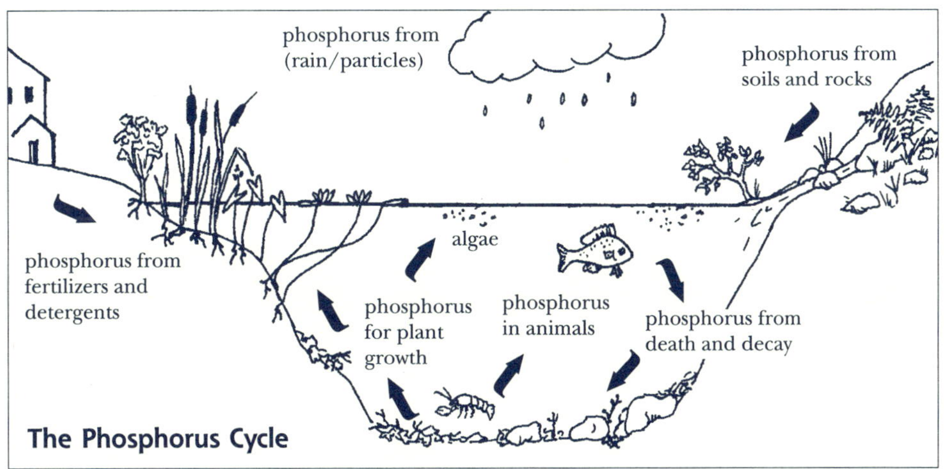

If a lake stays low in phosphorus, the natural aging takes place slowly. However, many human activities add more phosphorus than would normally be present. When excess phosphorus enters a lake, there is an "explosion" or bloom of fast-growing plants, and the lake is termed eutrophic. A eutrophic lake becomes rich with aquatic vegetation, including algae. After the aquatic plants die, bacteria, fungi and worms feed on the plants and decompose them, consuming a lot of the water's oxygen in the process. When the oxygen level becomes low it can be life-threatening to other species in the lake such as fish, which require a certain level of oxygen in the water to live.

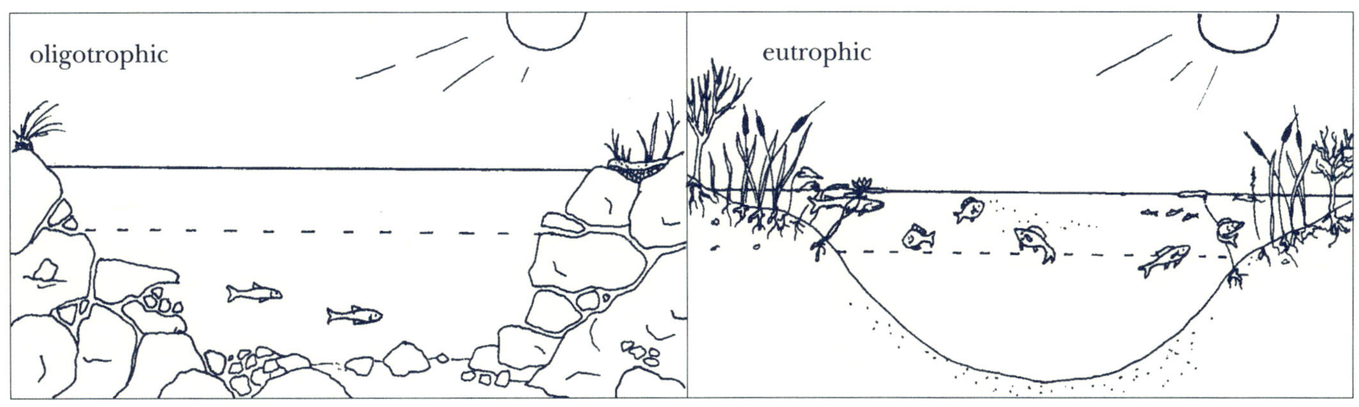

Some lakes around the world as well as parts of Lake Champlain have become eutrophic—they are loaded with excess nutrients, choked with plant growth and appear green and thick like pea soup! These excess amounts of nutrients speed up the natural aging process by adding organic matter to the lake. Where do these excess nutrients come from? Human activities within the Lake Champlain Basin are responsible for increasing the nutrient inputs to the lake. Routine human activities such as flushing the toilet, gardening or washing the car can impact the health of the lake.

Phosphorus also can enter the water naturally through the process of erosion. Next time you're out riding your bike or on a drive with your family, look for bare land where there is little or no vegetation growing. Nothing is holding this soil in place. It can easily be moved by wind and water. Look along road sides and stream banks. Phosphorus attaches to the sediment along the banks of tributaries and the lake. As the banks erode, the sediment flows into the water carrying the phosphorus with it. One way to help decrease this input of phosphorus is to stabilize the stream and lake banks by planting vegetation. The roots of the plants will hold the soil in place, not allowing it to flow into the water.

Eutrophication, accelerated by human activity, is a serious problem in the Lake Champlain Basin. However, there are things that we can all do to minimize the harms. One of the most important things is to understand the connections and impact between human activity and water quality.

HUMAN IMPACT

We share this land with other species including plants, mammals, fish, birds, reptiles, amphibians and insects. In general, all living things impact each other's lives by simply existing. Consider your own neighbors. When you mow your lawn, the noise affects your human neighbors as well as the lawn habitat and the animals that live there. A mosquito trying to survive and reproduce affects the lives of humans and other animals by extracting blood from their bodies, causing them to itch, roll in mud, swat their tails or grab for a bottle of bug repellent! Impacts such as these are all part of the natural life cycle of species on the planet earth. We are all connected. The action of one will affect the life of another.

How do we use the land and water within the basin, what effects do these land and water use practices have on the basin and why should we care about keeping the basin clean?

LIVING *in the* BASIN

How do you use land and water in the Lake Champlain Basin? In general, there are six major ways in which humans have an impact:

- recreation
- forestry
- agriculture
- transportation
- manufacturing
- developed land

Let's take a closer look at each of these categories.

RECREATION

• It's a beautiful summer day and you're out enjoying the mountains. A peaceful climb up Mt. Marcy in the Adirondacks provides a fabulous view of the Adirondacks.

• Strap on those roller blades and head for the Burlington bike path. You pass a biker. You get a good pace going and cruise the path all day long.

• What a day for a ride on the lake. The boat is full of gas, and you're off for a day of high speed fun and swimming on the Main Lake.

• Winter vacation! Ice-fishing season at last! Finally, you can ice fish all day!

The basin is a valuable recreational resource for residents and welcomed guests. It is rich in scenic beauty and a large source of income to the area. Despite these benefits, some aspects of recreation pose a threat to the health of the basin. Let's take a look at the lake itself in relation to these issues.

Today the lake is mainly used for recreation. Access points are becoming crowded and marinas are filling up. Boat traffic on the lake can be very congested and conflicts arise between sailboats and motorboats. The more boats there are on the water, the more fuel and engine oil enter the lake. The list can go on and on. Some people believe we have reached a limit in terms of how much activity the lake can take. Recreation needs to be managed in order to preserve this precious resource.

FORESTRY

• "My grandfather tells wonderful stories about the early logging days in the Adirondacks…how big the trees were back then, the two-person cross-cut saws slicing through bark and wood— back and forth, back and forth, and the horses used for skidding the logs out of the woods."

• "Our family has some land that is designated as a tree tarm. This means that we actively manage our woods. We have to follow some specific guidelines to be 'tree farmers,' but I'm glad we do. It helps to save our woods and make some money when we do harvest the trees and sell them to be made into furniture or paper."

• "My mom and I were traveling down Interstate 87 the other day. We got behind this logging truck. Huge logs stacked on top of one another. My mom asked me where I thought the trees were from. Then she asked me what I thought they would be turned into."

Today, forests cover 62% of the basin's surface area. In any given year, only

1% of this forested land is subject to harvest. Most of the forestland in the basin lies within the Adirondack Forest Preserve and is not subject to harvest. Therefore, forestry practices do not pose a large threat to the basin's health. However, poorly planned logging operations can cause major soil erosion, which leads to sediment and nutrient runoff into local streams and rivers.

AGRICULTURE

- *"We've got a hundred head of Jerseys. My family has been farming this land since the early 1900s."*

- *"We grow organic crops for the local community. Although the growing season is short, we love working the land and providing food for our neighbors."*

- *"Llamas are a unique agricultural enterprise. We raise them as breeding stock as well as selling their hair to be made into commercial products such as sweaters, blankets and scarves."*

Agriculture is an important way in which land is used and has been an important aspect of our history and culture. There are presently 3,100 farms in the U.S. portion of the basin, 2,080 of which are dairy farms. Farmers play a valuable role in our lives. Farmers provide us with the food and products we use every day. Think of how much milk you drink in a week, in a year—and thank the farmer! Farmers also provide food and agricultural resources for people and animals that live outside of the basin. Maple syrup produced within the basin is sold all over the United States. The milk from some of the basin's dairy cows is also sold in other parts of the country.

At the same time, agricultural practices impact the health of the basin. Any activity on the land, such as plowing, grazing, irrigation or pest management can potentially affect the quality of the water through runoff and infiltration.

The major threat to water quality from agriculture is the nutrient phosphorus. Manure and fertilizers are sources of phosphorus. When these phosphorus-rich products are put onto the land, they are either absorbed into the soil and plant root systems or they run off into a nearby stream or infiltrate down into the ground water. If the phosphorus reaches the surface water, the plants in the water use this nutrient to grow—and grow and grow. If too much phosphorus enters a body of water, an algal bloom will occur. This can affect the other plants and animals in and around the body of water.

Soil and You

by Fred Magdoff

WHAT *is* SOIL?

When you are walking in your backyard or garden or in a forest or alongside a stream, you are walking on soil. From this soil comes the nutrients and water that plants need to grow. Most of the nutrients that you need also come from the soil. Where does the calcium come from that helps make your bones strong? From milk? From vegetables? Well, yes. But how did it get into the milk? First plants grow and calcium enters the roots and moves up to the leaves and grain. Then a cow eats the hay and corn and uses some of the calcium to make milk. So the calcium inside you came from soil!!! So did the phosphorus and magnesium and nitrogen. The cotton shirt or socks you wear, the hamburger you ate last week, the cereal and orange juice you had for breakfast this morning all came from plants that needed soil.

There are many different kinds of soils, which scientists classify according to their properties. Some soils are deeper than others; some are more fertile than others. Soils may contain different minerals and have very different colors. Some soils are always wet, while some never contain enough water to grow plants.

Soils also play an important role in the environment. Soils store water during a rainstorm so that it doesn't run off into streams and rivers and cause flooding. The soil water is then used by plants or may percolate down to groundwater. Soils also serve as a filter for pollutants. Many people in the Lake Champlain Basin live outside of cities and big villages. The water from the kitchen sink and the bathroom go into a big septic tank buried near the house and then out to a trench or mound septic disposal field. As the wastewater enters the soil and flows downward, the soil filters out many bacteria and viruses and helps reduce the other pollutants as well.

HOW *is* SOIL MADE?

Soils can be formed in many different ways. The slow breakdown of bedrock or rocks ground up and pushed for hundreds of miles by glaciers can make soil. Rivers carry sands and clays down from mountains; the sands are deposited in the delta and the clays are pushed farther out into the lake. When lake levels drop, these sediments become soil. As plants start to grow (and then die) on the sediments, their remains become part of the soil, as well as the remains of insects, earthworms and larger animals that feed on the plants. This organic matter makes the soil more fertile. That's why many people put compost, manure or grass clippings in their gardens.

In the Champlain Valley there are many soils that were formed from materials that were once underwater. Do you know that the level of the lake was once about 500 feet above the current level? We have some soils that are very sandy—mainly old lake beaches and river deltas—as well as some that are very clayey—from parts of the old lake bed. But there are also rocky soils formed from glacial rocks and sandy loams alongside many rivers. The soils in the valley are pretty young—for soil, that is!—being only some thousands of years old. And because they are so young they contain many minerals that help keep the soil fertile.

WE *are the* CARETAKERS *of the* SOIL

There are many threats to our soil. Erosion by water and wind can be a major problem and cause loss of the fertile topsoil. Pollutants can contaminate soil, like when there is an accident and oil spills onto the side of a road. Also, new developments sometimes pave over large areas of soil for parking lots or buildings.

There are many ways to take care of the soil. Farmers are now trying to use crop rotations and other practices to reduce soil loss. Construction crews use straw or hay mulch to cover bare soil to decrease erosion. Loggers are being encouraged to select some trees in a forest to be harvested at one time—instead of taking all the trees at once—and this helps to protect soil from damage. Some states and private organizations are helping to keep soil from being paved over by purchasing land and then forbidding development in the future.

YOU can help protect soil by staying on trails when hiking in the mountains, helping to compost wastes and then putting the compost on your lawn or garden. And you can also be careful with wastes like paint or gas—don't pour them onto soil or down the drains where they will get into the water or soil. Soil is an important life-giving resource that helps us all—plants, animals and people—grow and stay healthy.

TRANSPORTATION

• *"We live in Vermont and my mom works in Plattsburgh. Five days a week she uses the Grand Isle Ferry to get to work and back again. The ride is peaceful. During the winter she sits inside and reads the paper. During the summer she hangs out on the deck, soaks up the sun and feels the cool lake breeze."*

• *"My family lives in rural New York. If we want to go shopping, I mean really shopping, we have to travel by car to Plattsburgh. There's no public bus or train, and it's way too far to ride our bikes!"*

• *"Have you ever driven on Route 7 south from Burlington between 4:00 and 6:00 p.m.? It's bumper to bumper traffic. There's been talk lately about running a train that would travel from Rutland to Burlington. If people commuting into Burlington took a train each day, think of all the fuel we'd save and traffic jams we'd avoid!"*

Ferries still provide an essential form of transportation from one side of the lake to the other. In 1995, 863,000 cars used the three ferry crossings run by the Lake Champlain Transportation Company. The Grand Isle-Plattsburgh ferry, which operates year-round, carried 679,000 cars in 1995.

Historically, the lake and its rivers served as the main transportation route for all the people who settled here. Canoes, bateaux, sailing ships and steam boats were used to travel from one place to another. Towards the end of the 1900s the railroad system replaced these ships as the major form of transportation. Although there are still trains, the system isn't as popular as it once was. Other forms of transportation, such as cars, motorcycles and airplanes, have replaced the rail system.

Due to the fact that the basin is mostly a rural region, public transportation is either inconvenient or not available. In today's fast-paced society, we need to be there NOW. It is quicker to jump in a plane or a car. The more urban areas, such as Burlington and Plattsburgh, provide public bus transportation within the city limits. This helps to cut down on traffic, save fuel and decrease the air pollution from the exhaust of all the cars.

MANUFACTURING

• *"I was at a science fair last week and International Paper Company had a display on making paper and how much water they use to make the paper. They were giving out pads of paper that were made at the plant in Ticonderoga."*

• *"Our class toured the Teddy Bear Factory this year. They showed us how they make the bears and the materials needed for stuffing and fluffing. Some of the materials they use are recycled."*

There are various forms of industry all over the basin. These industries may be located on the shores of the lake, such as International Paper in Ticonderoga, New York, or located near a tributary, such as IBM in Essex, Vermont. These industries provide people with products and help to bring people and jobs to the area.

These industries also use water during phases of their manufacturing processes. There are presently 28 industries that discharge treated water within the basin. This is called industrial effluent. It is important to make sure that the effluent is free of materials that may pollute the water. There are regulations designed to stop hazardous industrial effluent from entering the lake and its tributaries.

DEVELOPED LAND

• *"My parents just sold off my grandfather's farm. They told me a new housing development was going to be built there, and they're going to name the whole place after my grandfather!"*

• *"My mother is really upset about the Walmart that's going up in town. She said that there will be too much traffic on our road and we'll lose some of the scenic beauty."*

• *"I was at the mall yesterday when it started to rain really heavily. All this junk from the parking lot was in this little river and it all went down a storm drain."*

Developed land includes land used for residential home sites, roads, malls, construction sites, commercial developments, towns, cities and schools. Developed land makes up 3% of the basin's surface area. The common feature of most developed land is that the soil gets covered up by a hard surface. Water that falls onto these surfaces no longer filters through the soil. Water runs off these hard surfaces into a storm drain or directly into a body of water. The water can carry with it anything on the surface such as motor oil, pet feces, road salt or pesticides.

We may feel pretty comfortable now, but what will happen if all of these activities continue without being managed? Consider the following scenarios:

• It's a beautiful summer day and you're out trying to enjoy the mountains of the basin. You arrive at the trail head of Mt. Marcy and there is no place to park. There must be at least 2,000 people hiking the trail. You park half a mile away and finally reach the trail. As you hike along, you notice a lot of trash. You've passed 20 other hikers in the last 30 minutes! You reach the top of Mt. Marcy to find a crowd of people.

• Strap on those roller blades early in the morning and head for the Burlington bike path. You've learned that this is the best time to use the bike path. The middle of the day is a safety nightmare. You have to dodge strollers, bikers, walkers, bladers and runners. You're constantly slowing down or stopping to get out of someone's way...

• What a beautiful day for a ride on the lake. You arrive at the public access boat landing at 10:00 a.m. to find a waiting line to put the boat in the water. You finally motor off onto the lake at 2:00 p.m.

The Pine Street Barge Canal

by Nancy Bazilchuk

Lake Champlain's early history as a transportation corridor inadvertently became a twentieth century problem at the Pine Street Barge Canal Superfund site, a hazardous waste site on the shores of Lake Champlain.

In the early 1800s, engineers dug a large canal in a wetlands area of Burlington to allow barges from the Adirondacks to bring lumber to sawmills on Pine Street. A big square area called a turning basin allowed boats to turn around and head out into Lake Champlain again.

But once boats were no longer used to move timber, the canal fell into disuse. By 1908, when the Burlington Gas Works moved its operation to Pine Street, the canal took on another job; it became a convenient place to put wastes from the gas works, and that's when the trouble began.

The gas works took coal and cooked it in a kind of pressure cooker to produce something called water gas, which was piped throughout Burlington for lighting, cooking and heating.

Making the gas left sticky coal tar, essentially the same substance that paving companies use as asphalt. Some years the gas works was able to sell the coal tar for just that purpose. But even though coal tar is commonly used, it is not safe when sitting next to Lake Champlain, which supplies drinking water to about 166,000 people, including everyone in Burlington.

People do not agree on how the coal tar got into the barge canal. Those who ran the gas works said the Lake Champlain floodwaters spread the coal tar from tanks where it was stored during the last years of the plant's operation. But it is likely that in the early years, some of the coal tar was simply dumped in the canal. In any case, chemicals in the tar found their way into the groundwater.

By the time Green Mountain Power Company closed the gas works in 1966, an estimated 600,000 cubic yards of soil had been contaminated by the coal tar wastes. That's enough soil to fill a football field more than 100 feet deep.

The green of wetland vegetation hid the barge canal's woes until 1978, when the state decided that it would route a road through the wetland next to the canal. The road, called the Southern Connector, was seen by transportation experts as a way to ease congestion on roads like U.S. Route 7, and speed cars into Burlington's downtown. When engineers began drilling into the soil to see what was there, they found the sticky coal tar in everything—in some places as deep as forty feet.

Still, state officials weren't discouraged. They thought they could clean up the barge canal and build the road. But at the same time, the U.S. Congress enacted a new law that was supposed to help states clean up big hazardous waste sites like the barge canal. Some Burlingtonians, thinking that the new "Superfund" law would help pay for the cleanup, lobbied Vermont's senior senator, Robert Stafford, to have the Environmental Protection Agency (EPA) include the Pine Street site as one of the national sites needing cleanup.

Those Burlingtonians got their wish. But the complexity of the Pine Street site, combined with difficulties implementing the Superfund law, tied the problem up in red tape.

In November, 1992, 12 years after the Pine Street Barge Canal got named as a Superfund site, federal officials released a cleanup plan. But the plan didn't seem like a solution at all. Because there was so much contaminated soil, the EPA wanted to build a landfill right on top of the contaminated wetland. The landfill would have cost $50 million, and it would have been as big as the University Mall in South Burlington—a 25-foot-high, 23-acre structure that would have been larger than any other building in the city.

And because the landfill was going to be built on the squishy peat soils of the wetland, environmentalists were afraid that the weight of the landfill would squeeze all of the coal tar out of the peat and right into Lake Champlain, contaminating the lake. And even if the coal tar stayed in the peat, residents who lived near Pine Street were afraid that digging it up to pile in the landfill would release toxic vapors from the tar. Environmental groups, businesses and residents who read about the plan thought that it was crazy. The EPA was going to protect a wetland by building a landfill on top of it, possibly poisoning Lake Champlain or the neighborhood near to the barge canal? It just didn't make sense.

In fact, Vermonters were so outraged they flooded the EPA office in Boston with letters, phone calls and faxes. So the federal agency changed its mind and decided to let Vermonters study the barge canal site some more to come up with a more sensible plan. Out of this activism, the Pine Street Barge Canal Coordinating Committee was formed. This committee hopes to have a cleanup plan in place by 1997.

THE EFFECTS *of* POLLUTION *on* LAND AND WATER

Everything we do on the land affects the health of the basin in either a positive or negative way. Whether we are washing our car in the driveway or helping to pick up trash along the roadside, our actions have an effect on the basin.

Next time it rains in your area, think about where the water goes. What is the rainwater picking up as it travels toward a stream, lake, pond or puddle? Our land-use practices have a large impact on the quality of water throughout the Lake Champlain Basin.

Pollutants from land use are categorized in two large groups, point and nonpoint sources of pollution. Point sources of pollution enter the lake or a stream directly from one place, such as a pipe. This kind of pollution is easier to track and measure because researchers know exactly where the water is coming from and where it flows out into the lake or stream. Point sources of pollution usually are connected to industries and wastewater treatment facilities, which may include the outflow of chemical and industrial wastes.

On the other hand, nonpoint sources of pollution are a bit different. These are the pollutants that enter the lake and tributaries from dispersed sources on the land and in the air. They normally enter the water in surges of snowmelt or rainfall runoff. As the water travels over the ground, it picks up pollutants and carries them to a nearby stream or lake.

For the purposes of our discussion, pollutants in the Lake Champlain Basin can be placed into four categories:
- organic materials,
- inorganic materials,
- toxic pollution,
- thermal pollution.

Organic materials come from the decomposition of living organisms and their by-products. They enter the lake through both point and nonpoint sources. Materials such as grass clippings, manure, banana peels, urine and newspapers are examples of organic materials. Decomposing organic materials are great for the soil. However, in the water, decomposing organic materials can cause some problems.

OPPORTUNITIES FOR ACTION, a publication of the Lake Champlain Basin Program, says that 29% of the phosphorus entering Lake Champlain is from point sources. In 1992, the State of Vermont enacted statute 10 V.S.A. Sec. 1266a, which established a basin-wide phosphorus limit from point sources at 0.8 milligrams/liter. This regulation applies to point source discharges greater than 200,000 gallons/day. Research indicates that in order to maintain a balanced level of phosphorus in the lake, phosphorus inputs into the lake must be reduced by 200 metric tons/year.

In the water, these organic materials are broken down by microorganisms. This process requires oxygen. If there are lots of organic materials in the lake, thus lots of decomposition taking place, more oxygen is used, and the water will become low in oxygen. Some aquatic species do not tolerate low oxygen levels and will die or leave the area.

Inorganic materials include suspended and dissolved solids such as road salt and sand, minerals in the soil eroding from stream banks, and soil from construction sites, plowed croplands and dirt roads. When these inorganic pollutants enter the water, they may float around or settle to the bottom. Excess solids in the water can cause the gills of aquatic species to clog, making breathing difficult. Suspended solids also block light from reaching aquatic plants and interfere with photosynthesis. These solids are considered nonpoint sources of pollution.

Toxic pollutants are organic and inorganic chemical compounds that can poison living things. Sources of toxic pollutants can come from industrial sources and airborne contaminants as well as from our own homes. Issues relating to pollution from toxins in Lake Champlain, however, are centered around polychlorinated biphenyls (PCBs) and mercury. Most toxins are found in sediment. Therefore, the first species to ingest these toxins are the ones that live in the sediment and consume the particles such as midges and worms. A dragonfly nymph might consume several midges that are contaminated with toxins. The toxic material will accumulate in the dragonfly nymph. If a fish consumes numerous dragonfly nymphs that are all contaminated with toxins, that fish has all of those accumulated toxins in its body. Someone who catches 20 fish loaded with toxins and eats the fish then has all the toxins in his or her body.

When a toxin enters an ecosystem, its concentration sometimes increases as it moves up the food chain. This is called biomagnification. Although humans are susceptible to toxins in food, they are less vulnerable because of their ability to vary their diet. If, however, a person eats too many fish that are contaminated, there is a risk of a health problem.

Thermal pollution is a by-product of using water to cool something down. Some industries utilize water as a coolant; the water is heated in the process. Thermal pollution is considered waste heat. Although it is not considered to be a major problem in Lake Champlain, warmed water will affect the life of aquatic species.

THE IMPORTANCE *of* GOOD STEWARDSHIP

The best way to make sure that the lake and its tributaries are pollution-free is to take action, get involved! You can become part of a water testing program in your local area, conduct land-use surveys and monitor your own water use.

By testing the quality of water in a stream, you can learn important information. You may discover it has a lot of phosphorus in it. Now you're not only a scientist, you are a detective. What is causing the phosphorus to be high? Monitoring the water over a period of time, several times a year for five years, can tell you whether the water is healthy or polluted. You may see variations in your tests from season to season. Now that you've become involved, you have the responsibility to communicate your test results to the community. Many laws and regulations are changed in response to the results of citizen monitoring programs.

There are lots of different things to test for and techniques for testing them. The table below outlines the tests and their purposes. Most of these tests require some equipment that your school can purchase or make.

TESTING FOR WATER QUALITY

TEST	PURPOSE OF THE TEST
Dissolved Oxygen	*To determine the amount of dissolved oxygen in the water. Aquatic species need a certain amount of oxygen to survive.*
pH	*To determine how acidic the water is. Extreme low or high pH values create unsuitable living environments for aquatic species.*
Temperature	*To determine the temperature of the water. Warm water holds less oxygen.*
Turbidity	*To measure the clarity of the water. Murky waters can clog fish gills, block light and absorb the sun's heat.*
Total Dissolved Phosphorus	*To determine the amount of phosphorus in the water. Excess amounts of phosphorus can cause algal blooms and cultural eutrophication of the water.*
Benthic Macroinvertebrates *(bottom-dwelling invertebrates such as mayfly nymphs, leeches and snails)*	*To determine the species present in a certain body of water. Aquatic species have various tolerance levels for polluted waters.*

Aquatic Storytellers

The lakes, ponds, streams and even the puddles of the basin are full of very small aquatic species that can help tell us about the quality of our water. These species are called benthic macroinvertebrates.

Benthic means bottom-dwelling. Macroinvertebrates are invertebrates you can see with the unaided eye. Most macroinvertebrates are aquatic insects such as the water penny or the aquatic stage of insects such as a dragonfly nymph.

Macroinvertebrates have different tolerances for polluted water. By sampling a stream for macroinvertebrates, you can determine the quality of the water by simply identifying the collected species. All you'll need is a net or kitchen strainer, a bucket, a small cup for rinsing, a macroinvertebrate guide and good observation skills. Some of these macroinvertebrates are small and most of them are well camouflaged. Because they are so tiny they can be easily hurt. Find creative ways to observe them without touching them. Magnifying glasses or "bug boxes" that hold water and have a magnified lid work well.

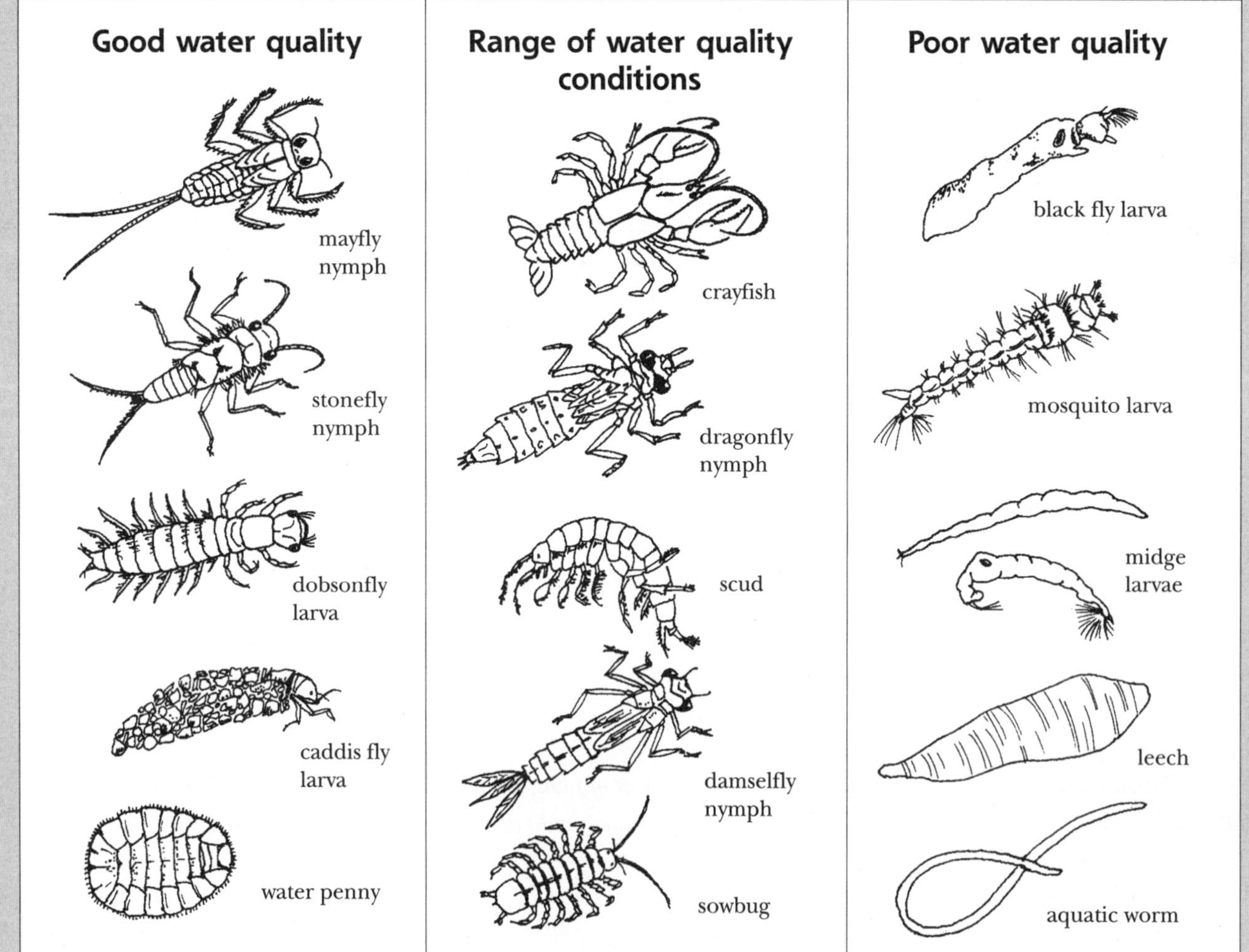

YOU CAN MAKE *a* DIFFERENCE!

People have been concerned about the health of Lake Champlain for a long time. In 1905, a U.S. Geological Survey was conducted and recommendations were made to improve water quality. The report clearly outlined the many problems facing the lake and deemed the water of Lake Champlain "unfit for domestic consumption," but little was done to design a comprehensive plan.

Many individuals over time became involved in water monitoring and lobbying politicians on specific issues. Over the years, Native Americans have protested and voiced their opposition to many land use practices that affect the quality of the water. The Lake Champlain Committee, formed in 1963, is a citizen's action group that has worked for many years on both sides of the lake.

In 1990, the Lake Champlain Basin Program (LCBP) was established to coordinate the activities of the Lake Champlain Special Designation Act. The Lake Champlain Special Designation Act, supported by Senators Leahy and Jeffords from Vermont and Senators Moynihan and D'Amato from New York, was to bring together people to create a comprehensive plan for protecting the future of the Lake Champlain Basin. A draft plan was released in October 1994 and adopted in the fall of 1996.

How can you insure that the Lake Champlain Basin we call home will continue to be a beautiful and useful resource in the future for all species? You have to take action! Many people in the basin participate in action projects. So can you!

You may not be a senator or serve on a big committee, but you can still work to help the Lake Champlain Basin. Ask yourself, what can I do to help keep the basin healthy? There are lots of simple yet critical action steps that we can all practice to make a difference. The following list offers just a few ideas. Meet with your family and friends to brainstorm some other ways you can make a difference and then put them into practice every day. We share this earth with many living things and are the caretakers of the earth for future generations. We all must do our part.

- Turn off the water while brushing your teeth.
- Test the water in your local community's ponds, streams and rivers.
- Ride your bike instead of traveling in the car.
- Car pool or take public transportation whenever possible.
- Write a letter to your local newspaper.
- Write a letter to your senator.
- Use environmentally-sound products to clean your home.
- Keep cars and boats in good working condition.
- Start a compost pile.
- Plant trees and shoreline vegetation to reduce soil erosion.
- Avoid using toxic materials.
- Dispose of toxic materials correctly—know about hazardous waste pick-up days in your community.
- Share your new knowledge about the basin with family and friends—you can be the teacher!
- Participate in a community clean-up day.
- Don't use too much fertilizer on your lawn.

The Ecology of the Lake Champlain Basin

Activities

There is an endless supply of wonderful educational activities relating to ecology and water. This section of the book provides you with a few favorite activities as well as a resource listing to find more. The key element, however, is to get the students out into the environment—take a close-up look at a mayfly nymph, plant willows along an eroded stream bank or simply take a walk in the woods.

In order to appreciate the beauty and richness of the Lake Champlain Basin, you and your students must take the time to be in the environment. As soon as your students have become more aware of the basin and begin to appreciate its resources, they are ready to take action. Foster their desire to be stewards of the basin by providing opportunities to complete community projects near your school or local body of water.

Above all, have fun and be prepared for exciting learning opportunities in and out of the classroom!

Water as a Universal

QUESTIONS

- Where is water?
- Where does water come from?
- What does water look like?

KEY RESOURCES

- Water Science *by Deborah Seed*
- Project WET—*Western Regional Environmental Education Council*
- Pond and Brook *by Michael Caduto*
- At the Water's Edge *by Alan Cvancara*
- Water *by Graham Peacock*

Word Bank

absorb
aquifer
atom
attraction
charge
covalent bonds
displace
droplet
electron
evaporate
freshwater
gas
gravity
groundwater
humidity
hydrogen
hydrologic cycle
hydrologist
ice
infiltration
lake
molecule
negative (charge)
percolation
positive (charge)
precipitation
ocean
oxygen
river
saltwater
solvent
transpiration
vapor

Activity: **Poetic Possibilities**

TEACHER NOTES *and* INFO

Learning about Lake Champlain can provide wonderful opportunities for writing poetry. Whole classes, small groups, or individuals can start by brainstorming a list of "water words" on the board, on an overhead or as a web on poster paper. A variety of activities may then be developed using this list, again either in small groups or as individual assignments.

STUDENT ACTIVITY

Brainstorm with your class some water words. Here is a sample from Sue Hardin's sixth-grade science class:

Water Words

rain snow ice lake flow cold aquatic dew condensation water scuba submarine river sewer moisture H_2O frost fog fish swim sink wet fluid boil dive drown bubble aquarium gurgle skating sparkles boat vapor Jacuzzi showers pool wet dog wetland swamp squirting juice spring splash spit saliva ice cream sleet wavey gulf precipitation spray squirt pacific pond marine waterbed brook water gun slippery sea sparkle canoeing hail skiing Atlantic hose falls overcast drops lobster damselfly tap dragonfly chlorine hydrophobia blizzard whale pleasure frog estuary well skipping stones stream shark trickling ice fishing snorkeling seal benthic shell algae clam depth habitat thunderstorm ocean l'eau foamy gushing

Poetic Possibility 1

Write a poem using at least five words from the list.

Poetic Possibility 2

Write a five-line poem in which the first word of each line begins with the letters of the word water.

Poetic Possibility 3

Write similies and metaphors for water or wetlands.

Poetic Possibility 4

Write poetic or punning definitions beginning with "Water is...."

"Water is a brook moving rapidly."

Poetic Possibility 5

Compose a wetland haiku (seventeen syllables, arranged in three lines of five, seven, five).

Sun peaks through the clouds.
The wetlands serve their purpose,
Soaking up the storm.
                    Samantha Price, Grade 6, South Burlington

The goose flies southward,
Comes to rest in a wetland.
Home away from home.
                    Kevin Stevenson, Grade 6, South Burlington

Poetic Possibility 6

Write a "shape" poem in which the words become graphic illustrations of their meaning, then mount them on construction paper cut to an appropriate shape. The shape poems provide a neat opportunity to play with words and to learn about computer fonts and typestyles as well:

WWWWATER LOVES TO WWWAVE

A brook rushes
                    down
                              the mountain,
                                        Tripping
                                                  over
                                                            stones.

Activity: **Water Diary**

TEACHER NOTES *and* INFO

This is a way for students to gather information about how much water people use in simple daily tasks.

STUDENT ACTIVITY

This activity can go for a week or longer. The "Water Diary" on which the students record their daily water use should be checked daily and can be recorded on a master class chart. If you want to extend this activity through-out the year and record seasonal changes in water use, you will need to set up another recording system.

Before handing out the worksheet, invite students to predict how much water is used for the tasks listed.

STUDENT HANDOUT - "How Much Water Do I Use?"

You will need:
- a diary for each student with a chart to help calculate water use. See "How Much Water Do I Use?"

Taking It Home

Brainstorm ways to conserve water for certain activities. Graph how much water you can save by changing water- use habits. Discuss with the class how they would like to share this information with their families and what action plan they might develop to conserve water.

Other Ideas
• When the activity is completed, have a small group of students calculate the total for each student in each category. Then calculate the total class use for each category. You will then have one figure for each activity, e.g. the class uses 175 gallons of water for their pets. Students can then each make a bar graph, or together they can make a large bar graph to display in the room.

How Much Water Do I Use?

DIRECTIONS: Use this chart to figure out how much water you used in one day.

PURPOSE	AMOUNT
Bath	40 gallons
Shower	30 gallons
Brushing teeth	1 gallon
Flushing toilet	5 gallons
Drink	1/2 gallon (food and drink)
Washing hands and face	2 gallons
Washing dishes	10 gallons (by hand), 15 gallons (by machine)
Watering lawn	240 gallons in 30 minutes
Washing clothes	30 gallons
Watering houseplant	1/16 gallon per plant
Pet waterbowl	1/4 gallon

DIRECTIONS: We all use water in different ways every day. We might drink it, wash with it or even water plants with it. Think about the things you do that use water. Record the amount of water you use in one day.

In the morning

I used water to: ________________________. I used about this much water ______.
I used water to: ________________________. I used about this much water ______.
I used water to: ________________________. I used about this much water ______.
I used water to: ________________________. I used about this much water ______.

In the morning I used __________ gallons of water.

At school

I used water to: ________________________. I used about this much water ______.
I used water to: ________________________. I used about this much water ______.
I used water to: ________________________. I used about this much water ______.
I used water to: ________________________. I used about this much water ______.

At school I used __________ gallons of water.

After school and in the evening

I used water to: ________________________. I used about this much water ______.
I used water to: ________________________. I used about this much water ______.
I used water to: ________________________. I used about this much water ______.
I used water to: ________________________. I used about this much water ______.

After school and in the evening I used __________ gallons of water.

DATE OF RECORDING: ____________   **I USED THIS MUCH WATER ON THIS DAY:** ______.

Activity: **The Drop Goes On!**

TEACHER NOTES *and* INFO

The following activity is a fun and creative way to teach about the never-ending process of the water cycle.

Find a large piece of rope and tie both ends together. The rope should be large enough for each child in your whole class to hold onto with both hands while standing in a circle. The one knot will signify the drop of water.

Note: If you or a student or parent "knows the ropes," splice the rope and make a slip knot that sits on the loop and can be transferred from one student to another.

You will need:
• a large rope

STUDENT ACTIVITY

Explain to your students that, together, they are going to tell a story about the life of a water droplet. The knot in the rope symbolizes a drop of water.

The first person to start is the person holding the knot. That person can have that drop of water do whatever he or she wants, as long as it ties in somehow with the water cycle. Encourage students to use the vocabulary they are learning, e.g. evaporate, precipitate, etc.

Example: *"The drop of water came out of the sky, it precipitated, and landed on the back of a frog."*

The speaker then hands the knot to the next person. The next person must take the drop of water from the frog's back and continue the story. Continue until everyone has had a turn. How much longer could the story go on? Forever! There is no end to the water cycle. Encourage your students to be creative: travel around the world, hook up with celebrities; the drop goes on!

Activity: **Believe It or Not**

The following three activities explore the qualities of water and can be set up as stations around your classroom. Directions for each experiment are on individual cards that can be handed out to pairs of students. Students will need to predict, test, observe and record their thoughts and results. The activities are from PROJECT SEASONS by Deborah Parrella. You can find more activities to explore the nature of water in this book.

You will need:
- several quarts of water
- clear plastic cups
- several plastic forks
- paper clips
- sewing needles
- magnifying glass

TEACHER NOTES *and* INFO

Step 1

The paper clip and needle are able to float because of the surface tension of the water. The water molecules at the surface are strongly attracted to one another and they form an elastic skin. If you can place these items horizontally on the surface, without breaking through this elastic skin, they will float. This is how some insects can walk on the surface of water!

Step 2

If you look closely at the water surface around and beneath the paper clip or needle, it appears dimpled. The water's skin appears to stretch and can suspend these light objects.

STUDENT DIRECTIONS *for* **Believe It or Not**

1. Fill a cup with water. Try to float a paper clip or sewing needle on the surface of the water. Use a fork to help place it gently. Why can the paper clip and needle float in the water, if placed correctly?

2. Once the paper clip or needle is floating, observe the water beneath it with a magnifying glass. What does the surface of the water look like?

 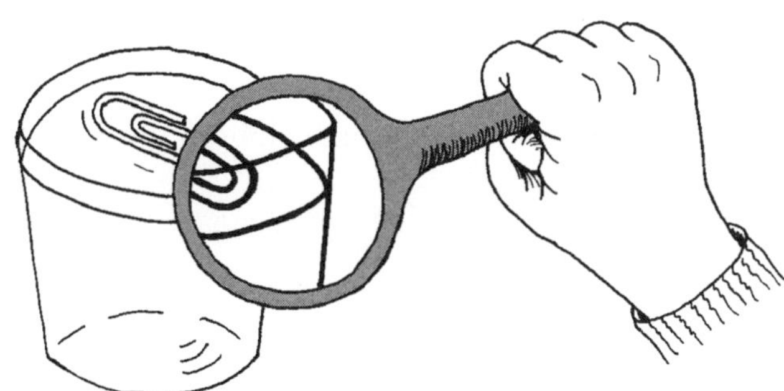

Activity: **Rising to the Top**

TEACHER NOTES *and* INFO

If you look closely at paper, you will see that it is made up of fibers. In between the fibers are air spaces. The water is attracted to these spaces and pulls itself into them, moving up the strip. The paper with the largest air spaces should provide the most surface area for the water. It is the most porous and water should move through it the fastest.

STUDENT DIRECTIONS *for* Rising to the Top

1. Gather four different kinds of paper to test in this activity. Using a ruler, pencil and scissors, cut the paper into strips one-inch wide by five inches long. Put a line across each of the strips at the four-inch mark. Number the strips one to four above this line. These are your "racing strips."

2. Fill two identical cups with one inch of water. You will place your racing strips into the cups at the same time, and the water will race to the finish line. Now it's time to place your bets. On which sheet will the water cross the line first? second? third? last? How long do you think it will take? Make your predictions. Then, on your mark, get set, flow!

3. What were the results? Can you explain how and why the water moves faster on some paper and slower on others? Use a magnifying glass to look for clues.

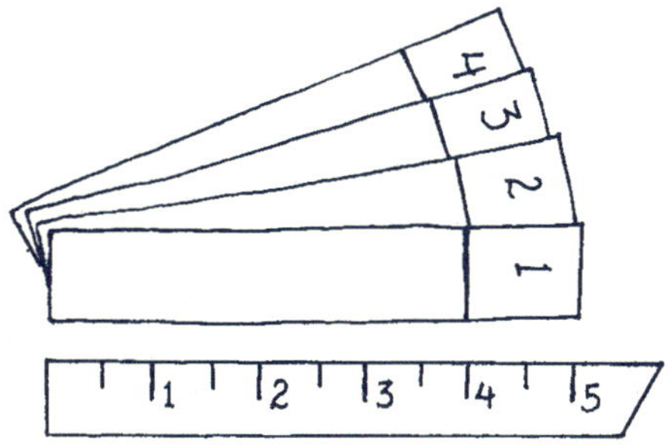
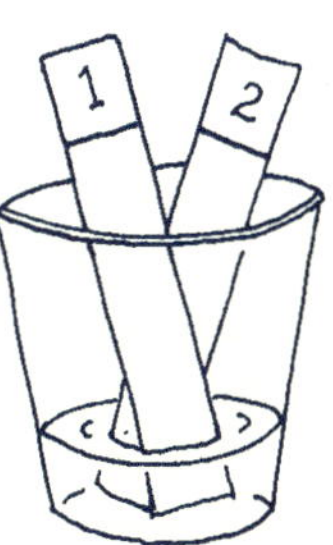
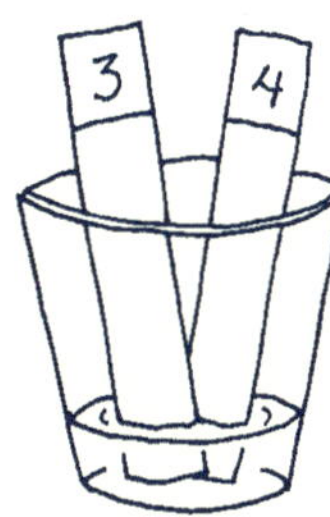

Activity: **Sink or Float**

TEACHER NOTES *and* INFO

The wooden block, crayon, lemon, walnut in the shell, pencil and twist tie, all float because they weigh less than the water that is pushing upwards beneath them. The metal jar lid may or may not float depending on how it is placed in the water. The cotton ball floats then sinks as it absorbs water. The plastic comb may sink or float, depending on what kind of plastic it is made of. The golf ball sinks.

STUDENT DIRECTIONS *for* **Sink or Float**

1. Begin by guessing which of the items on the following list will sink and which will float. Record your guess in the proper column.

2. Now test your guess by experimenting with each item in the basin of water. Record the actual result.

3. Look around the room and find at least two more objects to guess, test and record your results. Why do some objects sink and some float?

OBJECT	SINK *or* FLOAT?	RESULTS
Wooden block		
Crayon		
Lemon		
Walnut in the shell		
Metal jar lid		
Pencil		
Golf ball		
Plastic comb		
Cotton ball		
Twist tie		

Water Naturally

QUESTIONS

- What is a watershed?
- How many different types of habitats are in the basin?
- How much land makes up the Lake Champlain Basin?
- How does water travel within the basin?
- How is a river different from a stream?
- What happens to lakes and ponds in the winter?
- What types of species live in the basin and how are they connected?
- How do lakes and ponds change over time?

KEY RESOURCES

- Interactive Lake Ecology *by Mark Denencour*
- Project Seasons *by Deborah Parrella*
- Pond Life, a Golden Guide *by George K. Reid*
- Opportunities for Action—*Lake Champlain Basin Program*
- Pond and River, an Eyewitness Book *by Steve Parker*
- NatureScope: "Wading into Wetlands" —*National Wildlife Federation*
- Aquatic Project Wild—*Western Regional Environmental Education Council*
- WOW! The Wonders of Wetlands *by Britt Eckhart Slattery*
- Water: A Natural History *by Alice Outwater*

Word Bank

algae
Atlantic flyway
decomposition
density
dissolved oxygen
dormant
ecology
ecosystems
epilimnion
erosion
eutrophication
food chain
food web
gravity
habitat
hypolimnion
larva
lentic water
lotic water
macroinvertebrate
metalimnion
nutrient
nymph
oligotrophic
phosphorus
photosynthesis
phytoplankton
riparian
seiche
stratification
sub-basin
tributary
watershed
wetland
Wetland Restoration Project
Wildlife Management Area
zooplankton

Activity: **Where Are You in the Watershed?**

TEACHER NOTES *and* INFO

This activity gives students a chance to become familiar with topographic maps and learn how to recognize wetlands, watersheds and other features on these maps. Students will be able to identify where they are in the watershed.

STUDENT ACTIVITY

1. Get a USGS topographic map of your area and have the students find locations of interest—their homes, the school, the roads they travel. Explain that a contour line joins all points of the same elevation (height above sea level), that some of the contour lines have numbers on them and this is the elevation in feet or meters, and that contour lines that are close together indicate a steep area. Find some hilltops and valleys.

2. Have the students find the wetlands in your area. Are they associated with rivers, streams, lakes or ponds. If not, why are the wetlands where they are? Where are the wetlands located (elevationally) relative to other features?

3. Choose one wetland area and mark all the highest points around the wetland with an X or a large dot. Connect the points with a line to delineate the wetland's watershed (see below). Discuss how any land use activity in the watershed can affect the wetland: soil, fertilizer, pesticides and other pollutants can wash downhill into the wetland with surface runoff.

4. Use the topographical map to try to "travel" by water to the lake. Locate the nearest tributary and figure out what route to take to the lake. Students should be able to delineate what sub-basin they are in by outlining the area from their home to the lake.

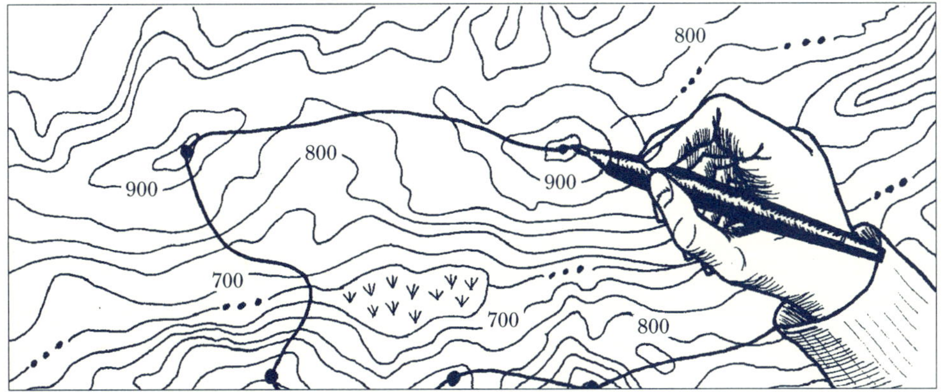

Credit: *Activity adapted with permission from DISCOVER WETLANDS, by Brian Lynn, Washington Department of Ecology, 1988.*

Activity: **Layering Activity**

Other Ideas
• Give students the materials and invite them to design an experiment that will demonstrate whether cold water acts differently than hot water and how they act together. Students will need to make a hypothesis, design a procedure then record what happens. Help them design questions that their experiment will answer.

TEACHER NOTES *and* INFO

Just as warm air rises above cool air, making the second floor of a building warmer than the first, warm water rises above cool water, making the top of the lake warmer than the bottom. Warm water is lighter or less dense than cold water. Discuss with students how this phenomenon affects the lake.

Every winter as the cold wind blows over the lake, it chills the surface water, which sinks. The warmer water below rises, gets cooled by the cold air, then sinks, too. This happens again in the spring as the water warms. The continual up-down movement of water is called "overturn." In this way, food and oxygen are constantly being turned over in the water.

STUDENT ACTIVITY

1. Add food coloring to the glasses of hot water. Slowly pour some of the water into a glass of cold water. What happens to the hot, colored water? Does it float on top of cold water or sink? Is it lighter or heavier than cold water?
2. Do the experiment again, pouring cold water over hot water. What happens?

Activity: **Junk in a Jar**

Note: *The good news is that detergents with phosphates are banned in New York and Vermont. The bad news is that phosphate may be hard to find for this activity. You can use plant food or fish fertilizer.*

TEACHER NOTES *and* INFO

This activity demonstrates what phosphorus that goes down the drain can do to our water. Phosphorus is an essential element for all plants and animals but it causes problems in surface waters when present in excessive amounts. In some places it is used widely in detergents.

STUDENT ACTIVITY

Organize students in small groups. Ask students to predict how excess phosphorus might affect pond water. Will it clean it? Change it? Harm it?
1. Collect enough pond water to fill each jar with an equal amount of water.
2. Using the eyedropper, add different amounts of the phosphate material to all but one jar. Leave this one jar alone as a control sample. Label each jar with the amount of detergent you put in. Put all the jars in a sunny windowsill and watch what happens to them over the next two weeks.

Activity: **Exploring Wetlands**

TEACHER NOTES and INFO

The most important part of teaching about wetlands is to visit a wetland. This often means getting wet and mucky; it sometimes means a ruined pair of sneakers and some dirty jeans but it's a mighty wonder. The following material is actually a series of activities about learning and visiting a wetland. As a humanities teacher who has added the study of the natural world of Lake Champlain in the past five years, wetlands were my door to the world of science and to the extraordinary pull the natural world has for children.

STUDENT ACTIVITIES

1. Preconceptions about Wetlands
2. Guided Imagery
3. Wetlands Metaphor
4. The Visit
5. Winding Down
6. Mudpoem

Activity:

Preconceptions about Wetlands

TEACHER NOTES *and* INFO

Since many students and their parents have negative attitudes about wetlands, it is helpful to explore these attitudes before your visit.

STUDENT ACTIVITY

Ask your students what they think of when they think of wetlands. Have them write their impressions in their thinkbooks.

> *"When I think of a swamp I think of mud, plants, gross animals like frogs and snakes. It's slimy, wet and ugly."*
>
> *thinkbook entry, Grade 5, Milton*

> *"When I think of a swamp it's not the best place to be. Sometimes it's neat to explore to see what lives there. But not for very long. It smells, it's wet and it's murky."*
>
> *thinkbook entry, Grade 5, Milton*

Note: The word "swamp" is loaded and you may choose to use "wetlands."

Taking It Home

Ask your students to ask their parents what they think of wetlands. Make up some questions with your students and ask them to copy them over and take them home to interview their parents. **Examples:** "What's the first word that comes to mind when I say swamp?" *green slime* "Do you know anything about swamps?" *mosquito-infested, frogs live there, lily pads*

Activity: **Guided Imagery**

TEACHER NOTES *and* INFO

Students should be seated quietly in a darkened room while you lead them through an imaginary walk through the wetlands.

STUDENT ACTIVITY

Shut your eyes and picture yourself in a very quiet place. It is warm and breezy and you can feel the wetness around you. There are trees and grasses and as you listen you can hear the sounds of birds. As you begin to walk you are aware of how soft and springy the earth is under your feet. You stop again and this time you can hear the CROAK of a bullfrog. It stops as you get nearer. You can hear the Zzzzz of mosquitoes and the ground is getting extremely moist under your feet. You're into some muck now and your feet are almost stuck as you pull them up to take your next step. (Make mud-walking noise.) Next you get to a small little hill and decide to sit there and watch all the birds and bugs fly by....

Activity: **Wetlands Metaphor**

TEACHER NOTES *and* INFO

This activity helps teach the unique characteristics and functions of wetlands. Begin by introducing wetlands to your class. Since the metaphor activity helps teach this material, this can be brief. Students should be familiar with the benefits of a wetland on the right hand side of the chart that follows.

Prepare a "Mystery Metaphor Container" (a pillowcase or box), filled with the following objects: sponge, small pillow, soap, eggbeater or mixer, small doll cradle or pictures of nursery items, picture of zoo, toy animal, sieve or strainer, paper coffee filter, antacid tablets, small box of cereal or crackers, package of wild rice. Use magazine pictures to represent anything that you

You will need:
- "Mystery Metaphor Container" with items listed on next page

can't locate. The following chart will help you but students always come up with other ways to explain their objects:

SPONGE: absorbs excess water caused by runoff; floodbuster; retains moisture for a time even if standing water dries up (A sponge stays wet even after it has absorbed a spill.)
PILLOW or BED: is a resting place for migratory birds
EGGBEATER: mixes nutrients and oxygen into the water
CRADLE: provides a nursery that shelters, protects and feeds young wildlife
STRAINER: strains silt, debris, etc., from water (keeps water supply clean)
COFFEE FILTER: filters smaller impurities from water (excess nutrients, toxins)
ANTACID: neutralizes toxic substances
CEREAL, RICE or PICTURE OF A GARDEN: provides nutrient-rich foods for wildlife and humans
SOAP: helps clean the environment as a whole
PICTURE OF ZOO or TOY ANIMAL: habitat for diversity of wildlife
PICTURE OF RESORT or SUITCASE: resting place for migrating waterfowl

STUDENT ACTIVITY

Divide the class into small groups. Ask each student to choose an object from the container. The group needs to find a metaphor for each object. **Example:** "A sponge is like a wetland because it absorbs moisture."

Encourage students to make any connections that help them understand the benefits of wetlands. There is not one right answer. Give groups some time to discuss and then have each student show his or her object and state its metaphor.

Review by asking the class these questions:

• Why are wetlands important?

• How do they help Lake Champlain?

Formalize with a short essay assignment or "Five Facts about Wetlands."

Credit: *Activity from AQUATIC PROJECT WILD by the Western Regional Environmental Education Council. Used with permission.*

Activity: **The Visit**

PREPARATION *for your* VISIT

Because of bird migrations some natural areas are closed at certain times of the year. Arrange the visit several weeks ahead. Some areas are designated hunting areas so this is a question of safety as well as courtesy. The area will be posted if it is restricted. Find out whether the wetland that you want to visit is privately owned or managed by a state or federal agency. Contact the person responsible.

Two weeks ahead, talk to the students about what they are going to need:
• "high waders" or a pair of old sneakers
• old clothes
• dry socks/pants to change into back at school
• warm jacket
• sometimes hats and mittens!
• sometimes bug repellent!
• chaperones!
Allow time for working out the logistics, e.g. "My brother has a pair of boots you can borrow."

TEACHER NOTES *and* INFO

When we visit the wetlands, we do two activities on site, the "Scavenger Hunt" and "Observing Water Creatures," described on p. 471 and 475. For the past four years, I have had a naturalist come with me so that we could split the class in half, each run one of the two activities, and then switch groups. Nine to eleven students is a maximum number for each activity. When Mary Dupont and I take a group together, she has taken a third group and run a workshop on dissecting cattails.

It is important to prepare the students for what will be happening and what they will be asked to do. I explain the schedule and show them the scavenger hunt. You don't want to have to explain much on site; at that point you turn them over to Mother Nature and let her do the instructing.

You will need:
• 12 clipboards
• pencils
• copies of the scavenger hunt (see p. 471)
I usually carry everything to the site in a big canvas bag.

STUDENT ACTIVITY

Hand out copies of the scavenger hunt, pencils and clipboards on site. Most of the walk is led in quiet; we try to stay still and see some birds and we sneak up on the beavers although they are always too smart for us.

At some point, when we have done our "work," we take time for some fun and exploration. If there is a safe place for them to explore the muck, I highly recommend letting them. The value of the exploring, observing, speculating and questioning always equals or surpasses the worth of the formal observation. When we've finished we walk to meet the other group, so the students can switch teachers and activities.

STUDENT HANDOUT - "Scavenger Hunt"

Activity: **Winding Down**

TEACHER NOTES *and* INFO

I have enjoyed scheduling the wetlands expedition mid-day so that we have some time in the classroom the same afternoon. We are exhausted and happy, the room is a mess and stinks of muddy socks and wet boots. The students change into dry clothes and have a snack and we sit around for a while and rave and laugh about how dirty and happy we are. The principal comes in and shakes his head, but leaves smiling.

We then settle down to a drawing/writing activity, which provides a welcome calm and a chance for students to tell their stories of their visit to the wetlands.

You will need:
- "Picture Page" (see p. 470)
- large, white drawing paper
- colored pencils
- glue
- scissors

STUDENT ACTIVITY

Each student gets a page with wetland "pictures" on it and a large piece of white drawing paper. The task for students is to write stories of their trips

using the pictures and their words. They may write the whole story on one page, or cut the paper into four to six sections and make a small book. Students always create variations to these possibilities and some artists choose to make all their own illustrations but use the "Picture Page" for ideas. We settle down to a peaceful time of drawing, writing, cutting and pasting. Instruct your students to either plan the story first or choose the pictures first. In any case, they should color the pictures before gluing them on.

• Color the pictures.
• Plan the page.
• Write the story.
• Glue pictures.
• Illustrate background. Students can trim, color frames or illustrate by coloring in skies or grasses.

"It was COLD today at the wetlands and it was fun. We got to see a BEAVER home and a lot of other things and my friend Jason got tons of muck on him. We saw a lot of DUCKS."
thinkbook entry, Grade 5, Milton

Activity: **Mudpoem**

TEACHER NOTES *and* INFO

After your visit to the wetlands, record the sensations of your visit by writing a poem!

STUDENT ACTIVITY

Ask students to brainstorm a list of the different sounds that they did hear or might have heard in the wetland. Individuals or groups of students can write their own creative versions of what a wetland sounds like, using any of the ideas on the board. As students read these aloud, the efforts become a group poem. Write the completed poem on the overhead. Read the poem while they make the sounds to accompany it. Practice a few times and produce a final tape for the classroom archive.

Possible sounds:
• frogs
• crickets
• birds
• bubbles
• mud
• dripping water
• lapping waves
• beavers slapping their tails on water
• beavers gnawing on trees
• mosquitoes
• a bear stuck in the mud
• bees
• a duck landing on water
• a heron silently watching for food
• a fish flopping over on water

Picture Page

Scavenger Hunt

Work in groups to find, but not take, these things.
Try to identify anything that you can. Draw pictures and describe:

ANIMALS

with wings: with a tail: with a tongue: with three colors:

The most interesting thing about animals I saw:

PLANTS

with a flower: with shiny leaves: that float: with roots:

The most interesting thing about plants I saw:

Find something...

dead: tiny: slimy: weird:

Find evidence of...

a home: a sponge: moving water: still water: decay:

Check off the animal signs that you see.
Identify them if you can and write down any others not on the list.

_____ tracks   _____ burrows

_____ droppings   _____ bones

_____ nests   _____ feathers

_____ lodges   _____ other: ____________________

_____ chewings   _____ other: ____________________

You are a guest in someone's home. Be a good one!

Rubies Pearls

Activity: **Silhouettes**

YOU WILL NEED:
- wet-on-wet watercolors
- watercolor paper—heavy drawing paper is best
- brushes or small sponges
- ice trays to hold water for painting
- newspaper to cover desk or tables
- colored or silver foil paper

STUDENT ACTIVITY

Class 1

1. Wet the colors in the kit—really stir and have a juicy, wet surface.

2. Wet the paper that you are going to paint on with clear water. Use a brush or small sponge and lots of water. Work fast. Cover the paper so it's wet like your skin after you come out of a bath or the lake.

3. Taking your brush, soak up two watercolors from your kit. Brush across the wet paper. Watch the paint sprawl, bleed, blend and mix.
Do this three or four times—each time soak the brush with two colors to create color blends. You may use two different colors each time or the same ones over and over. I wouldn't use brown or black.

Class 2

The next day, draw seaweed, shells, grasses and growth on the bottom of the lake. Color in totally with black markers. Blacken sand and bottom of lake also.

Class 3

Add small fish with colored foil paper. If you want a school of fish, fold the paper, then cut it, so all your fish are a uniform size. Make the contour of the fish a simple shape.

Human Impact

QUESTIONS

- How do humans use the Lake Champlain Basin?
- What are some positive human uses of the basin?
- What are some negative human uses of the basin?
- What role does soil play in the basin?
- How can I help keep the basin healthy?

KEY RESOURCES

- Pond and Stream Safari: A Guide to the Ecology of Aquatic Invertebrates
  —*Cornell Cooperative Extension*
- The Magic School Bus at the Waterworks *by Joanna Cole*
- Field Manual for Water Quality Monitoring *by Mark Mitchell and William Stapp*
- Testing the Waters: Chemical and Physical Vital Signs of a River *by Sharon Behar*
- Water: A Natural History *by Alice Outwater*

Little Ice Shanty:
The Lake Champlain Ice Fisherman
by Shelley Posen, December 1984

I am an old ice fisherman, On Lake Champlain I dwell;
At hooking ice fish, perch and smelt, There's none can me excel.

> *Little ice shanty, Ice shanty dear to me,*
> *In winter out on Lake Champlain, That's where I long to be.*

I take my shanty on the ice, When first it forms a skin,
I choose my spot most carefully, Before I do begin.
I bank the outsides up with snow, To keep inside the heat,
Then I take my Swedish auger in, And drill two holes so neat.

I rise from bed at crack of dawn, And stay out all the day,
My shanty keeps me nice and warm, Ice fishing on the bay.

For bait I use a piece of smelt, I skin off by the tail,
But if for perch I drop my line, It's perch eyes will not fail.
And when an ice fish takes my bait and tugs upon my line,
I weave my fish sticks back and forth, And land him double time.

My shanty keeps me from the wind; my gas stove keeps me warm,
A little drop of rye or rum, Don't do me any harm.
By night my bucket's full of fish, To be carried home and dressed,
We eat five pounds at suppertime, And in water freeze the rest.

Let those that want to tip-up fish, Outside do as they please,
Give me my shanty any time—, Why should I fish and freeze?
Let heave cracks thunder under foot, Let white-outs make me blink,
I'll ice fish on Lake Champlain, 'Til I have to swim or sink

And when I die and go to heaven, Where all ice fishers go,
I'm sure I'll find ice shanties there, Just like I had below.

> *Little ice shanty, Ice shanty dear to me,*
> *In winter out on Lake Champlain—*
> *Fish with me only on the ice,*
> *That's where I long to be.*

Dr. Sheldon I. Posen, folklorist and creator of the exhibit and book, "You Hear the Ice Talking," composed this song to the tune of "The Stern Old Bachelor" to describe ice fishing on Lake Champlain. Sung by Stan Ransom. Used with permission.

Activity:
Observing Water Creatures

TEACHER NOTES *and* INFO

*A note on teaching observation skills
from Judy Elson:*

Wetlands (or the grassy edges of a pond
or lake) are truly magical places to explore with students of all ages. Before
arriving at our observation spot, I like
to brainstorm with the students the
kinds of behavior that will ensure a successful visit. Eventually we cover every-
thing—respect, quiet, slow movements...“take only pictures, leave only
footprints.” If you have done some work in class on wetlands or water
environments, review what a wetland is and observe the basic characteristics of wetlands, such as moist soil and wetland plants.

The main objectives of our trip are:
• to strengthen students' observation skills,
• to enlighten their curiosity about an unknown area,
• to have fun.

We definitely accomplish all three. We also learn the names of some of
the plants, the life cycle of some aquatic insects and we solidify the connection of humans to the creatures and habitats of the wetland and the
water's edge.

Review with your class the observation skills and procedures they will be
using at the water's edge. Hand out “Taking a Closer Look” for each
student to have at the site. Students should review this sheet before
their visit and have a copy on site.

STUDENT HANDOUT - “Taking a Closer Look”

The staff at Vermont Institute of Natural Science
recites this poem as they put a creature back in
the water:

> *Swim away, stride away, crawl away, hop.*
> *You are free to go*
> *I'm not going to stop*
> *You from living your life*
> *You deserve to be free*
> *Thanks for sharing this time with me!*

You will need
for each group:
• a pad of paper and
  pencil
• a nature guide to ponds
  (optional)
• a small hand-dip net,
  a flat-bottomed net, or a
  kitchen sieve
• 2 or 3 clear containers
  half full of pond water
• a spoon
• trowels
• bucket
• a waterscope
• a magnifying glass
• flat-bottomed container
  with high sides to view
  creatures (use white
  enamel or clear glass
  with white paper under-
  neath it)

Taking A Closer Look

Tips for finding critters!

1. As you approach the water's edge, watch for tracks of animals in the mud or sand. Sketch the tracks on your pad of paper so you can look them up in your nature guide.

2. Look for insects such as water striders and dark whirligig beetles on the surface of slow-moving water, or for mosquito larvae under the water's surface. Catch a few insects with your dip net, and place them in a container of pond water. Some of these insects move fast so a viewer that can contain the insect, such as a magnifying insect bottle, is best. Use your nature guidebook to identify them.

3. Many insects hide near or on water plants. Sweep the dip net through the water close to plants and look under leaves. The slime beneath waterlily pads contains microscopic plants and animals that snails and insects eat. Look under rocks and small pieces of wood as well. How do the creatures attach themselves to things? Keep an eye out for dragonfly nymphs crawling about on the plants or stones, transparent freshwater shrimp that look like sow bugs, and dark brown leeches.

4. The bottom mud contains a surprising number of creatures. Use a spoon to dig up some mud and place it in a sieve. Wash the mud away with some pond water, then use the magnifying glass to look for aquatic worms.

5. Stand in the water and look at things with your microscope. Use the flat-bottomed net to catch minnows, large beetles or crayfish. Put them in a container of pond water, identify them, then return them to the pond.

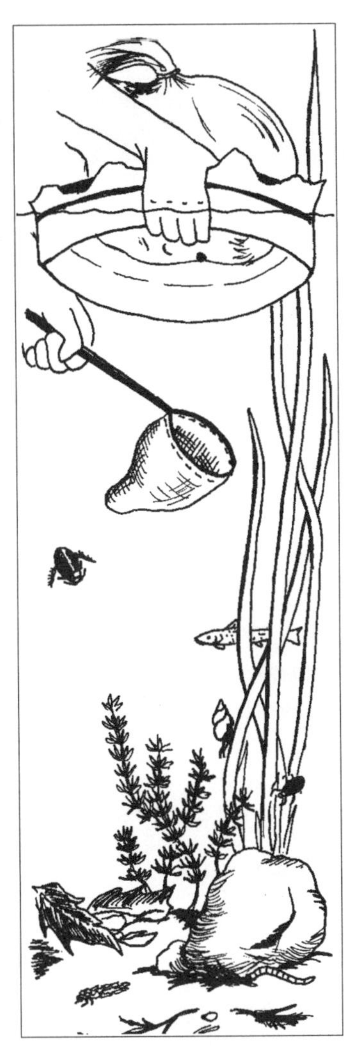

Making Your Own Tools

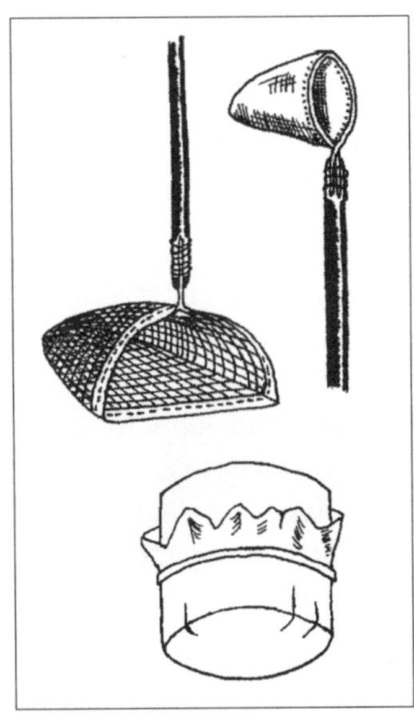

• A **hand-dip net** is good for collecting small insects and organisms on top of the water and among plants. Bend a coat hanger into a ring three inches in diameter. Sew a nylon stocking or piece of cheesecloth onto the ring. Fasten the ring to a stick or pole with wire. (A butterfly net works well too.)

• A **flat-bottomed net** is useful for collecting fish, minnows or beetles. Bend a coat hanger into a D-shaped frame about a foot wide. Sew a net bag made from cheesecloth onto the rim. Fasten the ring to a broom handle with wire.

• A **waterscope** is an ideal way to view tiny animals and plants without getting wet! Cut off the bottom of a plastic pail or ice-cream container. Cut a piece of plastic wrap to cover the bottom. Attach the wrap with large elastics. Use your waterscope on a sunny day in clear, still water.

Credit: *Adapted with permission from WATER SCIENCE by Deborah Seed.*

Activity: **Go With the Flow**

TEACHER NOTES *and* INFO

This activity introduces the concept of a watershed and the way that non-point source pollution flows within a watershed. Arrange students into small groups.

STUDENT ACTIVITY

1. Explain to the group that they will be designing their own watershed with the materials provided: aluminum foil (land), plastic cups or scrunched up newspaper (molds for the mountains) and the tray (bedrock). Place two or three plastic cups upside down on the tray. Have the groups mold aluminum foil over the cups to create the mountains, valleys and rivers.

2. When the watersheds are complete, invite the groups to discuss the types of land use that take place in their watershed: agriculture, industry, urban development, roads, recreation areas, to name a few! What effect do these land-use practices have on the water quality in your watersheds?

3. Ask the groups to sprinkle some pollution (the dry drink mix) over the land-use areas that they think may affect the water quality. Invite the group to make some predictions about what will happen when it rains on all this pollution.

4. Give the groups watering cans or spritzers to simulate a rainstorm in their watersheds. Where did the water travel? What happened to the color of the water after traveling though the land-use areas? Does this happen in real watersheds? What are some local sources of nonpoint source pollution in our local watershed? How can we decrease the amount of nonpoint source pollution reaching our water supply?

You will need:
- aluminum foil
- plastic cups or news-papers
- packets of unsweetened dry drink mix (grape or cherry)
- lunch trays or large platters/plates (lasagna pans are good)
- watering cans or plastic jugs with pin holes

Activity:
A Question of Development

TEACHER NOTES *and* INFO

After students learn about the importance of wetlands, this experience will help them formulate their opinions about the pros and cons of development on the lake.   It sets up an "us vs. them" mode for you and your students.

There are numerous role play scenarios in different sources such as PROJECT WILD and AQUATIC WILD.

STUDENT ACTIVITY

Explain the activity:

> *"Now you are all going to have a chance to be creatures of the wetlands. Imagine that you are a living thing in the wetlands on the Milton shore near the Sandbar [or other wetland]. You can be a very small creature or the largest living thing that might live in or near a wetland...a moose...a bear...? You may also choose to be a person...maybe you are a canoeist or hiker or bird-watcher who likes to walk through the wetlands in big, tall boots! Choose a creature that lives in or benefits from the presence of wetlands."*

Begin with:

> *"I am a developer and I want to build a 65-slip marina on these wetlands. Construction will mean draining the land and bringing in fill on which to put structures. It will mean the destruction of this habitat as you know it, but, of course, change is good. Don't tell me you have problems with this great plan!"*

As a closing for this activity, ask the students to write a position paper about what they think is the right thing to do. They can write them as a [fifth-grade student in Milton, Vermont], or speak as the characters they were during the role play. Students may choose to read their position papers orally when they have finished.

I maintain a strong position for building the marina and allow them turns in speaking out against construction. If needed, have a cattail for a microphone and ask them to pass it to each other and allow turns to speak. I prefer to do without this, however, so the crowd can build itself into a (well-orchestrated) frenzy.

In the second half of the activity, we switch positions: I am the lone opponent of the building of the marina and they are the local board of directors or selectpeople. I continue to press them with reasons why it shouldn't be built; they have an opportunity to explain to me why it must be built.

Activity: **Basin Bumpers**

TEACHER NOTES *and* INFO

This activity will give your students a chance to review all the problems that face Lake Champlain, consider solutions and speak out about a problem that they would like to solve.

STUDENT ACTIVITY

Brainstorm with your students all the problems that face Lake Champlain. Ask students to list the problems on the left-hand side of a worksheet. After you have completed the list, discuss and list solutions to each problem on the right-hand side.

Ask each student to choose one issue that he or she would like to design a bumper sticker for. Students can use space on the worksheet for a rough draft. Make final bumper stickers on oak tag, laminate them and display them in the school.

Your class may choose to have a contest and find a way to make real bumper stickers with the winning one!

You will need:
- worksheet
- oak tag pieces pre-cut to the size of a bumper sticker

Taking It Home

Ask your students to take home the list of problems that you have generated in class. Do families have any to add to the list? Ask students with their families to rank the problems in order of importance. What problems are the hardest to solve? What problems are the most serious and should be given priority? It would be interesting to have students share results in class and figure out a way to process and publicize the results.

Activity: **Soil on the Run**

Other Ideas

• Try this activity outdoors on a sloping plot of lawn. Remove sod from several plots and test various options: mulch, terracing, adding organic matter, etc.

• Make splash sticks to show how raindrops can loosen and move soil. Have small groups of students make their own splash sticks by attaching paper to three-foot lengths of lumber with thumbtacks. Explain that they will be holding these sticks vertically over bare soil with the paper touching the ground and using a watering can to simulate rain. How high will the raindrops carry bits of soil? Ask them to record and initial their predictions

TEACHER NOTES *and* INFO

Students will learn about soil erosion and how to control it. Arrange your students in small groups.

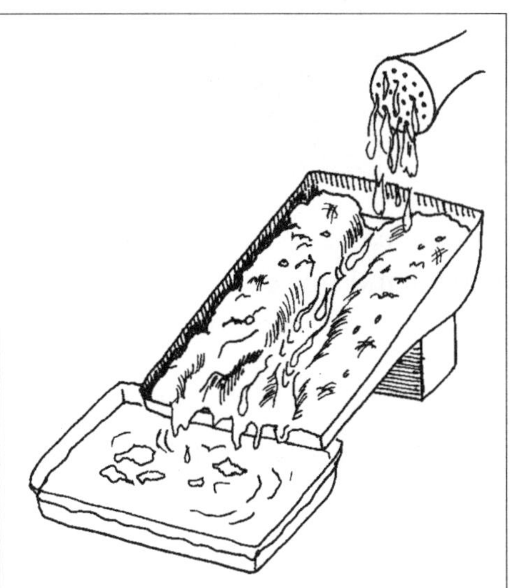

STUDENT ACTIVITY

1. Gather the students together for a demonstration. Explain that you are a New England hill farmer and you just finished harvesting and tilling your fields. Show the students a tray full of soil that is propped up on one side, creating a slope. Place a collecting basin beneath the tray that runs the width of the tray. Tell the students it has been a rainy fall and another storm is brewing. Ask them what will happen to the soil in this field during a rainstorm. Record their predictions. Then, using a watering can (held one foot above the tray), let it "rain" for one to two minutes.

2. Have the students examine the soil in the tray and observe the runoff collected in the basin. Pour it into a clear jar for closer inspection. (They should see gullies formed in the tray, and perhaps large areas where the soil was washed away. The water in the collecting basin will be muddy and full of sediment.) Have them test the soil at various depths to see how much water was actually absorbed. Discuss the results and what this means with regard to soil and plant health.

3. Explain to the students that soil erosion is a serious problem facing humans throughout the world. Every year three billion tons of topsoil are lost, and it is the topsoil that is responsible for soil fertility. Remind them it takes a hundred or more years to make an inch of new topsoil. Challenge the students to reduce the amount of erosion that occurs on sloping farm fields.

4. Divide the students into small groups and give each group two trays to be filled with soil. Tell them they will need to research and discuss options for controlling erosion in these fields. Possible options include mulch covers, contour plowing, cover cropping, terracing, and adding organic materials to the soil to improve water absorption.

5. Provide materials for students to use on their fields including compost, various forms of mulch, twigs, Popsicle sticks and toothpicks (for creating terraces, water bars and roots), and seeds. Decide with the students a time limit for research and preparations. It can vary greatly depending on the students' desires to experiment with cover crops and planting patterns.

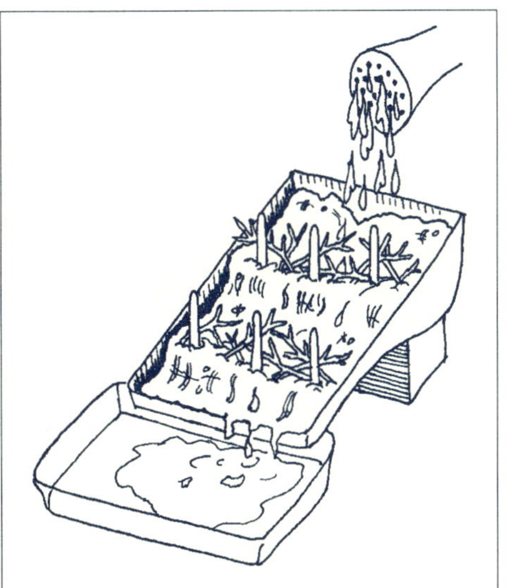

6. On the final day of the activity, set up trays and have students present their methods for erosion control. Have all groups pour the same amount of water from a set height onto the sloping fields. Examine the runoff of each field, noting clarity, color and amount collected. Which methods were most effective at controlling erosion?

Taking It Home

TEACHER NOTES *and* **INFO:** After students have gained some familiarity with pollution issues, send home the handout: "Pollution Sources in a Watershed." This structured interview will help generate awareness of where sources of pollution actually exist. Students will bring back some interesting information. **Example:** One student's father worked on a town road crew and there had been a concerted effort to decrease the amount of salt they put on the roads in the wintertime. This makes students think about the impact of specific jobs and learn about human impact in a more real way.

STUDENT ACTIVITY: Explain the questions on the worksheet and send it home. It's good to give a few days for this type of assignment.

STUDENT HANDOUT: "Pollution Sources in a Watershed"

Pollution Sources in a Watershed

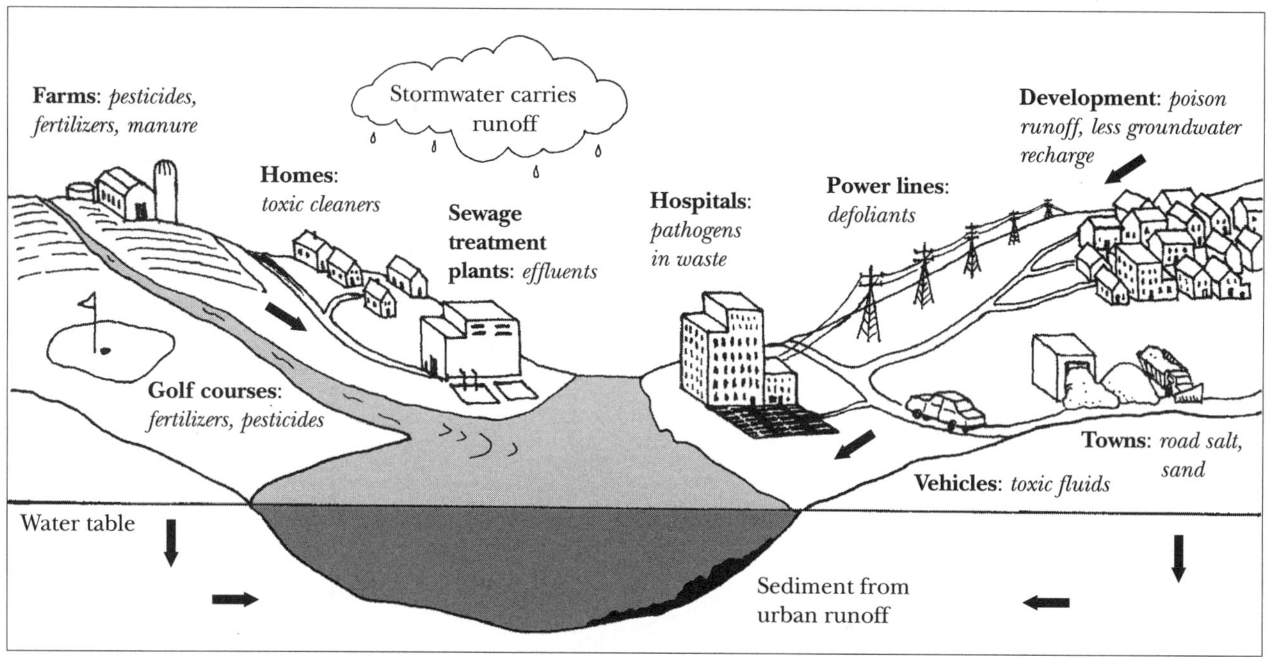

These questions should be completed with a member of your family.

A. Name three things that cause pollution in Lake Champlain.

1. ______________________________

2. ______________________________

3. ______________________________

B. Can you find something in the picture that you recognize?

Example: Specify where there is a hospital. Name the hospital. _______________

____

C. Are there any sources of pollution that a member of your family is involved in because of their job? Does he or she know whether things are being done to find a solution to the problem? Use reverse side for answers.

Signature of family partner ____________________________________

Drying Off

Certificate designed by Mandy Labrie, Grade 5, School Street School, Milton, Vermont

Celebrate Your Success

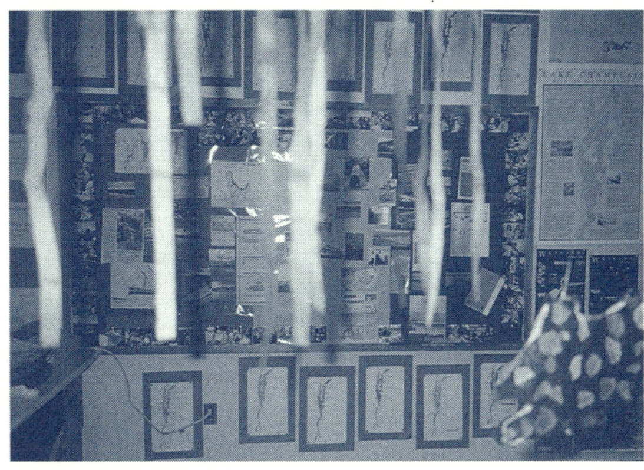

Culminating activities are important vehicles for students to:

• celebrate what they've learned,
• choose a different way to express what they have learned,
• share their successes with families and community,
• learn more by the process of observing, processing and recording what they know.

For you as a teacher, culminating events provide the opportunity to see what your students have learned. You will see evidence of having met your learning goals. If you have worked hard to help students learn to develop their opinions, for example, and then they stand up in front of 75 people and argue their position on development on the lakeshore, you can see the achievement of your goal. It's a pretty good feeling! When students plan a large portrait of their work, they are constantly retrieving information from the study. Even they will be amazed at how much they learned!

PLANNING *for the* BIG EVENT

The process of working together to plan a presentation is as important as the final product. Sometimes new learning happens in what starts out as a "review." It's also half the fun. When students work together, some good things happen to your community of learners.

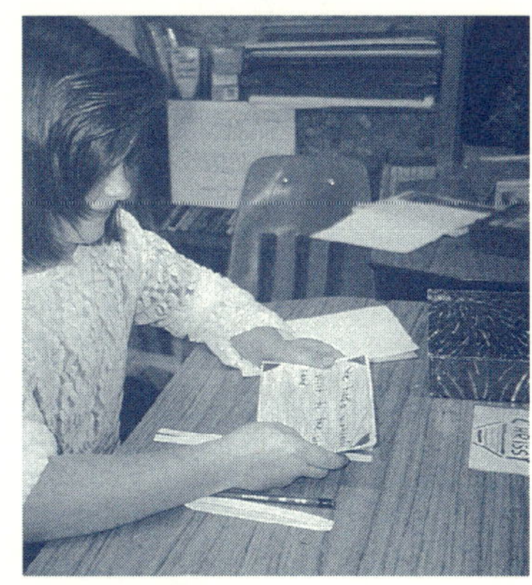

Usually I have some idea when I begin of what kind of event we will have but it is very important to involve your students as much as possible. I usually have had some kind of open house with displays and presentation, but that varies with the group that creates it. You are once again in that situation where you have to balance your own standards and expectations with the need to create choices for the students who must feel ownership of the final product.

I will review some ideas for an open house format and then offer some ideas of colleagues who have tried other things.

Other Ideas

• Make a magazine or "big book" for younger students. Each student can choose a topic about Lake Champlain and have one page to illustrate and write a paragraph explaining that illustration. Students should have the opportunity to read their book to younger kids.

What I think works for an open house is a display of student work-portfolios on desks, projects on the wall and a formal presentation. We also allow time for parents to walk through and marvel at all the work the students have done.

The following are examples of activities that can be done at an open house:

Skits. Some drama activities outlined in this book can be performed or skits can be created from the students' own writing. One year students wrote and performed a skit to the story "The Great Journey" (see p. 346).

Poems and speeches about the Lake Champlain study can be recited as a "chorus." For example, the following poem was written by Cara Basiliere, fifth-grade student in Milton, and recited at the Open House:

> **Wetlands**
> *Wetlands, wetlands, oh so mushy,*
> *Your globs of mud are, oh so gushy.*
> *Your filters make the water clean.*
> *You're one of the prettiest sights we've ever seen.*
>
> *Birds and geese, ducks, beavers and bugs,*
> *All make homes that are nice and snug.*

Creation of an underwater world in the classroom. One year, students made crepe-paper fish, which we hung from fishing line across the classroom. The room was dark and we had water music playing. We also dangled numerous facts about Lake Champlain that visitors could read on their underwater "swim."

A large map of Lake Champlain. Students projected an outline of the lake on poster board taped to the wall and made a large map. Different themes can be displayed on the maps. One group labeled shipwrecks and drew the ships with captions that sat on the map's edge.

Slide show with narration. One year, with a slide show in mind, I was uncharacteristically methodical about taking slides of each important moment of our study. Classroom activities, guest speakers and field trips were well documented and students organized the slides, wrote the narration and presented the show at the open house. I was lucky to have a parent who came in to work with the writers, which helped create a very well-written, organized production.

Miranda Bushey, fifth-grade student in Milton, wrote and delivered the introduction:

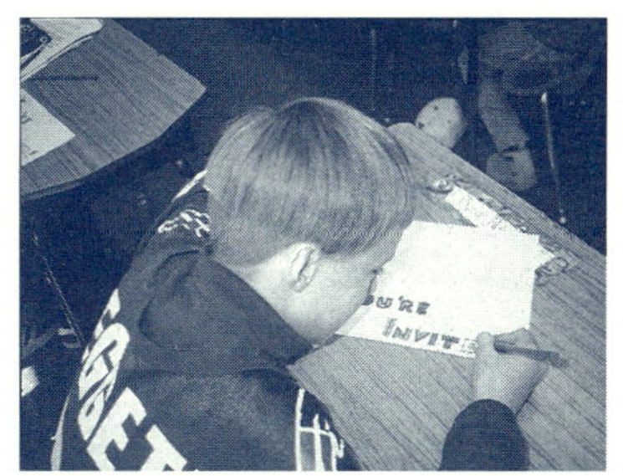

> *"On the slides coming up you'll see that during our Lake Champlain unit, we had lots of fun learning about Lake Champlain! We went on lots of field trips and had an exciting time on every one of them. We worked on our Lake Champlain unit for quite a few weeks! We learned many, many things we never knew. We did projects together and didn't complain who our partners were because in this class we work together as a team."*

Champ. One year a student made himself a wonderful costume out of some slippery green polyester. He was Champ and served as host for the big event.

Poster partners. One year I found myself in a situation where I didn't feel comfortable about the group dynamics of the class as they began to plan an open house. Some students were ready to go home and start building life-size replicas of boats (the *Philadelphia III*!), and other students had no clear idea what they wanted to do. I felt the need to pull the group together and offer some base to start from. The following is a letter I wrote to students the day after a frustrating planning session. We read and discussed the letter, used the chart of possibilities to choose topics and were under full sail within an hour.

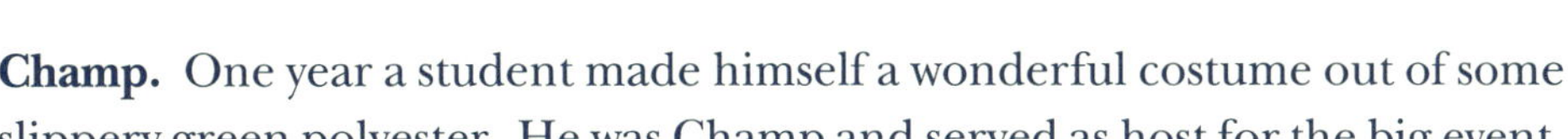

Dear Folks,

I have done some thinking after our discussion Friday, and I have a plan that I think will help focus our energies and get us going. I think it is a framework that you can get very creative with, and it gives us a place to start together, rather than going around in circles. I keep thinking about how much you know about our lake and what an important task you have of sharing your knowledge.

Two students will work together on making a poster with information (five facts) and an illustration. These posters will be displayed in the gym, unless connected to a specific display in our room. It is possible that some students may choose to work by themselves, and other students may pair up more than once! Aside from the basic format of the posters, you have an opportunity, after your posters are done, to create projects, displays, learning centers, skits...whatever time and your energy will allow!!!!

Here are some ideas... I bet you have more!

Information Poster

TITLE: Lake Champlain - General

FIVE FACTS: Could be even more!

GRAPHIC ILLUSTRATION: Scenes from the lake, tourist brochures you design, or each fact illustrated...

OTHER POSSIBILITIES: Game based on basic info, skit, survey of other students in the school about what they know.

Information Poster

TITLE: Pollution Problems

FIVE FACTS: About what threatens our lake, about how to prevent pollution.

GRAPHIC ILLUSTRATION: Something similar to the graphic we used on pollution problems in the watershed...or about a particular problem.

OTHER POSSIBILITIES: Bumper stickers or pins giving advice, skits on what to do or what not to do. Survey of practices that help or harm...

Information Poster

TITLE: Zebra Mussel

FIVE FACTS: You've got 'em! [*This had been a homework assignment.*]

GRAPHIC ILLUSTRATION: Life cycle or picture of clustering mussels.

OTHER POSSIBILITIES: Posters, brochures, buttons on how to prevent the spread of zebra mussels.

Information Poster

TITLE: Underwater Archeology

FIVE FACTS: On procedure or on diver safety.

GRAPHIC ILLUSTRATION: Grid system... underwater wrecks...

OTHER POSSIBILITIES: Larger model of shipwreck...

Information Poster

TITLE: Fish Hatchery

FIVE FACTS: How it works.

GRAPHIC ILLUSTRATION: Picture of how it works.

OTHER POSSIBILITIES: Glossary of fish words, artistic picture, life cycle of fish...

Information Poster

TITLE: Lake Champlain History

FIVE FACTS: Or more!!!

GRAPHIC ILLUSTRATION: Large "Time Quilt" or one large illustrated timeline...

OTHER POSSIBILITIES: Talking artifacts...

Information Poster

TITLE: Fish of Lake Champlain

FIVE FACTS: About different kinds of fish, their habitat...

GRAPHIC ILLUSTRATION: Pictures of fish, life cycle, cold-water and warm-water species.

OTHER POSSIBILITIES: Label drawing of parts of a fish...

Information Poster

TITLE: Lake Champlain Geography

FIVE FACTS: About what you think is important for people to know.

GRAPHIC ILLUSTRATION: Map!

OTHER POSSIBILITIES: Include important sites to us...

Information Poster

TITLE: *Philadelphia I & II*

FIVE FACTS: About each boat.

GRAPHIC ILLUSTRATION: Chronology of both boats.

OTHER POSSIBILITIES: Picture of Valcour Island, picture of launching of *Philadelphia II*, skit of firing cannon...

Information Poster

TITLE: Our study of the lake

FIVE FACTS: Highlights.

GRAPHIC ILLUSTRATION: Use pictures of our work and make a photo album....

OTHER POSSIBILITIES: Write a newspaper account of the things that we did....

Information Poster

TITLE: Alphabet of Lake Champlain

FIVE FACTS: If you used every letter, you would have 26 pictures!

GRAPHIC ILLUSTRATION: Illustrated alphabet.

OTHER POSSIBILITIES: A poem....

Information Poster

TITLE: Underwater Wrecks

FIVE FACTS: About preservation....

GRAPHIC ILLUSTRATION: Map with location of wrecks, picture of one wreck...

OTHER POSSIBILITIES: Horse ferry, model of shipwrecks...

Guest presenters. For two years, the Lake Champlain Basin Program has attended our open house and set up a display with literature. There are many groups that will be happy to share their information with a willing group of citizens and it adds class to your presentation.

OTHER CULMINATING ACTIVITIES *in the* BASIN
Colchester High School
Bill Romond and Betty Carvellas run a stellar interdisciplinary study of Lake Champlain at Colchester High School. Most years, they culminate the unit with a large public open house/science fair. This is very much a community event and many townspeople as well as parents attend. The students work hard to prepare their displays and are ready to teach the audience on the spot about their research.

A requirement for the final grade is for students to present their information outside of their class, e.g. to boy scouts, a gathering at a local library, the planning board or another classroom. Teachers accompany students on this presentation, which serves as their final exam.

Charlotte Central School
Cher Feitelberg, a fourth-grade teacher at Charlotte Central School, holds a large science fair at the end of their Lake Champlain study. Cher invites experts to attend and ask the students questions about their research.

Camel's Hump Middle School
Deb Higgins and Carol Livingston hold a simulated town meeting for parents. It is organized as follows:

A town (the class) is given an imaginary sum of money. Students are divided into cooperative groups whose task is to recommend how that money should be spent. The student groups represent citizens. Each group has a different interest:
- historians concerned about the preservation of historical sites and wrecks,
- developers interested in building a marina on the lake,
- citizens concerned about farm runoff,
- citizens wanting to clean up the barge canal,
- citizens wanting to rid the lake of lampreys and milfoil.

Science Fair
A science fair can be set up somewhat differently than an open house. Work is displayed and students are prepared to present and discuss their research with visitors.

Students do research and prepare reasons why the money should be spent on their cause.

At the town meeting, which is attended by parents, each group presents a resolution about the expenditure of funds. They present their argument with lots of background information. They also answer questions "from the floor" about their position. The "town meeting" of students and parents then votes on which "resolution" to support with the town's money.

Shrewsbury Mountain School
Grace Brigham takes her students on a boat ride together as a class (from Vergennes Falls to the mouth of Otter Creek, then southward to the Maritime Museum) on the M.V. *Carillon.* The class uses the time to reflect on the work they have done and celebrate the beauty of the lake. Her third grade wrote the following poem:

Sounds of Our Creek
Roaring, sound of thunder
Curtain of clouds falling
Water crashing, splashing
Wide pool at the bottom, smooth as glass

Curtain of clouds falling
Foamy pancakes wash toward us
Wide pool at the bottom, smooth as glass
River flows away from us, around a bend

Foamy pancakes wash toward us
Seven miles downstream, the river's mouth
River flows away from us, around a bend
Silence of Otter Creek as it becomes Lake Champlain

Seven miles downstream, the river's mouth
Water crashing, splashing
Silence of Otter Creek as it becomes Lake Champlain
Roaring, sound of thunder

Missisquoi Valley Union Middle School

The XStream Team, a seventh-grade interdisciplinary team at Missisquoi Valley Union Middle School, brainstormed this list of activities that could take place during a culminating event:

- produce a video explaining the process of the water study project,
- produce a tri-fold brochure about the project,
- provide student demonstrations on water quality testing,
- exhibit artwork including technical drawings of macroinvertebrates and maps,
- exhibit charts showing the results of the tests,
- have a special person give a congratulatory speech.

CLOSING

Include a closing celebration or ceremony at the end of your event. If your event is ongoing, be sure to tell your visitors when the ceremony will take place. Lois Thompson, who taught for many years at School Street School, always found special ways to acknowledge student accomplishment. She made certificates that were decorated and had each student's name carefully written in calligraphy. The same certificate can be given to every student and say something like: "Lake Champlain Expert" or "Lake Lover," or you can individualize the certificate to acknowledge a student's special accomplishment such as: "Leader in Class Discussion" or "Wetland Wizard." Laminate the certificates for an added touch of class.

Some teachers give prizes. I usually don't unless everyone gets one. One year I found little candies wrapped in foil that looked like the earth, so all my students got a "little earth" with their certificates, since they had shown themselves to be caretakers of the earth.

Culminating events can be an integral part of your assessment. You may choose to formally evaluate students' work. I don't usually formally grade the final presentation for the open house. I do ask them to do a written evaluation of what they learned.

Schedule time on the day after your big event to savor your success. The flip side of the excitement that builds as students prepare for a closing event is the quiet satisfaction they feel as they clean up and put things away. Sometimes the day after is a good time for students and you to reflect in writing on your success. Give students the opportunity to make any suggestions for changes and additions in your lake study or with future open houses. If you are putting away portfolios, a written evaluation could be included.

Whatever you choose to mark the end of your lake study, take time to congratulate yourselves and celebrate all that you have learned!

Bibliography

Arnosky, James. LITTLE CHAMP. New York: Putnam Publishing Group, 1995.

Atwell, Nancy. IN THE MIDDLE: WRITING, READING AND LEARNING WITH ADOLESCENTS. Portsmouth, New Hampshire: Boynton/Cook Publishers, 1987.

Beach, Allen Penfield. LAKE CHAMPLAIN AS THE CENTURIES PASS. Basin Harbor, Vermont: Basin Harbor Club and Lake Champlain Maritime Museum, 1994.

Beebe, Lewis. JOURNAL OF LEWIS BEEBE, A PHYSICIAN ON THE CAMPAIGN AGAINST CANADA, 1776. Philadelphia, Pennsylvania, 1935. (*out of print*)

Behar, Sharon. TESTING THE WATERS: CHEMICAL AND PHYSICAL VITAL SIGNS OF A RIVER. Montpelier, Vermont: River Watch Network, 1996.

Bellico, Russell P. SAILS AND STEAM IN THE MOUNTAINS: A MARITIME AND MILITARY HISTORY OF LAKE GEORGE AND LAKE CHAMPLAIN. Fleischmanns, New York: Purple Mountain Press, 1992.

Benson, Adolph B., ed. PETER KALM'S TRAVELS IN NORTH AMERICA. New York: Dover Publications, Inc., 1937.

Booth, Jerry. THE BIG BEAST BOOK: DINOSAURS AND HOW THEY GOT THAT WAY. Boston: Little, Brown and Co., 1988.

Bradley, Darby and Cheryl King, eds. A PORTRAIT OF THE LAKE CHAMPLAIN ISLANDS. Burlington, Vermont: Lake Champlain Islands Trust, 1979. (*out of print*)

Brandt, Clare. THE MAN IN THE MIRROR: A LIFE OF BENEDICT ARNOLD. New York: Random House, 1994.

Braus, Judy A., and David Wood. ENVIRONMENTAL EDUCATION IN THE SCHOOLS: CREATING A PROGRAM THAT WORKS! Washington, D.C.: Peace Corps Information Collection and Exchange, 1993.

Brink, Jeanne and Gordon M. Day. ALNÔBAÔDWA: A WESTERN ABENAKI LANGUAGE GUIDE. Swanton, Vermont: Franklin Northwest Supervisory Union, 1990. (*audiotape available*)

Bruchac, Joseph, ed. THE WIND EAGLE AND OTHER ABENAKI STORIES. Greenfield Center, New York: Bowman Books, 1985.

Bryant, Louella. THE BLACK BONNET. Shelburne, Vermont: New England Press, 1996.

Caduto, Michael and Joseph Bruchac. KEEPERS OF THE ANIMALS. Golden, Colorado: Fulcrum Publishing, 1991.

Caduto, Michael. POND AND BROOK: A GUIDE TO FRESHWATER ENVIRONMENTS. Hanover, New Hampshire: University Press of New England, 1985.

Cherry, Lynne. A RIVER RAN WILD. San Diego, California: Harcourt Brace and Company, 1992.

Calloway, Colin G. THE ABENAKI. Indians of North American Series. New York: Chelsea House, 1989.

_____. DAWNLAND ENCOUNTERS: INDIANS AND EUROPEANS IN NORTHERN NEW ENGLAND. Hanover, New Hampshire: University Press of New England, 1991.

_____. WESTERN ABENAKI, 1600-1800. Norman, Oklahoma: University of Oklahoma Press, 1990.

Cole, Joanna. THE MAGIC SCHOOL BUS AT THE WATERWORKS. New York: Scholastic, 1986.

Cone, Molly. COME BACK SALMON. San Francisco, California: Sierra Club Books, 1992.

Coolidge, Guy Omeron. THE FRENCH OCCUPATION OF THE CHAMPLAIN VALLEY FROM 1609 TO 1759. 1938.
Reprint. Harrison, New York: Harbor Hill Books, 1979.

Crisman, Kevin J. OF SAILING SHIPS AND SIDEWHEELERS. Montpelier, Vermont: Division for Historic Preservation, 1986. (*out of print*)

_____. THE EAGLE: AN AMERICAN BRIG ON LAKE CHAMPLAIN. Shelburne, Vermont: The New England Press, 1987.

Crompton, Anne Eliot. THE ICE TRAIL. New York: Methuen, Inc., 1980. (*out of print*)

Cvancara, Alan. AT THE WATER'S EDGE. New York: John Wiley & Sons, Inc., 1989.

Dalgiesh, Sarah. THE COURAGE OF SARAH NOBLE. New York: Macmillan Publishing, 1954.

Danziger, Jeff. THE CHAMPLAIN MONSTER. Shelburne, Vermont: New England Press, 1981.

Davison, Rebecca, ed. PHOENIX PROJECT. Burlington, Vermont: Champlain Maritime Society, 1981.

Denencour, Mark. INTERACTIVE LAKE ECOLOGY. Teacher's Guide. New Hampshire: New Hampshire Department of Environmental Services, 1991.

Everest, Allan S. THE WAR OF 1812 IN THE CHAMPLAIN VALLEY. Syracuse, New York: Syracuse University Press, 1981.

Grant, W.L., ed. VOYAGES OF SAMUEL DE CHAMPLAIN 1604-1618. New York: Charles Scribner and Sons, 1907.

Graymont, Barbara. THE IROQUOIS. New York: Chelsea House Publishers, 1988.

Guyette, Elise. VERMONT: A CULTURAL PATCHWORK. Peterborough, New Hampshire: Cobblestone Publishing, Inc., 1986.

Haviland, William A. and Marjory W. Power. THE ORIGINAL VERMONTERS: NATIVE INHABITANTS, PAST AND PRESENT. Hanover, New Hampshire: University Press of New England, 1994.

Hill, Ralph Nading. LAKE CHAMPLAIN: KEY TO LIBERTY. Woodstock, Vermont: Countryman Press, 1995.

_____. SIDEWHEELER SAGA. New York: Rinehart & Company, Inc., 1953.

_____. TWO CENTURIES OF FERRY BOATING. Burlington, Vermont: Lake Champlain Transportation Co., Inc., 1972.

Hoose, Philip. IT'S OUR WORLD, TOO! Boston: Little, Brown and Co., 1993.

Hullfish, William, ed. THE CANALLER'S SONGBOOK. York, Pennsylvania: The American Canal and Transportation Center, 1984

Jackson, Edgar N. GREEN MOUNTAIN HERO. Shelburne, Vermont: New England Press, 1961.

James, Charity. BEYOND CUSTOMS. New York: Agathon Press, 1974.

Johnson, Charles W. THE NATURE OF VERMONT. Hanover, New Hampshire: University Press of New England, 1980.

Klots, Elsie B. FRESHWATER LIFE. New York: G.P. Putnam's Sons, 1966.

Leopold, Aldo. A SAND COUNTY ALMANAC. New York: Oxford University Press, 1989.

Lonergran, Carroll Vincent. BRAVE BOYS OF OLD FORT TICONDEROGA. Interlaken, New York: Heart of the Lakes Publishing, 1987.

Lundeberg, Philip K. THE GUNBOAT PHILADELPHIA AND THE DEFENSE OF LAKE CHAMPLAIN IN 1776. Basin Harbor, Vermont: Lake Champlain Maritime Museum, 1995.

Lynn, Brian. DISCOVER WETLANDS. Olympia, Washington: Washington Department of Ecology, 1988.

Macrorie, Ken. THE I-SEARCH PAPER. Portsmouth, New Hampshire: Boynton/Cook Publishers, 1988.

Manning, Gordon P. LIFE IN THE COLCHESTER LIGHTHOUSE. Shelburne, Vermont: Shelburne Museum, 1958.

Marsh, George Perkins. MAN AND NATURE. Cambridge, Massachusetts: Belknap Press, 1965.

Meeks, Harold. VERMONT LAND AND RESOURCES. Shelburne, Vermont: New England Press, 1986.

Mitchell, Mark and William Stapp. FIELD MANUAL FOR WATER QUALITY MONITORING: AN ENVIRONMENTAL EDUCATION PROGRAM FOR SCHOOLS. Dexter, Michigan: Thomson-Shore, Inc., 1996.

Neering, Rosemary and Stan Garrod. LIFE IN ACADIA. Toronto, Ontario: Fitzhenry and Whiteside Ltd., 1976.

Ochoa, George. THE FALL OF QUEBEC AND THE FRENCH AND INDIAN WAR. Englewood Cliffs, New Jersey: Silver Burdett Press, Inc., 1990.

Outwater, Alice. WATER: A NATURAL HISTORY. New York: Harper Collins, 1996.

Ovecka, Janice. CAVE OF FALLING WATER. Shelburne, Vermont: New England Press, 1992.

Parrella, Deborah. PROJECT SEASONS. Shelburne, Vermont: Shelburne Farms, 1995.

Parker, Steve. POND AND RIVER. Eyewitness Books. New York: Alfred A. Knopf Inc., 1988.

Peacock, Graham. WATER. New York: Thomson Learning, 1994.

Peck, Robert Newton. FAWN. Boston: Little, Brown and Co., 1975 (*out of print*)

Peterson, James E. OTTER CREEK. Salisbury, Vermont: Dunmore House, 1990.

Posen, I. Sheldon. YOU HEAR THE ICE TALKING: THE WAY OF PEOPLE AND ICE ON LAKE CHAMPLAIN. Plattsburgh, New York: Clinton County Historical Association, 1986.

Randall, Willard Sterne. BENEDICT ARNOLD: PATRIOT AND TRAITOR. New York: William Morrow and Company, Inc., 1990.

Raymo, Chet and Maureen. WRITTEN IN STONE. Old Saybrook, Connecticut: Globe Pequot Press, 1989.

Reid, George K. POND LIFE. A Golden Guide. Racine, Wisconsin: Western Publishing Co., 1987.

Richter, Conrad. THE LIGHT IN THE FOREST. New York: Bantam Books, 1953.

Roberts, Kenneth. RABBLE IN ARMS. Garden City, New York: Doubleday, 1947. (*abridged version available from the Lake Champlain Maritime Museum*)

Schimmel Schimm. LETTERS FROM THE EARTH. Minocqua, Wisconsin: NorthWord Press, Inc., 1994.

Seed, Deborah. WATER SCIENCE. Reading, Massachusetts: Addison-Wesley, 1992.

Sharrow, Gregory. OUR TOWN: RECORDING AND PRESENTING LOCAL HISTORY AND FOLKLIFE, Teacher Handbook. Middlebury, Vermont: The Vermont Folklife Center, 1990.

______, ed. MANY CULTURES, ONE PEOPLE. Middlebury, Vermont: The Vermont Folklife Center, 1992.

Slattery, Britt Eckhart. WOW! THE WONDERS OF WETLANDS. St. Michaels, Maryland: Environmental Concern, Inc., 1995.

Speare, Elizabeth George. CALICO CAPTIVE. New York: Dell Publishing, 1957.

______. THE SIGN OF THE BEAVER. Boston: Houghton-Mifflin, 1983.

Stokes, Donald and Lillian Q. Stokes. STOKES NATURE GUIDE SERIES. New York: Little, Brown and Co., 1989.

Thompson, Zadock. NATURAL HISTORY OF VERMONT. Rutland, Vermont: Charles E. Tuttle Co., 1972.

Titus, Tim, ed. Crown Point and Its Powder Horns. Crown Point, New York: Crown Point Historic Site, 1985.

______. Teacher Resource Guide. Crown Point, New York: Crown Point Historic Site, 1994.

Van Diver, Bradford. THE ROADSIDE GEOLOGY OF NEW YORK. Missoula, Montana: Mountain Press Publishing Co., 1985

_____. THE ROADSIDE GEOLOGY OF VERMONT AND NEW HAMPSHIRE. Missoula, Montana: Mountain Press Publishing Co., 1987.

Weitzman, David. MY BACKYARD HISTORY BOOK. Boston: Little, Brown and Co., 1975.

Wickman, Donald. "Built With Spirit, Deserted in Darkness: The American Occupation of Mt. Independence, 1776-1777." Masters thesis, University of Vermont, 1993.

Wigginton, Elliot. MOMENTS: THE FOXFIRE EXPERIENCE. Nederland, Colorado: IDEAS, 1975.

_____. SOMETIMES A SHINING MOMENT. New York: Doubleday, 1986.

Williams, Jerry and Ralph Nading Hill. Lake Champlain Ferryboats. Burlington, Vermont: Lake Champlain Transportation Company, 1990.

Witten, Matthew, ed. A MARITIME HISTORY OF VERMONT. Barre, Vermont: SerVermont, Inc. and Lake Champlain Maritime Museum, 1996. (*written by Vermont students*)

Zarzynski, Joseph W. CHAMP: BEYOND THE LEGEND. Port Henry, New York: Bannister Publications, 1984.

Maps

"Lake Champlain Dive and Historic Sites." Williston, Vermont: Dive Research and Associates, 1991.

"Lake Champlain North, N.Y.-VT." 1:100,000. 1 minute by 2 minute Series (Topographic), #44073-E1-TM-100. Reston, Virginia: USGS, 1986.

"Lake Champlain South, N.Y.-VT." 1:100,000. 1 minute by 2 minute Series (Topographic), #44073-A1-PL-100. Reston, Virginia: USGS, 1986.

"Lake Champlain Region: Road Map and Guide." South Burlington, Vermont: Northern Cartographic.

"Lake Champlain Atlas of Navigational Charts." South Burlington, Vermont: R.W. Vogel (*author and publisher*).

"Ottawa/Montreal" Sheet 31 S.E. 1:5000,000. Ottawa, Canada: Canada Department of Mines and Technical Surveys, 1953.

"Raised Relief Map of Lower Champlain Valley: Glens Falls" and "Raised Relief Map of Champlain Valley: Lake Champlain." Chippewa Falls, Wisconsin: Hubbard. (*plastic topographical maps*)

"Lake Champlain Drainage Basin." Grand Isle, Vermont: Lake Champlain Basin Program.

Music

"Pipers Refrain" And So Will We Yet. Song about Black Watch at Fort Ticonderoga, sung by Ann Mayo Muir, Ed Trickett, and Gordon Bok. [audiocassette or CD C-116] Sharon, Connecticut: Folk Legacy Records.

"Champlain Valley Songs" from the Marjorie L. Porter collection of North Country folklore, sung by Pete Seeger. Washington, D.C.: Folkway Records.

"Songs of Lake Champlain," sung by Stan Ransom [audiocassette or CD] Hinesburg, Vermont: Connecticut Peddler Enterprise.

Organizations and Related Publications

Below is a listing of some of the important organizations relating to the Lake Champlain Basin. Publications that are noted below were referred to or used in THIS LAKE ALIVE! Most organizations have additional educational resources. Local addresses are given where possible; publications are available from national or central offices.

Clinton County Historical Association

48 Court Street

P.O. Box 332

Plattsburgh, NY 12901

  • The Original People: Native Americans in the Champlain Valley.
  Catalog of an Exhibition at the Clinton County Historical Museum.

Cornell Cooperative Extension

P.O. Box 388

Westport, NY 12993

  • Pond and Stream Safari: A Guide to the Ecology of Aquatic Invertebrates

Lake Champlain International Fishing Derby

P.O. Box 4503

Burlington, VT 05401

  • Fishing Lake Champlain

Lake Champlain Basin Program

54 West Shore Road

Grand Isle, VT 05458

  • Opportunities For Action
  • Lake Champlain Boat Study
  • *Newsletter and educational resources*

Lake Champlain Committee

14 South Williams Street

Burlington, VT 05401

  • Essays on Lake Champlain
  • *Newsletter and educational resources*

U.S. Fish and Wildlife Service–Lake Champlain Fish and Wildlife Resources Office

11 Lincoln Street

Essex Junction, VT 05452-3151

  • *Educational resources*

National Archives of Canada

Management of Inquiries

395 Wellington Street,

Ottawa, Ontario K1A ON3

National Wildlife Federation
Northeast Natural Resource Center

58 State Street

Montpelier, VT 05602
> • NatureScope: "Wading Into Wetlands"
> • NatureScope: "Geology: The Active Earth"

New York State Archives
The State Education Department
Cultural Education Center Room 11D40
Albany, NY 12230

New York Department of Environmental Conservation
Division of Water, Water Outreach Programs
NYS DEC Region 5
Route 86, Box 296
Raybrook, NY 12977

Office of Parks, Recreation and Historic Preservation
Lake Champlain Parks
Point Au Roche State Park
RD #2, Box 278
Plattsburgh, NY 12901

Special Collections
Bailey/Howe Library
University of Vermont
Burlington, VT 05405

Vermont Division for Historic Preservation
135 State Street, Drawer 33
Montpelier, VT 05633
> • An Introduction and Resource Guide to Underwater Archaeology in Vermont
> • Dive Historic Lake Champlain: Vermont's Underwater Historic Preserve System
> • Phoenix Project

Vermont Folklife Center
Box 442, Gamaliel Painter House
Middlebury, VT 05753
> • Legacy of the Lake (*video*)

Vermont Geographic Alliance
Leavenworth Hall
Geography Department
Castleton State College
Castleton, VT 05735

Vermont Institute of Natural Science
North Branch Nature Center
713 Elm Street

Montpelier, VT 05602

Vermont Historical Society
109 State Street
Montpelier, VT 05602
  • Green Mountaineer. 1981–88.

Vermont Geology Survey
103 South Main Street, Center Building
Waterbury, VT 05671
  • Paleontology of the Champlain Basin

Vermont Department of Fish and Wildlife
103 South Main Street, 10 South
Waterbury, VT 05676
  • Vermont Threatened and Endangered Species Education Guide
  • *Educational resources*

Vermont Department of Environmental Conservation
Water Quality Division
10 North Building
103 South Main Street
Waterbury, VT 05671

Western Regional Environmental Education Council
4014 Chatham Lane
Houston, TX 77027
  • Project Wild
  • Aquatic Project Wild
  • Project WET

Graphic Credits

Organizations

Chimney Point Museum: p. 290d, 291a
Clinton County Historical Association: p. 80, 81, 84, 85, 88, 90, 117, 129
Lake Champlain Basin Program: p. 56, 57, 62, 71a, 71B, 72D & F, 317, 320, 371, 382a, 387, 416
Lake Champlain Land Trust: p. 61
Lake Champlain Maritime Museum: p. 100, 109b, 203, 204, 207, 208
Lake Champlain Transportation Company: p. 221I
Lake Studies Center, University of Vermont: p. 290c
National Archives: p. 143
Northern Cartographic: p. 30, 32, 59, 69, 268b, 417
Original source unknown: p. 103, 202
Peabody Essex Museum: p. 79
Shelburne Farms: p. 290b
Shelburne Museum: p. 104, 105, 109a, 165, 187, 189a, 356
Skenesborough Museum: p. 290a
Special Collections, Bailey/Howe Memorial Library, University of Vermont: p. 107, 112, 139, 204
Teachout's Lakehouse: p. 289d
University of Pennsylvania: p.95, 357
Vermont Division for Historic Preservation: p. 106, 155, 156, 157, 170, 223, 224, 225, 221D-G
Vermont Historical Society: p. 150

Individuals

All paper cuts created by Bonnie Acker
Lou Borie: p. 18, 20, 33, 71A, 72C, E, G, H, I, J, 111, 189b, 342, 348, 364, 365, 366a & b, 369, 375, 376, 406, 412, 426, 427, 435, 436, 438
Holly Brough: p. 26a & b; 29, 31, 123, 128, 252, 264, 266, 298, 275, 279, 303, 350a & b, 351, 352, 353b- f; 377a, b, c; 378a-d; 379a, 389, 413, 414, 418a, 420, 422a, 425, 428, 429a & b, 444, 456, 457, 461, 470, 476a & b, 480, 481, 482
James G. Chapman: p. 164
Kevin Crisman: p. 99, 102, 206a, 210, 220A-D, 221E-H
Amy Demarest: all student photos unless otherwise indicated. Also, p. i, ii, iii, 9, 64, 27, 137, 159, 200, 206b, 282, 285a & b, 286, 287, 291b, 289a-c, 290b & d, 299, 319, 323, 340, 381b, 402
Tai Dinnan: p. 332
William Haviland: p. 82, 83
Nakki Goranin: p. 110a & b
Kris Kenlan: p. 268a, 269a
Elayne Sears: p. 92
Chuck Seleen: p. 205
Ruby Thibault: p. 405a & b
Peter Thomas: p. 396
Ron Toelke: p. 91
Mary Watzin: p. 380, 381a

People who are Part of
This Lake Alive!

Bonnie Acker is an artist who lives in Burlington, Vermont.

Nancy Bazilchuk is a staff reporter for the *Burlington Free Press,* where she covers environmental issues.

Lou Borie is the coordinator for the District 4 Environmental Commission in Vermont and is a freelance writer and photographer.

Lisa Borre works for the Vermont Agency of Natural Resources and coordinates the Lake Champlain Basin Program.

Sue Boyer is a sixth-grade teacher in Milton, Vermont.

Jeanne Brink is a basket maker and educational consultant for matters relating to Abenaki language and culture; she lives in Barre, Vermont.

Holly Brough is the publications assistant at Shelburne Farms, Shelburne, Vermont, and a graduate student in the School of Natural Resources at the University of Vermont (UVM) in Burlington.

Joseph Bruchac is a storyteller, songwriter, poet and author; he manages the Northeast Native American Education Center and Bookstore in Greenfield Center, New York.

Colleen Carter is a science teacher at Richelieu Valley Regional High School in Masterville, Quebec, and also teaches education at McGill University in Montreal.

Art Cohn is cofounder and director of the Lake Champlain Maritime Museum in Vergennes, Vermont and is a diver and underwater archeologist.

Kevin Crisman is a professor at the Institute of Nautical Archeology at Texas A&M University, College Station, Texas, and has been active in many archeological surveys in Lake Champlain.

Amy Demarest is a fifth-grade teacher in Milton and has been teaching and learning about Lake Champlain for eleven years. She lives in Burlington.

Barry Doolan is chair of the Geology Department at UVM.

Mary Dupont is a fifth-grade teacher in Milton, Vermont.

Jonathan Eddy is co-owner/manager of the Waterfront Diving Center in Burlington and has been diving in Lake Champlain for 28 years.

Laurie Eddy is the education director at the Lake Champlain Maritime Museum.

Judy Elson is the director of School Programs at Shelburne Farms and has been a leader in providing watershed education for teachers in the basin.

Steve Faccio is a naturalist who works for the Vermont Institute of Natural Science in Woodstock, Vermont.

Monty Fischer is the director of National Wildlife Federation's Northeast Natural Resource Center in Montpelier, Vermont, and past chair of the Vermont Citizen's Advisory Committee on Lake Champlain's Future.

Lori Fisher is the executive director of the Lake Champlain Committee.

Nakki Goranin is a writer and photographer who lives in Burlington.

Elise Guyette is the author of VERMONT: A CULTURAL PATCHWORK and lives in South Burlington, Vermont.

Sue Hardin is a sixth-grade teacher at the Frederick H. Tuttle Middle School in South Burlington.

Michael Hauser is an aquatic biologist and zebra mussel education and outreach specialist; he works at the Water Quality Division of the Vermont Department of Environmental Conservation in Montpelier.

Dale Henry works at the Lake Champlain Maritime Museum where he enjoys his life-long passion for water by serving as educator, boat-builder and blacksmith.

Jeff Howe is director of Museum Programs at the Delaware Museum of Natural History in Wilmington, Delaware.

Tom Hudspeth is a professor of environmental studies at UVM.

Don Jarrett is a fifth-grade teacher at St. Albans City School in St. Albans, Vermont.

Kris Kenlan is a sixth-grade mathematics teacher at the Frederick H. Tuttle Middle School.

Mark LaBar is a research biologist working for the Vermont Institute of Natural Science.

Gary LaShure is a teacher at Missisquoi Valley Union High School in Swanton, Vermont, and workshop facilitator for GREEN—Global Rivers Environmental Education Network in Ann Arbor, Michigan.

Garet Livermore is supervisor of School Programs at the Shelburne Museum in Shelburne.

Carol Livingston is a teacher of grades 7 and 8 at Camel's Hump Middle School in Richmond, Vermont.

Madeleine Little is a fishery biologist at the U.S. Fish and Wildlife Office in Essex Junction, Vermont.

Fred Magdoff is a professor of plant and soil science at UVM.

Charlotte Mehrtens is a professor of geology at UVM, where her specialty is sedimentary rocks in the Champlain Valley.

Karen Murdock is principal of Cumberland Head Elementary School in Plattsburgh, New York and has been active in the Lake Champlain Basin Education Initiatives.

Deb Parrella is the author of PROJECT SEASONS and is an ELF (Environmental Learning for the Future) trainer for the Vermont Institute of Natural Science.

Giovanna Peebles is the Vermont State Archeologist at the Vermont Division for Historic Preservation, Montpelier.

David Rider is a geography teacher at Bellows Free Academy in St. Albans.

Bill Romond is a science teacher and computer consultant at Colchester High School, Colchester, Vermont.

Joan Robinson is education director at the Flynn Theatre in Burlington, Vermont, and teaches storytelling and creative drama at St. Michaels College Prevel Graduate School of Education in Colchester.

Peter Thomas is Director of the Consulting Archeology Program at UVM.

Ruby Thibault is an art teacher for Grades 4-6 in Milton.

Tim Titus is the former educational outreach coordinator at the Crown Point Historic Site in Crown Point, New York.

Jill Vickers is a teacher of grades 4 and 5 in Ticonderoga Elementary School in Ticonderoga, New York.

Mary Watzin is an associate professor of natural resources at the School of Natural Resources at UVM.

Don Wickman is a historian and educator who works at the Lake Champlain Maritime Museum.